A.A. FEINGOLD
Flat 4. RIVERSDALE
ST ANNS ROA
PRESTWICH
MANCHESTER M25 9 GD

ARTSCROLL

SHAAR PRESS

0161 7736824
07876 3868
-43

NAVIGATION FOR
YOUR SOUL

BECAUSE LIFE'S A JOURNEY!

AN INSPIRATIONAL AND
ENJOYABLE GUIDE
TO SURVIVE & THRIVE
IN THE REAL GAME OF LIFE

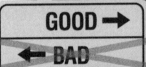

FOREWORD BY
RABBI BINYOMIN EISENBERGER

INSPIRED BY THE WRITINGS OF THE
NESIVOS SHALOM

YAAKOV SHAIN   **AVI FISHOFF**

Published by ARTSCROLL / SHAAR PRESS
Distributed by MESORAH PUBLICATIONS, LTD.
4401 Second Avenue / Brooklyn, N.Y. 11232 / (718) 921-9000 / ww.artscroll.com

Distributed in Israel by SIFRIATI / A. GITLER
6 Hayarkon Street / Bnei Brak 51127

Distributed in Europe by LEHMANNS
Unit E, Viking Business Park, Rolling Mill Road / Jarrow, Tyne and Wear, NE32 3DP/ England

Distributed in Australia and New Zealand by GOLDS WORLD OF JUDAICA
3-13 William Street / Balaclava, Melbourne 3183 / Victoria Australia

Distributed in South Africa by KOLLEL BOOKSHOP
Ivy Common / 105 William Road / Norwood 2192, Johannesburg, South Africa

ISBN 10: 1-4226-1177-9 / ISBN 13: 978-1-4226-1177-7

Printed in the United States of America

To contact the authors:
GPSforyourSOUL@gmail.com

GPS!
NAVIGATION FOR
YOUR SOUL

BECAUSE LIFE'S A JOURNEY!

BEWARE!

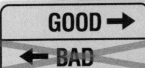

GOOD →

← BAD

This book, *GPS: Navigation for Your Soul* is dedicated
to all our
dear, sweet Einiklach

The Schuss Kids
The Kleinman Kids
The Freedman Kids

You give us such נחת and joy as we watch you grow
and develop your unique personalities.

We look forward בע"ה
to seeing you become בני תורה and בנות תורה
and contributing your כוחות
and talents to benefit כלל ישראל.

Every one of you has something very special
that you can use to be a "GPS"
to help guide those who need
to find the right direction.
May they look to you to show the way.

באהבה,

Zaidy Elly and Bobby Brochie Kleinman

וְהַעֲרֶב נָא ה' אֱלֹקֵינוּ אֶת דִּבְרֵי תוֹרָתְךָ בְּפִינוּ
וּבְפִי עַמְּךָ בֵּית יִשְׂרָאֵל.

GPS is an incredibly creative fresh, fun and sweet
approach that will b"Ezras Hashem bridge many future
generations of Yidden to Authentic Yiddishkeit!

Therefore, we feel it appropriate to dedicate this book
to our future generations, with heartfelt prayer that they
will all always follow their GPS and stay on course to
lead a life of Authentic Yiddishkeit!

Eli and Breindy Amsterdam:
Penina, Ari, Moishe, and Rena

Shmuly and Batsheva Werdiger:
Dovi, Chayala, Avi, Yosef and Adina

Avromi and Shoshana Schonfeld:
Ilana, Pessie, Rikki and Moishe

Sruli and Tiki Werdiger:
Meyer and Nechemiah

וְנִהְיֶה אֲנַחְנוּ וְצֶאֱצָאֵינוּ וְצֶאֱצָאֵי עַמְּךָ בֵּית יִשְׂרָאֵל,
כֻּלָּנוּ יוֹדְעֵי שְׁמֶךָ וְלוֹמְדֵי תוֹרָתְךָ לִשְׁמָהּ!

Shloime and Esther Werdiger

> *How great is your kindness and goodness, that you have been inspired to bring children back to their Father in Heaven .... You have now been motivated to produce a masterful work based on the concepts explored in the holy sefarim Nesivos Shalom of my mentor and father-in-law, the Slonimer Rebbe, zt"l ... presenting them ... so that thet they inspire and enlighten the spirit of every Jew, at his own level.*

ישיבת בית אברהם סלונים ירושלים (ע"ו)
YESHIVAT BETH ABRAHAM SLONIM JERUSALEM
מיסודו של כ"ק אדמו"ר בעל "נתיבות שלום" זי"ע

ישיבה גדולה · ישיבה לצעירים · בית מדרש גבוה לאברכים "צמח דוד" · מרכז תורני יד ואחי
תלמודי תורה ברכת אברהם · אמת ואמונה סלונים · בתי מדרש וכוללי אברכים ברחבי הארץ

נוסדה כברנוביץ - פולין
בשנת תרע"ח
ונוסדה מחדש כא"י
בשנת תש"ב

**Founded at
Baranowice Poland
In 1918
Founded in Israel 1942**

נשיא וראש המוסדות
כ"ק אדמו"ר מסלונים שליט"א

בס"ד, ירושלים עיה"ק, בחודש מנחם אב תשע"ו.

תקדמנו ברכות טוב תשית לראשו עטרת פז, איש חמודות
ונועם המדות, אוהב את הבריות ומקרבן לתורה, ידידי היקר
רב הפעלים, מו"ה **אברהם פישהוף** שליט"א.

אביעה רננות בעד פעליו, מה רב חסדו וטוב לבו, אשר נשאו רוחו לקרב לב
בנים לאביהם שבשמים, ברוב פעולותיו הכבירות בענוות חן והצנע לכת, שחז"ל
קראו עליו הכתוב "כְּפִי תִהְיֶה" (ברש"י ע"פ הגמ' בב"מ פה.) ולוקח נפשות חכם,
ועתה רחש לבכם להוציא מלאכת מחשבת מערכות דעת בעניני הקשר של יהודי
להקב"ה, ובנים אתם לה' אלקיכם, ע"פ היסודות המבוארים בספרים הקדושים
"נתיבות שלום" ממו"ח כ"ק אדמו"ר מסלונים זצ"ל, המגידים נפלאות ומפליגים
בשגב ערך יהודי ויעודו בבריאה, בתוספת נופך וסברה, כלשון הזהב של
הרמב"ם בהל' ליל הסדר "הכל לפי דעתו של בן", כדי להעיר ולהאיר נפש יהודי
באשר הוא. וברכתי ברכת ידיד שיברך ה' חילו וירחיב גבולו בתלמידים, וחפץ ה'
בידו יצליח, וכל אשר יעשה יצליח, ויקויים בכם מאמר הנביא (ישעיהו נח) וְתָפֵק
לָרָעֵב נַפְשֶׁךָ וְנֶפֶשׁ נַעֲנָה תַּשְׂבִּיעַ וְזָרַח בַּחֹשֶׁךְ אֹרֶךָ וַאֲפֵלָתְךָ כַּצָהֳרָיִם, וְנָחֲךָ ה' תָּמִיד
וְהִשְׂבִּיעַ בְּצַחְצָחוֹת נַפְשֶׁךָ וְעַצְמֹתֶיךָ יַחֲלִיץ וְהָיִיתָ כְּגַן רָוֶה וּכְמוֹצָא מַיִם אֲשֶׁר לֹא
יְכַזְבוּ מֵימָיו. ותעמוד לכם הזכות לראות בנים ובני בנים עוסקים בתורה
ובמצוות, כשאיפת אבות.

שלמה וינברג
חתן מרן בעל "נתיבות שלום" מסלונים זי"ע

רח' סלנט 21-17 פינת רח' אברהם מסלונים ת.ד. 5020 ירושלים 91050 טל. 6287756-02 פקס 6288682-02 info@slonim.org.il ע"ר 127-7-010-58
Salant St. Cor. Rabbi Abraham of Slonim St. P.O.Box 5020 Jerusalem 91050 Tel. 972-2-6287756 Fax. 972-2-6288682 info@slonim.org.il
Address in USA: Yeshiva Beth Abraham of Jerusalem Inc. 73W. 47th St. NYC 10036

ישיבת מיר ירושלים
YESHIVAS MIR YERUSHALAYIM

Founded in Mir 1817. In Jerusalem 1944   580037638 עיר   בס״יד נוסדה כמיר בשנת תקע״ז. בירושלים בשנת תש״יד
RABBI N.Z. FINKEL   הרב נ.צ. פינקל
DEAN   ראש הישיבה

כ״ו טבת תשע״א

לכבוד הידידים הנעלים והנכבדים, המסורים בלו״נ לחנוך צעירי הצאן בדרך
התוה״ק ה״ה הרב אברהם מנחם פישאהף שליט״א והרב יעקב יוסף שיין
שליט״א.

אחדשה״ט ושלו' כל אשר לכם, אבוא בזה בשערי הברכה לקראת הופעת ספרכם
החשוב אשר ניכר בו רב העמל שהשקעתם יען כי מונח בו ברכה מרובה להלהיב
את לבם של צעירי הצאן ולעוררם לשאוף ללכת בדרך התורה ולגדול בתורה וביראת
שמים. בדורנו אנו שרח״ל רבו אלו שיוצאים ממסגרת תלמודם, הרי הם בסכנה
רוחנית של ממש. ע״כ כל המוסר נפשו לזה שכרו מרובה מאד והוא בכלל חכם לב
יקח מצוות. אשרי מי ששומע את צעקתם של אלו המבקשים תחנונים ואומרים
הוציאה ממסגר נפשי להודות את שמך ואתם שזכיתם ע״י עבודת הקדש שלכם
וע״י ספרכם החשוב הרי אתם מקיימים בזה את מצוות ברוך אשר יקים את דברי
התורה הזאת ויהי׳ שכרכם כפול מן השמים במילוי כל משאלות לבכם לטובה.

הכו״ח בברכה מרובה ובכבוד ויקר,

הרב נתן צבי פינקל
ראש הישיבה

3 Beth Israel St. P.O.B. 5022 Jerusalem 91050 Tel. 02-5410999 Fax. 02-5323446 ● 580037638 עיר 02-5323446 פקס 02-5410999 טל. ירושלים 91050 ת.ד. 5022 רח. בית ישראל 3

"I received the sample of your guide .... I very much enjoyed your entire approach to attract hearts to Hashem. Your pleasant words are certain to have great impact on their readers and those who seek truth."

בס"ד.

שמואל קמנצקי
Rabbi S. Kamenetsky

2018 Upland Way
Philadelphia, Pa 19131

Home: 215-473-2798
Study: 215-473-1212

בס"ד ב' שבט תשע"ה

כב' חביבי ויקירי הר' אברהם מנחם עמו"ש
בן ידיד השם הר' בנציון פושמאן שליט"א

אחרי דרישת שלומו הטוב באהבה מרובה.

קבלתי הדוגמא למדריך דבקות השם יתברך שמוכן להוציא לאור. מאד נהניתי מכל מהלכו ודרכו לקרב לבבות להקב"ה. דבריו הנעימים בודאי יעשו רושם גדול להקוראים ולמבקשי האמת.

בטוח אני שספרו יביא וישא פירות בכל שטחי אחינו בני ישראל ויזכה להמשיך בזה מקרב את הרבים לקרבם לאבינו שבשמים.

בידידות נאמנה

שמואל קמנצקי

Rabbi I. Scheiner
Dean of Kamenitzer Yeshiva
51 Zephania St., Jerusalem
Tel. (02) 532-2512

הרב יצחק שיינר
ראש ישיבת קמיניץ
רחוב צפני' 51, ירושלים
טלפון 532-2512

בס"ד כ"ב אדר ב' תשס"ו ולאל ירושלם עיה"ק ת"ו

To my dear new young friends, Avi Fishoff שי'
and Yaakov Yosef Shein שי', שז רב לו!

First, I would like to thank you for
your wonderful G.P.S. "Kishmoi ken hoo", it's
a marvelous guide for young and old alike.
In your special idiom for the U.S. reader,
it just hits the spot, and I enjoyed every
word and still have a lot of reflection and
practice and internalizing to do. Thanks
and may you help many in the future, אי"ה.

I am thankful to ה' that our paths
have met again. As you both know this is
not the first time. I knew your Zeide Reb Moshe
Shein, ז"ל, and bobe ז"ל, of "All for the Boss".
and as you know my wife תי' 's Zeide Reb
Boruch Ber זצ"ל was a ben bais in their home.
Reb Moshe Aron ז"ל was a close younger colleague
in M.T.V. and Kamenitz many, many years. As
you know also, Avi, your great aunt Mrs. Deppelt
ע"ה cooked such delicious food on Wilson St in
my first years in M.T.V. My mouth still waters
when I remember her Quakers Oats, and through
recalling her ז"ל, I met your father שי' at
the recent convention.

It's a small world, and we have a Big
Father upstairs, and it's our job to get closer
and closer to Him ית', which your books so
admirably help us all do.

Yours,
בברכת התורה

בס"ד

RABBI MOSHE WOLFSON
1574 43RD STREET
BROOKLYN N.Y. 11219

הרב משה זואלפסאן
משגיח רוחני, ישיבה תורה ודעת
ורב דביהמ"ד אמונת ישראל

בס"ד, יום א' דחוה"מ פסח תשס"א

[handwritten Hebrew letter body]

נאם אברהם הלוי שארר

_____
RABBI AVROHOM SCHORR   רב אברהם הלוי שארר

[handwritten Hebrew postscript]

(718) 436-1133

RABBI YAAKOV PERLOW
1569 - 47TH STREET
BROOKLYN N.Y. 11219

יעקב פרלוב
קהל עדת יעקב נאוואמינסק
ישיבת נאוואמינסק - קול יהודה
ברוקלין, נ.י.

בס"ד   יום ד' י"א אדר ראשון תשע"א

One's journey through life is fraught with challenge and travail. The Sages and Teachers of Klal Yisroel have, thus, provided a Torah perspective and guiding principles to help a Jew understand and properly meet these challenges. They have taught that our Father in Heaven in his unending love for his children is a constant fountain of chizuk and instruction around which to build a solid foundation of spiritual growth.

Reb Avi Fishoff and Reb Yaakov Yosef Shain have beautifully elaborated on this theme in their book "GPS, Navigation for your Soul". They have elucidated from a richness of sources a sacred set of values and a Hashkofas Hayahadus, illustrating how the fundamentals of Yiddishkeit are to be applied in situations of real life. This book is a notable contribution to the Torah literature of our day.

בכבוד רב וביקר

R. Yaakov Perlow

> **GPS: Navigation for Your Soul** is written in a uniquely accessible way that enables anyone to tap into and connect to Torah Judaism. This *sefer* gives us all something to hold onto and, with Hashem's help, it will help our souls navigate through the many challenges of our times. ""

Rabbi Shmuel Dishon
1879 48th Street
Brooklyn NY 11204

A broken father once came to see the Imrei Emes ztz"l of Ger. With tears in his eyes he told the Rebbe that he had a son who was struggling with Yiddishkeit and his friends hurt him deeply by telling him the old saying: "the apple doesn't fall far from the tree," in essence blaming the father for his son's imperfections.

The Rebbe said that he should tell his friends that the saying applies only in a time where the winds are "רוח מצויה" (ordinary winds), but in a time of unusually strong winds,, an apple can be blown far, far from the tree!

Throughout our history we have suffered through many storms that have shaken the roots of our nation, such as: Christianity, Inquisition, Expulsion, Reform, Haskahlah, Communism, Socialism, and the Holocaust. The common denominator of all of these whirlwinds is that they caused hundreds of thousands of Jewish souls to be ripped away from their roots.

In our day, too, we feel whirlwinds that are shaking the core foundation of many Jewish homes, and we have all witnessed the terrible destruction that has been the result of these challenging times.

Many of us find ourselves helpless without knowing how to navigate ourselves and our children through these trying times. For this reason I am thankful to Hakadosh Baruch Hu for giving my dear ידיד נפשי Avi Fishoff נ״י the ability to compose a much needed book, *GPS: Navigation for Your Soul*. It is written in a uniquely accessible way that enables anyone to tap into and connect to Torah Judaism. This *sefer* gives us all something to hold onto and, with Hashem's help, it will help our souls navigate through the many challenges of our times. The tremendous *Siyata Dishmaya* that one sees while reading this book is extraordinary and this is certainly because "מגלגלין זכות על ידי זכאי", Hashem enables good people to do good things.

There is a famous saying: "An ounce of prevention is worth a pound of cure." I believe that this holy *sefer*, *GPS: Navigation for Your Soul*, has in it both qualities: It serves as much needed ounce of prevention to fortify us so that we may withstand the strong winds that seek to rip us away from our roots, and also it can serve as the pound of cure, for those who have already been affected by those terribly destructive winds.

May *HaKadosh Baruch Hu* help Avi to continue to be a source of tremendous *chizuk* to the many Yidden who seek his counsel, both verbally and now through his writings, *ad meah v'esrim shanah*, and may we all merit to see fulfillment of the promise: "והשיב לב אבות על בנים ולב בנים על אבותם", and he [Eliyahu] will turn back [to Hashem] the hearts of fathers with their sons, and the hearts of sons with their fathers.

Shmuel Dishon

MIRRER YESHIVA CENTRAL INSTITUTE
זצ"ל מיסודו של מרן הגאון רבי אברהם קאלמאנאוויץ • *Founded by* Rabbi Avrohom Kalmanowitz זצ"ל

1791-5 Ocean Parkway • Brooklyn, N.Y. 11223 (718) 645-0536 • Fax (718) 645-9251• mirreryeshiva@thejnet.com

Bais Medrash • Post Graduate School • Kollel • Mesivta • Yeshiva K'tana • Sephardic Division

בס"ד

Rabbi Osher Eliyahu Kalmanowitz
Rosh HaYeshiva

[handwritten letter in Hebrew]

> There is no doubt that [your work] will bring great inspiration to many people, who will find advice, concepts, and stories that will strengthen them in Torah and fear of Heaven.

ברכת אב

ע"פ "ויברך אותם משה" רש"י, יהי רצון שתשרה שכינה במעשה ידיכם!

From the desk of:
Y. B. Fishoff
108-38 69th Avenue
Forest Hills, N.Y. 11375
(718) 268-1061

ב"ה
יחיאל בנציון פישאהף

ברכת אב לבן - "בן חכם ישמח אב" (משלי)

לבני יקירי מחמד לבי, העוסק בצרכי ציבור באמונה
עסקן ופעיל רב בכל דבר שבקדושה הרה"ח ר' אברהם מנחם שיחי' לאוי"ט

שמחתי ונתרגש לבי לראותך הולך מחיל אל חיל, והנך מוציא
כעת לאור את ספרך השני "GPS" בו אספת דברי תורה ומוסר,
מדות טובות ויראת שמים, דברים היוצאים מן הלב ובודאי
יכנסו ללב השומעים!
דוגמתו בדבריך, ואין לי ספק שיביאו תועלת רבה וחיזוק לרבים,
שנכתבו בספרך עצות ונכונות, הנהגות וסיפורים, המביאים
חיזוק בעניני תורה ויראת שמים.
הוצאת ספר זה, הוא בעצם המשך לפעולותיך הנפלאות,
כאשר אתה עוזר לשבורי לב ונדכאים,
וסומך אתה את הנופלים, ומלמד לתלמידים בונה
וחד עם עזרתך: רעיתך היקרה בבית "HOME SWEET HOME"
ואני מברכך מעומקא דליבא בברכת אב אוהב,
ויזכה השי"ת שתראו כבוד ... תחי'!
להמשיך לעורר נפשות אחינו בני ישראל לתורה וליר"ש
ושלום השי"ת שיתן לכם ולחבריכם כוחות ברוחניות ובגשמיות
ותזכו לרוב נחת ועושר מכל צאצאיכם היקרים שיחיו ועניניכם כרצונכם ושמחות אי"ה

אביך אוהבך בלו"נ
יחיאל בנציון

והברכה מיוחדת לחתנא דביתא היקר
הר"ר יעקב יוסף שיין שיחי' לאוי"ט
שהשקיע יחד איתך מכוחו להוציא
לאור ספר יפה ומהודר.
והנני לברככם שתזכו עוד רבות בשנים
להגדיל תורה ולהאדירה מתוך
בריות גופא ונהורא מעליא!

" **This ... is the culmination of many years of growth and achievement ... You have created a very encouraging, motivating, and eye-catching work of art, written in a down-to-earth fashion. I am confident that your readers will mount your ספר on the dashboard of their hearts.** "

ברכת אב

כ"ב שבט תשע"א
January 27, 2011

To my dearest son Reb Yaakov Yosef שליט"א,

A great sense of happiness and pride fills my heart as your ספר called *GPS: Guidance for Your Soul* is about to go to print. This ספר is the culmination of many years of growth and achievement in those areas that make you the ideal person to author a ספר of such magnitude. Your experience in human relationships, שלום בית problems, kids at risk, problem solving, and lending an ear to anyone who needs help, is the foundation upon which this ספר was written.

With its publication you will be able to reach out to so many souls who will benefit from your loving guidance. You have created a very encouraging, motivating, and eye-catching work of art, written in a down-to-earth fashion. I am confident that your readers will mount your ספר on the dashboard of their hearts so as not to stray off the road of Torah and mitzvos.

May you enjoy the fruits of your labor as they blossom forth and may the wellsprings of a heart full of love for Hashem and his children continue to overflow to the multitude of souls thirsty for the word of Hashem.

May you merit to see much *nachas* from your beautiful family with health and happiness.

Your loving father,

Raphael Yitzchok Shain

I would like to express my great admiration for your co-author Avi Fishoff, who is famous for his work in *Kiruv Rechokim*. In addition, his many talents and innovations have enhanced the *sefer* in a special way to give it the potential to be a bestseller.

זכות דברי התורה שבמהדורה זו
יהיו לרפואת האשה היקרה
מרת רחל בת מרגלית שתחי׳
ישלח ה׳ דברו וירפאה
כרצון כל אוהביה וקרוביה
ולהקימה מחוליה וליתן לה חיים ארוכים

נר זכרון לעילוי נשמת אבינו
שהיה גומל חסדים
שלא על מנת לקבל פרס
אהוב, אוהב
ומשמח את הבריות

יצחק בן ויקטוריה שעיה מוגרבי זצ״ל
נלב״ע ל׳ כסליו תשס״ז

תנצבה

הונצח ע״י משה ורחל שעיה מוגרבי ומשפחתם הי״ו
ברוקלין יצ״ו

TABLE OF CONTENTS

Acknowledgments   21

The Nesivos Shalom: A Biographical Sketch   25

Introduction   29

Foreword: by Rabbi Binyomin Eisenberger   33

SECTION ONE: HASHEM LOVES YOU

Chapter 1: Unconditional Love   39

Chapter 2: Hashem ... Our Father   49

Chapter 3: Keeping Us Close   59

Chapter 4: Smokescreen   77

Chapter 5: Tough Love or Love Tough?   91

Chapter 6: Justice vs. Compassion   103

SECTION TWO: SOLID GOLD

Chapter 7: Essence or Circumstance   121

Chapter 8: The Spiritual CAT Scan   137

Chapter 9: A Rose Amongst Thorns   153

Chapter 10: Crazy Glue   163

Chapter 11: Who Is Your Biggest Fan?   173

Chapter 12: The Black Box   181

Chapter 13: Lifetime Membership   193

SECTION THREE: BUILDING MUSCLE

Chapter 14: Not a "Test" ... a "Challenge"! 205

Chapter 15: Custom-Tailored "CHALLENGES"! 221

Chapter 16: A Wake-Up Call 229

Chapter 17: The Right Attitude 241

Chapter 18: Acceptance 251

Chapter 19: Performance & Perfection 259

SECTION FOUR: THE BATTLE OF YOUR LIFE

Chapter 20: Heart & Soul 275

Chapter 21: Hindsight Is 20/20 287

Chapter 22: Atmospheric Combustion 299

Chapter 23: Twisted Reality 317

Chapter 24: Control Tower 329

Chapter 25: Losing Altitude 343

Chapter 26: Confusion 357

SECTION FIVE: LIFE TO THE MAX

Introduction 373

Concept One 385

Concept Two 393

Concept Three 407

Concept Four 421

Concept Five 439

Concept Six 455

OK, Now What? 467

Authentic Yiddishkeit 479

Meet the Authors 488

ACKNOWLEDGMENTS

I would like to take this opportunity to publicly thank:

The Ribbono Shel Olam:

> For letting me witness His guiding hand throughout my life. There were times that I realized it right away and there were many times when I only realized His loving guidance much later.

My dear parents, Rabbi Raphael Yitzchok Isaac and Yehudis Shain:

> You have guided me throughout my life, primarily by setting an example of how to succeed in every aspect of life. Your wisdom and patience, *shalom* and tranquility are appreciated much more now that I realize what is really important in life. You are *marbitz Torah* and teach students in a soft, mild manner that builds a lasting bond between Rebbi & Talmid. May you have much *nachas* from all your children and grandchildren.

My dear in-laws, Rabbi Raphael Yosef and Chummi Wallerstein:

> You personify energetic and selfless dedication to your family and the Klal. There are no words to describe all that I have learned and absorbed from witnessing your actions on a daily basis. You gave me the confidence to use strengths that I myself was not aware of. May you have much *nachas* from all your children and grandchildren.

My Grandmothers, Rebbitzin Rachoma Shain & Rebbitzin Chana Greenbaum:

> You are transmitters of greatness which you saw in the homes of your parents, Reb Yaakov Yosef Herman and Reb Shraga Feivel Mendolowitz, both pioneers of Torah in America at the beginning of this century. You are the pillars of our family. May Hashem grant you health and happiness for many years to come.

Rabbi Binyomin Eisenberger:

> You reignited the spark of Yiddishkeit in my soul and imbued me with a new love for learning. Your *Shiurim* are the highlight of my week. Your wisdom and guidance form the platform upon which I stand. May Hashem give you the strength to continue to be *marbitz Torah* and spread Yiddishkeit across the world.

To my chavrusah, Avi:

> Without you, *GPS* would have never happened. Your creativity and drive kept us going throughout the long process of writing this *sefer*. From learning to researching, from writing to editing, you made it for an enjoyable ride the entire time. May Hashem give you the *Siyata Dishmaya* to continue your *avodas hakodesh* and to inspire all those who seek your guidance on a daily basis.

To my partner in life, my wife Sima:

> There are no words to adequately thank you for all that you do for me and our family. All that I accomplish in life and all that I will accomplish is yours. May Hashem continue to shower us with *nachas* from all of our children; Elchonon & Racheli Jacobovits, Mimi, Yeshaya Dovid, Moshe, Bassie, Sara, Dovi, Shmuel.

The Gemara in *Maseches Shekalim* (7b) states: Dovid HaMelech prayed *"Agura B'ohalecha Olamim*— Let me dwell in two worlds." Asks the Gemora, how can one live in two worlds, either he is here on earth or he is in Olam Habbah? Answers the Gemora, Dovid HaMelech wanted his *Sefer Tehillim* to be prayed from long after he would pass away. This would keep him "alive" in this world even after passing on because his holy words were still having an impact. I pray that *GPS* should have a positive impact and inspire all those who read it and generate a chain reaction to affect others in a positive way that will last forever. *"Agura B'ohalecha Olamim."*

Y. Shain

After five years of writing our manuscript it was time to find a publisher that would appreciate and understand what we were trying to accomplish with *GPS: Navigation for Your Soul*. Rabbi Meir Zlotowitz and Rabbi Nosson Scherman who have been in the forefront of innovation for the last 30 years embraced our idea and we are eternally thankful to them for it.

We would like to thank Avrohom Biderman who was our guiding light throughout the publication process; Mrs. Frimy Eisner for proofreading the manuscript and giving us warm words of encouragement along the way, and Rabbi Moshe Rosenblum for turning his eagle eyes on the *Lashon Kodesh* quotations; Devorah Bloch for her creative talents in laying out the book and adding her special touch to enhance *GPS* in a professional way, and Eli Kroen for his expertise in photo-editing; Mendy Herzberg for coordinating the production and meeting all the deadlines.

THE NESIVOS SHALOM זצ"ל

Moreinu HaRav Shalom Noach Berezovsky
the Slonimer Rebbe זצ"ל
1911-2000

Shalom Noach was born August 8, 1911 (4 Av 5671) to an illustrious family of prominent Slonimer Chassidim in Baranovich, Poland. A diligent student, he absorbed the unique synthesis of the Talmudic system of the great Lithuanian yeshivos along with the lifestyle, values and thought system of Slonimer Chassidus.

Shalom Noach was a treasured student of both R' Moshe Midner זצ"ל (who was a close student of R' Chaim Brisker זצ"ל) and the Slonimer Rebbe; R' Avraham Weinberg זצ"ל (renowned for his collected Chassidic discourses under the title *Bais Avraham*). Under their personal guidance, he emerged with the spiritual dimensions of one who was destined for greatness. In approximately 1930, he was appointed to commit to memory and subsequently write up the discourses that the Rebbe delivered every Shabbos. These notes were subsequently published under the name *Bais Avraham*.

On a visit to Eretz Yisrael in 1933, the Bais Avraham arranged for Shalom Noach (to whom he lovingly referred as: "my most prized student") to marry the daughter of his first cousin R' Avraham Weinberg זצ"ל (author of *Birkas Avraham*), who became the Slonimer Rebbe in 1954. In 1935, Shalom Noach moved to Israel at the urging of the Slonimer Rebbe, the Bais Avraham.

In 1942, R' Shalom Noach received word of the annihilation of most of the Yiddishe population of Eastern Europe, including the yeshivah students of his beloved home town Baranovich and almost all of Slonimer Chassidus. After the indescribable near destruction of world Jewry, R' Shalom Noach responded with the enduring determination to rebuild. Abandoning a secure career, he moved to Yerushalayim and founded Yeshivah Bais Avraham, in memory and in the spirit of his beloved Rebbe the Bais Avraham, in order to replant and resuscitate the unique heritage and spirit of Slonimer Chassidus. Yeshivas Bais Avraham was the first of the yeshivos to re-open in Eretz Yisrael amidst the destruction of European Jewry. Although it began with only a few students and with almost no financial resources, it blossomed tremendously. Every student was personally molded by the Rosh Yeshivah, who instilled in his students a burning desire to live a committed life of Torah. His deeply rooted authentic Jewish wisdom, coupled with his princely spirit and impeccable character, made him a powerful role model for his students and many followers.

As well as being renowned for his genius in Torah and Chassidus, R' Shalom Noach became known as a master educator. With extraordinary insight he was able to penetrate and connect to the soul of any Jew — especially the youth — for his language was the language of the soul. In his inimitable fashion, he succeeded in pinpointing the individual abilities and character traits of every follower, giving them specific direction and curing their souls from any spiritual illnesses and complications. It is no accident that "Shalom Noach" is the exact numerical value of 434 which is the exact numerical value of "חנוך לנער," *to educate the young*, for his life was dedicated to educating Klal Yisrael.

In addition to his activities and influence within his own circles, he was also extensively involved for almost half a century with the spiritual direction of ALL the Yeshivos in Eretz Yisrael, as one of the heads of the *Vaad HaYeshivos* and *Chinuch Atzmai*. Also, as a respected member of the prestigious *Moetzes Gedolai HaTorah*, he was intimately involved with the many struggles facing the growing

Torah community. These activities were all part of his undying commitment to rebuild Klal Yisrael after the mass destruction of the Holocaust.

In 1981 (5741) at the age of 70, R' Shalom Noach was crowned the seventh Slonimer Rebbe after the passing of his father-in-law, the sainted Birkas Avraham, R' Avraham Weinberg. He became known as a titan of authentic Jewish thought and one of the spiritual giants that Hashem planted in our generation. His influence is felt, even after his passing, by means of his monumental work, *Nesivos Shalom*. Published in his lifetime, *Nesivos Shalom* has achieved extraordinary popularity throughout the entire spectrum of Torah communities, Chassidic and non-Chassidic alike. While its content and messages are deeply rooted in Kaballah and Chassidus, its language is clear and accessible to anyone who yearns for an elevated life. Rav Shach *zy"a* kept the *Sefer* on his desk and said, "The *Nesivos Shalom* is the *Mesillas Yesharim* of our generation!"

The Nesivos Shalom lived until almost 90, vibrant until the end. As one of the oldest Chassidic leaders who served as a bridge to an earlier era, he was venerated and loved by the entire Torah community. He passed away on August 8, 2000 (7 Av 5760) and was brought to rest on Har HaZaiysim.

זכותו תעמוד לנו להאיר לבנו
עד ביאת הגואל במהרה בימנו.

INTRODUCTION

After about 15 years working in the business world, I finally decided to go back to *kollel* for half a day. I decided to learn morning *seder*, but with whom? My wonderful nephew, Rabbi Sruli Gold *n"y*, found a wonderful *chavrusah* to learn with me for *Elul zman*, R' Chaim Simcha Elias *n"y*. But then I needed to find a new *chavrusah* for after *Succos*.

With great *Siyata Dishmaya*, I landed an **amazing** *chavrusah*. My good friend, fellow musician, and arch-enemy on the racquetball court, Yaakov (aka: JJ) Shain! Yaakov always learned or taught Torah the first half of his day before heading to his office, where he runs an importing business. Fortunately, he agreed to learn with me! But I made one stipulation; every day before learning Gemara, we must start off with 15 minutes of *Nesivos Shalom*. *"What's that?"* he asked. I explained that it is a *sefer* very close to my heart and I need my daily dose to inspire me! He reluctantly agreed to my request.

And so the "I" became "WE" and we started the winter *zman* learning *Mesechas Gitten* — but first, 15 minutes of *Nesivos Shalom* on Chanukah. The day after *Chanukah*, we began learning *Nesivos Shalom* on Purim. The day after *Purim* we began learning *Nesivos Shalom* on Pesach and **we** mamesh loved it! Fifteen minutes became thirty, thirty became sixty, and so on. We delved into the *sefer* and spent many many hours applying the holy words to our daily lives! The "history" of ancient Egypt became a living guide for our current life in America. The incredible words of the *Nesivos*

Shalom opened our eyes to understand many of our generation's spiritual struggles.

That's when my dear *chavrusah* couldn't take it anymore! *Avi — we need to share this incredible inspiration!* We decided to write an English *sefer* that would be based on what we learned. Our goal was to make sure that Jews of all ages and backgrounds would have access to the important lessons of our sages and a true understanding and appreciation of: *"Authentic Yiddishkeit."*

We took the concepts that inspired us, expanded, and elaborated on them, adding interesting examples and down-to-earth stories in order to make the information even more practical to apply. The final touch was when we decided to add pictures to each story, to bring out the message and to create a bookmark so the reader can easily reference a story that touched him.

What we present to you now is five years of daily work — a labor of love:

Section One helps us truly understand and internalize a major fundamental principle of Yiddishkeit: Hashem loves each and every Jew regardless of his situation!

Section Two focuses on the principle that every Jew is "Essentially" pure, good, and holy, since we have an indestructible piece of pure G-dliness inside of us that can never be damaged. That is why deep down every Yid always wants to be good!

So the obvious question is: If Hashem loves us so much and deep down we are essentially pure and good, then how come there is so much pain and suffering among Hashem's children? What is the purpose of life's challenges? That is the focus of Section Three.

Then in Section Four we draw a comparison between our present day *galus* and *galus Mitzrayim*, with the hopes that we can learn from the amazing parallels and use that information to navigate through our murky exile.

And finally, in Section Five we focus on how each person can break out of whatever is holding him back from raising himself up to a higher level. Although we use many extreme examples to bring out our point, the messages and tools we offer can benefit every person according to his level, from drug addict to saint. *(See letter from HaRav Yitzchok Scheiner shlit"a.)*

It is our sincere hope that you, dear reader, will find a fresh, easy, and enjoyable approach to the profound and often overlooked concepts of *Authentic Yiddishkeit*. It is our hope you will be able to use our GPS to navigate yourself — or someone you know — to a life of freedom, as we strive to do for ourselves on a daily basis.

Although we made these concepts very accessible by often taking a light and playful approach, you must know that every underlying concept we write about is derived only from the holy *Sefarim*. We even included the Hebrew quotes so you can see their beautiful words directly.

Certainly we would never use the phrase "Authentic Yiddishkeit" for something "we" made up. So when we say with confidence: "Authentic Yiddishkeit believes ..." it is only because this is what is written by the **authentic** leaders of Klal Yisrael throughout the generations.

We hope that you will be inspired to develop a strong bond with your Creator and find the peace of mind we all long for.

Avi Fishoff
Yaakov Y. Shain

Kislev 5772
November 2011

FOREWORD

"אם למדת תורה הרבה
אל תחזיק טובה לעצמך
כי לכך נוצרת!"

מסכת אבות פרק ב:ח

The משנה says:
"If you learn a lot of Torah,
don't give yourself a lot of credit,
for that is why you were created!"

One of the *mefarshim* explains, "אל תחזיק טובה לעצמך — don't keep the goodness all to yourself!" The message now reads: "If you learn a lot of Torah, don't keep this goodness all to yourself — spread the word! — for this is why you were created!" Therefore, when somebody is *zocheh* to learn and understand Yiddishkeit, it is important to share what he has discovered with others!

In addition, "אין חכם כבעל נסיון" — there is no wisdom like the wisdom gleaned from real life experience.

GPS is a combination of both of these concepts; (a) It is based on חכמת התורה of the many ספרים הקדושים that you cite, (b) it also has the benefit of wisdom derived from real life experience, since you are sharing what you have learned from your personal hands-on experience of helping many Yidden return to Hashem.

In our day and age we B"H have many wonderful *Sefarim*, however, what is unique about *GPS* is that it expounds upon the profound fundamental principles of Yiddishkeit, yet it is written in an enjoyable, down-to-earth manner that allows anyone to access them. *GPS* has the feel of a heart-to-heart conversation; intimate and warm, funny and inspiring. The insightful stories and creative parables will leave you deeply satisfied and spiritually uplifted. *GPS* does not preach "idealistic" concepts of what Yiddishkeit **should** be in a perfect world; rather, it offers "practical" advice to inspire a person to raise himself to what his Yiddishkeit **could** be in our very not-perfect world!

I would summarize the approach and flavor of GPS using the famous *vort* of the Baal Shem Tov.

"מְשׁוֹךְ חַסְדְּךָ לְיוֹדְעֶךָ

אֵ-ל קַנָּא וְנוֹקֵם".

"Extend Your kindness to those who know You,
O jealous and vengeful G-d."

The question is; if we are asking Hashem to bestow "kindness" upon us, then why do we address Him using the description: "vengeful G-d"?

The Baal Shem Tov explains with a powerful parable: Someone was once caught sinning against the king. When they brought him to the king, the ruler gave him a personal royal tour of his palace, his treasure houses of jewels, and he revealed to him all of the kind social services that he secretly provides for his people.

The advisors were shocked and they asked: "What are you doing? Not only aren't you punishing him — but you're doing the exact opposite! How will he ever learn a lesson?"

The king replied: "I know this man and I believe that he never meant to rebel against me. Because I showed him how kind and generous I am, he deeply regretted everything he did wrong and pledged his complete allegiance to me!"

This is the explanation of the *pasuk*: When we go against our inner pure will and we sin against our King, we ask Hashem to please help us get back on the right path by showering us with "kindness" so that we will deeply regret everything we did wrong and pledge our complete allegiance to Him!!

In today's times, we need to tap into this powerful *derech*. Instead of smacking, spanking, screaming, shouting, degrading, humiliating, and belittling, we must approach children, and ourselves, from a different angle. We must try to bring out how much Hashem truly loves us and how much He does for us each and every day!

People mistakenly think that the concept of "Unconditional love and acceptance" is a modern invention that will cause people to continue to sin against Hashem's commandments thinking, "If Hashem will love me unconditionally, then I don't need to be good!" The truth is that the exact opposite is true! For when you truly internalize this feeling, your inner desire will be, "How can I not be close to such a wonderful and kind G-d!"

This is the way to become inspired in our day and age. With so many spiritual challenges so readily available to young and old alike, today's battle is truly "uphill." *GPS* delivers Torah-true guidance for ourselves and our children. I don't want to call it a "book" because it is actually a *sefer* that strengthens and elevates the reader to live a *hechereh* life of meaning and purpose.

I really feel that there is nobody out there who doesn't need the type of *chizuk* that *GPS* provides. It's just that some people realize it, and some people still haven't realized it — but everybody needs it!

I give you a *brachah* that your *sefer* should find favor in the eyes of the masses and that you should be *zocheh* to inspire people למעלה מדרך הטבע.

Rav Binyomin Eisenberger

Kislev 5772

GUESS WHAT:
HASHEM
LOVES YOU

"Hashem loves you even more than you love yourself!"

"הקב"ה אוהב לאדם יותר משהאדם אוהב את עצמו."

ספר שמירת הלשון שער הזכירה פרק ב'

1

UNCONDITIONAL LOVE

*Analyzing the unique relationship
between parents & their children*

"לא נמצא רחמי
שום נמצא על זולתו
יותר מרחמי האב על הבן."

ספר העיקרים מאמר שלישי פרק ל"ז

SEFER HA'IKRIM:

*"We don't find any love
greater than the
love a father
has for
his child."*

HASHEM

**set up the world with an innate indestructible
love that every parent has for his child:**

"רחמי האב על הבן הוא
רחמנות הבאה מטבע כל
החיים כדרך הכלבים
והבהמות."

ספר אורחות צדיקים שער הרחמים

The mercy a parent feels toward his child is a natural instinct similar to that found in all other living creatures, such as dogs and other animals.

LET'S ANALYZE THIS FOR A MOMENT:

Just as you can build a relationship and create positive feelings toward another human being, so too those feelings can cool off and the relationship can dissolve. A person can detach himself emotionally from any relationship; you can split from a business partner, dissolve a friendship, and even divorce a spouse.

However, parents can NEVER STOP loving their children, because the relationship is not man-made; rather, it is a natural instinct created by Hashem.

But what about all the pain, agony, and frustration a child can sometimes cause his parents? Doesn't it sometimes seem that some parents "hate" their child?

When we see frustration, tension, and anger between parents and children, we are actually witnessing the manifestation of their indestructible bond, because when parents overreact and "freak out," that is the very proof that their internal love is still intact.

It would be much LESS painful and much EASIER for parents to cope with a difficult child if their loving bond would lessen as their relationship deteriorated. The proof is: Would they ever get this worked up because of their neighbor's child, their nephew, or anyone else in the world!?

Therefore, when a child sees how angry and frustrated his parents are because of the way he acts, he should realize that this proves how much they love him! For if they didn't love him so much — they wouldn't be so infuriated!

Furthermore, if the child would become deathly ill or in need of a kidney, these same parents — who seem so full of hate toward the child — would surely do whatever is necessary to help save their child! And what if the child would, G-d forbid, die? Who would bury the child ... mourn the child ... say *Kaddish* for the child ...?

Only parents grieve endlessly and even decades later still feel pain and longing for their child!

HERE'S A POWERFUL EXAMPLE OF THIS CONCEPT:

Dovid HaMelech's son, Avshalom, is the perfect example of a son gone entirely wrong. After all, what can possibly be worse than a son trying to murder his father!?

"וירגז המלך ויעל על עלית השער ויבך וכה אמר בלכתו:
בני אבשלום בני בני אבשלום מי יתן מותי אני תחתיך אבשלום בני בני..."

וְהַמֶּלֶךְ לָאַט אֶת פָּנָיו וַיִּזְעַק הַמֶּלֶךְ קוֹל גָּדוֹל **בְּנִי** אַבְשָׁלוֹם אַבְשָׁלוֹם **בְּנִי בְנִי!"**

שמואל ב' י:ה

Yet when Avshalom was killed, Dovid cried out eight times, "My son" and he could not be consoled! He even cried out, "If only I could have died instead of you!"

The lesson to us is clear: A child always remains a child **regardless** of what he does, and even when it seems that the child has destroyed his relationship with his parents, the internal connection is still completely intact.

We all know of many stories where parents and children made up with each other even after many years of horrific fighting and separation. Had someone else caused that much pain to the parents — there would be NO coming back. But with a child, emotions and tears pour forth with words of love as soon as the walls of separation come down.

The reason that children, and particularly young adults, have so much trouble understanding this concept is because of one sad fact: It simply does NOT work both ways!

"גָּדְלָה רַחֲמֵי הָאָב עַל הַבֵּן יוֹתֵר מִבֵּן עַל הָאָב!"

שפת אמת בראשית פרשת ויגש תרל"ט

The natural inborn love that a child has for his parents is not nearly as strong as the attachment the parents have for their child.

Therefore, until a person has his very own child, "unconditional love" is just a theoretical concept but not a feeling he can actually experience. He can hear the concept of a father risking his own life to save his child — even if the child is mentally challenged and physically ill — but he doesn't have anyone in his life for whom he would actually do that.

It is for this reason that a child can begin to comprehend and appreciate his parents' unconditional love for him only after he has his own child toward whom he will feel unconditional eternal love.

THE DIFFERENCE

This is the difference between the parent/child relationship and ALL other relationships. All other relationships begin when you meet someone and begin to develop a connection. At this point your association is purely external and is void of any internal feelings. However, as you continue to share life experiences together, you will develop an *internal* bond with that person.

Thus, every other relationship begins with *externally* getting along and "liking each other" and then it slowly works its way into the *internal* emotional zone of love.

Under normal circumstances, you can't develop a real emotional bond with someone you just met two weeks ago. You can really like them and enjoy being with them, but it takes time until that connection develops into internal emotional feelings.

FALLING FOR IT

This is why there is no such thing as "falling in love." "Falling in love" is an oxymoron and only morons fall for it. Love is a person's deepest emotion, and it takes years and years to truly develop real internal feelings for another human being. You cannot simply "fall" into it.

People claim to "fall in love" and then "fall out of love" over and over again, "falling" in and out, in and out. But the quicker you "fall in love" the quicker you "fall out of it," because it was never a true emotional connection and inner bond. In truth, you were never in love with anyone (other than maybe yourself)!

However, when parents create a child — the love they feel for their creation is not based on any external factors, since the baby has not done anything and is not doing anything to earn their love or respect.

"כי אין רחמים גדולים
כרחמי האב על הבן!"
רד"ק תהלים פרק ק"ג

Yet "internally," in the emotional zone of love, a parent's heart is completely in love with their child right away, from the very first minute!

CUTIE PIE

If someone would disturb your night's sleep demanding to be fed and changed — night after night — you would probably HATE that person with a passion and you'd call the cops!

Yet, this baby — who you only know for two weeks — gets away with it night after night ... and to top it all off — you even think that he's the MOST ADORABLE thing on the planet!

WHAT DID THIS BABY DO TO EARN THIS KIND OF EMOTIONAL ATTACHMENT?

Absolutely Nothing! And that is precisely why this love is:

Indestructible!

Thus, the basis of "true love" is an internal emotional connection that is an indestructible, unconditional, internal, eternal bond. You are emotionally attached to that person and that is not based on how well you get along or how strong your exterior *connection* is.

"כל אהבה שהיא תלויה בדבר: בטל הדבר בטלה אהבה;
ושאינה תלויה בדבר: **אינה בטלה לעולם!**"
אבות דר' נתן פרק מ'

When love is dependent on something external, then when that thing is taken away, the feeling of love — that developed only because of that external thing — will evaporate. However, when the love you feel for someone is not based on anything external, then it can NEVER be destroyed.

Therefore, the only way that true love can develop is if an internal emotional bond is created. This happens **slowly** over time by helping each other, giving to each other, supporting each other through hard times, etc. .... These things build a true **internal** connection between one person and another. After true love develops, even if the external factors fade away over time, the internal connection continues to grow stronger and stronger.

However, the deep feelings of love and attachment that a parent has for a child are inserted by Hashem directly into the internal zone of love without going through the external process. Therefore, it is **unconditional and indestructible.**

There is no internal joy like the "nachas" parents get from their child ... even a little baby cooing ... saying "mama" ... crawling in the mud ... eating melted chocolate with his hands ... it's all *"delicious"* to his parents. (Just to "his" parents!)

Conversely, there is no pain like the pain parents feel when their children give them *agmas nefesh* (grief); from little things that bother them way out of proportion, to big things that break their hearts in a way that no child can even begin to understand.

Yet even if the **outer** connection between parent and child is so damaged that they may even *seem* to hate each other, still and all, the **interior emotional connection** and inborn instinctive feeling of unconditional love remains completely intact.

As we have seen with Dovid HaMelech, his son Avshalom was ready to take his father's life — yet when Avshalom's life was taken, his father cried out in terrible pain. So too, regardless of what happens between parents and their child — nothing can break the eternal bond.

NOW WE CAN DISCOVER SOMETHING AMAZING:

> "כד ברא קודשא בריך הוא עלמא ברא ליה כגוונא דלעילא
> למהוי עלמא דא בדיוקנא דעלמא דלעילא."

זוהר כרך ה' (שמות) פרשת פקודי דף רכא.

The Holy *Zohar* teaches us that the physical world was created as an exact mirror image of the invisible mystical world above.

Just as we explained that a child cannot comprehend the concept of "unconditional love" because it does not exist in any of his relationships, so too, parents would never be able to comprehend this unique concept of "unconditional love" if they did not have this feeling toward their children.

We can now appreciate that the reason Hashem chose to create the concept of an instinctive unbreakable love from parent to child is specifically so that we could have some way to comprehend the concept of unconditional love! For if there was no earthly concept of "unconditional love," then we would have no way to wrap our minds around the idea that Hashem can love US unconditionally!

> "זה א-לי ואנוהו
> אלוקי אבי וארממנהו."

שמות פרק טו:ב

The Torah says that after the Splitting of the Sea we all sang to Hashem: "He is MY G-d and I will honor Him, the G-d of my father and I shall uplift Him."

During the last Shabbos of the *Divrei Shmuel's* life, he quoted the above verse, which is also found in our daily prayers, and then he passionately challenged the people around him:

> "זה א-לי? במה הוא א-לי שלי? מה מסרתי והקרבתי בעבורו?
> וכי שיניתי את הטבעיות והתשוקות שלי לכבודו יתברך?
> ומה זכותי שיקרא אלוקים שלי?"

מובא בנתיבות שלום חלק ב' דף רצ"א

"Is Hashem 'MY' G-d? How did He become 'MY' G-d? What did I do to *earn* that He should be 'MY' G-d? Did I overcome my natural tendencies and withhold my desires out of respect for His honor? What did I sacrifice to merit and acquire His love and devotion to me?"

Let's be honest; every relationship is a two-way street. To obtain love and affection from someone, you need to do **something** to "earn" it.

You can't simply pick someone out of the blue and proclaim, "This person is **MY** best friend," if you've done nothing at all to earn that title. Making mighty proclamations about your "close" relationship with Hashem, and grand statements like: "זה א-לי (He is **MY** G-d)" is spiritually dishonest if you have not done anything to *earn* this title!

Then the *Divrei Shmuel* explains: In every relationship one must *earn* the other person's affection; however, there is one exception:

WHAT A ZEESKEIT

Suri waited for five years to finally be blessed with a child. She could not stop talking about her "gorgeous zeeskeiyt," the cutest baby on the planet! But for some reason, whenever she introduced her baby to other people ... they replied, "Oh ... yes ... adorable ... definitely one of a kind ..." and found some excuse to quickly slip away.

"שבכדי להיות 'בן' אינו צריך למסור ולהקריב מאומה!
כי בין אם ימסור עבורו ובין אם לא ימסור:
הרי אביו הוא!"
מובא בנתיבות שלום חלק ב' דף רצ"א

To attain the title "child," you do not need to do anything at all. Once you are someone's child you will always remain that person's child and nothing will ever change that!

Since the only example on earth of indestructible love is the love of parents for their children, that is *davka* (specifically) why Hashem chose to call us — of all titles:

"בנים

אתם לה' אלוקיכם!"

דברים יד:א

"You are **CHILDREN** to Hashem your G-d!"

Hashem chose to call us His beloved **CHILDREN**, knowing full well the ramifications of this comparison — and He certainly meant it — in every sense of the word!

Interestingly, as seen above, the instinctive feeling of love that parents have toward their children is far stronger than the love children feel toward their parents. Accordingly, we can be sure that Hashem's love for us **far exceeds** the love we can possibly feel toward Hashem.

Authentic Yiddishkeit believes that the love parents feel toward their children is instilled by Hashem as a natural instinct and it is not dependent on anything at all. Now you know exactly why Hashem chose this specific way to describe His unconditional love toward each and every one of us!

Now you know beyond a shadow of a doubt that regardless of who you are and what situation you are in ...

Hashem loves ...
YOU!

2

HASHEM ... OUR FATHER

*Getting real with understanding
our relationship with Hashem*

"נמצא כי יפליג הכתוב
באהבת השם יתברך את
ישראל כאב לבן מכל צד
שאפשר שתהיה האהבה
ביניהם."

ספר העיקרים מאמר שלישי פרק ל"ז

SEFER HA'IKRIM:
*"The Torah emphasizes that
the love Hashem feels
toward Klal Yisrael is
comparable in
every way to a
father's love
for his child."*

HASHEM

**has been caring for us for a very long time;
let's roll back the tape to when we became
His nation:**

"כה אמר ה': **בני בכרי ישראל**!"

שמות ד:כב

"So said Hashem: **My firstborn son is Yisrael**!"

"My firstborn son" is a symbolic term of affection and love. Just as a firstborn has a special place in his parents' hearts, so too Klal Yisrael is Hashem's most worthy and beloved people!

Let's stop and think about this for a moment: If G-d decided to select one nation from the entire planet to be His "chosen" people for all of time, don't you think it should have been the most successful people on the planet?

"בחירת הקדוש ברוך הוא בישראל להיות לו לעם ...
לא היתה כאשר הם כבני מלכים, **אלא בהיותם בתכלית שפל המצב**!"

נתיבות שלום חלק ב' עמוד שס"ד

Imagine the SHOCK when He chose a broken people who were physically enslaved, emotionally broken, and spiritually corrupt!

We were extremely LOW in every category: **Physically**, we were poor and powerless slaves! **Emotionally**, we were swallowed up by our masters with no voice of our own! **Spiritually**, we had drifted far from the lofty levels of our Holy Avos and the twelve sons of Yaakov, and we were now lowly idol worshipers!

"במצב כזה שהיו שקועים במ"ט [49] שערי טומאה ונתונים בבית עבדים
שיא השפלות ברוחניות ובגשמיות קורא להם הקדוש ברוך הוא:
'בני בכורי ישראל' להודיע שלא מפני מעשיהם הטובים הם 'בני'
אלא הם בעצם בני בכורי וממילא אין נפקא מינה מה מצבם!"

נתיבות שלום ענייני חנוכה מאמר שני "חג האמונה והבטחון" אות ב'

It was specifically when we were in this terribly low situation that
Hashem referred to us with incredible **love** and **pride**, in order to
PROVE to us for all of time that we were NOT chosen because of
our ACTIONS; rather we are essentially His beloved child — and
therefore His love for us is **unconditional and indestructible!**

"שכדי להוציא את ישראל ממ"ט שערי טומאה הי-ה הכרח
שירד הקדוש ברוך הוא בגילוי שכינה אפילו בתוך מצרים, והכל לגודל
אהבתו יתברך את ישראל כדי להצילם ולעשותם עם הנבחר!"

נתיבות שלום חלק ב' ענייני פסח דף רס"ה

Hashem lowered Himself כביכול (so to speak) to "ערות הארץ,"
the most disgusting and perverted place on earth, in order to
personally rescue His beloved children who were gasping for their
last spiritual breath.

Hashem's extraction of an unworthy people who had already given
up on themselves, and then His appointing these people to be
His exalted chosen nation and ambassador to the world, was an
outrageously monumental event as shocking as a toothless janitor
winning the lottery and then being asked to marry the princess of
England on the same day!

"אתם עמוסים ונשואים מבטן ומרחם אמכם
וכן אשא ואסבול עלי אתכם עד שיבה ...
כל ימיכם לא אטוש אתכם!"

רד"ק ישעיהו מו:ג

Hashem told us: "You have been carried as a child in a mother's
womb, and so I will carry you and I will tolerate you until the end
of time ... all of your days [good and bad] and I will never leave
you forever." (What an amazing Hallmark card this would make!)

THIS ANSWERS ANOTHER QUESTION:

Why did Hashem rescue us from Mitzrayim specifically while we were immersed in the lowest level of *tumah*?

"ואף שהיה ביד הקדוש ברוך הוא לטהר אותם ממ"ט [49] שערי טומאה
ותפסוק זוהמתם עוד קודם יציאת מצרים, חפץ הקדוש ברוך הוא
להראות לישראל לדורות שהוציא אותם כשהיו בתכלית שפל המצב
ללמד שגם במצב כזה לא כהתה אהבתו יתברך להם!"

נתיבות שלום עניני חנוכה מאמר שני "חג האמונה והבטחון"

Had Hashem pulled us out of Mitzrayim when we were on a higher level, then in the future, if we would ever spiral down below the level we were on when Hashem took us out of Egypt, we might think that Hashem does NOT love us anymore!

When a son comes to his father with a test mark of "80" and his father still shows that he loves his son and is proud to be his father, then the son will only know that his father feels that way as long as he gets at least an "80." But if a son comes home with a "0" and the father STILL pours out his love, pride, and affection, then the child knows that his father's love is truly UNCONDITIONAL!

Had Hashem taken us out of Mitzrayim while we were on the "30th" level of spiritual contamination — then we would have no way to know that we are STILL the apple of His eye and He is STILL crazy about us if we would ever sink below that level in the future!

So it turns out that the reason that Hashem arranged that the Jews in Egypt 3,000+ years ago would be at the lowest level when He called them "My beloved firstborn child" was because He wanted to send **YOU — yes, YOU** — a clear message: **YOU should know and internalize that I truly love YOU, and nothing you do can ever diminish My love for you!!**

But it gets even better!

"ישראל נקראו **בנים** שנאמר: 'בנים אתם לה׳ אלקיכם.' (דברים יד:א)
ומלאכי השרת נקראו **בנים** שנאמר: 'ויבואו בני האלקים.' (איוב א:ו)
"ואי אתה יודע איזה אהוב מהם. כשהוא אומר:
'בני בכורי ישראל.' (שמות ד:כב)
[ישראל] אתם חביבין לפני יותר ממלאכי השרת!!!"
מסכתות קטנות מסכת אבות דרבי נתן נוסחא ב׳ פרק מ״ד

The Medrash says: "The Yidden are called Hashem's "children"
and angels are also called Hashem's "children" — but which
"child" does Hashem loves more?"

Now hold on a second — this is absolutely incredible! Angels
NEVER sin! Angels NEVER mess up! Angels NEVER go against the
will of Hashem! Yet, there is still a question of whether Hashem
loves YOU even more than He loves an angel!?! That's truly
amazing!

BUT THE ANSWER — IS EVEN MORE AMAZING!

The Medrash answers: "Since it says 'MY **FIRSTBORN** SON
YISRAEL' — and that is a term of love and affection — this proves
that the Yidden are **MORE BELOVED THAN ANGELS!**" This is
almost impossible to imagine!

BUT WAIT — IT GETS EVEN MORE AMAZING!

The PROOF that Hashem loves every Jew more than He loves
heavenly angels comes from the *pasuk* that Hashem used to
describe the Yidden while we were slaves in Mitzrayim and doing
what ...? That's right: SERVING IDOLS!

DO YOU REALIZE WHAT THIS MEANS?

Hashem LOVES a spiritually contaminated Yid who is defying G-d in the worst possible way — even MORE than He loves pure divine angels!

Yes, you read that right! This proves that even if you **REBEL** against Hashem in the WORST POSSIBLE WAY — He still LOVES YOU and wants to be close to you!

DON'T BELIEVE US? READ THIS:

"ה׳ אלקיו עמו: אפילו מכעיסין וממרים לפניו אינו זז מתוכן!"

רש"י פרשת בלק כג:כא

When the Torah says "Hashem, your G-d, is with you," it means that even if you **REBEL** and **ANGER** Him — He will NEVER leave your side!

Authentic Yiddishkeit believes that Hashem loves a Jew who is on the LOWEST POSSIBLE LEVEL — even more than He loves a perfect holy angel on the HIGHEST level!

"בן המלך נשאר תמיד בן המלך בכל המצבים שנמצא!"

הרב הקדוש מ׳רוזין זי"ע מובא בספר נתיבות שלום עניני פורים עמוד נ"ה

"A prince always remains a prince,
regardless of what situation he is in!"

Even if you are not loyal to Hashem and you do not uphold your side of the relationship — the fact remains that you are still a **SON** and Hashem is still your **FATHER** and this title can **never** be revoked!

THIS IS TRULY SOMETHING TO BE THANKFUL FOR — AND WE CERTAINLY ARE!

"**ברוך** המקום **ברוך** הוא **ברוך** שנתן תורה לעמו ישראל **ברוך** הוא.
כנגד ארבעה בנים דברה תורה:
אחד חכם, אחד רשע, אחד תם, ואחד שאינו יודע לשאול."

הגדה של פסח

Every year on Pesach we say these famous words from the Haggadah: "**Blessed** is He who is everywhere, **blessed** is He, **blessed** is He who gave Klal Yisrael the Torah, **blessed** is He! The Torah speaks to the four types of children: the wise, the wicked, the simpleton, and the one who does not know to ask."

Now let's look deeper and uncover an incredible message:

"ענין ההקדמה הזאת מהמגיד לומר ד' פעמים בלשון 'ברוך' והודיה
להשם יתברך היא על זה [גופא] שדברה תורה כנגד ד' בנים!"

ספר נתיבות שלום חלק ב' עניני פסח רנ"ג

The reason that the Haggadah begins with praising Hashem FOUR times, is to acknowledge and thank Hashem for wanting to engage each of the FOUR types of children!

In essence, we say: BLESS YOU, HASHEM, for accepting and wanting to have a relationship with EVERY kind of person; the WISE, the WICKED, the SIMPLETON, and even the one who doesn't even have a clue!

BUT WAIT — IT GETS SOOOO MUCH BETTER!!!

"היינו שיש בה עניני חיזוק בעבודת ה' לכל אחד באשר הוא
שבכל מצביו הרוחניים יכול להתחזק
כי לבן נחשב לפני המקום!"

ספר נתיבות שלום חלק ב' עניני פסח רנ"ג

The Haggadah is not just referring to four **different** people — it is also referring to EACH PERSON: Sometimes you proudly act like a WISE person. However other times, you may find yourself acting out like a WICKED sinful person! Then there are times that you act and think without any depth — just like a SIMPLETON! And sometimes you may find yourself in a situation where you are so lost that you just don't even know what to say!

THE MESSAGE IS VERY CLEAR:

"הן אם הוא במצב של בן חכם והן אם הוא במצב של בן רשע
יש לו את התואר 'בן' ויש לו תשובה על השאלות המעיקות עליו!"

ספר נתיבות שלום חלק ב' עניני פסח רנ"ג

 Authentic Yiddishkeit believes that whatever situation you will ever find yourself in, you will always retain your title of being Hashem's beloved SON, and Hashem is always ready, willing, and available to communicate with you!

NOW WE CAN UNCOVER SOMETHING VERY SPECIAL:

"ויאמר דוד: ברוך אתה ה' אלוקי ישראל אבינו מעולם ועד עולם!"

תפילת שחרית

Dovid HaMelech says:
"Blessed are You, Hashem, the Lord of Yisrael,
our Father **forever** and ever."

The word "עולם" can have two meanings: "forever" or "world." Although the simple meaning in this verse is "forever," we can also explain the verse using the meaning "world."

"פירוש: אתה אלוקי ישראל

הנך 'אבינו' באיזה 'עולם' שאנו נמצאים!

כמו שהנך אבינו במצב של 'אסק שמים שם אתה',

כך גם, 'ואציעה שאול - הנך אבינו!'"

ספר נתיבות שלום חלק א' דף נ.

The verse now reads: "Blessed are You, Hashem, the Lord of Klal Yisrael, OUR FATHER **regardless** of which 'world' we are in!" Just as when you find yourself immersed in a world of spirituality and holiness you know and believe that Hashem is your Father, so too, when you are immersed in filthy activities — you must know and believe that Hashem is still your **Father!** That is certainly something to thank Hashem for!

"החטא הגדול ביותר

כשיהודי שוכח שהוא בן מלך!"

ר' שלמה מקארלין מובא בספר פתגמים נבחרים

Therefore, the greatest mistake you can possibly make is to forget that no matter what — **YOU ARE A PRINCE!** The SON of the Creator and Master of the Universe!

THE TRICK IS TO LIVE WITH THIS FEELING ON A DAILY BASIS

"יהודי מזכיר את יציאת מצרים ב' פעמים בכל יום בבוקר ובערב

לידע שהקדוש ברוך הוא הוציא את ישראל מארץ מצרים

בהיותם משוקעים במ"ט [49] שערי טומאה, שזה יסוד האמונה

כי חלק ה' עמו יעקב חבל נחלתו!"

נתיבות שלום עניני חנוכה אות ב'

Every morning and **every** night of **every** day, **everyone** is required to recall that Hashem took us out of Egypt. Why on earth is this SO important to us that we need to always repeat the same story over and over?

The reason we recall this every "morning" and every "night" is to ingrain into ourselves that regardless of whether we are going through a period of "morning" or "night" — Hashem is right there by our side! We must INTERNALIZE that Hashem rescued us out of slavery even while we were on the LOWEST LEVEL of spiritual contamination! This is the foundation of our faith — not just our faith in Hashem — but **the faith that we must have IN OURSELVES!**

You can never do anything to cause Hashem to give up on you and "write you off" ...

So why give up on yourself?

3

KEEPING US CLOSE

Coming to terms with being loved
unconditionally by your Creator

"אלמלי הוו ידעין בני
נשא רחימותא דרחים
קודשא בריך הוא לישראל
הוו שאגין ככפיריא
למרדף אבתריה."

זוהר חלק ב׳ פרשת שמות ה:

"If man would comprehend the
great love that Hashem feels
for Yisrael, he would
run to Him
[Hashem] like a
roaring lion!"

HASHEM

**showed Moshe how far He is willing to
go to make sure that we don't slip away
from Him:**

"אמר רבי יוחנן אלמלא מקרא כתוב אי אפשר לאומרו: מלמד שנתעטף
הקדוש ברוך הוא כשליח צבור, והראה לו למשה סדר תפלה. אמר לו: כל
זמן שישראל חוטאין - יעשו לפני כסדר הזה ואני מוחל להם!"

תלמוד בבלי מסכת ראש השנה דף יז:

R' Yochanan said: Had the Torah not written this, we would
never be able to say it: Hashem wrapped Himself in a *tallis* like a
prayer leader and taught Moshe that whenever Yisrael sins, they
should say the following, and I WILL FORGIVE THEM!"

WHAT SHOULD WE SAY?

"ויעבר ה' על פניו ויקרא:
ה' ה' א-ל רחום וחנון ארך אפים ורב חסד ואמת
נצר חסד לאלפים נשא עון ופשע וחטאה ונקה."

שמות לד:ו

"Hashem passed before [Moshe] and proclaimed:

ה' ה'	Hashem, Hashem
א-ל	G-d
רחום וחנון	merciful and compassionate

ארך אפים	slow to anger
ורב חסד	and abundant in kindness
ואמת	and truth
נצר חסד לאלפים	preserver of compassion for thousands of generations
נשא עון ופשע וחטאה	carrier of our sins, willful sin, and error
ונקה	and He who cleanses

Let's take a journey into the famous "Thirteen Attributes of Mercy" in order to deeply understand how Hashem deals with YOU on a daily basis:

"כי השם הראשון הוא עצם ולא מידה, והשם השני מידה - והוא מידת
רחמים בלא תשובה ובלא שאלה, אלא כאב רחמן שהוא מרחם על בנו
ויודע בו מה שהוא צריך ונותן לו מבלי שישאל ממנו וכן הוא (ה') יתעלה
מרחם הוא על הרשע אפילו בלא תשובה!"

רבינו בחיי שמות לד:ו-ז

The first time the *pasuk* says the Name "Hashem," it is describing the essential Name of Hashem, Who is our merciful Creator.

However, the second time that it says "Hashem," it refers to the awesome character trait of EXTREME MERCY that Hashem has toward those who sin against Him, **even if they don't repent or ask forgiveness!** Hashem is a merciful Father who feels so bad for His child and therefore He has mercy even on a RASHA, even before he repents!

It is truly incredible that Hashem is even interested in you **after you sin.** But what's even more amazing is that of all the Names that Hashem could have chosen to represent Himself to you after you sinned against Him, He specifically chose "הוי-ה" which is the SAME Name used by the person who **DIDN'T SIN.** And to top it off — it is the Name reflecting Hashem's greatest level of — believe it or not — **MERCY!**

> ## DADDY DEAR
>
> *A father who wants his son to lovingly call him "Daddy" will not say, "If you do something wrong, then call me 'my mother's husband'"!*
>
> *A father always remains a father and a son always remains a son. No matter how much a son may mess up — he can always call out to his father: "**Daddy**, help me"!*

Hashem tells us: I know that you will sin! And I want you to know right from the start, that even if you cross the line and betray My will, I am willing to still relate to you in the **same exact way,** for I will always be your merciful **"ה'—Hashem"**!

CAN WE SHARE SOMETHING BEAUTIFUL WITH YOU?

הוי"ה בגימטריא כ"ו כנגדו כ"ו שבועות ימות החורף וכ"ו שבועות ימות החמה, ב' שמות של שם שהוא ברחמים בימות החמה ובימות הגשמים!"

ספר השם מרוקח עמוד כ"ה

The merciful Name of Hashem that is spelled in the Torah הוי"ה, has the numerical value of 26. The verse specifically says הוי"ה two times to teach us: whether we are in the 26 weeks of fall/winter or the 26 weeks of spring/summer, Hashem is always ready to relate to us with mercy!

Not only is Hashem our MERCIFUL FATHER when we spiritually "blossom" and grow closer to Him and when we actually feel the "warmth" of His Holiness, but even when we are "falling" from our spiritual level and our hearts are "ice cold" and we don't feel connected to Him — we can ALWAYS relate to Hashem as our merciful and compassionate Father Who is there for us and loves us!

Hashem never wants us to become distant from Him, so after we sin and slip away, Hashem closes the gap caused by **our** wrongdoings so that He can remain connected to us.

We can now understand that Hashem specifically created the many wonderful attributes of mercy in order to assist the sinner! Because if you never sin, then you do not need Hashem to be compassionate, slow to anger, forgiver of willful sin, etc.

Hashem's message is clear: I am a merciful G-d and I stand ready to bestow limitless patience, generosity, and kindness upon you: **even after you sin against Me!**

LET'S REVIEW THIS PLAY BY PLAY

Here's your contribution to the relationship: You mess up and sin. Once, twice, perhaps even many times. You have not yet repented for your sins. Your harmful actions cause you to slip away from your previous level of connection to Hashem.

Hashem lovingly responds with; "Oh, no, you don't — don't you separate from Me! I will now add onto **Myself** attributes of patience and mercy!"

But it doesn't stop there: The more we sin ... the lower we sink ... the farther we stray ... the **MORE** Hashem responds with even MORE patience, compassion, and mercy — specifically so that we don't disconnect from Him!

LET'S SEE HOW THIS WORKS:

After you sin, the first response from Hashem is that He will still deal with you in a merciful and compassionate manner. The Torah then goes on to tell us that Hashem's response to your sin is: "רחום" (mercy) and "חנון" (compassion).

"מה בין 'רחום' ל'חנון'? רחום: שהבורא יתברך מרחם עלינו כדרך
'כרחם אב על בנים' שישמרם שלא יפלו ...."

מובא בספר מעיין השבוע בשם אבן עזרא שמות פרק לד:ו

What's the difference between "רחום" (mercy) and "חנון" (compassion)? רחום means that Hashem has mercy on us like "a father has mercy on his child" and guards us so that we "should not fall."

"אבל לפעמים שומט הבן ידו של אביו, ורץ לבור שחת ונופל בו!
אזי פועלת מדת החנינה: 'וחנון' כדרך כי חנון אני (שמות כב:כב)
להושיע מי שנפל ולא יוכל קום!"

מובא בספר מעיין השבוע בשם אבן עזרא שמות פרק לד:ו

However, sometimes a foolish child **pulls his hand** from his father's grip and ends up falling into a deep pit! When you pull yourself away from G-d and cannot get up on your own, Hashem then employs His incredible trait of "חנון" (compassion) to rescue you! Just incredible!

If you stop reading here — you already got your money's worth! Understanding this unbelievably affectionate response from Hashem should inspire you to want to be close to such a wonderful G-d! Hashem is very understanding of your flaws and wants you to be in His inner circle. Got it? Okay — let's move on.

WHAT IF YOU STILL DON'T REPENT ... AND PERHAPS EVEN SIN SOME MORE?

If you still continue to stray and sin, amazingly Hashem responds with another helpful character trait: "ארך אפים" (slow to anger). What exactly is this?

"מאריך אפו ואינו ממהר ליפרע: שמא יעשה תשובה!"

רש"י שמות לד:ו

Hashem delays responding to your sinful behavior and does not punish you immediately, because eventually you might decide to repent! WOW! What an amazing response to a sinner!

Now, you might think that the sinner who receives such royal treatment must be someone really special. Probably a holy, righteous man who accidentally slipped and sinned against Hashem for the first time in his life, right?

"כי השם הוא ארך אפים **לרשעים** ולא לאשר לא חטאו!"

אבן עזרא שמות לד:ו

WRONG! Hashem is slow to anger when dealing specifically with **רשעים**, wicked people!

DOWN AND OUT

As usual, Charles was late with his mortgage payment and his banker was furious with him. Charles had promised to pay many times, but when he finally sent in a check, it bounced. After pushing it off for several months, the foreclosure team requested that the loan committee vote to foreclose on his home immediately. The president of the bank rose to his feet and said, "Ladies and gentleman of the board. Charles has been with our bank for over eight years and his reputation is well known to all of us. He is clearly a dirty-rotten-lying-scoundrel who has taken advantage of us over and over for many years. He took our patience and mercy and repaid it with lies! So here's what I think we should do: we should NOT take any action against him at all — after all, maybe one day he'll turn around, get an honest job, and decide to pay us back!"

Did you ever hear of a bank doing that?

This proves once again that the attributes of Hashem's patience and mercy were created specifically in order to deal with humans who are sinning!

BUT WHAT IF ALL THAT MERCY, COMPASSION, AND INFINITE PATIENCE STILL AREN'T ENOUGH TO BRING YOU BACK?

Then Hashem tosses on additional supernatural attributes: **"ורב חסד ואמת"** (abundance of kindness and truth). This means:

"חסד הוא לפנים משורת הדין ... אבל 'ורב חסד' הוא גודל חסדיו
של הקדוש ברוך הוא שיכול לעשות חסד על פי המשפט עצמו ...
על פי דין ממש מטהר את בני ישראל ביום הכיפורים,
שנתברר בדין: **כי אין החטא בהם בעצם!**"

שפת אמת דברים ליום כיפור

"**חסד**" (kindness) is when Hashem deals with you beyond the letter of the law, just like a judge who finds you guilty for speeding but instead of giving you points on your license, he merely demands that you pay a fine and take a 5-hour refresher course.

But "**רב חסד**" (abundance of kindness) is when Hashem does even more! Hashem proves to the heavenly court that you never really wanted to sin and your silly sinful action does not truly represent your sterling character and pure essence.

This is like a judge who dismisses all the charges against you because he realizes that there were circumstances that compelled you to act completely out of character.

NOW WE CAN PROPERLY UNDERSTAND OUR DAILY PRAYER:

"ומלוך עלינו מהרה אתה ה' לבדך בחסד וברחמים -
וצדקנו בצדק ובמשפט ברוך אתה ה' מלך אוהב צדקה ומשפט."

שמונה עשרה

"... and reign over us speedily, You Hashem alone, with **kindness** and **compassion**, and **justify us** with **righteousness** and **judgment**. Blessed are You, Hashem, the King who loves **CHARITY and JUSTICE!**"

On the surface this prayer may seem a bit confusing. How can we ask Hashem to reign over us utilizing the traits of "kindness" and "compassion," which are beyond the strict letter of the law, while and at the same time we ask Hashem to utilize "righteousness" and "judgment" and "justify us" within the court of law?! If we could be really found "righteous" within the world of "judgment," then we wouldn't need all that "kindness" and "compassion" to begin with!

The explanation is: We know very well that we would never be able to be judged favorably if the judge were to take our actions at face value.

"אנו מבקשים שכאשר הקב"ה דן אותנו
שיעשה את הדין בהסתכלות של 'חסד ורחמים' ואז הוא ודאי ימצא בנו
זכויות שיכולות להכריע את כף המשקל לטובה ואם כן אז יכול להיות
ש'וצדקנו' אפילו על פי החומר של הצדק והמשפט!"

ספר נתיבי אמת עניני תפילה

Therefore we plead with Hashem: When judging our actions, please view them through the lens of "חסד ורחמים" (kindness and mercy), and then "וצדקנו בצדק ובמשפט"; You will certainly find a way to justify our actions even within the system of justice as well!

Furthermore, although Hashem is a King who "loves charity and justice," His love for charity is listed before His love for justice. For Hashem knows that without His divine charity, we would never be able to survive the scrutiny of the justice system!

UNCOMMON CRIMINAL

The judge studied Mr. Goldfarb: A 60-year-old, nice-looking family man. Six children. All married and working. 18 grandchildren. Never arrested. A life of community service. Not your typical criminal. Mr. Goldfarb's lawyer asked that the judge allow testimony from people whom Mr. Goldfarb helped. Character witnesses filled the courtroom: his parents, his friends, and his children testified. People he

had helped, his Rabbi, and representatives from several community organizations testified on his behalf. It was all very impressive.

The judge decided to act with kindness and although he announced that his verdict was "guilty as charged," the sentence was only 5 years of community service — which Mr. Goldfarb was doing anyway since he was a community activist — and NO jail time whatsoever! Mr. Goldfarb's attorney was thrilled. But Mr. Goldfarb wasn't!

Mr. Goldfarb broke down and appealed to the judge, "Your Honor, I am so grateful that you are doing this for me. However please understand that after all is said and done, since I have been found guilty in a court of law — I will now have a criminal record, and this is too much for me to bear! I beg of you — help me! If not for me, then for the sake of my wife ... my children ... and my dear grandchildren ... their shame will kill me!"

The judge was overwhelmed with compassion and was visibly touched. Although he could not find any reason to let Mr. Goldfarb off the hook, the judge ruled, "Taking into consideration the lifetime of dedication to community service and recognizing that the defendant broke the law only due to extreme circumstances, I hereby find Mr. Goldfarb innocent!"

This is the message of "רב חסד" (abundance of kindness). Hashem does not merely blend the trait of "חסד" (kindness) with "דין" (judgment); rather, Hashem uses His special brand of **extreme kindness** to completely control the courtroom! This allows us to emerge INNOCENT even WITHIN the court of law itself! JUSTICE is truly served! How? By looking past our actions and uncovering our inner will and effort to be good!

AND WHAT IF EVEN AFTER ALL OF THAT, THE SCALE IS STILL NOT STACKED IN OUR FAVOR?

"ר' אלעזר אומר 'ורב חסד' מאזנים מעויינות, עוונות מכאן וזכיות מכאן,
והקב"ה חוטף שטר אחד משל עוונות וזכיות מכריעות ומניח העון תחת
פורפירין שלו, אלמלי כתיב אי איפשר לאומרו:
'נשאת עון עמך כסית כל חטאתם סלה!'"

פירושי סידור התפילה לרוקח עמוד תש"ט "א-ל מלך יושב" ועיין בבלי ראש השנה יז. "ורב חסד"

Hashem has some cute ideas up His sleeve — so to speak! When a person is being judged, there is a scale with mitzvos/credits on one side and sins/debits on the other. When Hashem sees that you're in trouble and your sins are outweighing your mitzvos, He grabs one of the sinful debits and hides it under His cloak, so to speak, and suddenly the credits outweigh the sins and the person emerges victorious from his court case!!

BUT WHAT IF ALL THAT MERCY, COMPASSION, PATIENCE, ABUNDANCE OF KINDNESS & TRUTH STILL DOESN'T WORK?

Well, then Hashem adds another attribute onto Himself and He chooses to be: "נצר חסד לאלפים" (preserver of compassion for thousands of years). This means that Hashem credits us for the good deeds done by our ancestors. Wow — this is really cool!

BUT LISTEN UP — BECAUSE IT GETS EVEN BETTER THAN THAT:

Hashem has a very advanced "computer program" (so to speak) that has a running meter calculating every time you do a mitzvah.

It calculates the "value" of your mitzvah, based on all kinds of things, such as how difficult it was for you, how much effort you put into it, if you did it with *simchah* (happiness), etc. ....

It also calculates the impact you have on other people. So if your *davening* inspires the person next to you to *daven* better, the program calculates your impact on him and credits your "account."

In addition, if you have an impact on a person who then inspires others, and they inspire others, etc. ... your account is credited for all of that as well!

Plus, if the person you inspire — or anyone who ever gets inspired from anyone you inspire — *davens* better and gets a better *shidduch* and raises a better family, or makes more money and gives more charity, etc. ... you are continuously CREDITED for whatever IMPACT is traced back to you ... **forever!** Pretty amazing stuff!

But, as good as all this sounds, Hashem goes much much further for us:

”אינו מסתכל בּעבירות שעתידין לחטוא

אבל במצות מסתכל הוא במה **שעתידין להטיב** ומיטיב עמהם!“

עץ יוסף כ:יח על מדרש רבה במדבר כ:כ

When you are being judged, Hashem does not consider the sins that you will do in the future; however, He DOES look into the future to see the mitzvos that you will do — and guess what? He credits you NOW based on them! WOW!!!

Not only does He credit you for the ripple effect that will emerge from all the good deeds that you have already done, He also takes into consideration the good deeds that you will do in the future! You have not even done these mitzvos yet and your loving Father in heaven is already crediting your account! **Get up and dance**!

LET'S SEE SOME EXAMPLES OF THIS AMAZING TRAIT:

”ר' ברכיה ורבי לוי בשם ר' שמואל בר נחמן אמר:

אברהם לא ניצול מכבשן האש אלא בזכות יעקב!“

מדרש ויקרא רבה פרשה לו:ד

Example #1: Avraham Avinu was saved from the burning furnace in the merit of his grandson Yaakov, who was not even alive yet!

"... בשביל שתי פרידות טובות [רות המואביה ונעמה העמונית]
חס הקב"ה על ב' אומות גדולות ולא החריבן ...."

תלמוד בבלי מסכת בבא קמא לח:

Example #2: Hashem instructed Moshe not to destroy two nations, Ammon and Moav, since they would one day produce two very special people.

שבת פ"ט: "בשעה שהקדימו נעשה לנשמע קראת להם **בני בכורי ישראל;**
רש"י: שהי-ה גלוי לפניך שהן עתידין לומר לפניך בסיני נעשה ונשמע
לקבל עולך מאהבה **כבנים.** והיינו דמשום כך זכו
שכבר במצרים קרא להם הקב"ה 'בני בכורי ישראל'!"

נתיבות שלום משפטים קפ"ב

Example #3: Since Hashem foresaw that when He would give us the Torah we would enthusiastically respond with the loving words: "we will do and we will hear," that is why He called us "My beloved firstborn son" way back when we were still serving idols in Mitzrayim!

CASHING IN

Going back to our story: What would have happened if Mr. Goldfarb had not helped many people yet? No personal testimonies about his charitable nature. No letters on his behalf. No record of selfless community service. He would be in big trouble!

Now imagine that out of nowhere, a group of people appeared. They formed a line that went out of the courtroom and down the hallway... out of the courthouse and down the road .... Hundreds of people ... they kept coming and coming ... all ready to testify on Mr. Goldfarb's behalf!

The judge was shocked. "Who are all these people?" Mr. Goldfarb was even more shocked than the judge, as he also didn't recognize any of them! The lawyer explained that he magically called upon all the people who WILL ever be helped by Mr. Goldfarb in the future! The lawyer pleaded, "Look at how much Mr. Goldfarb WILL do to make the world a better place! Look at his great potential and please take that into consideration even now!"

 Authentic Yiddishkeit believes that Hashem in His infinite mercy calculates: (1) all the good deeds that you have already done, (2) plus He calculates the ripple effect caused by you, and (3) **He even calculates all the good deeds that you will ever do!** CAN YOU STILL THINK THAT HE ISN'T ON YOUR SIDE??

BUT WHAT IF ALL OF THAT MERCY, COMPASSION, PATIENCE, ABUNDANCE OF KINDNESS & TRUTH, AND EVEN TAKING INTO CONSIDERATION ALL OUR FUTURE GOOD DEEDS STILL DOESN'T WORK?

Then Hashem responds with: "נשא עון ופשע וחטאה"; Hashem carries the burden of our sin, willful sin, and error. This means that Hashem carries and tolerates your sins, but in a way far deeper than we can ever comprehend:

"הקב"ה ... נושא וסובל העון, וכמו שהוא זן העולם כולו –
זן ומפרנס המשחית הזה!"

תומר דבורה פרק א' ד"ה נושא עון

When a person does a good deed, he creates a good angel and when a person does a bad deed, he creates a bad angel.

The mystics teach that the "bad" angels created from sin want to immediately attack the sinner. However, since Hashem wants to

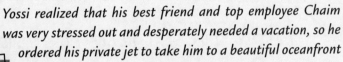
give a person the opportunity to repent, Hashem restrains them from immediately seeking out and destroying the sinner!

UNUSUAL BENEVOLENCE

Yossi realized that his best friend and top employee Chaim was very stressed out and desperately needed a vacation, so he ordered his private jet to take him to a beautiful oceanfront villa in Hawaii — with Yossi's credit card on file!

While Chaim was vacationing, the accounting department discovered that he had been stealing money from the company for many years! It seemed that things would never be the same between Yossi and Chaim. Yet, incredibly, Yossi still continued to cover the hotel bill, the room service, and all the spa treatments! Yossi even sent the private jet to Hawaii to bring Chaim home after his vacation.

The accountant asked him, "Why are you doing all this for this lowly, ungrateful crook?"

Yossi replied, "Well ... maybe one day Chaim will truly mend his ways and apologize for what he did to me!"

Hello!!! Are you listening to this? Not only did Hashem teach us that He will not distance Himself from us after we "steal" from Him through sin, on the contrary — the **more** we succumb to sin and slip away from Him — the **more** He utilizes unbelievable amounts of patience, mercy, compassion, and infinite unconditional love to keep us close to Him!!! And to top it all off – when there are "bills" to pay — HE CONTINUES TO PAY THEM FOR US!

"כשיטיב ה׳ ברחמיו לאיש **הגם שיחטא** לא יפחות מטובו דבר
ותהיה המידה שהיה בה קודם מתנהגת גם אחר שחטא!"

אור החיים הקדוש שמות לד:ו

In fact, even after a Yid rebelliously defies Hashem's will, Hashem still does not hold back from bestowing **ANY** kindness upon him and relates to him in the **same exact way** as before!

You're probably thinking, that's pretty amazing in theory, but does Hashem REALLY treat us with this incredible infinite mercy?

FASTEN YOUR SEAT BELTS FOR A SHOCKING MEDRASH:

When we left Mitzrayim we found ourselves living in the desert with no possible way to survive. In order to sustain us, Hashem performed an open miracle and delivered heavenly food for us.

Now listen to this: Some people took this miraculous food that was sent down by G-d Himself, and defiantly, appallingly, served it to their idols!

One would imagine that after G-d saw such an obnoxious sin, lightning would immediately strike these sinners and fry them on the spot! Next day's lunch should have been — "fried sinners"!

After all, how could they take the gift of food sent directly by Hashem — an open miracle — and use that same food to serve worthless pieces of wood and stone? Is there any worse instance of repaying good with bad?!

"... שהיו נוטלין מן המן ומקריבין לפני עבודת כוכבים ...
וחוזר ויורד (המן) ביום האחר! הוי לך ה' הצדקה!"

שמות רבה (וילנא) פרשה מ"א בשם ר' יהודה ב"ר שלום

Yet, listen to this — the very next day Hashem sent down the heavenly sustenance once again as if nothing had happened! Hashem's patience is endless! לך ה' הצדקה

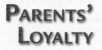

PARENTS' LOYALTY *Baruch was 16 and rebelling terribly against his parents. After reading an amazing book, Baruch's father bought him an expensive leather jacket to show that he loved and accepted him for who he was. A few weeks later, Baruch's sister was getting married and his father hoped that Bobby,*

as he now wished to be called, would dress properly and at least make an attempt to blend in and not be an embarrassment to the family.

Showing up two hours late and high as a kite, "Bobby" made a grand entrance wearing his new leather jacket and told everyone, "Do you like my new jacket? My dad bought it for me just for the wedding!"

Although his parents were embarrassed and sickened by their son's action, when the night ended and Baruch was lying on the floor, drowning in his own vomit, it was his parents who cleaned him and carried him home ... bathing him and then tucking him into his bed. To top it off — the next day his father went to buy him a new leather jacket ... after all, the old was totally ruined!

This is how Hashem treats us on a daily basis. We take His miraculous gifts and use them to sin against Him. Yet He continues to give us those same gifts day after day.

THE MESSAGE IS CLEAR:

Judaism is not just for saints; in fact, much of the Torah speaks directly to sinners! Hashem's response to even the worst sinner is: I love you, I am rooting for you, and I am patient beyond your comprehension! Come back to Me ... I want you here next to Me, where you belong!

Authentic Yiddishkeit believes that the MORE we distance ourselves from being connected to Hashem — the MORE mercy and patience Hashem showers onto our relationship, so that no matter what the situation is, the door is wide open for us to reconnect to Hashem, our wonderful, amazing, incredible Father in Heaven!

So no matter where YOU are right now ...
It's time to walk through that door!

Oh, by the way ...
we almost forgot to mention one more thing:

"ר' הונא בשם ר' אבא אמר:
כביכול אין שכחה לפניו ובשביל ישראל נעשה שכחן! מה טעם?
דכתיב (מיכה ז:יח) 'מי א־ל כמוך נושא עון ועובר על פשע.'
וכן דוד אמר: (תהלים פה:ג) 'נשאת עון עמך כסית כל חטאתם סלה!'"

פסיקתא דרב כהנא פיסקא כ"ה סליחות

Although Hashem never forgets anything,
in order to help us out,
Hashem sometimes acts forgetful!

4

SMOKESCREEN

Finding the light within the darkness

"מתוך כעס - רצון,

מתוך אפילה - אורה,

מתוך רוגז - רחמים,

מתוך צרה - רווחה,

מתוך ריחוק - קירוב,

מתוך נפילה - קימה!"

מדרש תהלים מזמור כ"ב

"Through anger — desire,
through darkness — light,
through fury — mercy,
through suffering —
salvation,
through distance —
bonding,
through falling —
rising!"

HASHEM

**sometimes has to punish us for our sins ...
and that's the part of the job He hates the
most:**

"השמרו לכם פן יפתה לבבכם וסרתם ...
וחרה אף ה' בכם ועצר את השמים ולא יהי-ה מטר ...."
דברים יא:יז

The Torah says: "Beware lest your heart shall stray and leave the right way ... and Hashem will become **extremely angry** with you, and He will stop the rainfall, and the ground will not give produce, etc. ...."

The obvious question is: Since we already proved that Hashem truly loves us regardless of our spiritual level and He responds to sin with incredible patience and compassion, how can we understand that Hashem gets **"extremely angry"** at us when we sin?

Let's carefully examine one of the most severe examples of harsh judgment ever decreed by Hashem: the destruction of our Holy Temple.

"מקדש ראשון מפני מה חרב? מפני שלשה דברים שהיו בו:
עבודה זרה, וגלוי עריות, ושפיכות דמים."
תלמוד בבלי מסכת יומא דף ט:

The first Bais HaMikdash was destroyed because of idol worship, adultery, and murder.

Klal Yisrael abandoned Hashem and the unfortunate result of our attitude and actions was the destruction of our beautiful home.

Now think about this: How do you envision Hashem during the destruction? Many people have the vision of an angry old school principal, a bitter and cold-hearted boss, or an enraged jealous spouse. *Chas v'Shalom!*

LET'S GET A TASTE OF WHAT HASHEM WAS TRULY FEELING DURING THE DESTRUCTION OF OUR HOLY TEMPLE:

"... אני דומה היום לאדם שהיה לו בן יחידי ועשה לו חופה -
ומת בתוך חופתו!!!"

איכה רבה פתיחה כ"ד רבי יוחנן

Hashem said: "I feel like a father whose only child just died while standing under the chuppah at his wedding!"

"לאיזו אומה דמיתי אתכם? לאיזה אומה גאלתי ביד חזקה והבאתי על
אויביה עשר מכות? לאיזו אומה קרעתי הים והורדתי את המן
והגזתי את השלו והעליתי להם את הבאר?"

איכה רבה פרשה ב'

"Which nation can I compare you to? Which nation did I redeem with a mighty hand and punish her enemies with ten plagues!? For which other nation did I split a sea, send heavenly food, special meat, and fresh water streaming from a rock!?"

"איזו אומה הקפתי ענני כבוד וקרבתי לפני הר סיני ונתתי להם תורתי?
הבת ירושלם הבת שיראה ומשלמת לי, מה אשוה לך ואנחמך?"

"For which other nation did I dispatch heavenly clouds to surround and protect them, and which other nation did I bring to Har Sinai and give MY HOLY TORAH!? Only to the daughter of Yerushalayim, **My dear child who MAKES ME COMPLETE! There is no comparison to you!** How can I possibly comfort you!"

"באותה שעה היה הקב"ה בוכה ואומר:

אוי לי על ביתי, בני היכן אתם, כהני היכן אתם, אוהבי היכן אתם,

מה אעשה לכם, התריתי בכם ולא חזרתם בתשובה!"

איכה רבה פתיחה כ"ד רבי יוחנן

"At that time, Hashem **cried** and said: Woe unto My Home, where are My children? Where are My *Kohanim*? Where are My **BELOVED**? What can I do for you now? I warned you but you did not repent!"

NOW HANG ON A SECOND ... DID HASHEM REALLY SAY "BELOVED"?

Why was Hashem still referring to us as His **"beloved"** even after we betrayed him and caused the destruction of His beautiful Home!? Where is the disgust and the anger, the venom and the hatred?

Reading these amazing words we can perhaps begin to feel the immense pain of the **ULTIMATE FATHER** crying for His beloved children!

A FATHER'S PAIN

A case came before Judge Markowitz. There was overwhelming evidence against a young man and it was impossible to consider any leniency whatsoever. The judge had warned him many times and had given him chance after chance to stay out of trouble, but it was obvious that he needed a life change that could only come from strict punishment. The judge called for a brief recess and went alone into his private chambers. No one in the courtroom knew that this young man was none other than the judge's own son! Alone in his chamber, he wept bitterly, knowing that he had no choice but to severely punish his own flesh and blood. Heartbroken, he walked back into the courtroom and sentenced his son.

Hashem feels exactly the same way toward His precious children;

even though it is our own poor choices that bring about the need for us to be punished, Hashem still cries for us:

"אמר [הקב"ה] אם אין אתה מניח לי לבכות עכשיו,
אכנס למקום שאין לך רשות ליכנס - ואבכה!"

איכה רבה פתיחה כ"ד רבי יוחנן

While Hashem was destroying the Bais HaMikdash, He said [to the angels]; "If you do not allow Me to cry now, I will go into a place where you have no permission to enter — and I will cry."

LET'S DELVE INTO THIS TOPIC ON A DEEPER AND MORE MEANINGFUL LEVEL:

TERRIBLE TWOS

Mrs. Brownfeld sat her young son Chaim down for a serious discussion. She carefully and sternly explained the importance of not eating anything on the brand-new white living room sofa that they finally bought after saving up for many years. Naturally, just a few short hours after their serious talk, cute little Chaim'l saw some chocolate bars and sat on the new white sofa and "somehow" it got over his hands and ... well ...

When Mrs. B. saw what happened, she yelled "Chaim Yitzchok Moshe Yaakov HaKohain Brownfeld, come over here right now!" Chaim tried to run but his stubby little feet couldn't move fast enough and his Mommy caught up with him. Now poor little Chiam'l faced Judgment Day. His mother decided that Chaim'l would have to stay home with a babysitter while the family went on the upcoming Chol Hamoed trip. Chaim would learn to listen to his parents.

When Mr. Brownfeld came home that evening, he entered a very sad home. Mrs. B. was very upset and Chaim'l was in his bed crying. He asked his wife, "Why are you so upset — what happened?"

Let's take a journey into the psyche of Mrs. Brownfeld to properly understand all the reasons she was upset:

First of all, she was upset because:

(1) Her precious new beautiful white sofa was ruined!

The sadness over the new sofa being ruined would be exactly the same had the damage come from a leaky roof or any other circumstance for which there is no one to blame. This pain has nothing to do with "who" caused the damage.

But she is also upset about something else:

(2) Her child did not listen to her specific instructions!

It is always upsetting to parents when their child does not listen to them, but even more so when the disobedience comes at the expense of a brand-new sofa!

However, beneath the surface the mother is also feeling another emotion:

(3) She is upset because her beloved child is in pain!

Simply put: Parents feel pain when their child is in pain — for whatever reason! Whether the child is in pain because he is sick, he fell off a bike, his feelings were hurt, and yes — even if his pain results from a well-deserved punishment from his parents! The bottom line is that parents always feel hurt when their child is in pain.

Delving a little deeper, we will discover that there is yet another source of anguish lying deep inside the mother's subconscious:

(4) She's upset at the one who caused her son to be in pain!

Imagine if someone else caused her child's pain. Wouldn't she be upset at that "other" person for hurting her precious child?

In our case it was little Chaim'l himself who caused himself to be punished because he did not listen to his mother. We can hear her thinking, "Why did he have to do such a foolish thing that caused him to be punished and lose the special treat of joining the family on the fun trip?!"

So we now see that she is also upset with Chaim'l for causing her beloved child (Chaim himself) to cry and be hurt!

But there's something still deeper:

(5) She's upset that she had to punish her own child!

It is an upsetting experience for parents to punish their own flesh and blood — even if they deserve it.

Had Chaim been punished in school, she would feel the pain of #1 through #4, but she would not feel this aspect of pain. But in our situation, Mrs. B is upset at being the one who punished her own beloved Chaim'l — even though she knows that she did the best thing for HIS OWN growth.

But there's something still deeper:

(6) She's upset at Chaim'l for causing her to punish her own child!

Punishing someone you care about hurts you more than punishing someone you don't care about! Who caused Mrs. B. to make her beloved Chaim'l cry? Chaim! So she is also upset at Chaim'l for causing this to happen!

Authentic Yiddishkeit understands that even though kids sometimes think that their parents' ANGER and frustration toward them is a sign that they do NOT love them and care about them, the reality is that the complete opposite is true! For if the parents no longer cared about the child, they would be far LESS angry about the situation!

Now we can understand the concept of Hashem becoming "angry" on a much deeper emotional level, since Hashem feels all the emotions listed in our example of Mrs. Brownfeld — and much, much more:

1. Hashem created a world of peace and tranquility. Sin destroys

the world, as we have seen with Adam and Chavah (evicted from Gan Eden due to their sin), Noach's times (when the entire world was destroyed due to corrupt actions), Sodom and Amorah (uprooted due to their sins), and the destruction of our holy Bais HaMikdash (torn down due to our sins).

"בשעה שברא הקב"ה את אדם הראשון נטלו והחזירו
על כל אילני גן עדן ואמר לו: ראה מעשי כמה נאים ומשובחין הן
וכל מה שבראתי בשבילך בראתי,
תן דעתך שלא תקלקל ותחריב את עולמי!"

קהלת רבה (וילנא) פרשה ז:יג

When Hashem created Adam, He gave him a tour of all the trees in Gan Eden, and said to him, *"Look how beautiful all of this is, and everything that you see here was created for YOU — please be careful not to destroy my world!"*

Whenever we sin, we bring destruction to the world and so Hashem becomes upset that His "white couch," the beautiful peaceful world that He created, is damaged.

2. As we know, Hashem called us "בנים" (His children)! Therefore, Hashem is upset that we disobey His specific instructions and stray from the proper path!

3. The outcome and consequence of our sins is our own pain — and that is precisely what hurts Hashem most:

"א"ר ינאי: מה התאומים הללו
אם חשש אחד בראשו חבירו מרגיש,
כן אמר הקב"ה כביכול: עמו אנכי בצרה!"

שמות רבה פרשה ב'

Just as with twins — if one has a headache, the other feels pain — so too Hashem says: "I am with you in your pain!"

NATURAL CONNECTION

"My twin brother and I just turned 18. When we were 9, my brother lived with our grandmother for a few months while we remained in the city. One night I suddenly woke up and wouldn't stop crying; I seemed to be choking but I wasn't. I kept trying to reach over to my brothers' cot. Then my parents called my grandmother to check on my brother. My grandmother found my brother (who has asthma) choking! He was rushed to the hospital and recovered. My father said I stopped crying only after my grandmother said the ambulance had arrived. My brother and I have a bond so strong that nothing can break it. We know what the other is thinking and we know when the other is in trouble."

Source: twinsrealm.com

4. He's upset at the one who caused His beloved child to suffer.

If someone hurt you, Hashem would be very angry with that person for harming His precious child. So too, if you hurt yourself through unwise decisions, Hashem is now angry at YOU for causing pain and suffering to His precious child — YOU!

5. He's upset that He must punish His own beloved child:

"שמעתי בת קול שמנהמת כיונה ואומרת: אוי לבנים שבעוונותיהם
החרבתי את ביתי ושרפתי את היכלי והגליתים לבין האומות!"

תלמוד בבלי מסכת ברכות דף ג.

Reb Yosi told Eliyahu HaNavi: "I heard a heavenly voice moaning like a dove: Woe to My **children**; because of their sins I destroyed **My** house, burned **My** chamber, and dispersed them among the nations."

"ואמר לי חייך וחיי ראשך לא שעה זו בלבד אומרת כך
אלא בכל יום ויום שלש פעמים אומרת כך!"

תלמוד בבלי מסכת ברכות דף ג.

"And Eliyahu responded: It wasn't only said the time that you heard it — it is said three times every single day!"

Did we deserve to be punished? YES! Still — three times a day — every single day — Hashem bemoans the destruction of the Bais HaMikdash and the exile of His beloved children!

6. Last but certainly not least, Hashem also is upset that we put Him in the position where, as Master of the universe, He must mete out judgment against His very own beloved child!

"אם האדם גורם על ידי עוונותיו שמוכרח הקב"ה לענשו ...
אז יגיע עונש גם על זה שגרם צער להקב"ה
שמוכרח לשלוח לו יסורים וצער!"
באר מים חיים פרשת בא דף קי"ט

There is nothing more upsetting to Hashem than having to punish His beloved children. So when a person causes Hashem to punish him, he receives an additional punishment for forcing Hashem to punish him!

NOW WE CAN UNDERSTAND WHY HASHEM BECOMES "ANGRY"

1. His beautiful world is being damaged!

2. His beloved child disobeyed His specific instructions!

3. His beloved child must be punished and be in pain!

4. Someone (that "someone" is the person himself!) caused His child to be in pain!

5. He had to punish His own beloved child!

6. Someone (that "someone" is the person himself!) caused Him to have to punish His own child!

What comes out of this is the deep understanding that when Hashem punishes you — that is when His LOVE for you is most awakened!

ALLOW US TO BRING THIS OUT ON A DEEPER LEVEL:

There are three levels of love that a father can have for his child:

"באהבת האב לבנו יש שלוש אופנים:
יש האהבה כפשוטה בשעה שהבן קרוב אליו
ונמצא במחיצתו והאב משתעשע עמו באהבתו."

ספר נתיבות שלום ענייני בין המצרים במדבר עמוד קצ"ו

LEVEL 1: First there is the "regular" level of love that one has toward his child who lives with him and is always around him.

"ויותר מזה היא האהבה כאשר הבן מצוי הרחק מאביו
ואינו יכול להתראות עמו, שאז האב מתגעגע אליו מאד,
וככל שהוא רחוק יותר הגעגועים יותר חזקים."

ספר נתיבות שלום ענייני בין המצרים במדבר עמוד קצ"ו

LEVEL 2: Then there is a love that becomes aroused when the son is NOT near his father and they don't see each other often. The further the son is — the MORE the father yearns to be near him once again.

"ויש עוד בחינה אהבה העולה על כולנה:
בשעה שהבן חולה אנוש וצריכים לעשות לו ניתוח קשה להציל את חייו,
והאב הוא הרופא המנתח שצריך לחתוך בבשרו!"

ספר נתיבות שלום ענייני בין המצרים במדבר עמוד קצ"ו

LEVEL 3: However, there is another level of love that is much higher than those other situations: If the child becomes extremely sick and needs to undergo a painful surgery to save his life — his father would hurt so much for his beloved child! Now imagine that the father himself is the doctor and he is the one who must cut his own child's flesh!

"שאמנם מצד אחד הוא יודע שעליו להציל את חיי בנו בניתוח זה,
אך מאידך לבו נקרע בקרבו כשהוא צריך לחתוך בבשר בנו שסובל

בינתיים יסורים קשים ומרים,
שבבפנימיות הלב מתעוררת אז האהבה החזקה ביותר!"

ספר נתיבות שלום עניני בין המצרים במדבר עמוד קצ"ו

Even though he clearly knows that this is for his child's benefit and this is what he must do to save his son's life — still and all — his heart will break inside knowing that he must cut his child and cause him to be in terrible pain.

"וכעניין זה יש באהבת הקדוש ברוך הוא לישראל שהיא אהבה עזה
וגדולה בלי גבול ובלי סוף כמו דכתיב: 'אהבתי אתכם אמר ה'.'"

ספר נתיבות שלום עניני בין המצרים במדבר עמוד קצ"ו

Now you are BEGINNING to feel the tremendous pain that Hashem has when He must impose punishment and pain upon His beloved children!

BUT IT GOES EVEN FURTHER:

"תניא, רבי שמעון בן יוחי אומר: בוא וראה כמה חביבין ישראל לפני
הקדוש ברוך הוא: **שבכל מקום שגלו - שכינה עמהן!"**

זוהר חדש כרך א' פרשת אחרי מות דף עט: ותלמוד בבלי מסכת מגילה דף כט.

Rebbi Shimon Bar Yochai says: "Come and see how **beloved** Yisrael is before Hashem. For every time they were sent into exile — which was only due to our excessive sins — **Hashem went with them**!"

WOW! What an eye-opener! In order to see how much Hashem really loves each one of us, don't just look at how Hashem treated us when we were GOOD. Rather, take a look at the way He dealt with us when we were TERRIBLE! Even when Hashem had no choice but to destroy our beautiful home, and throw us into a long bitter exile — look Who packed up and went with us!!!

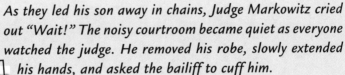

UNBREAKABLE BOND

As they led his son away in chains, Judge Markowitz cried out "Wait!" The noisy courtroom became quiet as everyone watched the judge. He removed his robe, slowly extended his hands, and asked the bailiff to cuff him.

Stunned, the people asked, "But you didn't do anything wrong — why should you suffer in jail?" The great judge replied, "What you don't know is that this young man is my own SON! I love him so much and I cannot bear to be without him! So I will go where he goes ... even if it means giving up my glory as a successful judge and being dragged through the low and disgusting life in prison for many, many years!"

"אף על פי שאנו באורך הגלות הוא אוהב אותנו אהבה שלימה
ואהבתו אלינו אהבה עיקרית וקדמונית!"

דרשות ר"י אבן שועיב פרשת תולדות

When Hashem destroyed our beautiful Temple, His Home on Earth, even though WE were totally to blame, Hashem did not discard us and forget about us. He did not give up on us and choose another nation to be His new Chosen People! Instead, He followed along with us into the dark, bitter, and painful exile. Why? Because the only place He wants to be ... is right next to His "**beloved**" children!

"חייך לא שבקית ולא אשבק ...
בין חייבין בין זכאין!"

מדרש אסתר רבה פרשה ז'

I [Hashem] swear that I will never abandon or forsake you ... whether or not you deserve Me!

So if Hashem will never leave you ...

Why would YOU ever leave HIM?

5

TOUGH LOVE OR
LOVE TOUGH?

*Looking at punishment
through heavenly eyes*

"רבון העולמים: אמר
לו דוד לעולם אין
[אתה] בא עלינו בדין
אלא במדת רחמים!"

פסיקתא רבתי (איש שלום) פיסקא מ' בחודש השביעי

DOVID HAMELECH SAID:

*"Master of the universe,
You never deal
with us strictly,
ONLY WITH
MERCY."*

HASHEM

**is the ultimate loving Father, so let's see how
He deals with rebellious children:**

"בכל מקום במה שנזכר פעם ראשונה בתורה שם הוא שורש הדבר."

פרי צדיק במדבר ראש חודש תמוז

In order to understand a concept, we must examine the very first time that concept is mentioned in the Torah, for there we will find the source of the matter.

So let's travel back in time and examine the very first major human failure. Nu, so who do you think was the very first human failure? You got it! The very first human ever created! And guess how long it took for him to make such a massive mistake that would forever change the entire vision of G-d's new project, "Earth"? Yup, you got it — he messed up on the very first day!

"ויקח ה' אלקים את האדם וינחהו בגן עדן."

בראשית פרק ב:טו

The Torah says: "Hashem took Adam
and placed him in Gan Eden."

Hashem created a beautiful world. There was no sickness, no death, no stress, no hardship, no labor pains, and no need to ever work! All the challenges and difficulties we experience in our daily lives were simply not there! The world was a perfect place: heaven on earth.

"ומעץ הדעת טוב ורע לא תאכל ממנו כי ביום אכלך ממנו מות תמות."

בראשית פרק ב:יז

"You may not eat from the tree of knowledge of good and bad,
for on the day that you eat from it you shall die."

Unfortunately, Adam and Chavah were unable to restrain
themselves from this **one** restriction and the ramifications were
horrendous! Hashem's beautiful, serene, and perfect world was
completely DESTROYED with just one bite!!

"וישלחהו ה׳ אלקים מגן עדן ... ויגרש את האדם ...."

בראשית פרק ג:כג-כד

"... and Hashem sent him out of Gan Eden...
and He banished the man ...."

CURIOUS GEORGE

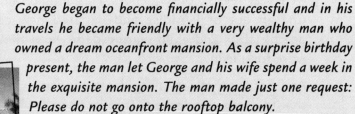

George began to become financially successful and in his
travels he became friendly with a very wealthy man who
owned a dream oceanfront mansion. As a surprise birthday
present, the man let George and his wife spend a week in
the exquisite mansion. The man made just one request:
Please do not go onto the rooftop balcony.

When George and his wife arrived, their mouths dropped
open as they walked around the home and gazed in awe
at the perfectly manicured property. They were truly
enjoying themselves; however, each time they passed by
the staircase leading to the roof, they had to suppress
an inner urge to see what the magnificent view would
look like from up there.

George's wife Chavah started talking to him about
how wonderful it would be to be able to go onto the roof.
After all, what could possibly be better than watching
sunrise from there? He tried to talk her out of it but after
a while, his curiosity got the better of him. At 4:25 a.m.,

they woke up to watch the sunrise. They quietly ... carefully ... slowly ... opened the latch and pulled down the staircase leading to the roof ... slowly they climbed stair after stair and ascended to the roof ... when suddenly ... CRASH! They fell through the broken glass roof and dropped three stories! They ended up in full body casts and wheelchair bound for the rest of their lives!

The owner was furious with them: I told you not to go up on the roof because I knew the glass sunroof was broken and it was UNSAFE for you to go there! I made the request for YOUR BENEFIT and you couldn't listen???

Hashem gave Adam and Chavah everything ... but asked that they refrain from just ONE thing! They didn't listen and indeed, there were very severe consequences. Hashem literally threw Adam and Chavah out of Paradise and initiated new concepts: sickness, death, labor and child-rearing pains, and the need to painfully work for a living.

Another outcome of eating the forbidden fruit was the realization that they were unclothed. This was a pretty big problem for them since they were really far away from Woodbury Commons! So what did they do? They actually tried to make clothing for themselves by sewing fig leaves together. That's right — leaves!

Hashem was watching this situation unfold. It was pretty sad and a little funny, seeing them figure out how to sew leaves together and trying to tailor them to actually stay on and fit properly.

THEN THE TORAH TELLS US SOMETHING
ABSOLUTELY REMARKABLE:

"ויעש ה' אלקים לאדם ולאשתו כתנות עור וילבשם."
בראשית ג:כא

"Hashem made leather garments for Adam
and his wife and He clothed them."

Hashem decided to step in and help them with their wardrobe predicament! Incredible! Amazing! Why on earth did Hashem do this for them? What did they do to earn this personal treatment — especially when you consider that the only reason they needed clothing in the first place was because they defied the will of Hashem!?!?!

"רצה ליחס פעולת ההלבשה אליו יתברך להורות על
אהבתו וחמלתו על יצוריו שאף על פי שחטאו לא זז מחבבן!!!"

רבינו בחיי בראשית ג:כא

Brace yourself for this amazing answer: Adam and Chavah might have mistakenly thought that after they messed up and were consequently thrown out of Paradise, Hashem no longer cared about them! And that attitude would have been passed down to their children and the entire world would have been founded on the false impression that Hashem doesn't care about us humans anymore!

Hashem performed this menial tailoring task Himself specifically to prove to Adam and Chavah that in spite of their horrific failure to adhere to His one and only request, **His love and care for them was not diminished whatsoever!**

"והוא (ה') בעצמו השתדל בתקונם ובגמילות חסדים עשה להם מלבושים
מעולים ונכבדים מעור ויתעטפו כל גופם דרך כבוד!"

רבינו בחיי בראשית ג:כא

Hashem Himself helped them with their clothing crisis and personally made them **high-quality** and **distinguished** leather clothing that covered them in a **comfortable** and **honorable** way!

Hashem didn't make them low-quality clothing! "Here's jeans and a t-shirt!" No way! "Only the best for My precious children!"

You would think that they had done something really special to deserve such great personal treatment!

BUT WAIT — IT GETS EVEN BETTER:

From where did Hashem take this leather material?

"ויעש לאדם ולאשתו **לבושי כבוד** מעור הנחש!"

כתר יונתן בראשית פרק ג:כא

The leather came from the very snake that caused them to sin!

Perhaps Hashem specifically chose to use the leather skin of the snake so that Adam could comfort himself by remembering that it was only due to the outside influence of the scheming snake that he now needed clothing to cover his pure holy essence!

In addition, there is a deeper lesson to be learned as well:

CROWNING GLORY

There is a well-known story of R' Amnon Yitzchok shlit"a who held up a boy's ponytail in front of a large audience and said; Do you know how long it takes to grow one of these? This is what young people are willing to give up to return to Torah." He held the ponytail high and with a big smile he proclaimed; "Zeh shel Ashkenazi ... blondie!" Then he lifted another pony and said; "V'zeh shel Taimoni ... krinkie!" and he showed everyone the frizzy hair of a Yemenite boy. Then he pulled out a very long black ponytail "V'zeh shel Sepharadi!" He then explained that these boys would only give up their ponytails if they were really convinced that the Torah was true.

He then held up a box with hundreds of earrings and proclaimed to the audience, "After Klal Yisrael left Mitzrayim they gave their earrings to make an Eigel

HaZahav [Golden Calf]. Today these men are giving up their earrings to return to Torah! When we have enough, we will use them to make a crown for a Sefer Torah!" Immediately a young man came forward from the audience, removing his earring as he walked. He was followed by another and another. Scores of earrings were dropped into the box to build the Sefer Torah's new crown.

Source http://www.rabbiyy.com/essays/Amnon%20Yitzchak.htm

Perhaps the reason that Hashem chose to create their new garments specifically from the snake that caused them to sin was to emphasize that even the biggest failure of your life — can be used to clothe yourself with honor!

BUT WAIT — IT GETS EVEN BETTER:

"שהלבישם הקב"ה מיני מעלות ומאורות
מן האור העליון שהיו בגן עדן כעין משה שזכה להן בהר!"

רבינו בחיי בראשית ג:כא

Hashem enveloped them in a spiritual light, from the light of Gan Eden, similar to the light that Moshe Rabbeinu received at the pinnacle of his attachment to Hashem on Har Sinai!

All of this shows us that even after we messed up in such a terrible way, Hashem still: (1) supplied us with magnificent clothing, (2) inspired us to not give up on ourselves, (3) and gave us a spiritual light to enable us to repent and return to Him.

LET'S LEARN ANOTHER AMAZING LESSON FROM THIS STORY:

"ויעש ה' אלקים לאדם ולאשתו כתנות עור וילבשם."

בראשית ג:כא

We know that "ה" reflects מדת הרחמים, the characteristic of mercy, and "אלקים" reflects מדת הדין, the characteristic of strict justice. When the Torah describes Hashem making these amazing garments for Adam and Chava, it refers to G-d as "ה׳ אלקים."

The Torah shows us that even Hashem's מדת הדין (which we mistakenly think is the angry, uncaring, strict arm of the law) also agreed to personally care for Adam and Chavah's clothing needs — even after their horrific sin!

Consequences? YES!

Turn My back on you? NEVER!

Although Adam and Chavah had to be severely punished, the fact was that now — for whatever reason — they had a need for clothing and they had no idea how to make clothing for themselves. Hashem's response was: My dear children, even though you have this need only because you defied My explicit command, I still love you and care about the needs you have in whatever situation you find yourself!

Hashem showed us by example that
the need to punish is not the need to hate!

Authentic Yiddishkeit believes that not only should we not lose any affection for those we must punish, Hashem showed us by example that it is UP TO THE "PUNISHER" to make sure that the "PUNISHEE" never feels that you don't care about him anymore.

SOUL WARMING

It seemed hard to believe that after raising four wonderful children, that child number five would be so difficult. The parents tried everything ... yet Naftali fell more and more.

His father begged him not to hang out with certain boys in the neighborhood, but Naftali didn't listen. One thing led to another and things became completely unmanageable at home. Naftali became Neil and dropped out of school. He

WHERE'S MY STIMULUS PACKAGE ??!!

would stay out all night, get into all kinds of trouble, and he did not respect anything his parents asked of him.

Naftali sank down the slippery slope of the underground street world. No kashrus, no tefillin, no yarmulka, no Shabbos, and no respect for any of the things so dear to his family for dozens of generations. It didn't take long for Neil to become jobless, penniless, and homeless.

On the first cold winter day Naftali had a surprise visitor — his father. "It's getting really cold outside and I figured that you probably don't have a proper coat, so I bought you a really nice, expensive name-brand leather jacket with a fur lining — the one you always wanted!"

When a child realizes that you truly care about him — then he might utilize your punishments properly and it can have a positive effect on him. Whereas if the child thinks that since he disappointed you, you now care less about him — the punishment will not have as much of a positive effect on him and, in fact, it may have a negative effect on him.

HOW DOES THIS APPLY TO YOU AND ME?

When you take an honest look at your real inner spiritual level and connection to Hashem and you consider how many foolish sins you've done, your automatic instinct may be to shrink away from facing Hashem and from Yiddishkeit. After all, you are a "flop" to Hashem, a "disaster" to your religion, and a "loser" to your nation!

But now you know that such reasoning is completely false! In fact, it was never your *Yetzer Tov* that led you to that conclusion; it was the *Yetzer Hora* that caused you first to sin and then convinced you that you are no longer wanted by Hashem, your religion, and your nation!

Your mission now is to stop allowing those crooked thoughts to control you and to begin to think like Authentic Yiddishkeit:

"אהבתו יתברך לישראל היא אהבה
שאינה תלויה בדבר ואינה בטלה לעולם!"

נתיבות שלום חלק ב' דף רנ"ב

Hashem's love toward you is not contingent on anything that you need to do! That is why, even if you commit the worst sins and fall to the lowest spiritual level — His love toward you is not diminished whatsoever and can never be damaged.

Authentic Yiddishkeit believes that Judaism is not just for saints; in fact much of the Torah speaks directly to sinners and constantly teaches us the same message, over and over! Hashem's response to even the worst sinner is: YOU are My child! I LOVE YOU! I am rooting for you and I am patient beyond your comprehension! Don't ever think that I am sick of you! Come back to Me ... yes — even after what you did I still want you right here next to Me, where you belong!

WE STILL HAVE ONE MORE THING TO THINK ABOUT:

"ומעץ הדעת טוב ורע לא תאכל ממנו כי ביום אכלך ממנו מות תמות."

בראשית פרק ב:יז

"You may not eat from the tree of knowledge of good and bad, for on the day that you eat from it you shall die."

"רבונו של עולם ... לא כך גזרת עליו כי ביום אכלך ממנו מות תמות?"

פסיקתא רבתי (איש שלום) פיסקא מ' בחודש השביעי

In fact, the angels asked Hashem, "Didn't You decree that the punishment for eating from the tree is that Adam would die THAT DAY — how then did Adam continue to live?"

"שלא פירש לו אם יום משלו או יום של הקדוש ברוך הוא שהוא אלף שנים! ... והוא חיה תשע מאות ושלשים והניח לבניו שבעים שנה."

פסיקתא רבתי (יש שלום) פיסקא מ' בחודש השביעי

Hashem explained that when He said that on the "day" you eat from it you shall die, He did not specify whether it meant a "day" in human time — 24 hours — or one of Hashem's days, which is equal to 1000 human years — which is over 8,700,000 hours! Pretty innovative!

We see that even when we think that our fate is signed and sealed, Hashem's endless compassion and mercy can always find a way to help us and we don't need to worry about "how" it will work out with the letter of the law! Hashem is the greatest Lawyer in the world and He knows every trick in the book! You're in good hands!

"חיי דוד המלך שבעים ואלו שבעים שנה חסרו מאדם הראשון."

אוצר המדרשים פנחס בן יאיר

Indeed, because of the sin, Adam was sentenced to live for "only" ONE of Hashem's days, meaning ONE THOUSAND years! Adam then "donated" seventy of his years to Dovid HaMelech and lived for 930 years.

"אמר דוד: רבון העולמים:
אילולי שדנת את אדם הראשון ברחמים ... לא היה אפילו שעה אחת ...."

פסיקתא רבתי (איש שלום) פיסקא מ' בחודש השביעי

Dovid HaMelech said:
"Master of the universe: Had You not judged Adam with mercy,
I would have not lived for even one moment!"

"וכשם שדנת אותו ברחמים כן אתה דן את כל הדורות אחריו לעולם!"

פסיקתא רבתי (איש שלום) פיסקא מ' בחודש השביעי

"And just as You judged him with mercy ...
may You judge all future generations forever!"

אמן ואמן!!!

6

JUSTICE VS. COMPASSION

---

*Understanding how we can
"beat" the system of justice*

"מי יתן ויכלתי לאהב
את הצדיק הגדול
בישראל, כשם שהשם
יתברך אוהב את הרשע
הגדול בישראל!"

בעל שם טוב מובא בספר פתגמים נבחרים

*"If only I would love the
greatest tzaddik as
much as Hashem
loves the
greatest
rasha!"*

Hashem

created a perfect system of justice ...
with just one loophole:

"אף על גב דקודשא בריך הוא רחים ליה לדינא
כמא דאת אמר 'כי אני ה' אוהב משפט' (ישעיה ס"א)
נצח רחימוי דבנוי לרחימו דדינא!"

זוהר - רעיא מהימנא כרך ג' פרשת אמור דף צט:

"Although the Torah states: 'I, Hashem, love Judgment,'
Hashem's immense love for His children
conquers His love of justice."

MISGUIDED PARENTING

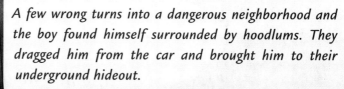

After a long string of events, the wild and rebellious teenager stole his father's new car in the middle of the night and went for a joyride.

A few wrong turns into a dangerous neighborhood and the boy found himself surrounded by hoodlums. They dragged him from the car and brought him to their underground hideout.

The gang leader called the boy's father to demand a ransom for his prize possession and was shocked by his response: "Well, my son has really been rebellious lately and he doesn't listen to any of my rules. Stealing my new car was last straw and I'm just not interested in getting him back. Baruch she'ptarani!"

The hoodlum shouted, "But we will torture him!"

The dad replied, "Good! Maybe then he'll finally learn to act like a mentch!"

We all realize that no father would ever respond like that! Even if a father wants his son to learn a valuable lesson, a normal father would never abandon his child under **ANY** circumstances!

JUDGE BERNSTEIN

Judge Arthur Bernstein was known to be the most prestigious judge in the history of the federal court system. He knew how to see through complicated cases and figure out exactly what really happened. For over thirty years he handed out verdicts exactly according to the letter of the law. "It is the only way society can exist," he stated.

One day a case came before him. Although the prosecution made a strong case against the defendant, the judge ruled that although the exact letter of the law would require the boy to sit in a maximum security prison for five years, in this case, the boy was sentenced to only one month in a minimum security camp.

The judge explained to the shocked crowd, "Although I truly believe in pure justice and I devoted my entire life to upholding the exact letter of the law, this defendant is my son and I love my son even more than I love justice!"

That is the lesson of the *Zohar HaKadosh*: Yes, Hashem really does love justice; however, Hashem's love for EACH AND EVERY YID — regardless of his spiritual status — is simply much more powerful than His great love for justice!

> "אף על פי שבאמת על פי דין וסדר לא מגיע לו
> **אך על ידי שיודע ומרגיש 'כי אבינו אתה'**
> נמשך עליו רחמים למעלה מן הדין והחשבון!"
>
> ספר נתיבות שלום על חנוכה

Authentic Yiddishkeit believes that even when there is no way to win according to normal courtroom proceedings, by truly feeling that Hashem is your loving FATHER, you unleash the enormous reservoir of compassion and mercy that is ABOVE the justice department!

It is this powerful concept of "אבינו — our Father" that has brought salvation to the Yiddishe nation when all other doors were closed:

> "מעשה ברבי אליעזר שירד לפני התיבה
> ואמר עשרים וארבע ברכות ולא נענה. ירד רבי עקיבא אחריו,
> ואמר: **אבינו** מלכנו אין לנו מלך אלא אתה!
> **אבינו** מלכנו למענך רחם עלינו! וירדו גשמים!"
>
> תענית כה:

In the days of the Mishnah, there was a terrible drought and everyone poured out their hearts to beseech Hashem to end the suffering; nevertheless, the drought continued. Even the holy Tanna Rebbi Eliezer *davened* fervently, yet he was not answered. Finally, Rebbi Akiva prayed, "Our **FATHER** our King! We have no other king! Our **FATHER** our King! Have mercy on us!" The decree was nullified and it began to rain!!

LET'S EXAMINE THIS STORY A LITTLE DEEPER:

The Torah (*Devarim* 11:17) openly states that if Hashem will ever hold back the rain, it is because the Yidden are **NOT** behaving properly. So in the time of Rebbi Akiva, it was OUR sins that brought about the drought in the first place.

Behind the scenes in the heavenly court, everything was being processed precisely in accordance with the rules of the universe as per Hashem's creation of the justice system. The Yidden sinned and therefore, the appropriate punishment of "withholding the rain" was implemented.

Yet we see that Rebbi Akiva still felt that he could approach Hashem using the emotional title "**FATHER**" — and by evoking this powerful title he was able to overturn the decree!

THIS PROVES TWO REMARKABLE THINGS:

1. Although the masses of Yidden sinned to the point that Hashem had to hold back the rain — which is really bad — Rebbi Akiva was still able to call Hashem: "אבינו," our Father!

This proves that even when we sin and we must be punished, we still have not relinquished our status of: "בנים," Hashem's precious children, as the Gemara brings down from R' Akiva's disciple:

"רבי מאיר אומר: בין כך ובין כך אתם קרוים בנים!"
קידושין לא.

"Whether you do Hashem's will or not,
you are ALWAYS Hashem's child!"

2. Even though Hashem created a perfect justice system and once a decree is set forth based on factual calculations of our sinful actions it cannot be easily overturned, we can still beseech Hashem to please save us (from the results of our own sins) because He is not bound by any of the rules and regulations of the justice department!

The president of the United States is able to issue presidential pardons! This pardon is not REQUIRED to fit into the rules and regulations of the justice system — it is a completely different approach! The presidential pardon doesn't claim the person is INNOCENT — in fact, he might very well be GUILTY of the crime ... yet he will still be set free!

"וְהַיְינוּ שֶׁהָיָה אָז קִטְרוּגִים עַל יִשְׂרָאֵל וּמִשּׁוּם כָּךְ לֹא נַעֲנָה רַבִּי אֱלִיעֶזֶר,

אַךְ רַבִּי עֲקִיבָא אָמַר 'אָבִינוּ מַלְכֵּנוּ', הַשֵּׁם יִתְבָּרֵךְ 'אָבִינוּ',

וּמִכֹּחַ זֶה מִסְתַּלְּקִים הַקִּטְרוּגִים!"

ספר נתיבות שלום חלק ב' עמוד קמ"א

Now we can understand: Rebbi Eliezer tried to find a way to overturn the decree within the justice system; however, the decree could not be annulled, since it was a perfectly suitable punishment based on the facts.

However, Rebbi Akiva did not try to appeal to the department of justice — rather, he ran directly to the highest authority — the President of all presidents, King of all kings — OUR FATHER IN HEAVEN!

NOW WE CAN UNDERSTAND THE FOLLOWING:

"שַׁעֲרֵי תְפִלָּה פְּעָמִים פְּתוּחִים פְּעָמִים נְעוּלִים,

אֲבָל שַׁעֲרֵי רַחֲמִים אֵינָן נִנְעָלִין לְעוֹלָם!"

מדרש תהלים מזמור ד'

"The Gates of Prayer are sometimes open and sometimes closed. However, the Gates of Mercy **never** close!"

The justice system is rigid and has many rules and regulations, and also has hours of operation! However, "mercy," by definition, has no limitations, no boundaries, no logic, and therefore: NO hours!

MISPLACED SYMPATHY

One day Shaindel was standing at the bus stop next to an elderly man holding a full bag of groceries. Suddenly the bottom of the bag plotzed and the groceries rolled in all directions. The elderly man was annoyed that Shaindel didn't try to help him and snapped, "Young lady, maybe you can give me a hand?"

Shaindel replied: "I'm so sorry but I was working on the character trait of chessed (helping people) last week. This week I'm working on feeling another person's pain — and I really do feel bad for you!"

You can't be truly merciful and compassionate from 9:00-12:00 and then if someone needs your help afterward, you reply: "Oh sorry, it's my lunch break!" For if you are **truly** merciful and compassionate — and you **really** care about people — then that mercy compels you to help people at ANY time — even if it is not convenient for you!

FREE ADVICE

A doctor and a lawyer were attending a cocktail party when the doctor was approached by a man who asked advice on how to handle his ulcers. The doctor mumbled some medical advice, then turned to the lawyer and grumbled, "I hate it when people seek free advice from me at parties."

The lawyer replied, "I know just what you mean — it happens to me all the time."

"How do you handle it?" asked the doctor. "After all, it seems rude not to answer a question when you are asked for advice during a social function."

"I just send the person a bill for the time," replied the lawyer, "and then he never asks me again."

"That's good," said the doctor. "I'll have to remember that." The doctor went home and thought about sending a bill to the man who asked about the ulcer, but when he woke up the next day it had already slipped his mind. However, the night's events came rushing back to him the next day when he opened his mail. In it, he found a bill for $100 from the lawyer for "consultation services rendered."

A tzaddik who lives a pure and holy life, completely dedicated to Hashem, can perhaps do battle within the system of justice based on his piety and well-deserved merits!

However, everyone else surely cannot win in the strict courtroom of Divine justice! So what should you do now? Give up?

> "בגלל שר' עקיבא הוסיף **וחידש** בתפילתו תואר 'אבינו'
> והקדים אבינו למלכנו על כן מיד נענה!"
>
> ספר נתיבות שלום חלק ב'

Absolutely not! Rabbi Akiva showed us a new path to victory! He approached the bench (so to speak) with the emotional title "TOTTY" and brought out the feelings that Hashem has to His beloved children ... and was immediately answered!

We aren't just bringing this down just to teach you nice ideas — this knowledge is PRACTICAL ADVICE for you as you go through your life! Whenever you encounter ANY kind of difficulty, please remember:

> "והדרך להמשיך בחינה זו של 'אביכם שבשמים,'
> שאפילו במצב של **לא מעלי** יהיו בבחינת 'בנים אתם לה' אלקיכם'
> **הוא בכח האמונה** שיהודי מאמין כי 'בנים אתם לה' אלקיכם'
> **ובעצם כח האמונה ממשיכים את המדרגה הגבוהה הזאת בחינת 'בנים'**!"
>
> נתיבות שלום חלק ב' עמוד של"א

The way to ensure that Hashem treats you as His beloved child — even though you may currently be unworthy of the title — is by increasing your belief that you really are His child! So by calling out "Totty, help me," you actually awaken Hashem's mercy and He responds as a father running to help his lost child from even the worst possible situation!

> "כאשר יהודי מאמין שישראל הם **בנים בכל המצבים,**
> הרי כיון שמאמין שהוא **בן** ורוצה להתנהג **כבן** הריהו ממשיך בחינה זו!"
>
> נתיבות שלום חלק ב' עמוד של"ב

For if you BELIEVE that you are Hashem's son and you truly WANT to act like a PRINCE — you will arouse the powerful love that Hashem has for you! NOTHING can stand in the way of a loving father who wants to rescue his beloved child!

IN FACT — THE FACT THAT YOU ARE LESS WORTHY AWAKENS MORE OF HASHEM'S LOVING MERCY:

"יש שני בחינות של עת רצון שמתעורר אצל המלך על בנו:
כאשר הבן חכם ונבון, והמלך מתפאר בחכמתו לפני שרי המלוכה,
הריהו מעורר רצון אצל המלך למלא את רצונו וליתן לו כל משאלותיו."

מובא בספר נתיבות שלום מספר בית אברהם (פ' פנחס)

LOTS OF NACHAS

There was once a king who had two sons. The king gave each son his own province to rule. The older son was a brilliant leader and his province thrived under his courageous leadership. He made treaties and developed trade with neighboring countries, creating a prosperous economy. He was his father's pride and joy, and he brought power and prestige to the throne.

The other son however, was quite a different story! He was a לא יצלח (big-time loser). He was a terrible leader who couldn't manage to get along with any of his neighboring rulers. His people were poor and angry about his lack of leadership skills. He brought great shame to the king's name.

The king made a wedding for a third child and afterward both sons came to bid him farewell. First the older, successful prince walked in and naturally the king was very happy to greet him. The prince requested that his father grant him a tremendous amount of money for important *projects that would spread the king's good name to even more continents. Hearing his dear son's ambitious plans aroused the king's great mercy and he was eager to grant his dear prince whatever he requested.*

"אך יש עת רצון כאשר יש למלך בן מפגר אשר לא יצלח

למאומה, ומצד מעשיו היה ראוי לגרשו מעל פני המלך,

אך הרי עצמו ובשרו הוא, ומפני מצבו האומלל שאינו

מסוגל לכלום מתעוררת עליו גודל הרחמנות של אביו,

ומרחם עליו עוד יותר מאשר על הבן המוצלח!"

מובא בספר נתיבות שלום מספר בית אברהם (פר' פנחס)

MORE MERCY

Then the second son came in and pleaded with his father to help him as well. Not with expanding the king's glory throughout the world; rather, he needed help just to get out of the horrible mess he was in. He couldn't take care of even the most basic needs of his people! Without his daddy's help, he would be in deep, deep trouble!

Another kind of mercy was aroused in the king's heart, for he realized that he MUST help this son out, because if he didn't help him — no one else would! He recognized that this child needs even MORE MERCY and compassion than his brother, because this loser would never be able to survive on his own!

LISTEN CAREFULLY:

There are **two** types of children who arouse Hashem's mercy:

The righteous "good" child is a constant source of great pride to Hashem and Hashem watches over him and assists him in glorifying His great name throughout the world.

However, Hashem's boundless mercy is also awakened when the "לא יצלח" loser son beseeches Him. For Hashem knows that if He doesn't help this kid ... he'll NEVER make it on his own!

Who needs MORE MERCY from Hashem? The righteous "GOOD" son? Or the one caught in the web of sin, transgression, insubordination, defiance, and disobedience?

"כבן אצל אביו' אשר גם כשהוא מטונף ביותר בא וחוסה בצל אביו על אף שמלכלך אותו בידעו כי אין מי שיכול לעזור לו זולת אביו!"

ספר נתיבות שלום חלק ב' עניני יום כיפור

Yup — you guessed right! Just as a small child who is incredibly filthy can still run to his father to hold him and clean him, because the father knows that NO ONE ELSE would help this child right now, so too with our Father!

"וכל כמה שהבן פחות מסוגל מתעורר יותר עת רצון!"

מובא בספר נתיבות שלום מספר בית אברהם (פר' פנחס)

The children who are STRUGGLING need MORE mercy! Therefore, the LESS worthy the child is — the LOWER he is — the DIRTIER he is — **the MORE mercy is awakened!** So it's a really good thing that Hashem has lots 'n lots of mercy always in stock!

HASHEM'S WAREHOUSE

"באותה שעה הראה לו (למשה) כל אוצרות של מתן שכרן של צדיקים ... והוא שואל האוצר הזה של מי הוא? והוא אומר של בעלי תורה, והאוצר הזה של מכבדיהם ...."

מדרש תנחומא (ורשא) פרשת כי תשא סימן כ"ז

Hashem took Moshe on a royal tour of many heavenly treasure houses set aside for those who will earn them. Moshe asked, "Hashem, who is this for?" Hashem replied, "This is for the Torah scholars." "And who is this for?" "... for those who honor the Torah scholars ...."

"הראה לו אוצר גדול מכולם ואומר רבש"ע האוצר הגדול הזה של מי?
אמר ליה מי שיש לו מעשים טובים אני נותן לו משכרו,
ומי שאין לו: חנם אני עושה ונותן לו מזה!"

מדרשת תנחומא (ורשא) פרשת כי תשא סימן כ"ז

Then Hashem revealed a humungous treasure house that was larger than all the others, and Moshe asked, "And who is this for?" Hashem answered, "When people have good deeds, I pay them from the other warehouses, but when someone does not have ANY good deeds at all, then I give him from this warehouse!"

"יש שיהודי עומד במצב שכל הדרכים חסומות בפניו ואינו רואה שום
מוצא אך: 'והרבה עמו פדות' - להשם יתברך **יש הרבה דרכי פדות** שאינן
יכולות בכלל לעלות על הדעת! הקדוש ברוך הוא **נתן דרכים ליהודי בכל
המצבים** איך להמשיך ישועה ורחמים!"

נתיבות שלום עניני פורים בשם מרן הסבא קדישא מלכוביץ, זי"ע

There are many times in life when you will find yourself in a very difficult situation, physically, emotionally, or spiritually, and you will not see any way out. It is in those dark times that you must believe with all your heart that Hashem has no shortage of "פדות" (redemption) — He is ready and willing to generously dispense as much redemption as you need in ways that you could never even imagine.

"ההבטחה של 'אביכם שבשמים'
היא הבטחה נצחית לכל יהודי ויהודי! 'ואשריכם ישראל'
בזה במיוחד שבעוד שאתם 'מלוכלכים' הריהו גם כן **אביכם** שבשמים!"

ספר נתיבות שלום חלק ב' עניני יום כיפור

The guarantee that Hashem is YOUR FATHER is an ETERNAL guarantee to each and every Yid regardless of your situation! How fortunate are we indeed that even when we are filthy and low — when NO ONE else can help us and when we have NOWHERE else to turn — Hashem is still our LOVING FATHER! That is truly something to dance about!

SO LET'S NOT FORGET:

"צריך יהודי להרגיש בכל המצבים הקשים והחשכים:
'שבכל מצב שהוא הריהו בן המלך!'"

הרב הקדוש מרוזין זי"ע מובא בנתיבות שלום עניני פורים עמוד נ"ה

As you go through life whenever you find yourself in difficult and dark situations;

Remember: YOU are a **PRINCE!**

AND SO ... YOU MUST LIVE UP TO THAT TITLE!

"המוסר החזק ביותר
שהקדוש ברוך הוא אומר לאיש יהודי הוא: **בני אתה!**
ומכיון שהנך בן המלך, **אל תמאס את עצמך בהנהגה בלתי הולמת!**"

מרן הסבא קדישא מסלונים זי"ע מובא בנתיבות שלום

Internalizing that you are the son of Hashem means that you have a **RESPONSIBILITY TO ACT** like the prince of the King of the universe and you should not lower yourself to act in ways not befitting your lofty status.

This incredible knowledge also changes the way you will approach all of your service to Hashem:

"כל עבודתו של יהודי מרוממת לאין ערוך כאשר עובד בבחינת בנים
שאם לומד תורה או מתפלל מתוך הרגשה שהוא בן המלך
אז לימודו ותפלתו מתרוממים למדרגה אחרת!"

נתיבות שלום עניני חנוכה: זאת חנוכה

When you learn Torah, *daven*, and just live your life with the feeling that you are LITERALLY the King's SON, your learning and davening will become elevated to an entirely different level! As you go through your day — ALL of your Yiddishkeit will feel completely different when you internalize that you are a beloved son yearning to connect to your loving father!

BUT THE GREATEST MOST INCREDIBLE BENEFIT OF ALL IS:

"והנה בשעה שיהודי מגיע להרגשה האמיתית בלבבו 'כי אבינו אתה'
ולא די שאומר כן בפיו, כי הרי כל לבבות דורש ה' היודע תעלומות לב,
אלא שמרגיש באמת כן בלבבו 'כי אבינו אתה'
אזי אין בקשה שאינו יכול לבקש בשעה זו!!"

נתיבות שלום חלק ב' עמוד רי"ג

Authentic Yiddishkeit understands that when you actually internally believe that Hashem really is your loving Father — you don't just say it — you really FEEL that way in the depths of your heart — then you tap into a **supernatural power that allows you to receive ANYTHING that you request from Hashem!**

Pretty amazing ...

No?

PARTING WORDS...

Now we can finally properly understand the words of the Holy *Zohar*:

"אלמלי הוו ידעין בני נשא רחימותא
דרחים קודשא בריך הוא לישראל
הוו שאגין ככפיריא למרדף אבתריה!!!"

זוהר חלק ב' פרשת שמות ה:

If YOU would truly comprehend the infinite unconditional love that Hashem feels for YOU at every moment of every day, regardless

of your physical, emotional, psychological, or spiritual condition, you would roar like a lion to run after Him!

Start running!

חזק ואמץ

YOUR ESSENCE IS:
SOLID GOLD

"The root of the Yiddishe soul is in holiness; it is the root of all good traits and holy merits."

"שורש נשמת ישראל בקדושה שורש כל מדות טובות ומעלות קדושות."

ערבי נחל בראשית לך לך דרוש ג'

7

ESSENCE OR CIRCUMSTANCE

*After all the good and bad that I do ...
who am I really?*

"אמר רבי אבא בר זבדא
אף על פי שחטא
ישראל הוא!"

תלמוד בבלי מסכת סנהדרין דף מד.

"Even after he sinned,
***he is still a
Yid!"***

Hashem

gave every Yid the status: "YISRAEL"
and there's nothing you can do to lose it!

"שלשה שותפין יש באדם:
הקב"ה ואביו ואמו."
תלמוד בבלי מסכת נדה דף לא.

"There are three partners in the creation of man:
Hashem, father, and mother."

Spiritually speaking, Hashem **invests** into your being by inserting a piece of His holiness, called a נשמה (soul), as the Torah says: "Hashem blew a living SOUL into his nostrils."

"ויפח באפיו נשמת חיים: מאן דנפח מתוכו נפח!"
בראשית ב:ז תקוני זוהר מובא בפרי צדיק פרשת וילך

Just as when a person blows out, the air comes from within him, so too, when the Torah says that Hashem blew a soul into man, where did that soul come from? From within Hashem! (So to speak.)

An essential part of every Yid is a "חלק אלוק ממעל," an actual piece of G-dliness inserted directly by Hashem, Creator of the universe. Therefore, **the core of every Yid is pure and holy**. This is known as "the pintele Yid."

This eternal, enduring, infinite, pure G-dliness **within** us is an indestructible supernatural power with the ability to prevail over the raging flames of evil that constantly attempt to disconnect us from Hashem.

"זרע האבות זרע קודש מחצבתם
ואם חוטאים מיצר הרע
קדושת טבע תולדותם עוזרם לתשובה!"

מהרז"ו על מדרש רבה במדבר ב:טז

Physically, we are also rooted in pure holiness, since we are the direct offspring of the אבות הקדושים (holy forefathers) who uplifted their physical beings through a life of purity and holiness, thereby morphing into physical manifestations of G-dliness. Thus, even the physical aspect of every Yid is pure and holy.

NOW WE CAN UNDERSTAND:

"ישראל - אף שחוטאים זהו רק במקרה מצד היצר הרע
אבל עצם נפשם טובה ולא יתכן הנפילה להם לגמרי!"

עץ יוסף על מדרש רבה במדבר ב:טז

Since we are created from pure goodness, it **cannot** be that we sin because we are "essentially" bad and it **cannot** be that our sins have the ability to change our "essence" from good to bad. Therefore, when you sin, it is not because your **ESSENCE** is corrupt; rather, it is only because of **circumstances** brought upon you by the Evil Inclination!

"החטאים הוא רק כהוצי הסובבים לפנימיות הלב הישראלי
שהוא אסא והדס המעלה ריח טוב."

פרי צדיק ויקרא קונטרס עמלה של תורה אות ו'

Therefore, we must understand that sinning is merely an EXTERNAL act brought upon you by the יצר הרע, Evil Inclination. A person's sins are only like **external** thorns that merely surround but never affect the **internal** goodness of a Yid, who is like a sweet-smelling myrtle branch!

YOU SEEM A LITTLE SKEPTICAL —
SO LET US PROVE THIS TO YOU:

"הן עשו אחי איש שער ואנכי איש חלק."

בראשית פרק כז:יא

The Torah says: Behold, my brother Eisav is hairy, whereas I am a smooth-skinned man.

"רבי לוי אמר: משל לקווץ וקרח עומדין על שפת הגורן ועלה המוץ
בקווץ ונסתבך בשערו עלה המוץ בקרח ונתן ידו על ראשו והעבירו."

בראשית רבה פרשה ס"ה

There were two people standing at the edge of a granary; one of them was very hairy and the other one was completely bald. Suddenly a big wind came and blew loose chaff all over them.

The bald guy simply wiped his head and all the chaff slipped off. However, the chaff became entangled in the hairy man's thick bushy hair, and he had a very hard time getting it all out.

So too with Yaakov and Eisav, the extremes of good and bad:

"כך עשו הרשע: מתלכלך בעוונות כל ימות השנה ואין לו במה יכפר,
אבל יעקב: **מתלכלך בעוונות כל ימות השנה**
ובא יום הכפורים ויש לו במה יכפר!"

בראשית רבה פרשה ס"ה

Throughout the year, the wicked Eisav becomes filthy with sin and has no way to properly clean himself, whereas **Yaakov** (meaning every Jew) **becomes filthy with sin throughout the whole year** but then Yom Kippur wipes the filth away!

We learn two amazing things from this Medrash:

1. The Medrash does not say that the difference between Yaakov and Eisav is that Eisav sins all through the year whereas Yaakov **never sins! This shows us** that the Torah understands that human

beings — even though we are precious, pure, and holy — can still sin every single day of the year!

2. The Medrash clearly shows us that there is a fundamental difference between Klal Yisrael and the rest of the world: A Yid's sins do not cause internal corruption. Therefore, even after you sin all year, you can cleanse yourself with one quick swipe, just as the bald man wipes the *shmutz* off his head. Why? Because it isn't really a part of you.

WATERLOGGED *My cell phone dropped into a bathtub full of water. Obviously it stopped working and I was sure that it was ruined. A friend suggested that I put the phone into a closed bucket of uncooked rice for 24 hours. Skeptically, I followed his advice, and to my great surprise, the phone worked like new! I was sure the water had destroyed my phone's ability to receive signals from the satellite way up in the sky. However, I learned that those connections were perfectly intact and once the water evaporated — the phone worked like new! (Try it — it works!)*

The lesson is clear: Even if you are **COMPLETELY SUBMERGED** in the destructive murky waters of sin and your connection to Hashem becomes "waterlogged" — the reality is that if you completely immerse yourself within the pure confines of the Holy Torah, allowing your soul to "dry up" from "sin damage," you will discover that you have not lost the ability to once again connect to purity and holiness.

This concept is not just a hypothetical, obscure, far-fetched thought — it is the foundation of our religion and it affects our daily lives. Here's proof:

In Jewish law, a person can divorce his wife only **willingly**. If a man refuses to divorce his wife, the rabbinical court may use **force** to "convince" him to "reconsider" and give the divorce of his own "free will," and it is a proper divorce. The question is, if they forced him to give the divorce, then how can this qualify as giving the divorce **willingly**?

THE EXPLANATION IS AS FOLLOWS:

"מפני שהנפש השכליי חפיצה בחפץ פנימיי לעשות רצון בוראה!
... אלא שיצרו הרע הוא שתקפו לבטל מצוה או לעשות עבירה
וכיון שהוכה עד שתשש יצרו **שוב כבר עשה ברצונו**....."

מדברי שו"ת יד חנוך סימן ט' ד"ה לפיכך נלפע"ד, בביאור דברי הרמב"ם פרק ב'
מהלכות גירושין הלכה כ'

Internally, every person always wants to fulfill the will of Hashem, Creator of the universe. Therefore, when a person has trouble doing what he is supposed to, we understand that his Evil Inclination is not allowing his inner pure self to do what he **really wants** to.

"בהא דכופין עד שיאמר 'רוצה אני' משום **דבאמת רוצה**!'"

רמב"ם הלכות גירושין פרק ב' הלכה כ'

This is why we can physically beat the husband! We need to knock his Evil Inclination out of the equation and FREE him to do what he really wanted to do all along — and that is: what is RIGHT in the eyes of Hashem!

WITH THIS ELEVATED PERSPECTIVE, WE CAN UNDERSTAND HOW HASHEM LOOKS AT US WHEN WE SUCCUMB TO SIN:

"לא הביט און ביעקב ולא ראה עמל בישראל,
ה' אלקיו עמו ותרועת מלך בו!"

במדבר פרק כג:כא

The Torah says: "Hashem did not see any sin amongst Yaakov or any perversity amongst Yisrael. Hashem his G-d is with him, and the friendship of the King is within him!"

"דלכאורה איך יתכן ש'לא הביט און ביעקב' - והרי אית דין ואית דיין
'וכל האומר הקדוש ברוך הוא ותרן יוותרו חייו'?!"

נתיבות שלום חלק ב' עניני ראש השנה דף קט"ו

This sounds really good, but come on — how is it possible that Hashem just ignores our sins — isn't there any justice system?

The reason is revealed to us at the end of the *pasuk*:

"היינו: דגם בשעה שהוא חוטא וממלא תאוותו
ואין לו כח להתגבר על יצר הרע הבוער בו גם אז לבבו נקרע בו:
איך אני עושה דבר שהוא נגד רצון ה' אלוקי?!?!"

נתיבות שלום חלק ב' עניני ראש השנה דף קט"ו

The words: "Hashem his G-d is WITH him" refers to during the sin! This means that even when you don't have the strength to overcome the Yetzer Hora and you fulfill your desire — deep down inside of you — your heart is torn to shreds as you cry: "How on earth can I go against the will of my G-d?"

Since this is how you really feel deep inside of you while you engage in the sin, Hashem does not take your sinful actions at face value and does not consider it as if you truly meant to rebel against Him!

HERE'S THE PLAY BY PLAY:

The prosecuting angels come running to Hashem: "Look what Moishy is doing!" But Hashem looks past his action and sees Moishey's broken heart, and responds: "This is what you are bringing Me? A distraught Yid who is so upset about doing something against My will?!"

"מלאך שנברא על ידי עשיית העבירה
איננו שלם - כי הפעולה אינה שלימה!"

ספר מנורת זהב צ"ח בשם רבי זושע זי"ע

Since every time you sin, you regret going against the will of Hashem, you don't sin with a truly happy heart. For this reason, the bad angels created by your sins are never whole — for deep down, your heart is not completely in it!

EVEN AFTER SO MANY SINS — YOUR ESSENCE IS STILL INTACT:

"שהניצוץ יהדות אי אפשר לכבות לגמרי על ידי ריבוי החטאים
דאם לא כן לא היה מתעורר לשוב כלל!"

פרי צדיק ויקרא קונטרס עמלה של תורה אות ו'

Your internal "pintele Yid" can never be extinguished — **even by an abundance of sin!** For then it would be impossible for a big-time sinner to ever be able to return to Hashem!

Authentic Yiddishkeit clearly believes that even after sinning over and over, day after day, year after year, all the receptors that connect us to Hashem are still completely intact and ready to be used! They don't become musty, dusty, or rusty!

"דמה שפושעי ישראל היותר גרועים
יכולים ברגע אחד להתעורר לשוב לה' יתברך במסירות נפש
זהו על ידי התעוררות הנקודה דשורש נפשם!"

פרי צדיק ויקרא קונטרס עמלה של תורה אות ו'

The fact that one who intentionally rebels against Hashem can completely turn around in one moment and stand ready to literally die for Hashem is only possible because he possesses an indestructible spark of G-dliness deep inside him!

OVER THE CENTURIES KLAL YISRAEL HAS WITNESSED
THIS PHENOMENON HUNDREDS OF TIMES.
HERE'S JUST ONE STORY:

IT'S NEVER TOO LATE

During the terrifying years of the Holocaust, the Nazis, yimach shimam, gathered all the Yidden of a town into the main shul on Yom Kippur. The Yidden were squashed together, gripped in fear, not knowing what would happen to them. They knew that the Nazis were capable of burning them alive in the shul, as they had done elsewhere.

After hours of waiting, the Nazis ym"sh burst into the shul with their top Jewish informant. This was a non-religious Jewish thug who had sunk to the lowest depths of the underworld. Before the Nazi invasion, he would terrorize the religious people and extort money from them. He was such a dangerous thug that when anyone even heard his name mentioned, they cringed in fear. Since the Nazi invasion, he tried to find favor in the Nazi's eyes by being an informant. Now, the Nazis roughly shoved this Jewish thug into the shul. They had an agenda.

They opened the Aron Kodesh, took out a Sefer Torah, unrolled it on the floor, and commanded the Jew to relieve himself on the Torah! To everyone's shock, he refused! The Nazis beat him mercilessly; however, he would not shame the Torah. They beat him and beat him until he died right there on the spot. The next day, the Rabbis decided that this **holy Yid**, who was murdered Al Kiddush Hashem, should be buried with the Sefer Torah for which he gave his life.

Source: Umasuk HaOr on Megillas Esther, p. 263

NOW WE CAN UNDERSTAND
THE POWERFUL WORDS OF THE MEDRASH:

"אפילו בוגדיו, רשעים שבישראל - צדיקים הם!
שנאמר: ועמך **כלם צדיקים**!"

פסיקתא זוטרתא בראשית פרק כ"ז

Even a seemingly rebellious wicked Jew is really ... are you ready for this?

A TZADDIK!

NOW WE CAN UNCOVER A POWERFUL INSIGHT INTO
OUR RELATIONSHIP WITH HASHEM AND LEARN
HOW WE CAN GROW AND CONNECT TO HIM:

"שובה ישראל עד ה' אלקיך
כי **כשלת בעונך**."

הושע פרק יד:ב

The Prophet Hoshea says: "Return, Yisrael, **until** Hashem your G-d, for you have stumbled with your sins!"

IF YOU CAREFULLY ANALYZE THIS VERSE,
YOU WILL HAVE THESE QUESTIONS:

1. The prophet should have said "return **TO** Hashem," not: "return **UNTIL** Hashem."

2. Every Jew thinks to himself: (or at least should!)

"יהודי חושב לעצמו איככה יוכל
להגיע להיות דבוק בה' אחרי כל חטאיו שיצרו מחיצות

ברזל ומסכים המבדילים בינו לבין השם יתברך:
הרי אין ארור מתדבק בברוך!?"

נתיבות שלום חלק ב' בין כסה לעשור דף קנ"ד

Come on — let's be really honest: after all the rebellious, revolting, hideous, horrible, horrific, dreadful, appalling, disgusting, awful, sickening, repugnant, horrid, ghastly, grisly, and slimy sins that I knowingly committed directly against the will of Hashem, is it really possible for me to return "עד ה' אלקיך" all the way back UNTIL Hashem? How can a low-life spiritually contaminated sinner like me actually still connect to the ultimate of all purity and holiness?

3. The prophet should have told us to return to Hashem "because you **sinned and messed up your life!**" Why, then, does he say, "come back and return to Hashem — because you STUMBLED with your sins" as if to cover up the severity of our sins and suggesting that we just somehow ... kinda ... you know ... accidentally... "stumbled"?

"בכחך לשוב עד ה' אלקיך מפני שכל החטאים שלך
הם רק 'כשלונות', ואינם שינוי בעצם מהותך!"

נתיבת שלום חלק ב' ענייני ראש השנה דף קט"ו

The answer to all of these questions is: **YES!** Even after all the sins you did — **YOU CAN STILL** return literally all the way "עד ה' אלקיך" **UNTIL** Hashem! **Why?** "כי **כשלת בעונך**". Because each time you sinned, it was **ONLY** because you "stumbled" due to the Evil Inclination!

MISFIT *Reuven was a really good yeshivah boy. When his friend Chaim got married, Reuven rented a car and drove eight hours to be at the wedding. At the wedding someone "spiked" the soda with vodka and without even realizing it Reuven had alcohol in his system. The wedding was over*

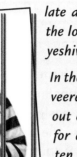

late and Reuven was pretty tired ... but he set out for the long drive back home in order to be back in time for yeshivah the next morning.

In the darkness of the night, he dozed off ... BOOM! He veered into the other lane and hit a car ... which spun out of control ... and hit a tree. Reuven was arrested for driving under the influence and was sentenced to ten years in jail.

Throughout the ten years Reuven sat in jail, his parents NEVER missed a chance to visit their beloved son. They knew that even though he did a terrible thing, outside factors were to blame for this horrible occurrence. When they visited their precious child and saw him in a prison jumpsuit, treated like a common lowlife ... their hearts went out to him ... and they suffered along with him! Their poor child was in the same jail as thieves, drug dealers, and drunks — yet they knew and believed that he was NOT one of them! Seeing their dear son in this lowly situation only <u>magnified</u> how **different** he was from them ... and how much he did NOT fit in with these criminals!

THE SAME APPLIES TO EACH ONE OF US:

"ואפילו כשיהודי חוטא במרד ובמעל, אין זה אלא 'כשלון'!!!
כי אם הי' יודע ומכיר את גדלות הבורא כראוי לא הי' חוטא ...
אם כן דינו כאדם החוטא מבלי דעת!"

נתיבות שלום חלק ב' בין כסה לעשור דף קנ"ד

Even if it seems that you are sinning against Hashem out of **defiance and rebelliousness** — it is really only due to a **stumbling block!** The truth is that the only reason you sinned is because the Evil Inclination managed to wrap himself around your better judgment and somehow NUMB your brain to the point that you were in a fog — like a drunk man who can't focus on the ramifications of his actions! It was never your **internal will** to sin — YOU never signed off and agreed to this and you surely aren't proud of what you did! **Therefore, you will be judged as someone who sinned unintentionally!**

"יהודי ירד לעולם הזה כדי להגיע למשהו של השגה בגדלות הבורא,
ולבסוף תמורת זאת שקוע ומבולבל בשטויותיו והבליו,
והרי זה בבחינת 'כי כשלת בעוונך' שהכל בגדר 'שוגג'
אפילו החטאים החמורים ביותר שיהודי עושה במזיד
הרי זה רק משום שאינו מבין את כבוד הקדוש ברוך הוא!"

ספר נתיבות שלום

You were sent down to this world on a mission to live with some sort of comprehension of the greatness of G-d and your commitment to follow His command, but in the end, you got sidetracked and confused and became immersed in stupidity and nonsense. No sane person would ever do that. So the sins that you did while in a dazed and confused state of mind — even those that you did on purpose — were not while you clearly felt and perceived the true greatness of Hashem!

Did you know what you were doing? Well, technically you did — but did you understand what a terrible thing you were really doing and the consequences of your stupid idiotic actions? NO WAY!

The proof is, that while thinking clearly — you would NEVER do those things! That is why Hashem will have mercy on you and purify you from all of your sins!

How can you be sure? It's really quite simple: If at that moment of your sin — you would have truly recognized the incredible infinite greatness of Hashem — would you have still sinned? Absolutely not! If you would be standing in the Bais HaMikdash — would you do this sin? Of course not! At the Kosel? Never! On Yom Kippur during Neilah? No way!

Therefore, there is nothing that can BLOCK YOU from returning to Hashem:

SO WHAT DOES THE YETZER HORA DO TO US?

"דהנה היצר הרע מתגבר במיוחד על יהודי שלא יחזור בתשובה!
כי יודע היצר הרע כמה גדול כח התשובה!"

ספר נתיבות שלום חלק ב' קנ"ג

The Yetzer Hora knows that if you really try to get back on track and become better, you will succeed in improving your life! That's why it works really hard to make sure that you don't even try!

"ועל כן מעמיד הוא בפני יהודי 'כאילו' כבר אינו יכול לשוב בתשובה,
שהרי כבר כל כך הרבה פעמים עשה תשובה ולא עמד בתשובתו וחזר
לכמות שהיה - **ומה יועיל לו עתה אם יעשה תשובה עוד פעם?!**"

ספר נתיבות שלום חלק ב' קנ"ג

The evil twisted Yetzer Hora tries to convince you that it's too late for you to return to Hashem. After what you did?!? Forget about it! Hashem's never seen anything like that before! Besides — you already made up your mind to be good so many times and still and all you FELL again and again — so what good is it if you would pick yourself up again!?

But the truth is that we know and believe that Hashem understands our personal difficulties and struggles, and Hashem takes into consideration our inner pain stemming from our distance from Him. Therefore, when we do what we can, He accepts us back with open arms! Time after time!

"אל יפול ברוחו ובל ימנעוהו מעשיו
מלהשיג את התשובה הראוי' כי כל מה שיהודי חוטא
אינו בעצם אלא כשלון! כי נשמתו של יהודי היא חלק אלוק ממעל!"

נתיבות שלום חלק ב' בין כסה לעשור דף קנ"ד

Authentic Yiddishkeit understands that you should not despair and you should not give up on trying to repent, rebuild, and reconnect to Hashem, because every sin you did is only due to external stumbling blocks and it does NOT properly represent who you really are, for your **ESSENCE** is a pure soul, and your pure soul is a piece of G-d — so how can you be bad!?!

"חביבין הן ישראל
שאף על פי שהן טמאין **שכינה ביניהם**!"

במדבר רבה (וילנא) פרשה ז'

The Jewish people are so **beloved** that even when they are spiritually bankrupt — Hashem still remains with them! There is no thought or action you can possibly do that will ever cause Hashem to stop loving you! In spite of your sins, Hashem has NEVER left your side, and He will never leave your side!

THIS IS WHY HASHEM LOVES YOU EVEN AFTER YOU SIN:

"אָבִי הוא **קודם** שיחטא האדם
וְאָבִי הוא **לאחר** שיחטא האדם!"

נתיבות שלום

Hashem is your LOVING FATHER before you sin —
and He is still your BELOVED FATHER after you sin!

8

THE SPIRITUAL CAT SCAN

What's really going on inside that mind of yours?

"ודבר זה מתנה
טובה שנתן הקב"ה
לישראל כי מעמקי
לבם דבוק בה'."

פרי צדיק ויקרא קונטרס עמלה של תורה אות ה'

"Hashem gave a special gift to His precious children: **Deep in our hearts we always remain connected to Him."**

HASHEM

does not just look at your actions...
He sees deep into your core!

"לבוחן לבבות ביום דין ...
לגולה עמוקות בדין ... ליודע מחשבות ביום דין ...."
תפילה לימים נוראים

One of the most emotional aspects of Rosh Hashanah and Yom Kippur is the awesome realization that we are standing before a Judge who "examines hearts ... reveals hidden depths ... and knows all our thoughts ...." Yikes!

It's bad enough that Hashem judges our sinful ACTIONS as our violations are displayed on a life-size, high-def, full-color, 3D, slow-motion video. But along come these heart-wrenching words, revealing that Hashem, our Judge, does not only see what we actually did wrong, but He also knows our sinful thoughts lurking beneath the surface! OY! How can you not die of embarrassment as EVERY sinful thought and feeling you had during the entire year is openly revealed in Hashem's heavenly court!?

OUT OF CONTROL *The prosecutor began the case against Herman by playing a video showing him entering a liquor store at 2:19 a.m. to purchase a huge bottle of vodka. Then came the testimony of a police officer who saw Herman wandering through the park at 3:30, completely intoxicated. Herman's credit*

card receipt showed that he purchased gas for his car at 3:45. And finally, a video taken at 4:05 by a bystander crossing the street clearly showed Herman speed straight through a red light, running over the innocent video guy himself! With the camera on the ground, still filming, the video captures Herman stumbling out of the car drunkenly screaming, "OIY VEY! What did I do ... how did I do this .... HELP!"

This was clearly an open-and-shut case. How could Herman defend himself? Could he deny what happened? Of course not! And now, he was about to be judged ....

The feeling of knowing that we are "cooked" happens to us each and every year and we just don't know how to deal with it. So let's take a look back in time and we will find that it actually happened to ALL of us as an entire nation ....

ROLL CLIP:

After we finally got out of Egypt with the Egyptians chasing us in hot pursuit, we found ourselves trapped on all sides, with our path blocked by a sea. Hashem then commanded the sea to split for us, but a very interesting event occurred:

"בעת קריעת ים סוף טען הקטיגור לפני הקב"ה על ישראל ואמר:
הללו [המצרים] עובדי עבודה זרה והללו [ישראל] עובדי עבודה זרה
[כי במצרים היו מישראל נוטים לעבודה זרה]
ולמה אתה קורע להם את הים?"

תורה תמימה בראשית פרק מח:יא בשם מדרש שמות רבה כא:ז זוה"ק ח"ב קע"ב

The heavenly command got caught up (so to speak) in "red tape" and the prosecuting angels interjected: "These Jews worship idols just as these Egyptians do! So how can You command us to split the sea for one group and then drown the other, when they are both essentially THE SAME!?"

SECURITY CLEARANCE

The Prime Minister called the head of airport security with a direct command: At 2:00 p.m. today a flight from Iran will be landing. Forty men named Ishmael Aleli Ikbamakubaku will try to get into our country. They were all trained by the same terrorist group. I hereby command you to escort the first twenty of them right through security and the next twenty of them should be shot dead on the spot!

The head of security replied: I'm sorry, Mr. Prime Minister, but we have rules and regulations that we must follow! How can we possibly do this — they are all the same!?!

Based on our actions, we were in big trouble with no way to defend ourselves, just like our friend Herman and just like each one of us feels every year as we stand to be judged.

"ומהי באמת התשובה
על קיטרוג זה מאחר ששוים במעשיהם?"
ספר נתיבות שלום חלק ב' עמוד ער"ה

But as we all know, Hashem did rescue us from the Egyptians! Nu, so how did He get around the prosecuting angels' rational objection?

"כי מלאכים ושרפים רואים רק את המעשים בפועל,
אך אינם יודעים את המחשבות, ואינם יכולים להבחין **בין עצם למקרה**
על כן טענו הללו והללו עובדי עבודה זרה!"
ספר נתיבות שלום חלק ב' עמוד ער"ה

The explanation is as follows: heavenly angels can only see our exterior **actions** but they have no way to know what we are **thinking**. Therefore they cannot differentiate between "**ESSENCE**" and "**CIRCUMSTANCE**." That's why they mistakenly thought that the two groups of idol worshipers were exactly "THE SAME"!

"הקדוש ברוך הוא היודע מחשבות ומבין כל תעלומות לב
רק הוא ידע שאין הללו כהללו! ... שאפילו כשיהודי חוטא
אין זה בשאט נפש, אלא לבו נשבר מאד בקרבו מכשלונו!"

ספר נתיבות שלום חלק ב' עמוד ער"ה

However, Hashem — Who sees **deep inside** of us — knows that there is **NO comparison** between a Yid (even while doing the worst sins imaginable) and idol-worshiping Egyptians! Hashem knows that you would **never ever willingly agree to sin against Him!** In your internal mindset you never meant to sin at all and you are completely dedicated to Hashem and to following all His commandments!

RABBI GOLDSTEIN

Rabbi Shimon Goldstein was perhaps the most popular Jewish figure in America. He lived in Washington and was the top Jewish liaison to the president. The president often publicly said that if he would ever convert to Judaism — Rabbi Goldstein would be his Rabbi!

One late night on the way home from visiting the president, he came head-to-head with a gang of idol worshipers! They put a gun to his head and said: "Hey Rabbi — either bow down to our idol or we will blow your brains out!" Defiantly the Rabbi retorted: "I will NEVER bow down!"

The hoodlums placed the idol on the ground and brutally swung a bat at the Rabbi's stomach, cracking his ribs! Reb Shimon doubled over and fell on his hands and knees in intense pain. They then snapped a picture, and sent it to all the newspapers. The next day every paper featured the picture with the caption: "The president's Rabbi becomes an idol worshiper!"

Dear reader: Did Rabbi Goldstein physically bow to the idol? YES! Do you think that Rabbi Goldstein is an idol worshiper? Of course not! He was merely unable to fend off the gang members who forced him to bow down! If he knew karate or carried a weapon, he certainly would have fought them!

THIS IS EXACTLY WHAT HASHEM TOLD THE PROSECUTING ANGELS:

"שֵׁירד ס"מ ואמר לפניו רבונו של עולם לא עבדו ישראל עבודה זרה במצרים ואתה עושה להם נסים? והיה משמיע קולו לשר של ים ונתמלא עליהם חֵמָה ובקש לטבען! מיד השיב לו הקב"ה: **שׁוֹטָה שֶׁבָּעוֹלָם** וכי לדעתם עבדוה והלא לא עבדוה אלא מתוך שעבוד ומתוך טרוף דעת **ואתה דן שוגג כמזיד ואונס כרצון?!?!"**

ילקוט שמעוני תורה פרשת בשלח רמז רכ"ה

When the angels questioned our loyalty, Hashem responded: "**You fools!** Can you compare those who sin because they are **FORCED TO SIN** to those who willingly sin!? Did Klal Yisrael worship idols because they wanted to — or because they were under the extreme pressure of their enslavement and under the influence of their contaminated surroundings!?"

Now let's remember: If Hashem would have judged us based on our ACTIONS, we would have been wiped out by the pursuing Egyptian army. So we see that this concept is not just a "nice thought"; rather, our **entire existence** as a nation came about because this is truly the way that Hashem evaluates us!

Although they may have externally engaged in the action of "bowing to idols," they certainly were NOT — by any stretch of the imagination — "idol worshipers!"

And so it is with each one of us: you may "_____" — but you certainly are not a "_____er"!!!

"כי באמת במעמקי לבם כולם צדיקים וקדושים
והפגמים רק מהשאור שבעיסה ההוצי המקיף!"

פרי צדיק ויקרא קונטרס עמלה של תורה אות ו'

In reality, every Yid is essentially **righteous and holy**, and anything he does wrong is ONLY due to the thorny Yetzer Hora that constantly pokes him!

"אתה רואה את החיצוניות בלבד
ואני רואה הן את החיצוניות והן את הפנימיות שבפנימיות
יודע אני את גודל הכאב המחלחל בפנימיות נפשם
אשר צעק לבם אל ה' על שפל מצבם!"

נתיבות שלום עניני פסח דף רנ"ח

While the Jews were still slaves in Mitzrayim, Hashem told Moshe: You only see their **outside**, which **seems** like they have given up on their true Jewish identity and they **seem** to be comfortable living a life immersed in טומאה (spiritual impurity). Whereas, I, Hashem, see the same exterior that you see, but I also see what lies **deep within** their souls. I see their intense יסורי נפש (internal agony), heartache, and misery churning deep within them as they scream out to Me regarding their low spiritual state and depressing situation.

NOT A GOOD SHABBOS

Mr. Greenstein was walking quickly down Ocean Parkway on a cold and dark Friday night after attending his weekly shiur, when he chanced upon a few rebellious-looking teenagers. He tried to walk past them quickly, hoping they weren't dangerous, when suddenly one of them spitefully shouted at him "Gut Shabbos, Rabbi" while taking a drag from some kind of cigarette and gulping down a shot of vodka straight from the bottle. The other boys chuckled.

His heart nearly stopped as he realized that these dangerous-looking kids were actually Yiddishe boys! Anger boiled within him as he could not understand how they

> were not ashamed to act like that in front of him! He became disgusted at their spitefulness in wishing him a "gut Shabbos" while desecrating it right in front of him at the same moment! Fuming with anger, he told his family, "These stinkin' kids are trash and we should throw them out of the neighborhood! They aren't even 'recyclable' because they can never become anything good! Just plain TRASH!"

When we see a "rebel," we may think that he is content with his life and he isn't interested in improving. We may think he really is "worthless" and just a piece of junk. But that is only because we can see only his **external** actions and the tough front he puts up. On the outside he may **seem** happy and content with his life. He may look tough and rebellious. He may look like he is having so much fun partying and spitting in the face of Yiddishkeit.

However, Hashem, Who sees the deep pain inside his heart regarding his sad spiritual status, knows that nothing is further from the truth! No one wants to be far away from Hashem. **No one** really wants to be a rebellious ungrateful person. **No one** wants to waste his life and waste his potential!

Hashem would tell the Mr. Greenstein inside of each one of us: When you judge any Yid at any age or stage, remember that you can only see the exterior; the kid-at-risk or post-risk, the angry person, the miser, the hypocrite, the *kuchleffel*, the fighter, the *ganuf*, etc. ... etc. .... However, I, Hashem, also see **deep within him** and I can tell you that he is in tremendous pain and agony over his situation and he **wishes** that he could improve!

Hashem, Who also sees the **hidden** parts of us, can hear the muffled screams emanating from deep within their souls, crying out in pain over their low spiritual situation: **HASHEM — PLEASE SAVE ME!**

"כי כאשר יהודי חוטא לבו שותת דם על התרחקותו מהשם יתברך
ורק שאינו יכול לעמוד בפני גודל התגברות היצר הרע עליו!
ואילו בפנימיות נפשו **אינו חוטא כלל** ואין הללו 'עובדי עבודה זרה'
והעצם של יהודי קדוש וטהור חלק אלוק ממעל!"

ספר נתיבות שלום חלק ב' עמוד של"ב

Whenever you go against the will of Hashem, deep deep inside you feel absolutely horrible! After all, what **fool** would ever want to do that!?! You know that these actions are not in **your best interest** and you never fully internally agreed to do these sinful actions and thoughts! Therefore, it is as though you were hijacked and forced to go against your true wish and desire to be close to Hashem.

NOW WE CAN LOOK AT THIS PRAYER WITH A FRESH OUTLOOK:

" לבוחן לבבות ביום דין ... לגולה עמוקות בדין ...
ליודע מחשבות ביום דין ...."

"הקב"ה רואה לא רק את המעשים הרעים שעשינו, ולא רק על המחשבות הגלויות שלנו, אלא הוא יתברך מעמיק יותר עד לשורש ושם הוא גולה עמוקות ורואה **את הרצונות והמחשבות הטובים שלנו הטמונים בתוך־תוכנו בעומק הלב והנפש!!!**"

ספר נתיבי אמת

We now understand that these words are not meant to be said in grief: **"Woe is to me that Hashem is going to reveal my deep dark thoughts and secrets! OY VEY!"** On the contrary — it is a heartfelt PRAYER! "PLEASE Hashem; as the prosecutor displays all of my disgusting sinful external actions, please delve past ALL the confusion and corruption, and look DEEPER and DEEPER into my true core essence; reveal to the heavenly court how brokenhearted I am each time I sin, how much I regret sinning against You, and how my true inner desire is to never sin against You again!! YES!

Hashem, look deep into my heart and reveal all of my deep PURE feelings and my inner longing to always be GOOD!"

BEHIND THE SCENES

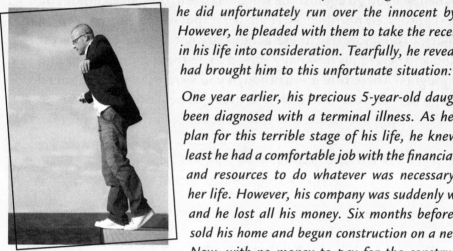

Back to Herman: Herman asked to address the jury. He explained that he was indeed guilty of the horrific crime! Yes, he was drunk, he did speed through the red light, and he did unfortunately run over the innocent bystander. However, he pleaded with them to take the recent events in his life into consideration. Tearfully, he revealed what had brought him to this unfortunate situation:

One year earlier, his precious 5-year-old daughter had been diagnosed with a terminal illness. As he tried to plan for this terrible stage of his life, he knew that at least he had a comfortable job with the financial security and resources to do whatever was necessary to save her life. However, his company was suddenly wiped out and he lost all his money. Six months before, he had sold his home and begun construction on a new house. Now, with no money to pay for the construction, he had to stop the project and the bank took the home away from him. His entire life quickly unraveled. He did not have the money to help his daughter find the best medical treatment possible— and his daughter died. He began to suffer from chest pain and developed diabetes. As a result of all the stress, his beloved wife had a breakdown and was committed to a mental institution. He was shattered. Penniless. Homeless. In his broken and twisted mind that night ... he was hoping — not to kill — but to be killed! He planned to jump from a cliff. This horrible accident occurred while he was driving to the cliff.

He stood before the jury ... weeping ... and pleading .... "Please don't send me to jail for the rest of my life! Please execute me and put me out of my misery, for I can't bear to live any longer!"

> *The jury now understood that Herman was not an "evil person" — rather, he was a broken "good person." They realized that he does not need to be "punished" as much as he needs to be "repaired"! It is true that he may have "killed" — but he was NOT "a killer"! They sentenced him to spend one year in a state-of-the-art rehabilitation center, to be funded by the state, in order to help him deal with his past trauma and build a new life for himself.*
>
> *Indeed, after just one year at the facility, Herman left the facility like a new man, with the rest of his life ahead of him. Greeting him at the front door were the judge and the entire jury. They celebrated his new lease on life and they all wished him well. The same jurors, who were originally prepared to convict Herman of murder, became his biggest fans, rooting for him and buying him gifts in order to lift his spirits.*

Now we can understand how Hashem looked at us when we left Egypt: Instead of focusing on our corrupt actions — He focused on our pure **ESSENCE** and incredible POTENTIAL! These souls did not need to be PUNISHED — they needed to be SAVED! They did not need to be DROWNED — they needed to CROSS THAT SEA and GET AWAY from their past so that they could build a new life for themselves! Indeed, just 49 days later we heard the voice of G-d speaking directly to us at Har Sinai! (Not bad for a seven-week *kiruv* program!)

NOW THAT WE HAVE REVEALED HOW HASHEM LOOKS AT US, WE MUST LEARN TO LOOK AT OURSELVES IN THE SAME INSPIRATIONAL WAY!

"שיר המעלות ממעמקים קראתיך ה'."
תהלים פרק קל:א

Dovid HaMelech writes: "A song of elevation; from the **depths** I call out to Hashem." The simple meaning of "from the depths" is that the person is calling out to Hashem from a very difficult and dismal situation.

"היינו: ממעמקי הנפש!"

נתיבות שלום חלק ב' עניני פסח דף רנ"ח

However, it can also mean that I am calling out "from the depths" of: my own heart and soul! Meaning:

"דאף כאשר יהודי נמצא במצב שבחיצוניות כבר אינו מסוגל לקרוא לה'
הרי 'ממעמקים' קראתיך ה'!
במעמקי נפשו הרי הוא מיוסר וכאוב ונפשו משוועת לה'!!!"

נתיבות שלום חלק ב' עניני פסח דף רנ"ח

Even if you sink so low that **externally** it already seems (even to you!) that you are no longer reaching up and calling out to Hashem, still, "ממעמקים" (from the depths), meaning: from the depths of YOU — **deep deep inside** — you are in pain and agony over the sad state of your low spiritual situation, and your soul is screaming for salvation!

"ולפי זה מובן למה נקט דוד לשון של 'שיר המעלות' ולא 'תפילה לעני'
וכדומה, לומר שהדרך 'להתעלות' הוא דוקא כשיודע
שבמעמקי נפשו עדיין קורא לה'!"

כלילת יופי

Perhaps this is why Dovid HaMelech specifically began this verse with the words "שיר המעלות — a song of **elevation**," for the KEY to being able to raise yourself up from a low level and ELEVATE yourself, is to tap into the fact that "ממעמקים" — deep inside your soul — you are not happy with your current low situation and "קראתיך ה'!" — you are still yearning to be closer to Hashem!

NOW WE CAN UNCOVER
A DEEPER REVELATION IN OUR PRAYERS:

"ושמע צעקתנו יודע תעלומות."

תפילת אנא בכח

"Hear our screams, the One Who knows hidden things."

At first glance, it seems that the attribute doesn't correctly match the description; for if we are "screaming," then why refer to Hashem as the "One Who knows **HIDDEN** things" — hello — it's not HIDDEN if we are SCREAMING! Wouldn't it be better to describe Hashem as "שומע צעקות — He who **hears our screams**"!?

"אפילו כאשר היהודי נמצא במצב כה שפל וגרוע שאינו יכול אפילו
לצעוק, הקב"ה שהוא 'יודע תעלומות' שומע **למכאוביו הפנימיים**
אשר צעק 'הושיעני אבי!!'"

ספר נתיבי אמת

This is the inner beauty of the prayer: Even when I am so messed up that I cannot even manage to cry out over my low spiritual situation, and it may even seem like I am okay with the way things are, Hashem, Who is a "יודע תעלומות," hears the bitter screams of intense pain emanating from deep within my soul!

FASTEN YOUR SEATBELT
WHILE WE REVEAL AN AMAZING CONCEPT:

"וישמע יהושע את קול העם ברעה ויאמר אל משה: קול מלחמה במחנה.
ויאמר: אין קול ענות גבורה, ואין קול ענות חלושה:
קול ענות אנכי שמע!

שמות פרק לב:יז-יח

When Moshe Rabbeinu descended from Har Sinai, Yehoshua heard shouting coming from the camp: "The voice of WAR is in the camp!" Yehoshua understood that if the camp was in such an uproar, it must have been because the camp was under attack; either they were they were winning and chasing the intruders while shouting victoriously, or they were losing the battle and screaming in pain. However, our wise leader, Moshe Rabbeinu, responded: "I do not hear shouts of victory or screams of weakness. I hear only sounds of **DISTRESS**."

"אמר משה: אדם שהוא עתיד להנהיג שררה על ששים ריבוא
אינו יודע להבחין בין קול לקול?!"

תלמוד ירושלמי מסכת תענית פרק ד' דף ס"ח

There is a fascinating Talmud Yerushalmi: Moshe's words to Yehoshua carry an implied rebuke, as if to say that the future leader of Klal Yisrael should be able to differentiate between the sound of "war" and the sound of "pain"!

"מהי הטענה על שאין לו כשרון זה להבחין
בין קול לקול בקולות הנשמעים מרחוק?!"

ספר מעין בית השואבה עמוד רכ"ד

The obvious question is: What was so terrible about Yehoshua's inability to differentiate between distant screams of victory and screams of anguish? If you were far away from a football stadium and heard 40,000 people shouting at the top of their lungs, would YOU be able to tell the difference between the crowd screaming "Defense!" or "Go! Go! Go!"?

"ויש לומר שבאמת הבחין יהושע שהיה קול של הוללות ושכרות
רק שחשב שהוא קול מלחמה של מרידה כנגד הקב"ה!"

ספר מעין בית השואבה עמוד רכ"ד

The explanation is that both Yehoshua and Moshe heard and understood that the shouting emanated from a drunken crowd that was dancing around a golden calf. However, Yehoshua concluded that this behavior must represent that they were waging

a WAR against Hashem! Therefore he cried out: **"קול מלחמה במחנה**
— The voice of **war** is in the camp!"

"ועל זה ענהו משה רבינו שבאמת הוא קול 'ענות', קול של צער ועינוי
נפש, שעל ידי שחשבו שהם נעזבים וגלמודים במדבר בלי מנהיג
התחילו בשכרות והוללות **אבל אין זה מתוך מרידה אלא מתוך צער!**"

ספר מעין בית השואבה עמוד רכ"ד

However, our holy teacher, Moshe, who knew and understood us
very well, rebuked Yehoshua for this interpretation of our wrongful
acts and taught him a fundamental principle. Moshe looked past
the **external actions** of the rebellious nation and saw the anguish
and inner pain that arose because they felt abandoned in a desert
without a leader! He understood that even though they were
drunk and dancing around an idol, the **source** of their behavior
was NOT a rebellion against Hashem; rather, it was because they
thought that their beloved Moshe — their GPS — had left them
and they felt completely lost!

"וכדרך האנשים שמרוב יאוש וצער
הרי הם עוסקים בשכרות והוללות של הבל!"

ספר מעין בית השואבה עמוד רכ"ד

As we see openly in our day and age, people who suffer inner pain
and turmoil try to escape by drinking, doing drugs, and partying!

"ולזה הי' טוען על יהושע,
שראוי למי שעתיד להיות מנהיג שידע להבחין אם קול של עוברי עבירה
ופורקים עול מלכות שמים בא מתוך שמחה של קלות ראש,
או מתוך צער ויאוש ועינוי נפש, כי אז יש תקוה להשיב בנים לגבולם!"

מעין ספר בית השואבה עמוד רכ"ד

This is what Moshe told Yehoshua: The future leader of Klal
Yisrael MUST be able to know whether those who stray from the
right path and throw off the yoke of heaven are doing so out of
happiness and lightheadedness, or if the reason they are acting

out is really because they are filled with depression, hopelessness, and inner pain — because only with this proper understanding can we hope to bring these lost souls back home!

BREAK- DANCING

There is a famous parable of a man who caught a fish and his young son watched in amazement as the fish wildly flipped and flopped on the ground. The boy thought the fish was dancing, overjoyed to be "saved" from the water! So the boy pumped up the music and started to clap and dance along with him! "Papa, look how well this fish break-dances!" They danced and danced until the fish died. The naive child thought the fish was having fun, but the wise man understands that the fish was actually ... gasping for life.

Authentic Yiddishkeit believes that someone may seem to be "enjoying" himself and "partying" out of control, but that does not mean that he is satisfied with his life! In fact, the partying might very well be a manifestation of tremendous inner pain that is eating him up to the point that he cannot deal with it any other way. He is not "dancing" — he is gasping for life!

Understanding this is our only hope of returning those lost souls to Hashem,

... and that includes our own souls as well!

9

A ROSE AMONGST THORNS

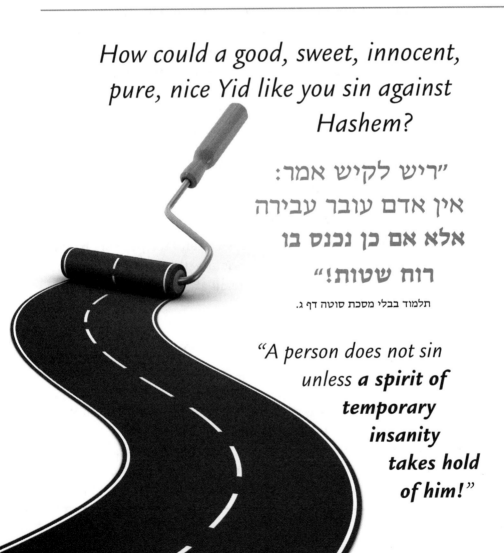

How could a good, sweet, innocent, pure, nice Yid like you sin against Hashem?

"ריש לקיש אמר:
אין אדם עובר עבירה
אלא אם כן נכנס בו
רוח שטות!"

תלמוד בבלי מסכת סוטה דף ג.

"A person does not sin unless **a spirit of temporary insanity takes hold of him!**"

HASHEM

**sees every time we sin against Him,
so let's understand how we look in His eyes:**

"יהודי בעצם הוא דבוק לגמרי בהשם יתברך,
ואף כשחוטא **אין זה בעצם אלא במקרה מחמת 'רוח שטות'**
שנתגבר עליו יצרו ולא הי' יכול לעמוד כנגדו
אבל לעצם שלו לא הגיע הפגם!"

נתיבות שלום חלק ב' עניני פסח דף קע"ד

Every single Jew is בעצם — completely connected to Hashem. Even though you may sin, your sins are not due to a corruption of your pure and holy essence; rather, it is only because you are overwhelmed by circumstances that bring about "temporary insanity," so that you are simply not strong enough to withstand the pressure to sin! For this reason, "sin damage" does not affect the ESSENCE of who you really are and what you really are all about.

"העושה עבירה נחשב לשוטה."

ערבי נחל פרשת כי תצא דרוש ב' ד"ה ופירשתי

Someone who sins is considered "insane."

A שוטה (insane person) does not have the mental ability to properly evaluate his actions and therefore often chooses instant gratification over internal satisfaction and fulfillment. Examples include: eating too much candy ... not going to sleep on time ... playing in the cold without a coat ... and other immature things ....

On the flip side, a healthy person has the mental capacity to put things into perspective and make intelligent, mature decisions. However, even a mature human brain has a major flaw; it can lose clarity and make decisions strongly resembling those of an insane person.

| INSANITY PLEA | *The temporary insanity plea argues that a defendant was briefly insane, but is now sane. A defendant found to have been temporarily insane will often be released without any requirements of psychiatric treatment.*   Source: Wikipedia |

Authentic Yiddishkeit understands that no one in his "right mind" would ever willingly "choose" to go against the will of his Creator by engaging in any form of sin. Therefore, your sinning against Hashem was obviously only caused by outside influences that temporarily seized control of your mind and caused you to act against your true inner will.

BREAKING IT DOWN:

(1) Let's be honest: it is completely insane and suicidal to sin against Hashem Who created you and the entire universe, and Who has complete control over every single thing in the world!

He can make you happy and successful, or He can make you suffer, give you aggravation, physical or mental illness, or simply decide that you have no more reason to be around ... and then: poof! Buh-bye!

"שכל יהודי אילו היה מכיר ומשיג את גדלות הבורא **לא היה חוטא כלל**
שמי שמבין את גדלות הבורא ברוך הוא אינו מסוגל לחטוא!"

ספר נתיבות שלום דברים דף ר"נ (אלול)

No one in his right mind would ever sin against Hashem, Creator of the entire universe! That's a really dumb idea!

> **GUTSY JOEY** *Little Joey was your typical 8-year-old schoolyard bully who thought he was the toughest kid in third grade. But he went a little too far when he picked a fight with the toughest kid in eleventh grade!*

Would you ever go up to a black belt and pick a fight with him? Would you ever attack a soldier holding an automatic weapon? Never! Multiply that by an infinite number and ... well, you get the idea!

"אַרְבָּעָה מֵתוּ בְעֶטְיוֹ שֶׁל נָחָשׁ.
רַשִׁ"י: בַּעֲצָתוֹ שֶׁל נָחָשׁ שֶׁהִשִּׂיא לְחַוָּה
וְלֹא בְחֵטְא אַחֵר, שֶׁלֹּא חָטְאוּ."

תַּלְמוּד בַּבְלִי מַסֶּכֶת שַׁבָּת דַּף נה:

Yet, while we all know that no sane person would ever rebel against Hashem, there were only four people in the history of the world who NEVER committed any sin against Hashem! That means that ALL the other BILLIONS of humans ever created on this planet, without exception, DID sin against Him! So what on earth is going on here?

(2) Aside from the fact that a sinner is going against the wishes of the Almighty Creator and Controller of the universe, there is yet another aspect of complete insanity when a person sins:

> **POWERFUL ATTRACTION** *The new upscale restaurant "Taiyvah" opened with a huge advertising campaign. The entire city was swamped with full-color advertisements of the most incredible-looking restaurant anyone had ever seen.*
>
> *One day Chaim met Moshe "Hey, Moish, where are you going?"*

Moish replied; "I'm going to check out Taiyvah — the ads look so great!"

"Okay — let me know how it is!"

The next day Moish called with his report: "Chaim — it looked so good but I'm soooo sick from it! I'm never going back there!"

Three days later Chaim met Moish: "Hey, Moish, where are you going?"

"I'm going to Taiyvah."

"But why? It made you so sick!"

"That's true, but the ads look SOOOO great — I just NEEEED to go!"

Again Moish went ... and again he got terribly sick!

After seeing Moish go and get sick and go and get sick and always regret going to Taiyvah — Chaim made the only rational decision: He went to check it out for himself — after all — the ads look SOOOO good!

Think about this: How many times would a normal person revisit something that makes him feel so sick about himself? And why would a sane person do something when the people who have already experienced it told him that they completely regret doing it?!

LET'S BRING IT HOME:

If YOU perform a sin, and then afterward YOU really feel terrible, and YOU really deeply regret what you did, and YOU decide to NEVER do it again, and yet YOU keep on repeating this same sin over and over again — is there a greater insanity than that!?

Whenever you sin, your mind loses the ability to control yourself, and your emotions go numb, just like a drunk loses much of his physical and emotional feeling.

Sin causes you to be as lost and confused as a drunk trying to find his way home ... stumbling ... unable to walk straight ... unable to think straight ... unable to see clearly ... making wrong decisions that make it even harder to get home ....

L'CHAYIM

Shmeel Moishe had a really tough week at work. After a beautiful heartfelt Shabbos morning davening he was invited to several kiddushim to celebrate various simchos. At each one his good friend making the simchah asked him to join him for a l'chaim and Shmeel Moishe didn't say NO.

The only thing worse than getting drunk before going home to have a seudah with your family, is when your family is invited to your in-laws! By the time he got to his in-laws, Shmeel Moishe wasn't able to see straight or walk straight — let alone think straight! Losing his balance he accidentally knocked over a very expensive vase that had been in the family for generations.

Does Shmeel Moishe need to feel sorry for what he did? Of course! Does he need to ask forgiveness for the damage he did? Of course he does! Does he have to make sure that he never drinks that much again — sure he does! But would he have done this if he wasn't drunk? No way!

In the very same way, you can find yourself acting like a drunk person who is simply not able to properly control himself! You know what is right and what is wrong, but you don't always have the self-control to stick to your inner pure will to do the right thing.

Since any sin that you do goes AGAINST your TRUE INNER WILL, therefore, logic dictates that you must be judged like a person who sinned AGAINST his will!

How many people say: "I know that this is the worst thing for me and this is not going to bring me any real happiness," and yet they can't stop sinning! How many people destroy not just their spiritual lives, but even their physical lives because of their sins?! Clearly they are unable to control their actions and they have — to some degree — lost their minds!

NOT TO BLAME

People with a disorder called Tourette syndrome display unusual movements or sounds over which they sometimes have little or no control. For instance, they may repeatedly blink their eyes, shrug their shoulders, or jerk their heads. In rare cases, they might even blurt out obscenities or do other things that are beneath their dignity.

These kinds of movements and sounds are called "tics," and for people with the disorder, they can be extremely distressing. With great effort and concentration, people with Tourette syndrome can stop themselves from having these tics or can temporarily hold back the tics. Source: Wikipedia

When reading the above description, one cannot help noticing the similarities between the uncontrollable physical outbursts of someone with Tourette syndrome and every person who struggles with his Evil Inclination!

Even a completely normal, rational, and stable person can undergo the most primitive struggles with controlling his eyes, his thoughts, his speech, and maybe even his actions.

"יהודי אפילו בשעה שהוא פועל און אינו עבד לשני אדונים
ורק שהוא בבחינת 'אנוס' שאינו יודע לשית עצות בנפשו להתגבר על

יצרו וכולו מלא כאב על כך וגם אז ה' **אלקיו עמו הקדוש ברוך הוא**
הוא אדוניו היחיד ואינו עבד לשני אדונים!"

ספר נתיבות שלום עמוד שס"ה

That is why you need to remember: Even when you sin, it does NOT mean that you are no longer loyal to Hashem. All it means is that you are being temporarily overwhelmed by a powerful force that is coercing you to do things that you are really against doing! Even though you may seem interested and even excited to go ahead with the sin, on a deeper level you are in PAIN and disgusted with yourself. Therefore — even while you sin — Hashem is really your only Master.

Authentic Yiddishkeit understands the concept of a mature, normal, functioning adult losing control to the point that he can make incredibly wrong decisions that are inconsistent with his true ideals and life's mission.

NOW WE CAN BEGIN TO UNDERSTAND HUMANS FROM HASHEM'S PERSPECTIVE:

"אמר להם הקב"ה כשם שהתינוקת הזו כשהיא קטנה והיא חוטאה על
אבותיה, אין אבותיה מתרעמין עליה - למה?
שהיא קטנה! כך הם ישראל **כשהם חוטאים אין הקב"ה מעלה עליהם!"**

מדרש רבה במדבר ב:טז

Just as a normal parent does not (should not!) become upset and hurt when an immature child does something wrong, so too, when a Yiddishe child acts out in an immature, small-minded, and foolish manner, Hashem our Father does not hold it against them.

Hashem knows that He created us with flaws and that our mature adult minds can become confused and disoriented to such extent that we can actually lose the ability to make the correct decisions that we truly know are best for us!

SO — DO YOU STILL THINK THAT HASHEM DOES NOT
UNDERSTAND YOU AND THAT JUDAISM EXPECTS
MORE FROM YOU THAN YOU CAN DO?

We didn't think so!

10

CRAZY GLUE

Even while we stray,
Hashem "sticks" with us!

"יהודי מחויב להאמין
כי הקדוש ברוך הוא
בחר בנו מכל עם ושוכן
אתם אפילו בתוך
טומאותם!"

ספר נתיבות שלום חלק ב' עמוד רנ"ד

"A Yid must believe that
Hashem chose us to be
His nation and He
remains with us
even while we
are spiritually
contaminated!"

HASHEM

will always CARRY YOU
even while you sin against His wishes:

"תינוק שיש בידו אבן בשבת
מהו ליטול בשבת?"

מדרש תנחומא פרשת שלח יד:כז הוספה סימן ז'

Jewish law states that a person may not move a stone on Shabbos.
The question arises: If your child is holding a stone, can you pick
up the child, thereby effectively moving the stone?

THE LAW IS DERIVED FROM AN AMAZING CONCEPT:

"מדור המדבר אתה למד:
שהקב"ה נושאם במדבר כביכול ...
כאשר ישא איש את בנו - והיתה עבודה זרה בידם!"

מדרש תנחומא פרשת שלח יד:כז הוספה סימן ז'

We know that Hashem carried Klal Yisrael (so to speak) through
the desert just as a father carries his son — even though they were
still holding idols in their arms! So too, one may carry a child
on Shabbos, even though the child is holding something that is
prohibited.

Now hang on a minute — while Hashem carried us and cared for
us as we traveled through a barren dessert — we were holding
WHAT????? That is absolutely incredible!

LET US THINK ABOUT WHAT WE
JUST EXPERIENCED WITH OUR OWN EYES:

1

"לכל האתות והמופתים אשר שלחו ה'
לעשות בארץ מצרים לפרעה ולכל עבדיו ולכל ארצו
ולכל היד החזקה ולכל המורא הגדול אשר עשה משה לעיני כל ישראל."

דברים פרק לד:יא-יב

We openly saw the יד ה' (hand of G-d) smite our Egyptian rulers with the awesome מכות (plagues) that mocked the Egyptians and proved that Hashem controls every facet of the world.

2

"וילך מאחריהם - להבדיל בין מחנה מצרים ובין מחנה ישראל,
ולקבל חצים ובליסטראות של מצרים."

רש"י שמות פרק יד:יט

We saw Hashem create ענני כבוד (heavenly clouds) to protect us from the Egyptian army chasing in hot pursuit, and we witnessed with our own eyes how these heavenly clouds absorbed the arrows being shot at us by the Egyptian marksman while we crouched defenseless and powerless.

3

"כשהייתי מהלכת במדבר והיה עמוד האש והענן הולכים לפני והורגים
נחשים ועקרבים ושורפין הקוצים והברקנים לעשות הדרך מישור."

רש"י שיר השירים פרק ג'

We saw the עמוד אש (pillar of fire) appear out of nowhere and escort us through the desolate desert like a heavenly navigation system while also clearing the path of dangerous scorpions, snakes, and animals.

SOLID GOLD **165**

4

"דרש ר' נהוראי: היתה בת ישראל עוברת בים ובנה בידה ובוכה
ופושטת ידה ונוטלת תפוח או רמון מתוך הים ונותנת לו"

שמות רבה (וילנא) פרשה כא:י

Then we again witnessed the hand of G-d, as we walked in shock
through an actual sea, while experiencing the stunning miracle of
water standing in an upright position and forming walls reaching
the sky, carrying within them fresh fruit for mothers to give to their
children!

This is just a small sampling of the many amazing miracles Chazal
revealed to us!

BUT IT GETS EVEN BETTER:

"וכן את מוצא כשעברו בים - צלמו של מיכה עבר עמהם!
ובכל כך לא הניחם הקב"ה!"

מדרש תנחומא פרשת שלח יד:כז הוספה סימן ז'

Even while Hashem openly revealed His love and compassion
to us as never before and split the sea for us — we still could
not abandon our worthless idols that did absolutely nothing
to redeem us from slavery and protect us from harm! This goes
against common sense!

But even more remarkable is that although we were still clinging
to our stupidity, Hashem did not present us with an ultimatum
and say:

Ok guyz — here's the deal: If you drop the idol nonsense — then I
will save you, but if not; well ... I sure hope you're good swimmers!

On the contrary, Hashem showed us that He is willing to break
the rules of nature in order to save His precious children through

supernatural means — even while we acted like small-minded ingrates!

A SIDE NOTE TO PARENTS:

Similarly, with rebellious children, if you respond to their rebelliousness by fighting with them or constantly pestering them to become better, you are in danger of possibly alienating them and adding fuel to their rebellion! Many times, the anger and frustration that kids feel after their parents respond to their initial rebelliousness does a lot more damage to the child than anything that they did wrong!

If you walk in the footsteps of Hashem, you learn to respond in the opposite manner. The more the child rebels, the more the child needs to feel your love and affection. You must continue to draw him closer and closer while adding more attributes of mercy and patience onto yourself. And you must do this while carrying the shame and burden of their rebellion completely on your own shoulders!

BUT HANG ON ... IT GETS EVEN BETTER!

"דידוע דהמלאכים הם יותר גבוהים מישראל מחמת קדושתם,
אפס כשהשם יתברך מראה אהבתו לעמו ישראל ואוהב את ישראל,
אז ישראל הם למעלה מכל מלאכי מעלה!"
ספר קדושת לוי שמות פרשת בשלח יד:יט

Angels are intrinsically holier than Klal Yisrael. However, that does not mean that Hashem loves them more than He loves us. In fact, when Hashem shows His great love for us, we see that it is even greater than His love for the angels.

"והנה בעת קריעת ים סוף הראה הקב"ה אהבתו לישראל
והיו ישראל למעלה מכולן (מהמלאכים)!!!"

ספר קדושת לוי שמות פרשת בשלח יד:יט

Specifically at קריעת ים סוף Hashem showed that He loves us even more than He does His heavenly angels!

So let's put it all together:

During קריעת ים סוף we were carrying idols in our hands, and yet of all times, it was at this very moment Hashem showed that He loves us even more than He loves perfect heavenly angels! WOW!!!

Now ask yourself: Am I more spiteful and rebellious than someone clinging to his idols even while Hashem is openly revealing Himself and miraculously saving him from certain death?

"רבון העולמים:
גלוי וידוע לפניך שרצוננו לעשות רצונו, ומי מעכב?
שאור שבעיסה [יצר הרע] ושעבוד מלכיות."

תלמוד בבלי מסכת ברכות דף יז.

OF COURSE NOT! When we sin, it is only because we are too weak to overpower our animalistic desires after 2000 years in the cold darkness of גלות (exile)!

Authentic Yiddishkeit believes: If while we clung to worthless idols Hashem still loved us even more than He loved perfect heavenly angels (who never sin or mess up), then He certainly loves each and every one of us — regardless of what sins we are currently doing!!! For our ACTIONS never affect our true RELATIONSHIP with Hashem!

This incredible revelation should cause your heart to overflow with joy, tears of happiness should flow from your eyes, and you should dance in the streets! Now you have proof that Hashem really does love you!

SO HOW SHOULD YOU FEEL
AFTER YOU FALL AND SUCCUMB TO TEMPTATION?

"שגם לאחר החטא
לא ירגיש יהודי שהנ"י 'מנותק מהשם יתברך'!"
נתיבות שלום תולדות דף קפ"א

After you sin you should never feel that you are cut off and unwanted by Hashem.

So what exactly happens when you sin and go against the will of Hashem time after time, over and over again — does He get sick of you and move away from you?

I THINK BY NOW YOU KNOW THAT THE ANSWER IS:
NO!

But if you have some time, let's use an example to help us internalize this concept:

SHUA AND YANKEL *Shua was walking with his friend Yankel on 13th Avenue and they got into a terrible argument. Shua became so enraged that he stormed away and walked to 12th Avenue. After Shua's anger subsided, he wanted to patch things up.*

HERE ARE THREE POSSIBLE SCENARIOS:

1. As Shua walked away, Yankel, also infuriated, turned and walked away from Shua. Yankel is now on 14th Avenue. So to make up with Yankel, Shua must travel two avenues to find him.

2. Although Shua stormed away, Yankel remained where Shua left him and waited for him to return. So all Shua has to do to reconnect with Yankel is simply walk back to where he turned away from him.

3. As Shua stormed away, Yankel exercised extreme patience and followed behind him. He stood behind Shua, anxiously waiting for him to turn around so they could patch things up right then and there — without Shua having to journey back to find Yankel!

One of the biggest misconceptions about our relationship with Hashem is the idea that when you sin, rebel, or otherwise disengage from feeling close to Him, Hashem also purposely moves away from you, as described in scenario #1.

However, we hope by now you realize that Hashem, Creator of the universe, does not walk away from you just because you faced a נסיון (challenge) that you did not overcome.

This may bring you to think that the correct answer is scenario #2. Now you envision Hashem waiting right where you left Him.

This is a more mature understanding of your Creator. He's not vengeful — yet He's firm and steadfast, and if you distance yourself from Him, it is now "up to you" to work your way back to where you left Him and He will then graciously accept you with open arms. Beautiful!

HOWEVER, THIS DOES NOT PROPERLY DEMONSTRATE THE DEEP FEELINGS OF OUR LOVING FATHER.

The real truth is that with each step you take to move away from Hashem, He takes one as well — but in the same direction as you! He follows right behind you, just as in scenario #3, patiently waiting for you to "turn around" and embrace Him.

"יהודי שאינו מסוגל להתחזק ולעמוד בתפלה
אפילו אחרי שעבר את העבירה החמורה ביותר
לא דרכו רגליו על מפתן היהדות!"
ר' משה מקוברין זי"ע מובא בנתיבות שלום חלק א' דף ל"ג

Even after transgressing an extremely immoral sin, if you feel that Hashem does not want to hear your prayers and you've lost your connection to Him, then you do not comprehend what your relationship with Hashem is all about (and you should go back to page 1!).

> "... מחויב להאמין כי אף לאחר שעבר העבירה החמורה ביותר שבתורה
> הקדוש ברוך הוא מקבל אנחתו וצריך להיות מסוגל
> לשפוך לבבו לפניו אז גם 'נוכח פני ה'!'"

נתיבות שלום חלק ב' דף קנ"ו

You must believe that even if you did the WORST SIN POSSIBLE, Hashem is ready and willing to accept you back into His embrace! Therefore, even when you find yourself in such a low situation, you should be ready and willing to pour your heart out to Him!

> "יהודי שאינו מאמין שהקדוש ברוך הוא
> נמצא ושוכן עם ישראל בכל המצבים
> **ואף בתוך טומאותם - הרי הוא גם כן אפיקורס!**"

הרב הקדוש בעל בת עין זי"ע מובא בספר נתיבות שלום חלק א' דף נ'

You can never end up in a situation where you blew it and now there is no way to return and once again become close to Hashem. Never!

Therefore, **Authentic Yiddishkeit** understands the unbreakable, unconditional love Hashem has for each and every Yid to be precisely as we described in scenario #3: Hashem has been following behind you step by step, even as you descended into the depths of sin, and He is standing behind you RIGHT NOW, anxiously waiting for you to just turn around and feel close to Him again!

> "מעולם היה קשה לו פירוש הפסוק:
> 'תעיתי כשה אבד' (תהלים פרק קי"ט)
> דהיה צריך לכתוב כשה 'נאבד'?"

ספר גן הדסים כ"ו בשם הרב הקדוש ר' יחזקאל משינאווא זי"ע

Dovid HaMelech says in *Tehillim*, "I have strayed like a lost sheep." The word "אבד" means that the sheep lost its way and doesn't know where its owner is. He should have really used the word "נאבד," meaning, "I have strayed like a sheep that is actually lost from its owner."

NEVER LOST

A young sheep wandered off from the flock. After a while, the sheep realized that it couldn't find its way back and it felt lost and alone.

The shepherd, watching from the top of the mountain, saw exactly where the young sheep was. He protected it from the wolves with his long-range rifle and eventually helped it return to the flock.

This sheep was not actually LOST because the shepherd knew where it was and was protecting it, but the sheep FELT LOST since it could not see the shepherd.

"וזהו כוונת הכתוב: תעיתי ממך כביכול כשה אובד אשר אבד את הרועה,
כך אנו שוכחים השם יתברך, אבל אין אנו אבודים חס ושלום
מאתו יתברך כי הוא משגיח עלינו תמיד!"

ספר גן הדסים כ"ו בשם הרב הקדוש ר' יחזקאל משינאווא זי"ע

Now we can fully appreciate the message: Dovid HaMelech said, "I feel that I've lost my way and I cannot feel You in my life." This is how we feel when we forget Hashem — but we are never truly LOST from Hashem, since He always keeps a watchful eye on us!

So just turn around …
and smile …

He's right there, waiting!

GPS!
NAVIGATION FOR
YOUR SOUL

11

WHO IS YOUR BIGGEST FAN?

Hashem's faith in YOU is not based on your track record!

"אלה אלקיך ישראל: לא היה
צריך לכלותן? אלא אפילו באותה
שעה **לא זז מחיבתן!** לוה להן ענני
כבוד ולא פסקו מהן המן והבאר!"

מדרש במדבר רבה כ:יט

THE MEDRASH RABBAH:

"When we proclaimed the Golden Calf as our god, shouldn't we have been annihilated? Yet, even then, Hashem did not stop LOVING us and CARING for us! He continued to shelter us with heavenly clouds, He fed us heavenly food, and He gave us fresh water from a rock."

HASHEM

is the ultimate INVESTOR
Who keeps INVESTING in YOU every day!

"בטח בה' - ועשה טוב."

תהלים ל"ז

Dovid HaMelech says:
"Trust in Hashem and do good."

When analyzing the *pasuk*, it seems that the statement is out of order. Shouldn't it say: (1) "Do good," and then say: (2) "Trust in Hashem"? For only after a person does at least "some" good does he deserve Hashem's protection and mercy! Only after depositing funds into your bank account can you start writing checks!

"הי-ה מקום לומר:

שאם אין לאדם חלק הטוב במה יבטח?"

נתיבות שלום פורים דף ח'

However, if there is NOTHING GOOD about me, then what right do I have to think that Hashem will take care of me and protect me?

"כלומר: אף על פי שאין בידך מעשים ותדע בעצמך שאתה 'רשע'

עם כל זה בטח בה' כי הוא בעל רחמים וירחם עליך!

כמו שנאמר 'ורחמיו על כל מעשיו' רצה לומר צדיקים ורשעים!"

רמב"ן בספר האמונה פרק א'

The order of the *pasuk* teaches us that even BEFORE you do ANY *mitzvos*, and you know in your heart that you are a "**רשע**," you can still trust that the all-merciful G-d will surely have mercy on you. As it says, "He has mercy on ALL His creations." ALL means **ALL**! The righteous good ones and, yes — the wicked evil ones as well!

Authentic Yiddishkeit clearly believes that no matter how low you sink, Hashem will **always be on your side!** Believe it or not, there is actually **nothing** you can possibly do to make Hashem **stop** rooting for you — and therefore you can **always** put your full trust in Him. He's on your side! Why should He help you? Because He *wants* to!

You see, originally we were going to charge $100.00 for this book — but we knew that you wouldn't think it's worth so much. But now that you see how much it's really worth — please mail us the balance immediately!

WITH THIS UNDERSTANDING, WE CAN UNCOVER A DIAMOND:

"אהבת עולם בית ישראל עמך אהבת!"

תפילת מעריב

In our evening prayers we say: "**אהבת עולם** — with an everlasting love, **בית ישראל עמך** — the house of Yisrael Your nation, **אהבת** — You loved."

The simple translation of "**אהבת עולם**" is, "*with an everlasting love*"; however, an alternative translation is, "*loving the world.*" Using this translation the phrase now means:

"אפילו כאשר 'בית ישראל'

שקועים 'באהבת עולם' ובתאוות עולם הזה,

אפילו אז 'עמך אהבת' 'הנך אוהבם מפני שהם עמך!'"

מובא בספר נתיבות שלום חלק ב' עמוד רמ"ג בשם ר' אהרן הגדול מקארלין זי"ע

Even when "בית ישראל — the Jewish people" are engrossed in "אהבת עולם — the pursuit of worldly desires, "עמך אהבת — they are still Hashem's beloved chosen nation!"

Although this sounds SO GOOD, with our limited human understanding, we may often find ourselves questioning this concept. After all, how patient can Hashem be? I mess up time after time! Isn't He sick of me already? Doesn't He just wish that I would stop trying to get close to Him only to once again be a major disappointment? How many times can He agree to work with me — especially since I always make deals and promises and yet I continuously don't keep my end of the deal!

THE ANSWER IS VERY CLEAR:

"ויתן לך האלקים

מטל השמים ומשמני הארץ ורב דגן ותירש."

בראשית פרק כז:כח

The Torah tells us: ויתן לך האלקים — and G-d shall give you מטל השמים — from the dew of the Heavens, ומשמני הארץ — and from the fat of the land, ורב דגן ותירש — and much grain and wine.

"רבי אחא אמר: ויתן לך האלקים

ויתן לך אלקותא! אימתי? לכשתצטרך לה!"

בראשית רבה פרשה סו:ג

ויתן לך — What will Hashem give you? He will give you: אלקים — the ability to connect to His Divine Holiness — for that is the greatest gift of all! When will Hashem give this to you? WHEN YOU NEED IT! When will you need it? AFTER YOU LOSE IT!

Furthermore, it really should say, "יתן לך האלקים — Hashem will give you." Why does it say, "ויתן לך האלקים — **AND** Hashem will give you"?

"ויתן לך: יתן ויחזור ויתן לך!"

בראשית רבה פרשה סו:ג

The "**AND**" teaches that no matter how often you may "lose" the incredible gift of being close to Hashem, Hashem will "continuously" give it back to you, over and over again!

SO WE LEARN TWO IMPORTANT LESSONS:

(1) Hashem is offering you the gift of: אלקותא — the opportunity to connect to His Holiness, and:

(2) He is ready to give you this gift OVER AND OVER!

UNLIMITED FUNDING

As each of his children turned 20, a very wealthy man said, "My dear child, it is time for you to go out and learn to make money yourself. Your future success is up to you; however, I will give you the chance to make it big. I deposited ONE MILLION DOLLARS into your account. What you make of yourself depends on what you accomplish with this gift. Good luck."

Each child knew that he had a tremendous opportunity to become successful — but he also knew that this amazing opportunity would never come again! If he would lose this money – he'd be broke for the rest of his life! The pressure was almost too much to bear!

However, imagine if the father would say: "My dear child, DO NOT WORRY! If you lose this money, I will not sit idly by and watch you become homeless! I am prepared to give you another million! And another! As many times as you need it! Even if you lose this money, you will always have another chance to try again!" Then the son would not just have the million dollars to invest, but he would also feel confident knowing that he has the support of his father's entire empire behind him!

Hashem understood that you may lose the Divine inspiration and closeness He so graciously bestowed upon you, and that you will then think that you have lost the opportunity to connect to Him. That is why He told you up front: DO NOT WORRY! I AM PREPARED TO GIVE IT TO YOU AGAIN! AND AGAIN! AND AGAIN! AND AGAIN! AND AGAIN! AND AGAIN! AND AGAIN! AND AGAIN! AND AGAIN! AND AGAIN! AND AGAIN! AND AGAIN!

This clearly shows us how Hashem views us when we sin. Why should we be more negative than the One Who created us?

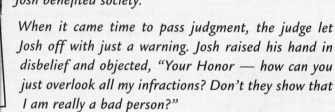

GULITY CONSCIENCE

Josh was arrested for speeding. The presiding judge looked at Josh's driving record, consisting of several other infractions. However, the judge also looked at the ways Josh benefited society.

When it came time to pass judgment, the judge let Josh off with just a warning. Josh raised his hand in disbelief and objected, "Your Honor — how can you just overlook all my infractions? Don't they show that I am really a bad person?"

Hashem clearly says that He isn't interested in focusing on your bad actions and He does not define you by them. So why should you?

We must know and believe that we are NEVER unwanted by Hashem — regardless of the sins we may have done:

"וזהו סוד האמונה של איש יהודי: **כי תמיד יש לו דרך אל הקב"ה!**"

מובא בנתיבות שלום חלק א' פרקי מבוא דף ל"ג

Authentic Yiddishkeit believes that no matter what you did in the past, and no matter what situation you are currently in, Hashem is always waiting for you with open arms and there is always a path leading you right back to Hashem. ALWAYS!

ABSURD BAILOUT

*September 2008: The U.S. government seized control of AIG (American International Group), in a deal that revealed its concerns of the danger a collapse could pose to the financial system. The federal government had been strongly resisting AIG's requests for an emergency loan or other intervention to prevent the insurer from bankruptcy. Not long before, the government had allowed Lehman Brothers to go under. This time, the government decided **AIG truly was too big to fail.***

(Source: Wall Street Journal)

September 2009: AIG burned through the first $85 billion lifeline and continued to hemorrhage cash. The government helped three more times.

(Source: Associated Press)

Hashem specifically told us: I KNOW you WILL sin and I want you to know that: "יתן ויחזור ויתן" — I am prepared to keep on investing in you and to continuously repair our connection over and over again ....

WHY?

Because in Hashem's opinion:

YOU ARE TRULY TOO BIG TO FAIL!!

12

THE BLACK BOX

Revealing your indestructible essence

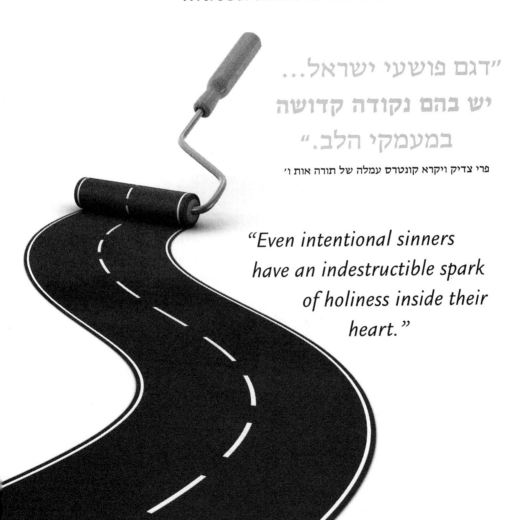

"דגם פושעי ישראל...
יש בהם נקודה קדושה
במעמקי הלב."

פרי צדיק ויקרא קונטרס עמלה של תורה אות ו'

"Even intentional sinners
have an indestructible spark
of holiness inside their
heart."

HASHEM

decided that it was time to redeem us from Egypt and He taught us a timeless lesson:

"ומשה היה רעה את צאן יתרו ...
וירא והנה הסנה בער באש והסנה איננו אכל."

שמות פרק ג'

One day, Moshe was tending his sheep when suddenly he saw a bush completely engulfed in flames — yet it was not being consumed by the fire. Moshe intently watched this burning bush in amazement when suddenly a heavenly voice spoke to him. Hashem told Moshe that the time for גאולה (redemption) has arrived and that Moshe would be His שליח (messenger) to redeem the Jewish people.

We must understand: Why did Hashem specifically choose a "bush not being consumed by fire" in order to get Moshe's attention? Hashem could have done many other things, such as ... a mountain floating in the air ... a tree flipping slowly upside down ... or some other spectacular phenomenon.

THERE MUST BE A DEEPER MESSAGE LYING BENEATH THE SURFACE:

"והיינו שמשה רבינו ראה את הסנה בוער באש:
שכוחות הטומאה הולכים ומכלים את כלל ישראל!"

נתיבות שלום ענייני פסח דף רנ"ח

The burning bush was a representation of the situation the Yidden were in at that time. The bush was a symbol of Klal Yisrael and the fire represented the heated passion of spiritual contamination engulfing the Jewish people.

"ויאמר משה: אסרה נא ואראה את המראה הגדל הזה מדוע לא יבער הסנה:
פירוש: אם הם שרויים בכזו טומאה, ומשוקעים במ"ט שערי טומאה
איך זה יתכן שעוד לא נשרפו לגמרי מגודל הטומאה?!"
נתיבות שלום עניני פסח דף רנ"ח

Moshe wondered in amazement: "If Klal Yisrael is completely immersed in the flames of spiritual contamination, how is it possible that their inner connection to Hashem is not completely destroyed?"

Therefore, in order to prepare and train Moshe for the task of taking the Yidden out of גלות (exile), Hashem had to first make something crystal clear:

"והסנה איננו אוכל - שאינם נשרפים לגמרי!"
נתיבות שלום עניני פסח דף רנ"ח

Just as this bush was fully engulfed in flames and yet Moshe saw that its **essence** could not be destroyed, so too כלל ישראל can **never** be spiritually extinguished — even while being engrossed in spiritual contamination!

HOWEVER, THE TORAH CONTINUES:

"ויען משה ויאמר: והן לא יאמינו לי ולא ישמעו בקלי
כי יאמרו לא נראה אליך ה'!"
נתיבות שלום עניני פסח דף רנ"ח

Moshe internalized Hashem's message regarding the eternal core of Klal Yisrael. But then he faced a problem: since only he saw the burning bush, how would he be able to transmit this new concept to the general assembly of Klal Yisrael, who had already given up on themselves?

A WILD IMAGINATION

Imagine for a moment how this would play out in our day and age: A great sage gathers all the Yidden together for an assembly. He takes the mic and begins, "Testing 1, 2, 3 ... ahem ... dear friends ... an amazing thing happened to me today ... while I was out driving all alone on the highway ... my car overheated so I pulled over ... and suddenly I noticed that there was a bush ... and it was on fire ... (eyes start to roll ...) and ... and ... incredibly the fire did not consume the leaves ... (skeptical looks from the audience ...) and then — well — a voice came out from the bush — yeah — the one on fire (people begin to look uncomfortable ...) and it was G-d — and He was talking to me! (Oh boy ... maybe HE'S the one who overheated ...) and G-d told me that I am now your supreme leader (oy vey! What's he drinking?) and I will take you to Yerushalayim ... (yeah right — as if Hashem still wants us!).

For this purpose Hashem showed Moshe a heavenly sign that would effectively prove to all Yidden that in spite of their shattered self-worth ingrained in them by their many sinful actions, they could once again become attached to Hashem.

"ויאמר אליו ה' מה זה בידך? ויאמר מטה.
ויאמר: השליכהו ארצה, וישליכהו ארצה,
ויהי לנחש - וינס משה מפניו!"

נתיבות שלום עניני פסח דף רע"ח

Hashem began by asking Moshe: *"What is in your hand?"* Moshe replied, "מטה, a stick." Hashem then instructed Moshe, *"Throw it down to the ground"* — and behold, it turned into a snake. The Torah then says that Moshe became frightened and ran away from the snake.

THERE ARE SEVERAL OBVIOUS QUESTIONS:

1. Didn't the Creator of the universe know what was in Moshe's hand? What was the purpose of the question: "What's in your hand?" and the obvious answer given by Moshe: "It's a stick"?

2. On the surface this whole exchange seems a bit silly. Hashem asks: *"What's in your hand?"* Moshe answered: *"It's a stick,"* and Hashem replies: *"A stick? Oh, great! We can use the old stick-turns-into-a-snake trick! An oldie but a goody!"* Obviously, this requires a deeper understanding.

3. How could it be possible that Moshe Rabbeinu was afraid of a snake, while talking directly to the Master of the Universe?

TRUE TRANQUILITY *One Motza'ei Shabbos, soldiers burst into the Alter of Novardok's home and began threatening the people there. The Alter was reciting Havdalah, and despite the tumult, not even one drop of wine spilled from his brimming cup, so calm and unruffled was he.*
Source: Aleinu l'Shabei'ach Shemos, p. 236

We all "say" the words: "I will trust in Hashem and not be afraid," but the Alter really **meant it and felt it** in every fiber of his being!

How much more so Moshe — on his level — could not possibly have been afraid of a snake while speaking directly to Hashem!

These three questions make us realize that there must be something much DEEPER going on over here!

LISTEN UP AND YOU WILL BE AMAZED!

A stick has two distinct, diametrically opposed purposes; each purpose is represented by its own Hebrew name:

"'מקל' הוא מעולם החורבן כעניין מקל חובלים,
ואילו 'מטה' הוא מעולם הבניין שעליו נשענים!"

נתיבות שלום עניני פסח דף רנ"ח

A stick is called a מקל when it is used to hit someone. This usage comes from the עולם החורבן (world of **de**struction), because it hurts people.

However, a stick can also be described as a מטה, which is a walking stick used to support someone. This usage comes from the הבניין עולם (world of **con**struction), since it helps people.

NOW WE CAN GO BACK AND RE-EXAMINE THE DIALOGUE BETWEEN HASHEM AND MOSHE AND REVEAL AMAZING MESSAGES:

"וזה ששאלו הקב"ה 'מה בידו?'
'מטה' מעולם הבניין או 'מקל' מעולם החורבן?'"

נתיבות שלום עניני פסח דף רנ"ח

Certainly Hashem knew that Moshe was holding a "stick" — but Hashem wanted Moshe to think about what KIND of stick he was holding: Was it the **con**structive kind used to <u>support</u> someone, or the **de**structive kind used to <u>hurt</u> someone?

"ויאמר: 'מטה' היינו מעולם הבניין!"

נתיבות שלום עניני פסח דף רנ"ח

Moshe replied: "מטה, *it is my walking stick, which is used for support.*"

"ויאמר 'השליכהו ארצה' היינו: שישליך אותו בתוך הארציות,
'ויהי לנחש' מקור הסטרא אחרא - שהנחש שורשו מעולם החורבן
שאינו מביא שום תועלת ואינו כי אם מזיק!"

נתיבות שלום עניני פסח דף רנ"ח

Hashem then commanded Moshe to throw it to the ground and it turned into a snake, whose existence comes from the

"עולם החורבן," since it is destructive with no inherent beneficial use; you can't plow your field with it and it sure makes for a lousy pet!

> "והיינו שה' הראה לו שאפילו 'מטה' ששייך כולו לעולם הבנין,
> הרי כאשר נופל בארציות נהפך הוא לנחש מקור עולם החורבן!"

נתיבות שלום עניני פסח דף רנ"ח

The point was that Hashem clearly demonstrated that even a "מטה," which is from the עולם הבנין (the constructive and helpful world) — when thrown to the ground — will turn into a dangerous snake, seething with evil, from the עולם החורבן (world of destruction)!

The underlying message is to show that the transformation of כלל ישראל from lofty levels of holiness to the lowest levels of spiritual contamination was only as a direct result of being "thrown down" into "ערות הארץ," the most spiritually depraved atmosphere in the entire world — Egypt!

NOW WE CAN UNDERSTAND
WHY MOSHE BECAME SO FRIGHTENED:

It was extremely frightening for Moshe Rabbeinu to witness how something from the **constructive** world of "בנין" could transform right before his very eyes — to such an extreme — that it now represented "חורבן," the **destructive** root of all evil!

FALLING FROM GRACE

In today's day and age it is unfortunately quite common to see Yiddishe kinderlach fall into the materialistic immoral world.

It truly frightens us to witness with our own eyes how something created from a pure and holy source, such a cute boy, who once said the "alef-beis" and "Shema Yisrael" with such zest and joy, can turn into a seething angry creature full of venom and hatred!

Indeed, watching the horrific transformation of someone whose true essential existence comes from the pure source of goodness, to the extent that he now conducts himself in the opposite manner, really is frightening to all who witness it!

THEN LOOK WHAT HAPPENED:

"ויאמר ה' אל משה: שלח ידך ואחז בזנבו
וישלח ידו ויחזק בו ויהי למטה בכפו!"

נתיבות שלום עניני פסח דף רנ"ח

Hashem told Moshe: *"Stretch out your hand and grasp its tail."* Moshe stretched out his hand and grasped it **tightly**, and it suddenly transformed back to a staff in his palm.

Now, when we normally think about this miracle, it seems that the impressive sign was completed when the stick transformed into a snake. That was the "WOW" factor! A stick turned into a snake! That would show the Jews that Moshe really did speak with Hashem. Then after completing this amazing miracle, Hashem told Moshe to change the snake back into a stick seemingly just so that he would have his walking stick back.

BUT OF COURSE THERE IS A MUCH DEEPER LESSON TO BE LEARNED:

One might think that the transformation of something from the world of **building** to the world of **destruction**, from the root of **goodness** to the root of **evil**, from the highest connection to holiness and purity to actively pursuing perverse pleasures is a **permanent internal change** that can never be reversed. Therefore:

"ושוב אמר לו הקב"ה: 'שלח ידך ואחז בזנבו'
ויהי 'למטה' בכפו — שחזר להיות מעולם הבנין!"

נתיבות שלום עניני פסח דף רנ"ח

Hashem commanded Moshe to reach out and grab the evil snake by its tail. Moshe grabbed it (notice, he wasn't frightened anymore

— proving that he was never afraid of the snake physically hurting him!), and amazingly, it turned back into a walking stick in his hand!

With this heavenly sign, Hashem illustrated that merely with the power of Moshe's holy embrace, he was able to return the object to once again become a positive force in the עולם הבניין — world of construction!

"המשמעות בזה: שדבר שביסודו הוא 'טוב' בבחינת 'עצם'
ונפילתו אינו אלא בבחינת 'מקרה'
יכול לשוב לשורשו ומקורו ולהפוך בחזרה לטוב!"
נתיבת שלום עניני פסח דף רנ"ח

The lesson is clear: When you are dealing with something that is **essentially good,** even if it is THROWN WAY DOWN and *appears* to be thoroughly corrupted, it can revert back to its internal essence of pure goodness.

THAT IS WHAT WE YIDDEN ARE ALL ABOUT.

Authentic Yiddishkeit believes that since essentially we come directly from the source of goodness, even if we find ourselves completely transformed into a state of impurity and spiritual corruption, we can always return, re'JEW'venate, and reconnect to our pure source of holiness!

BUT, HEY — WHY DID HASHEM TELL MOSHE TO GRAB THE SNAKE BY THE TAIL? WHY NOT JUST GRAB IT STRAIGHT ON?

The *Yayin Saraf* sharply explains, as only his brilliant mind can: When trying to transform someone who is snaking through earthly swamps, you must show that you understand who he is and prove that you love and accept him in spite of your full knowledge of his "tail" activities.

This is why the Torah wrote: "ויהי למטה בכפו — and it returned to being a *Mateh* **in his grasp.**" Do you know what causes the transformation from evil back to the world of goodness? The incredible power of your embrace — because you "hold" of him — ווייל דו האלטס פון אים!

8-STEP PROGRAM

Your unconditional love and embrace — the fact that you show him that you "hold" of who he is and what he can become — is what will give him the inspiration and willpower to return to the world of good and will ultimately save him!

WE ALSO CAN LEARN ANOTHER INSIGHT:

When Moshe witnessed his good, helpful walking stick transform into an evil, seething, slithering snake, he became frightened — just as many people become so frightened when they witness pure Yiddishe kids fall away from the right path. But Hashem said — No! Don't be frightened! You can't run away from the kids-at-risk issue; in fact you MUST do the exact opposite! Go back to that scary situation — find the child — and **embrace him**! You don't need to know what to say! No mussar schmooze is necessary! No great words of wisdom to impart! The power of your embrace is ALL that he needs!

That is exactly what Hashem did. When He saw Klal Yisrael worshiping idols, He lovingly declared: "I love you" and embraced them! Only by utilizing this method can we hope to return this "snake" to his level of glory — which is where he truly belonged all along!

Authentic Yiddishkeit believes that no matter how "bad" someone is "acting," you can always tap into his pure essence that has **not been affected** and return him to his place in the "world of building."

This applies to ANYONE —

EVEN YOU!

13

LIFETIME MEMBERSHIP

---

*You can never lose your membership
in Hashem's exclusive club!*

"וֹאֲפִילוּ מוּמָר
לְכָל הַתּוֹרָה כּוּלָהּ
בִּכְלַל שְׁמִירַת בְּרִית הוּא!"

רבי עקיבא איגר מסכת עבודה זרה דף כז.

REB AKIVA EIGER:

*"Even if one ignores the
entire Torah ... he is
still considered
as a part of
the Yiddishe
covenant."*

HASHEM

**made a pact with Avraham Avinu and his
descendants ... and it's not dependent on any
of our actions!**

"קונם שאני נהנה לערלים:
מותר בערלי ישראל ואסור במולי עובדי כוכבים. שאני נהנה למולים:
אסור בערלי ישראל ומותר במולי עובדי כוכבים!"
תלמוד בבלי מסכת נדרים דף לא:

The Mishnah says: "If someone promises not to derive benefit
from an "**uncircumcised**" person, the law is: He MAY benefit from
an uncircumcised Jew and he MAY NOT benefit from any gentile
— even one who is circumcised. And if someone promises not to
derive benefit from a "**circumcised**" person, then the law is: He MAY
NOT benefit from any Jew — even one who is uncircumcised, yet
he MAY benefit from any gentile — even one who is circumcised."

The simple logic behind the ruling is: Since most Jews are
circumcised and most gentiles are not, the term "uncircumcised"
generally refers to non-Jews and the term "circumcised" generally
refers to Jews. We therefore conclude that although there may be
an uncircumcised Yid or a circumcised gentile, that exception was
not what this person had in mind when he made his declaration,
since he intended to refer not to an individual but to a general
group that is or isn't circumcised.

HOWEVER, ON A DEEPER LEVEL
THE MISHNAH HAS ANOTHER UNDERSTANDING:

"הערלה אינו בעצם הלב
רק על ידי היצר הרע היושב על שני מפתחי הלב!"

פרי צדיק ויקרא קונטרס עמלה של תורה אות ו'

When a person cuts off contact from "all circumcised" people, the reason that it includes ALL Jews — even those that are NOT circumcised — is because even a non-circumcised Yid is still included in the category of "circumcised," since that is his ESSENCE!

So too, even when you feel that your heart is covered over and blocked from sensing holiness and spirituality, you must know that it is only due to the Evil Inclination preventing you from feeling connected to Hashem! But nothing is wrong with your essence!

LIGHTS OUT

2:00 a.m.: The Greenbergs just got home from a family wedding, when suddenly ... pooof! All the lights went out! The parents scrambled to find candles and somehow managed to get all nine kids into pajamas and tucked into bed. Mr. Greenberg was worried that perhaps the entire house would require rewiring ... walls would have to be ripped out ... the family would need to move out and rent a temporary house for a few months ... who knows what expense and difficulty this would bring!

The next day, the electrician came and Mr. Greenberg was relieved to find that the electrical wiring was completely intact and fully operational; the problem was just that the main cable from the street had become disconnected. Once the "outside" connection was repaired, the **"internal"** wiring worked perfectly.

Authentic Yiddishkeit believes that only your outer "circuit breaker" can stop functioning properly. However, your internal spiritual wiring is always functional and ready to carry spiritual currents throughout your holy essence.

"ואפילו הגדיל עבירות וכבר נכנס היצר ממפתחי הלב לפנימיותו ונעשה
בעל הבית מכל מקום שורש היהדות ישנו במעמקי הלב רק שמעוטף
בהרבה לבושי שק וה׳ אשר יראה ללבב רואה גם אז בו
אותה הנקודה הנותנת ריח טוב!"

פרי צדיק ויקרא קונטרס עמלה של תורה אות ו׳

Therefore, even if you've already performed so many sins that your Evil Inclination moved in, got comfy, and even took control of your mind and heart — even in this miserable situation, your "pintele Yid," rooted deep inside of you, is completely intact! It's merely covered with many disgusting thick layers of *shmutz!*

Hashem, Who sees past your **external** flaws and mistakes, sees the indestructible goodness deep inside you, that always radiates holiness and G-dliness!

"כל יהודי הוא כמו יהלום!
וגם אם הוא בשפל המצב ומשוקע בבוץ **אין להתייאש ממנו**
רק להרים אותו ולנקותו כי אז יוחזר אליו אורו הנוצץ כבראשונה!"

ספר נתיבות שלום חלק א׳ עמוד כ׳ מאת מרן הסבא קדישא מלכוביץ׳ זי"ע

Every Jew is like a diamond. Even if it is lying in filth, you just need to lift it up and clean off the dirt to reveal its original shine.

Let's analyze this analogy: Most things are affected when they come into contact with exterior elements, as the dirt becomes ingrained into the essence of the objects, thereby causing them to lose their original shine and become essentially changed forever.

However, a diamond simply does not absorb any outside elements, and therefore its interior essence can never be penetrated and internally affected.

Therefore, the focus of those who work with diamonds is not to improve the actual diamond itself, since there is nothing lacking in the actual stone. Their focus is only to remove the exterior layers of *shmutz* that were merely blocking the diamond's glorious shine that was there all along.

"כך גוף ישראל אשר היה בו קדושה רמה נשמה עליונה
ואז לא היו יכולים הנמצאים השפלים ורוח הטומאה להדבק בו!"

ערבי נחל במדבר חקת - דרוש א'

So too, our heavenly נשמה (soul), an actual piece of G-dliness, cannot absorb any outside dirt; **therefore its essence can never be penetrated and affected.**

"וגם בוגדיו ופושעי ישראל יש בהם ריח גן עדן!"

פרי צדיק ויקרא קונטרס עמלה של תורה אות ו'

Even rebels and intentional sinners have the sweet pure scent of Gan Eden emanating from within them!

Authentic Yiddishkeit understands that when dealing with a Yid who has fallen from grace, the focus is not to **improve** the actual נשמה, because nothing is **essentially** wrong with the נשמה — it is still radiating purity and sweetness! Rather, our focus is to remove the **exterior** layers of *shmutz* that are merely **blocking** its glorious shine!

Although this concept seems simple and crystal clear, we may still find that when we sin, we still cannot stop "feeling" distant from Hashem.

This feeling can be motivational, as it may spur you to repent and work your way back to Hashem. However, you may find that the Yetzer Hora takes advantage of your situation and hijacks your mind. It will try to convince you that although Hashem stuck with Klal Yisrael until now, this time YOU went too far and it's all over. It will push you to feel more distant and detached from Hashem, until you become convinced that it is simply not **possible** for Hashem to still want you to be near Him. And even if you would accept that maybe Hashem would accept you back if you completely change your ways and work your way back to Him, you still believe that Hashem certainly does not want to hear from you from the low situation you are in right now! Right? WRONG!

SO THE QUESTION IS:

WHY? If all the holy *Sefarim* and all our great Torah leaders tell us not to feel that way, then what is it that causes us to feel distant from Hashem? What or who is it that can twist things around so much and make us feel the opposite of what we are supposed to?

"אין כוונת יצר הרע בהכשילו האדם בעבירה לעצם העבירה,

כי אם בעיקר לנפילת הרוח והיאוש שאחרי העבירה.

כי על ידי שמרגיש את עצמו מרוחק ומנותק —

נהיה באמת מרוחק ומנותק!"

בעל יסוד העבודה חלק ג׳ פ״ד

You guessed it! This too is the working of the Evil Yetzer Hora! His main objective is not just to make you sin – it has a much bigger agenda! It wants you to sin so that afterward it can deflate your spirit and pull you into a state of despair. First it pulls you to do the sin and now it comes to you like a tzaddik and demands: "Look what you just did! You are such a rebellious lowlife!" He causes you to feel ashamed and separated from Hashem and once you FEEL SEPARATED — then you BECOME SEPARATED!

The evil Yetzer Hora capitalizes on the situation (that it trapped you into to begin with), and focuses all its energy on convincing you that **you** are now unwanted by Hashem! You blew it! Your lifetime membership has been revoked! You are being stripped of your badge!

Once you have bought into this completely false concept and you "feel" that you have become a "נדח" — unwanted ... cast away ... a perpetual loser who can never succeed ... then the game is over — and then you really are a loser!

BUT IS THAT THE TRUTH? NO!

"בכלל תכלית הבריאה הוא: 'לבל ידח ממנו נדח' (שמואל ב' יד:יד),

שזהו רצונו יתברך!"

נתיבת שלום חלק ב' עניני שבת דף פ"ה

Included in the purpose of reation is expressly expressed in *Sefer Shmuel*: *"The one who is pushed away shall not be pushed away!"* That is the will of Hashem. Hashem does not want us to ever feel pushed away from Him!

The expression, *"the one who is pushed away shall never be pushed away,"* seems odd. If we are worried that this person is being pushed away **now**, then that means that he wasn't *already* "pushed away." So why is he called a "נדח" someone who is **already** pushed away? Shouldn't it rather say, "לבל ידח ממנו יהודי," so that a nice good Jew should not get pushed away"?

The explanation is: only a person who already considers himself a נדח — pushed away from his connection to Hashem — is at risk of actually becoming "pushed away"!

For if you would believe that NO MATTER WHAT you say or do, you will always remain a beloved child to Hashem and a member of Klal Yisrael, then nothing could ever make you feel "pushed away"!

"תרגיש ותאמין שהקדוש ברוך הוא שוכן אתם בתוך טומאותם
ואפילו במצבים השפלים ביותר עדיין הוא אלקיך
לעולם אינך אבוד מאתו יתברך!!"

ספר נתיבות שלום חלק ב' עמוד קנ"ד

Authentic Yiddishkeit understands that Hashem remains WITH US even if we fall to the lowest possible spiritual level! We must know and remember that we can **NEVER** become separated from Hashem!

THIS KNOWLEDGE SHOULD MAKE YOU GET UP AND DANCE!

"גם כשעובר על התורה כולה
אינו חדל מלהיות יהודי וקידושיו קידושין!"

נתיבות שלום חלק ב' ענייני פסח דל"ד
רמב"ם הלכות איסורי ביאה פרק י"ג הלכה י"ז

Even if a Yid transgresses ALL the commandments of the Torah, his status of being a "Yid" is not revoked and he may Halachically still marry a Jew.

If you manage to internalize that no matter what the Yetzer Hora causes you to do against the will of Hashem — even if you transgress the entire Torah — you are still a beloved and wanted son to Hashem, then no force could ever push you away! Face it: you were born into the holy Jewish nation and **nothing you do can ever change your status!**

"כל ישראל יש להם חלק לעולם הבא
כמו שנאמר: ועמך **כולם צדיקים**!"

משניות סנהדרין י:א

The Mishnah says: Every Jew has a portion in the World to Come, as it says: and Your nation is ALL righteous.

Now hang on just a second; can we honestly say that every single Jew **acts** like a pure and holy tzaddik?

"רצה לומר אפילו אותם שאינם כן!"

פרי צדיק ויקרא קונטרס עמלה של תורה אות ו'

The answer is: YES! In Hashem's eyes EVERY SINGLE JEW is considered to be a pure and holy tzaddik — **even those who are NOT currently acting like one!**

Authentic Yiddishkeit believes that EVERY single Yid has a pure נשמה whose internal infinite power can never be tainted, defiled, or removed, even after he may have sinned repeatedly and fallen to the lowest levels of spiritual impurity. EVERYONE .... Yes — **Even you!**

NOW LET'S MAKE YOU SMILE FROM THE GESHMAK OF TORAH!

"אל תסתכל בקנקן אלא במה שיש בו."

אבות פרק ד'

"Don't evaluate the contents in a jug based on the appearance of the jug." Or, as the famous saying goes: "Don't judge a book by its cover!" In the same vein, we can now confidently state: **"Never judge a Jew by his behavior!"**

"ואומרים על צד הצחות על 'ונקה לא ינקה' (שמות לד:ז)
שאם תסיר מן 'ונקה ינקה' [אותיות] 'קנקן' -
ישאר 'יהו"ה' שם הרחמים!"

ספר חיים של תורה בראשית דף ר' ומרכבת המשנה לר"י אלאשקר על אבות פרק ד'

The Torah says: "ונקה לא ינקה — If somebody sins and repents, then Hashem cleans him; and if he doesn't repent, then Hashem does not clean him." However, since we just noted that we must not look at the קנקן — exterior, therefore, we should remove the letters קנקן from "ונקה ינקה."

וּנַקֵה יְנַקֶה

Surprise! We are left with the letters of ו־ה־י־ה, and when you unscramble it — you have י־ה־ו־ה, which is the Name of Hashem reflecting MERCY!

The practical lesson is: Only by looking past the קנקן — exterior — of every Jew can you expose the inner G-dliness within him!

But hang on — there's more! In order to complete the Four-Letter

Name of Hashem, we need to take two letters from the word "ונקה" — which represents the group of sinners who repent, but we also need to take two letters from the words "ינקה" — which represents the group of sinners who did NOT repent!

This teaches us that the spiritually superior "clean" group of Yidden cannot form the Name of Hashem on their own! The only way to complete the Name of Hashem is when both groups of Yidden join together as one!

DON'T STOP READING NOW — IT'S ABOUT TO GET EVEN BETTER!

The Holy *Sefarim* teach us that the letters י and ה of Hashem's Name are on a **higher** level than the letters ו and ה.

Now if you look again carefully, you will notice something absolutely incredible: The word ונקה — referring to those who are forgiven and cleansed — utilizes the letters ו and ה from Hashem's Name, whereas the word ינקה — referring to people who are not yet worthy of being purified — utilizes the letters י and ה, which represent MORE MERCY from Hashem!

Most people would be shocked and unable to comprehend: HOW is this possible!?! However, YOU were smart enough to buy (or borrow) this *sefer*, and, if you didn't just open up to this page and you actually read until here, then you know that the answer is simple:

Authentic Yiddishkeit believes that the FURTHER away you are from Hashem, the **MORE MERCY** you need to bring you back home and therefore Hashem is ready to bestow **MORE MERCY** upon you! Why?

BECAUSE:
Hashem LOVES YOU AND
YOUR ESSENCE IS SOLID GOLD!

AHHHHHH GEVALDIG!

BUILDING MUSCLE

"Challenges are sent to us ONLY in order to make us GROW!"

"הנסיון הוא רק בשביל לגדלן שהנסיון גופא מגדל אותנו!"

ספר נתיבות שלום פרשת לך לך דף ע'

14

NOT A "TEST" ...
A "CHALLENGE"!

A challenge is the VEHICLE to carry you to a higher destination.

"כי על ידי נסיון
מתעלה האדם למדריגה
עליונה כי נסה הוא לשון
הרמה כמו: שאו נס."

שפת אמת בראשית פרשת לך-לך

"For through 'challenges' a person rises to a higher level."

HASHEM

created the world with a
built-in system for personal growth:

"אין הקב"ה מעלה את האדם לשררה עד שבוחן ובודק אותו תחלה,
וכיון שהוא עומד בנסיונו הוא מעלה אותו לשררה!"

במדבר רבה (וילנא) פרשה ט"ז

Hashem does not elevate a person to a higher level without challenging him first. Once the person proves his dedication by overcoming his tailor-made challenge, Hashem raises him to a higher level.

You can never grow — and you certainly cannot achieve your true potential — unless you are properly challenged. Whether you choose to be a Rabbi, doctor, lawyer, accountant, plumber, electrician, or even a lifeguard, you will only receive your degree AFTER you work hard and pass the test!

The MORE difficult it is for you to pass the test, the MORE elated and accomplished you will feel when you hold the diploma in your hands!

LET'S GO BACK TO THE BEGINNING

In an era when the entire world was bowing down to pagan idols, one young lad opened his eyes and recognized that there must be a Creator. One young boy stood up to his family, his city, and the entire world. One man went on a life quest to discover the true G-d and to develop a close relationship with Him.

We would imagine that Hashem would have been so thrilled (so to speak) that someone finally "discovered" Him, that He would have showered him with the easiest life imaginable! Avraham should have been quickly transported to Jamaica with a billion dollars deposited into his bank account, to relax in comfort and tranquility for the rest of his life!

YET WE FIND THAT
THE COMPLETE OPPOSITE OCCURRED:

"עשרה נסיונות נתנסה אברהם אבינו ועמד בכולם"

משנה מסכת אבות פרק ה:ג

Our patriarch Avraham was tested with ten major life-altering challenges! It's not easy to pick up and leave your hometown at age 75 or to have your wife abducted by the authorities, and we cannot even fathom being commanded to slaughter your beloved child!

Why was this necessary? Wasn't Avraham the ONE person who DID NOT NEED challenges? After all — he was the one who saw the truth!?

"נסיון אחר נסיון וגידולין אחר גידולין
בשביל לנסותן בעולם בשביל לגדלן בעולם!"

בראשית רבה (וילנא) פרשה נה:א

The explanation is: Avraham was given opportunities to prove his complete devotion and unwavering faith in Hashem, in order to be propelled to unparalleled greatness!

Authentic Yiddishkeit believes that by remaining steadfast to your belief that the difficult challenge is being presented to you by a loving G-d — THAT IS THE VEHICLE that brings you to a closer relationship with Hashem.

TRUE LOYALTY

The administration of the Greenwald University decided they must somehow become the most prestigious institution in the nation. The board of directors came up with an ingenious idea. They would pay top students from all around the country to join their university program and soon enough they would acquire the title "most prestigious college in the nation."

Their research identified one particular student who they felt must be convinced to join them. If this KEY student would switch to their school, their plot would certainly be successful. They tried to recruit him, but his allegiance to his current university was strong. They offered him scholarships, a long-term teaching contract after graduation, health benefits, a home, etc., but nothing worked! His loyalty to his professors and mentors was simply too strong and he would not budge. When his current professors discovered his loyalty to their university, they honored him with their highest title and they gave him all those wonderful benefits that he had turned down, and he immediately became a member of the school faculty!

NOW WE CAN BETTER UNDERSTAND OUR OPENING STATEMENT

Our sages don't tell us that Avraham was given ten life challenges merely as an interesting tidbit of trivia. Rather, it is to TEACH US that all of the lofty spiritual levels that Avraham reached were possible ONLY because he went through those incredibly difficult challenges and passed each of them with flying colors!

So now we understand that the opportunity to be challenged like this was actually the "chance of a lifetime" given to Avraham by Hashem. These challenges were not OBSTACLES and DISTURBANCES to his growth potential! On the contrary! It was these very challenges that TRANSFORMED "Avraham" into becoming "AVRAHAM AVINU" — the great patriarch of our nation!

A GIFT — AN OPPORTUNITY

Understanding and internalizing this concept allows us to begin to view challenges and difficulties as a "gift" and an "opportunity" for us to grow and achieve spiritual success in our lives.

Now I know what you're thinking:

It's okay with me — let someone else have this great gift!

But think of it this way: Giving up on your personal "challenges" means giving up on your personal growth and development, thereby forfeiting your destiny of greatness. Is that what you really want?

Now we can begin to understand why Dovid HaMelech uses the word "fortunate" when he refers to challenges:

"אשרי הגבר אשר תיסרנו י-ה!"

תהלים מד:יב

"Fortunate is the one whom Hashem disciplines!"

Now wait a second — did Dovid HaMelech really say.....

"FORTUNATE"???

"באמת [יסורים] הוא האושר האמתי והתכלית העליון לאדם
כי היסורין מצרפים לב האדם ומזככו לטוב!"

פירוש עץ יוסף על מדרש בראשית רבה פרשה צ"ב סימן א'

YES, HE CERTAINLY DID!!! Because the truth is that the pain and suffering you experience throughout your life compel you to analyze your true self and cleanse your heart and mind to be true to Hashem.

"רק אולי ידמה האדם שלא כן הוא

כי נוח הי-ה לו אם ישב בשלוה ואז הי-ה עוסק בעבודת ה'..."

פירוש עץ יוסף על מדרש בראשית רבה פרשה צ"ב סימן א'

However, you probably might be thinking: *"If I had the opportunity to live in peace and tranquility, then I would certainly be able to dedicate myself to serving Hashem! So why is all this suffering and difficulty really necessary? Isn't it just distracting me from all the good that I want to do?!?"*

"ילמוד מתורתו יתברך מה שקרה להאבות

שהיו צדיקים גדולים ובודאי בשלוותם היו עוסקים בכבוד ה' –

ועם כל זה בא עליהם יסורים ולא הקפידו כי ידעו כי לטובתם הוא!"

פירוש עץ יוסף על מדרש בראשית רבה פרשה צ"ב סימן א'

The answer for this can be found when you study what transpired in the lives of our holy Avos (forefathers). They were completely righteous and certainly did not need any motivation to purify their hearts and minds! If they had just been "left alone" to sit in peace, without troubles and problems, they would certainly have spent all their time dedicated to spiritual growth!

Yet each of them constantly received painful life-altering challenges, and THEY DID NOT COMPLAIN. WHY? Because they understood that the ONLY way to earn the title: "Patriarch of G-d's chosen people" was to go through those difficult challenges/opportunities.

Going through those painful difficulties was the PROCESS that TRANSFORMED them into PATRIARCHS!

"על ידי הנסיונות הריהו הולך ומתעלה!"

ספר נתיבות שלום פרשת לך לך דף ע'

Authentic Yiddishkeit believes that a נסיון/test is actually a "challenge" whose sole purpose is to give you the "opportunity"

to bring out the potential buried deep within you — and which could otherwise never be revealed.

The physical world clearly teaches us that without "challenges" a person cannot physically grow. A person who decides to build muscle must steadily work out and challenge his body, pushing himself "beyond" his current ability. The success of his muscular growth will be in direct correlation to the amount of resistance and strain with which he challenges his muscles.

AS THE WORLD SAYS: NO PAIN — NO GAIN!

There is NO way to lift 300 pounds without first starting off with lifting 50 pounds and **building up** your muscles with consistency and dedication. Similarly, you cannot do 300 sit-ups or 100 push-ups without first starting off doing the few that you can, and consistently working hard to build up your muscles.

It is common knowledge that you can't possibly reach your physical potential WITHOUT GOING THROUGH the muscle-building process. That is precisely why people actually use their free time and pay money to **work out**. People actually **look for new ways to challenge** their bodies in order to build themselves up faster! They actually do research to find out where they can go to RECEIVE the best CHALLENGE! Why do they do this? Because they know: The MORE difficult the challenge — the MORE they have the opportunity to achieve their goals.

So too there is just NO POSSIBLE way to become an **emotionally** or **spiritually** strong person without going THROUGH the muscle-building process!

HARD TO SWALLOW *With a proper outlook and a deeper understanding, life's daily נסיונות/challenges can be compared to vitamins. Although they may be very uncomfortable to swallow, their sole purpose is to make you stronger.*

"שלכל השגותיו ומדרגותיו הגיע
אברהם אבינו על ידי הנסיונות שעברו עליו!"

נתיבות שלום פרשת בהעלותך ד"ה על פי ה'

Avraham Avinu did not have an easy life by any stretch of the
imagination, but it was specifically those challenges that were
the VEHICLE that carried him to his ultimate level of incredible
accomplishment: becoming the father of Klal Yisrael and
transmitting the ability to serve Hashem under any and all
conditions to his offspring for generations to come.

THE SAME APPLIES TO YOU:

"ענין 'נסיון' ידוע שפירושו נסיון
וגם פירושו הגבהה מלשון 'ארים נסי-ה' (ישעיה מט:כב)."

ערבי נחל בראשית חיי שרה דרוש ב'

The word "נסיון" actually has a dual meaning. It means "a challenge"
and it also means "to raise up," as it says: "lift up your flag"! For
after you surpass your challenge, your personal flag is raised!

"כל נסיון שיהודי עובר הוא אמנם קשה מאוד
אבל בעמידתו בנסיון הוא נעשה יותר גבוה מקודם
שהוא עתה יהודי שכבר עבר נסיון כזה!"

מדברי נתיבות שלום פרשת שלח לך לך דף ע'

Every challenge that you go through is truly very difficult, but
overcoming your challenge will elevate you to a higher level, for
now you are someone who has already conquered that previous
level of difficulty!

GROWING HIGHER *When young Meir first started playing the new video game,
he was overwhelmed by the challenge. Yet, after hours of
dedication, he learned how to maneuver and not get out*

right away. As he began the 6th level, he found himself facing a brand-new enemy with greater power than ever before. However, he didn't give up. Eventually, he learned how to conquer the 6th board. Now he was a much better player than before, for he was a player who could conquer the 6th board!

The **greater** the challenge, the **more** of an **opportunity** is being extended to you to grow quicker and to greater heights ... and that should make you feel energized and excited to stand up and face the challenge head on!

As Winston Churchill said: "A pessimist sees the DIFFICULTY in every OPPORTUNITY; an optimist sees the OPPORTUNITY in every DIFFICULTY!"

THE MEANING OF LIFE

"זהו סדר החיים של יהודי: חיים הרצופים נסיון אחר נסיון
אך כל זה מביא לנסוע ולהתעלות למדרגות גבוהות!"
מדברי נתיבות שלום פרשת בהעלותך ד"ה על פי ה'

You were put on this world to GROW. Since you cannot GROW without being challenged, that is why your life is a process of going from one difficult challenge to the next. With the wrong attitude, these difficulties can get you down and break your spirit. Therefore, you must realize that it is these very difficult life challenges that raise you up and enable you to develop into a spiritually elevated person.

In between life's difficulties and challenges is when you go through your routine and await your next challenge. The fact is: the weeks or months that you live without challenges are the times that you will grow the least!

SPECIAL CHANCES

Moshe got a job at ABC Worldwide Corporation and received an annual salary of $100,000. The manager realized that Moshe could be trusted to do difficult technical analyses for the business, and throughout the year Moshe was given special research projects to work on during his spare time. He received a $10,000 bonus for each special project. Each opportunity took 10 hours of his private time — and he usually needed to work straight through the night — but it was well worth it. Between opportunities, he went back to being just a regular employee doing the best he could as he waited anxiously for the next amazing opportunity. Looking back at his year, he realized that although he worked 50 weeks for the company at his regular pay, his huge savings account had been filled due to the special difficult opportunities given to him.

When you look back and review your life, you will see a lot of "regular time," without much growth, and then occasional bursts of tremendous growth that will benefit you and your descendants. Those GROWTH SPURTS come from the turbulent times of pain, difficulty, and challenges that you went through.

NO PAIN NO GAIN

The karate teacher noticed one student who took karate very seriously. He decided to give this particular student a special opportunity to grow and skip ranks. When the student walked in the next week, the teacher told him that he would fight a huge kid from a higher rank. The kid was frightened but the teacher assured him that he could certainly beat him. "I know that you have it in you to crush this guy!"

The kid nervously entered the ring but, boy, did he get a beating! He complained to the teacher, "What are you doing to me? Don't you like me? Why are you punishing me like this? I'm the student who is so dedicated to you!"

The teacher said, "You have it in you to beat this guy and move up in ranks much quicker than if you just stick to the regular process. Go home and rest up, because next week you'll be back in the ring with him again!"

Week after week the student fought and he lost. But he NEVER gave up!

After many months of extra work and dedication, pushing himself physically and emotionally, the student finally realized that he CAN beat this guy. He conditioned his body and his mind, pushing himself ever harder. He kept losing, but he didn't give up. By the end of the season, he BEAT the guy and swiftly moved up the ranks! His teacher proudly said, "I knew you had the inner potential to beat him! You just needed to not give up!"

LET'S REVIEW THE STORY
AND SEE WHAT WE LEARNED THUS FAR:

Question #1:

Why did the teacher pick this student for this golden opportunity?

   A. Because he hated him.
   B. Because this student always came late.
   C. Because he knew that this student had the most ability.

Question #2:

Why did he make his prized student suffer more than the others?

   A. Because his parents always paid late.
   B. Because deep down he really hated this kid.
   C. Because that was the QUICKEST way for the student to GROW.

"וּמַאן דְּלָא רָחִים לֵיהּ קוּדְשָׁא בְּרִיךְ הוּא ...
סְלִיק מִנֵּיהּ תּוֹכַחָה סְלִיק מִנֵּיהּ שַׁרְבִּיטָא!"

זוהר כרך ג (ויקרא) פרשת בחוקותי דף קיד:

When you don't care about someone, you don't bother to challenge him. If a teacher doesn't care about a student, he'll just leave him in the back of the classroom and let him rot away without learning a word. If a boss doesn't care about an employee, he'll never give him the opportunity to earn his way up the corporate ladder.

Conversely, the MORE you care about someone — a student, a child, or anyone whose growth you are responsible for — the MORE you will push him and challenge him in order to bring out his inner potential and help him RISE HIGHER!

"וְהָאֱלֹקִים נִסָּה אֶת אַבְרָהָם עַל נָכוֹן,
לְהוֹצִיא עֲבוֹדָתוֹ מִן הַכֹּחַ אֶל הַפּוֹעַל
לִהְיוֹת זֶה סִבַּת טוֹבָתוֹ!"

ספר הכוזרי מאמר ה'

When the Torah says: "Hashem challenged Avraham," it means that Hashem decided to bring out Avraham's untapped potential into reality — for his own benefit!

LET'S EXAMINE THE MOST DIFFICULT TEST:

Avaraham was asked to sacrifice his only child — the one he had waited for his entire life! To a normal person, this would have been a life-crushing, horrific experience that could possibly kill him or cause him to have a nervous breakdown!

Yet to Avraham, this extreme challenge was clearly a once-in-a-lifetime OPPORTUNITY to completely prove his unwavering loyalty to Hashem and to thereby connect on a much higher level.

Therefore he woke up EARLY the next morning! Avraham would

not have chosen to pass up this amazing OPPORTUNITY for anything in the world!

Some people spend their entire life mopping the floors of a huge multibillion-dollar corporation ... while others work their way up the ranks to run it. A person who is truly determined to be as successful as possible would surely welcome even the most difficult challenges so that he can reveal his inner potential and earn his stripes in the corporation.

He would come home and say, "I can't eat supper ... I can't relax ... I can't go out and have fun ... I can't go to sleep early ... I have this huge chance to prove myself to my boss and work on this project that he asked me to do ...."

Everyone enjoys going swimming and lying out in the sun, yet the achiever would laugh at someone who chose to do so instead of working his way up the corporate ladder!

NOW WE CAN APPRECIATE THE LANGUAGE OF THE PREVIOUS CHAZAL:

"עשרה נסיונות נתנסה
אברהם אבינו ועמד בכולם."

משנה מסכת אבות פרק ה:ג

The common translation is: Avraham Avinu passed through ten **נסיונות** and he stood up to all of them. However, why does it specifically use the term "ועמד בכולם — and he stood up to all of them"; it really should have said "ולא נכשל בהם — and he didn't stumble on any of them"!?

"ועמד בכולם: לא רק שעמד בהנסיונות
אלא שעמד על גבי הנסיונות!"

ספר נתיבי אמת פנימי

With the understanding that challenges make you grow and

become a more elevated person, we can now understand that after you withstand a challenge, you actually are standing on top of it — for you are higher than you were before!

You must believe and internalize that every bit of pain and difficulty you ever encounter comes from your loving Father Who is sending you a custom-made opportunity designed for your maximum growth. After you CONQUER the challenge — you are GREATER, STRONGER, and MORE ELEVATED than you were before!

So the next time something goes **"wrong"** in your life, realize that maybe something just went **"right"**!

Reviewing his weekly schedule on Motza'ei Shabbos, all Shloimy wanted to do was to get through the week without being thrown off schedule — after all — his schedule consisted of the maximum amount of Torah and mitzvos humanly possible, and he wouldn't want to miss out on any of it!

As he encountered trouble with his business and had to work around the clock for several days, he became upset — not so much about his business difficulties, but because his beloved schedule was ruined and he had missed several opportunities to daven with minyan, learn Torah, and help other people who needed his advice. When he complained to his Rebbi that he could not keep up the spiritual parts of his day, he was shocked to be informed that his thinking was completely wrong!

His Rebbi told him: "YOU don't know what YOU need - more than Hashem knows what YOU need. YOU set up a schedule that YOU think brings out the best in YOU by doing all those wonderful things, and that may be true — but if Hashem wants YOU to have a different kind of week, then embrace it and recognize that there is MORE growth waiting for you THIS way!"

"כל יהודי נושא שליחות עליונה
שלמענה ירד לעולם למלא שליחות זו
ועל ידי הנסיונות שעובר - ממלא הוא שליחותו!"

ספר נתיבות שלום פרשת וירא עמוד קי"ז

Authentic Yiddishkeit understands that life's difficulties are NOT a distraction that **gets in the way** of your REAL life. On the contrary — those difficulties and challenges are what your life is REALLY all about! It is your specific hardships and challenges that SHAPE who you are and CARRY you to fulfill your personal mission in this world.

GRAND SLAM  The Kleelas Yoifee once told the Nesivei Emes: "The harder the ball is thrown at you, the more potential it has to travel!"

The Nesivei Emes responded with a twinkle in his eye: "True — but you have to know how to hit it!"

So step up to the plate ...
and smash that fastball out of the park!

15

Custom-Tailored "Challenges"!

*Searching for YOUR personal
growth opportunity*

"אמר רב אחא משום רבי
לוי: מאי קרא: (תהלים ק"א)
'חסד ומשפט אשירה לך ה'
אזמרה'? אם חסד - אשירה,
ואם משפט - אשירה!"

תלמוד בבלי מסכת ברכות דף ס:

*"When you treat me with kindness
I will sing praise to You, and
when You treat me
harshly I will sing
praise to You!"*

HASHEM

custom designs every single event in our lives to guide us to fulfill our potential:

"אמר רבי חנינא: אין דבר רע יורד מלמעלה!"

בראשית רבה פרשה נ"א

We must internalize a fundamental principle of Yiddishkeit:

"Nothing bad comes from Heaven!"

You must believe that the all-powerful Creator of the universe is not "out to get you," and nothing "BAD" or "WRONG" or "UNFAIR" comes forth from Hashem. When you internalize and really believe that this is true, then you are ready to accept the next step:

"אין רע יורד מן השמים והכל הוא **לטובת האדם** כדי שיתקן בזה את השייך אליו שעל ידי זה ישיג יעודו ותפקידו בעולמו!"

נתיבות שלום לך לך עמוד ס"ב

If NOTHING BAD comes from Heaven, that means that whatever happens to you — regardless of how painful it is — must be ... are you ready for this? **GOOD!** As it says:

"טוב ה' לכל ורחמיו על כל מעשיו."

תהלים קמה:ט

"Hashem is GOOD to all and He is compassionate to all His creations."

"הקב"ה מעמיד לכל אחד את כל הנסיבות והתנאים שיוכל **על ידם**
לתקן את אשר תפקידו לתקן ולמלאות יעודו ותפקידו בעולמו!"

נתיבות שלום לך לך עמוד ס"ב

Authentic Yiddishkeit believes that EVERY detail of your life; who you were born to, what school you went to, how much money you have, where you live, how many siblings you have, and every single thing that ever happened to you — have all been designed to SET UP YOUR LIFE so that you can reach your specific destiny and purpose.

LET'S TAKE THIS A STEP FURTHER:

"ואף **המצבים הקשים** בחיי האדם
הם גם כן אמצעים שניתנו לו בכדי שיגיע אל תיקונו!"

נתיבות שלום לך לך עמוד ס"ב

Furthermore, as you encounter life's **difficulties and hardships,** these painful "situations" are precisely given to you in order to help you reach your ultimate goal.

Almost any person who accomplished anything for the greater good, did so by overcoming personal pain and suffering. ONLY by going through the pain and suffering in their life did they elevate themselves and help mankind!

No longer can you think: *"OY! WHY did Hashem make me: lose money/ get into a fight/marry this person/have in-laws like this/have difficult children/have sick children/have mean parents/injure myself/get sick/etc. "*

For there are no accidents!

 LIFE SAVINGS *A Yid in Bnei Brak was diagnosed with a horrific, rapidly advancing disease that would surely kill him in a short time. The family was brokenhearted because the doctors gave up any hope for his survival. The patient decided to*

pour out his heart to Hashem by saying the entire Tehillim at the burial place of R' Shimon bar Yochai in Meiron. On the way to Meiron, he stopped off at the home of the Gadol Hador, HaRav Chaim Kanievsky shlit"a, to receive his blessing. Rav Chaim asked him, "Do you remember that I was in your house eight years ago?" Of course the Yid remembered.

The reason Rav Chaim had visited his home eight years before was because of an incident that happened to the Yid's wife: Twelve years before that visit from Rav Chaim, somebody did something horrible to her and as a result, someone in her family died. After a while, the person who did this terrible thing got married, but did not have any children. This is why Rav Chaim had come to visit their home. He showed the Yid's wife a piece of paper on which he had written, "I completely forgive this person." The Rav asked the wife to sign the paper! She replied that if the Rav is requesting it, of course she will sign, but she knows that she cannot bring herself to truly forgive the person for what had happened. He replied, "Please work on yourself to forgive this person with a full heart and sign the paper!" After many long minutes of deep thought and introspection, she somehow managed to bring herself to forgive the person with a full heart and she signed the paper! Rav Chaim instructed them to save the paper and keep it in a safe place.

Now eight years later, Rav Chaim told this Yid: "Take that paper with you to Meiron and daven that you should be saved in the merit of the forgiveness of your wife!" After returning from Meiron, the Yid underwent a new set of tests and the doctors were dumbfounded as they found him to be perfectly healthy!

Eight years earlier, his wife thought that by forgiving

that terrible person, she was helping THAT person have children — but in actuality she was really saving her own husband's life!

Source: Umasuk Haor on Megillas Esther, p. 114

Authentic Yiddishkeit believes that it is not only when someone EARNS 10 million dollars that he has an opportunity to grow and fulfill his life's potential, but even when someone LOSES 10 million dollars, this painful loss is given to him because he NEEDS this in order to reach his potential and complete his life's mission!

"מנין שכשם שמברך על הטובה כך מברך על הרעה?
תלמוד לומר: אשר נתן לך ה' אלקיך - דיינך, בכל דין שדנך,
בין מדה טובה ובין מדת פורענות!"

תלמוד בבלי מסכת ברכות דף מח:

This is what Chazal mean when they say: "The SAME way that you thank Hashem for what you think is GOOD for you, you must also thank Hashem for what you think is BAD for you." Why? Because that too, is for YOUR benefit!

LET'S TAKE THIS A STEP FURTHER:

This concept does not refer only to difficult situations that you will encounter, but it even refers to your own inborn deficiencies:

"ולא רק התכונות הטובות מביאות אותו אל יעודו
אלא גם התכונות הרעות שעל ידי שמתגבר עליהם
ומשבר מידותיו הרעות מגיע לתפקידו ויעודו בעולמו!"

נתיבות שלום לך לך עמוד ס:ג

Not only do your **GOOD** qualities help you achieve your life's mission, but even your **UGLY** qualities were given to you specifically so that you can reach your destination! For by overcoming, controlling, and refining them, you will fulfill your purpose.

No longer can you think: *"OY! WHY did Hashem make me so angry/mean/haughty/jealous/lustful/stingy/self-centered/etc."* (add in whatever is not perfect about your personality — if you aren't sure, then just ask your spouse for a list!)

FOR THERE ARE NO ACCIDENTS!

"הביאו לפניו צורת משה רבינו
והכיר בו כל המדות רעות והשיבו לו **שעל ידי כך**
זכה למעלה גדולה הזאת כי כפה את כלם לעבודת הבורא ב"ה!!!"

מראה יחזקאל דברים פרשת וילך בשם אחד מהחכמים

Moshe Rabbeinu had a long list of terrible character traits! However, he was able to reach such lofty levels only by having those bad traits within him and forcing himself to control himself and use them only for good!

We are each given natural impulses and urges to help us achieve greatness by CONTROLLING and UTILIZING these traits for our service to Hashem:

"אדם שמטבעו אינו בעל תאוה
אינו יכול לעבוד את ה' 'בכל לבבך'!"

ר' צדוק הכהן מלובלין זי"ע מובא בספר פתגמים נבחרים

A person who by nature is NOT a passionate person cannot truly serve Hashem as well as one who is very passionate and uses his passion and lust for the right reasons. Highly successful people are not "blah." They have an extra dose of passion rushing through their veins and they utilize this to motivate themselves to go the extra mile.

If you feel that you are extremely passionate — this is a SIGN that these inborn feelings were given to you to be utilized for you to become **extraordinary!**

Authentic Yiddishkeit believes that even your **character flaws and personality deficiencies** are specifically placed in you by Hashem as part of the **"set up"** that you need in order to fulfill your individual purpose in life.

BUT IT GOES EVEN DEEPER THAN THAT:

"וגם כאשר פחז עליו יצרו
ידע שזוהי **מתנה** מן השמים!
שרק על ידי זה יוכל להגיע ליעודו!"

נתיבות שלום לך לך עמוד ס"ו

You should know that even when your Evil Inclination attacks you — THIS TOO is a GIFT from heaven! For only by overcoming this battle can you reach your destination and fulfill your mission!

YES! You read that right! Every piece of you and every situation you encounter is specifically designed by Hashem for YOUR BENEFIT! Even your inner desire and temptation to sin — were also specifically placed within you by Hashem!

No longer can you think: *"OY! WHY did Hashem give me such a huge Yetzer Hora/bad friends/all these spiritual challenges/bad influences/etc."*

For there are no accidents!

This puts a whole different spin on how you must face your own personal difficulties and challenges!

We tend to keep our focus on the parts of our lives that we have under control and we're doing great at! We think that those are the things that define our true character.

But the truth is that our entire life's mission is really about facing and dealing with our **imperfections** by: (1) developing the inner strength to try and prevent ourselves from falling and (2) developing the inner strength to try to recover after falling so that we can stay in the game of life.

So refocus on your
DEFICIENCIES and **PERSONAL STRUGGLES**
and get ready to ...

FIGHT!

16

A WAKE-UP CALL

---

*A once-in-a-lifetime opportunity —
every day!*

"דבאמת מאתו [מה']
לא תצא הרעה ...
רק הכל טובות!"

קדושת לוי כללות הניסים

•

*"In reality no bad comes
forth from Hashem. Rather, it
is all for our benefit!"*

HASHEM

sometimes has to put us in our place; how should we react?

"מוסר ה' בני אל תמאס ואל תקץ בתוכחתו,
כי את אשר יאהב ה' יוכיח וכאב את בן ירצה!"

משלי פרק ג:יא-יב

Shlomo HaMelech, wisest of all men, said, "Do not become **disgusted** when Hashem chastises you, for Hashem reprimands those whom He LOVES and He desires to have a father-son relationship."

RUDE AWAKENING

Chaim was driving back to Lakewood from a wedding in Montreal. He tried keeping himself up by opening the window and blasting the latest Solid Gold album but he still kept nodding off. At 4:10 a.m., he fell asleep as his car cruised at 65 miles per hour. His end was surely near. Driving behind him, his good friend Moishe noticed Chaim's car veer slightly off the road. Realizing that something must be wrong, Moishe put the pedal to the metal, pushing his yeshivishe 1978 station wagon into overdrive. As he pulled alongside Chaim's car, Moishe saw him enjoying a blissful sleep.

Moshe was in a dilemma; on the one hand, he must honk his horn to wake Chaim before it was too late, but on the other hand, he really felt bad to disturb his good friend Chaim while he was in such a yummy peaceful sleep!

> *Moishe couldn't decide what to do .... What would you do?*
> *Foolish question, huh?*

Many times we find ourselves cruising down the highway of life, asleep at the wheel, oblivious to the danger ahead. Because Hashem loves **YOU** and cares for **YOU**, sometimes He needs to wake **YOU** up in order to save **YOU**, guide **YOU**, and redirect **YOU**. He may have to "honk His horn" to startle **YOU** and shake **YOU** out of your trance.

Which word sticks out in the above paragraph? That's right — the word: "**YOU**" — because this is all about **YOU**! After all, what other purpose could there possibly be for Hashem to waste His time and effort *(so to speak)* to give pain, challenges, and difficulties to puny human beings? Do you really think that Hashem is "bored" and "mean"? Of course not! *Chas v'shalom!*

But sometimes while going through something painful, somewhere in your confused mind you may somehow sort of think that it seems like Hashem wants to give you a hard time and He's just playing around with you .... Ask yourself this: Couldn't He do a much better job?

A REALLY BAD DAY

The following urban legend was printed as fact in several newspapers: A man was working on his motorcycle on his patio. He was racing the engine on the motorcycle and somehow, the motorcycle slipped into gear. The man, still holding the handlebars, was dragged through a glass patio door along with the motorcycle and dumped onto the dining room floor inside the house. Hearing the crash, his wife ran into the dining room, and found her husband lying on the floor, bleeding, cut, and in pain. She ran to the phone and called an ambulance. Because they lived on a fairly high hill, the wife went down the several flights of long steps to the street to direct the paramedics to her husband. After the ambulance arrived and transported the husband to the hospital, the wife went to clean up the mess. Seeing that gas had spilled on the floor, the wife mopped up the gas and wrung out the mop, draining the gas into the toilet.

The husband was treated at the hospital and was released. After arriving home, he looked at the shattered patio door and the damage done to his motorcycle. He became despondent, went into the bathroom, sat on the toilet, and smoked a cigarette. After finishing the cigarette, he flipped it into the toilet bowl while still seated.

The wife, who was in the kitchen, heard a loud explosion and her husband's screams. She rushed into the bathroom and found her husband on the floor. His trousers had been blown away and he was suffering burns all over the back of his body. The wife ran to the phone (again) and called for an ambulance. The same ambulance crew arrived (again) and the wife met them (again) at the street. The paramedics loaded the husband on the stretcher and began carrying him down the many stairs. On the way down, one of the paramedics asked the wife how the husband had burned himself. She told them what happened and the paramedics laughed so hard that they tipped the stretcher and the husband fell out. He rolled down the remaining steps and broke his arm! This story redefines what it is to have a bad day.

As bad as a person may have it, couldn't Hashem make it worse? Why can't a person wake up one day with his head turned around so he can't drive or even walk straight! That would be really bad! How about meteors randomly falling from the sky every day? That would surely rattle those little humans! How about eyeballs randomly popping out of their sockets — that's a good one — no?

However, while experiencing pain and suffering, it is very hard to appreciate the goodness of Hashem. You may ask: WHY? WHY? WHY? But once you start asking WHY — the list never ends!

WHY, OH WHY

WHY do pharmacies make sick people walk all the way to the back of the store to get their prescriptions filled while healthy people can buy cigarettes at the front?

WHY do people order double burgers, large fries, and a diet coke?

WHY do banks leave vault doors open and then chain the pens to the counters?

WHY do they sell hamburgers in packages of ten and buns in packages of eight?

WHY does the sun lighten our hair, but darken our skin?

WHY don't you ever see the headline "Psychic Wins Lottery"?

WHY is it that doctors call what they do "practice"?

WHY is lemon juice made with artificial flavoring and dishwashing liquid made with real lemons?

WHY isn't there mouse-flavored cat food?

WHY don't they make the whole airplane out of the material used to make the indestructible black box?

WHY don't sheep shrink when it rains?

WHY are they called apartments when they are all connected?

And the "WHY" list goes on and on ...

HEAVENLY ANSWERS

The Holy Ramban had a student who became deathly ill. The Ramban requested of his dear student that after he dies, he should ascend to the highest heavens and ask several important questions that were bothering him concerning the pain that Klal Yisrael was going through.

Shortly after the student passed away, he appeared to his Rebbi. He reported that he ascended to the highest levels of heaven and they showed him that from the holy and pure heavenly perspective — there are NO questions. Everything is conducted with a precise measure of perfection for the ultimate benefit of each and every Yid.

Source: Lekach Tov Devarim 1, p. 282

Although deep down every person knows that if Hashem was really "out to get him," he would have been gone a long time ago, nevertheless, as a person suffers through difficult times, the natural human reaction is to feel isolated and disconnected from Hashem. This can bring you to complain about your seemingly "unfair" situation and to conclude that Hashem, Master of the universe, is somehow "mean" or "not fair." If YOU were in charge, things would be much better!

A PAINFUL OPPORTUNITY

Zeesha couldn't believe that he overslept on this very important day! He jumped out of his bed right into his crisp new suit. Zeesh ran out with his shirt untucked, tie hanging open around his neck, and briefcase unzipped with papers half falling out. "It's okay," he thought, "I'll finish getting dressed in the taxi."

As he approached the sidewalk to hail a cab, a passing car hit a huge puddle and poor Zeesh got soaked! He shrieked, "Aarrrggghhhhhh!!!" as all his papers flew out of his briefcase and into the murky puddle! At that moment he did not think, "Boy, does Hashem love me!"

Throughout history, those with strong faith in a loving G-d suffered unspeakable horrors and yet they understood that there is a perfect, precise calculation for everything. They **did not** question Hashem's ways. They **did not** question that Hashem is the ultimate Good. They **did not** question that Hashem is their loving merciful Father.

It is the people who lack proper faith and trust in Hashem who complain. They may sometimes think: *"I feel like Hashem is toying with me."* As if Hashem has nothing better to do than to think up new ways to playfully mock their entire existence.

"מה האלוקים הי-ה זה

אילו הייתי אני צריך ללמדו כיצד ובמה לעזור!"

ר' זושה מאניפולי זי"ע מובא בספר פתגמים נבחרים

What kind of G-d would Hashem be
if He needed ME to advise Him on how to run the world!

CLEAR VISION

When the Chofetz Chaim was a young lad of only eight years old, his teacher asked the boys in the class, "What would you do if you were Hashem?"

One boy said: If I was Hashem I would send money to the family in our town that has no food!" Another boy said: "I would heal my friend's dying mother!" Each boy came up with another beautiful idea that they would do to "improve" the world if they were Hashem.

The Rebbi then turned to little Yisrael Meir and asked him, "And what would you do if you were Hashem?"

The child, wise beyond his years, responded, "Nothing! If something could be done better — Hashem certainly would have done it that way!"

Authentic Yiddishkeit believes that the foundation of Yiddishkeit is coming to grips with the fact that the Master of the universe is not something that we can understand or figure out. Much like trying to fit the sun into a soda can, it is impossible for a physical, tiny human mind to grasp Hashem.

HERE'S AN EXAMPLE THAT BRINGS OUT THIS POINT:

"רבי מני הוה שכיח קמיה דרבי יצחק בן אלישיב

אמר ליה: עתירי דבי חמי קא מצערו לי. אמר: ליענו ואיענו.

אמר: קא דחקו לי. אמר: ליעתרו, ואיעתרו."

תלמוד בבלי מסכת תענית דף כג:

Rebbi Munny would frequently visit Rebbi Yitzchok. He once complained to him that the wealthy people in his in-laws' hometown were bothering him. So Rebbi Yitzchok replied: "Let them become poor," and they become poor. Afterward, Rebbi Munny complained that since they had became poor, they bothered him for money, and so Rebbi Yitzchok said: "Let them become rich," and they once again became rich.

"אמר: לא מיקבלי עלי אינשי ביתי.

אמר ליה: מה שמה? חנה - תתייפי חנה, ונתייפת. אמר ליה: קא מגנדרא עלי.

אמר ליה: אי הכי תחזור חנה לשחרוריתה - וחזרה חנה לשחרוריתה!"

תלמוד בבלי מסכת תענית דף כג:

Another time Rebbi Munny complained that his wife was not pleasing to him. Rebbi Yitzchok asked: "What's her name?" and he said "Chanah." Rebbi Yitzchok said: "Chanah should become beautiful," and that's exactly what happened! Later, Rebbi Munny complained that since she had gained self-esteem and independence, she was abusing him! Rebbi Yitzchok said: "If so, let her return to the way she was," and so she did!

"הנהו תרי תלמידי דהוו קמיה דרבי יצחק בן אלישיב
אמרו ליה: ניבעי מר רחמי עלן דניחכים טובא!
אמר להו: עמי היתה ושלחתיה!"

תלמוד בבלי מסכת תענית דף כג:

Afterward, two students asked Rebbi Yitzchok to pray for them that they should become exceedingly smart! He replied: "I once had the power to change things around — and I sent it away from me!"

We see that after trying to IMPROVE the way Hashem set things up, the great Tzaddik realized that he wasn't improving things at all, because everything that Hashem does is PERFECT and CANNOT be improved!

If you really internalize the concept that any challenging situation given to you is designed specifically for you by Hashem, and the purpose of the challenge is for YOUR personal growth, then you will be able to face your difficulties with determination and perseverance and you will even LOOK FORWARD to greeting your next challenge!

YOSEF HATZADDIK

Yosef HaTzaddik suffered through many hardships. At the young age of seventeen, he was sold by his brothers to be a slave. He rotted in jail for twelve years, away from his beloved father. Yet Yosef always had faith that all the challenges he encountered were presented to him for his benefit.

Indeed, if not for these challenges, he would never have been able to reach his position of power, enabling him to reach his full potential. He became the savior of his family! The same family that had sold him out and disgraced him. They wanted him dead. Yet his deep wisdom understood that it was Hashem Who had sent him ahead so that he would be in the position of power to save his family from starvation.

"הים ראה **וינוס** ראה ארונו של יוסף יורד לים
אמר הקב"ה: **ינוס** מפני הנס שנאמר:
ויעזוב בגדו בידה **וינס** ויצא החוצה!"
ילקוט שמעוני תהלים רמז תתע"ג

In fact, the sea split for Klal Yisrael only in the merit of Yosef. That means that by withstanding his intense immense challenges, he actually earned enough credit to SAVE THE ENTIRE NATION OF KLAL YISRAEL!

MITZRAYIM

"וכן בגלות מצרים הראה לו ה' יתברך
איך כל שלות המצריים להאבידם הי-ה לטובה ....."
פרי צדיק שמות פרשת כי תשא

Hashem showed Moshe how everything that transpired in Egypt over the painful 210 years of horrific enslavement was actually all in order to benefit Klal Yisrael!

ALL EXILES

"וכן הוא באמת כל הגלויות **לטובה**
אך בהווה לא יוכל האדם לעמוד על זה!"
פרי צדיק שמות פרשת כי תשא

The same will be in the end of time when Moshiach arrives and the horrific 2000 years of our exile will all come together, and we will understand how the hardships we suffered through were all part of a precisely planned story with a picture-perfect ending. We will clearly see all the pieces come perfectly together as Hashem wove our nation's history from persecution and difficulty to redemption and victory!

YOUR PERSONAL PAIN

The same applies to you: When you look back over the sands of time, it will become easier to clearly see the good hand of Hashem in everything. As the saying goes, "Hindsight is 20/20."

"אל תמאס מוסר ה'
כשיקרו לך קצת רעות גופיות ...
(כיזה) יהי-ה סבה למנוע ממך התועלת
אשר בעבורו היה זה התוכחות!"

רלב"ג משלי פרק ג:יא

However, if you become "**disgusted**" when Hashem puts you through painful situations, you will forgo the benefit for which Hashem sent you the hardship in the first place! Then all of the pain and sadness will **takeh** be for no reason — and that's **takeh** a real shame!

After you finish your earthly life and everything is clear to you from the heavenly perspective, you will see how it was your life's challenges that consistently raised you higher and higher. Then you will really ask Hashem "WHY??? WHY did I not MERIT to receive MORE pain, MORE difficulty, and MORE troubles?!?"

Challenges are meant to drive you to become a stronger and more refined person. This life-change will improve and upgrade who you are and thereby help you move toward a more productive life, look forward to a satisfying eternal afterlife, and provide your children and grandchildren with merits for generations to come:

"יען אשר עשית את הדבר הזה:
כי ברך אברכך."

בראשית כה:טז

As the Torah says: "Because you [Avraham] did this incredible thing [surpassing the challenge of Akeidas Yitzchak] I shall certainly bless you!"

The blessings showered on Avraham for generations to come were bestowed upon him only as a direct result of his withstanding his incredible personal challenges sent specifically to him by Hashem — in order to give him the greatest payoff imaginable!

"כל יהודי נושא שליחות עליונה
שלמענה ירד לעולם למלא שליחות זו
ועל ידי הנסיונות שעובר – ממלא הוא שליחותו!"

ספר נתיבות שלום פרשת וירא עמוד קי"ז

Authentic Yiddishkeit understands that life's difficulties are NOT a distraction that gets in the way of your REAL life. On the contrary — those difficulties and challenges are what your life is REALLY all about! It is your specific hardships and challenges that SHAPE who you are and CARRY you to fulfill your personal mission in this world.

With so much to gain, if you had the spiritual guts, you would actually look forward to your next challenge!

17

THE RIGHT ATTITUDE

*Learning the correct way
to face life's challenges and difficulties*

"כי השם יתברך יוכיח
את **אשר יאהב** וירצה
להתנהג עמו כאב את הבן
שייסר אותו לטוב לו!"

רלב"ג משלי פרק ג:יב

*"Hashem chastises one whom
He loves and Hashem wants to
interact with us like a Father
who punishes and
corrects His beloved
son **in order to
improve
him!**"*

HASHEM

wanted us to be able to understand the hidden world ... so He created the visible world in the same way:

"כד ברא קודשא בריך הוא עלמא ברא ליה
כגוונא דלעילא למהוי דא בדיוקנא דעלמא דלעילא."
זוהר כרך ב' (שמות) פרשת פקודי דף רכא.

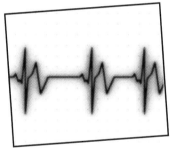

Everything in the physical world is an exact representation of the way things operate in the spiritual realm as well.

With this in mind, we must wonder: Why is it that when you look at an EKG (electrocardiogram) you see that the human heart is shown to go up and down?

"כי אצל האדם יש זמנים של עלי-ה וזמנים של ירידה ...
אחר כל עלי-ה ירידה! ואחר כך שוב עלי-ה!"
מאור עינים (פר' יתרו) מובא בנתיבות שלום שבועות שמ"ט

A normal healthy human life is comprised of cycles of ups and downs. After every "UP", you can be sure that there will be a "DOWN." After that "DOWN" you can rest assured that once again will come another "UP," then a "DOWN" and then an "UP" then "DOWN" then "UP" "DOWN" "UP" DOWN" "UP" "DOWN" "UP" ....

The very essence of the human existence is the experience of rising up and falling down. Once you "flat-line," your life is over.

AVRAHAM AVINU

"כאשר הבטיחו ה' בל ינסהו עוד - היינו שעל ידי העשרה נסיונות כבר
עלה אל אשר בחק האפשרי שיעלה, וכאשר ראה כל זה,
לכן עלה בדעתו שיסתלק מהעולם הזה ולכן השביע את אליעזר!"

ערבי נחל בראשית חיי שרה - דרוש ב'

After Avraham successfully endured his ten major life challenges,
Hashem assured him that he would not be put through any
additional challenges. Upon hearing that, Avraham assumed that
his life must be coming to an end! For with no opportunity to
meet challenges and prove his commitment to Hashem — what
purpose could there be to be alive?

MOSHE RABBEINU

We also find the same thing with Moshe Rabbeinu:

"האדם צריך להיות מהלך תמיד ממדריגה למדריגה.
ועל כן אמר משה רבינו ע"ה ביום מותו 'לא אוכל עוד לצאת ולבוא'
(דברים לא:ב). שאמר שאין לו שום עסק בעולם הזה כיון שלא יוכל
לצאת לא יוכל לבוא לדרגא גבוה יותר!"

מדברי פרי צדיק בראשית פרשת לך לך וקדושת שבת מאמר ד'

On the day that Moshe Rabbeinu left this world, he said: "I can
no longer go and come." This means that he had reached such
a high spiritual level of clarity that there was no longer anything
that could test his allegiance to Hashem. He could not "go" —
meaning to go away and FALL from his level, and then "come"
— meaning to come back to Hashem. Once the process of sinning
and returning was not applicable to him, he realized that his time
on this world was over.

A **stick** can be used for two completely opposite purposes. It can be used to **HIT** and **HURT** someone, or it can be used as a walking stick to **HELP SUPPORT** someone.

This is a great way to understand challenges; a נסיון/test/challenge/opportunity/gift/life is exactly like a stick: **IT IS UP TO YOU TO DECIDE** whether you will use it to **build** yourself up or **break** yourself down!

As Rav Sorotzkin said so eloquently: "A rock in your path can be either a stumbling block — or a stepping stone!"

Two people can go through the same exact pain and difficulty. One embraces it and grows from it, while the other becomes shattered by it and it destroys his life. Was it the painful situation that broke him — or was it his attitude?

"ואלמלא היה להם לב להבין
היה להם להתלהב ולהשתוקק ולכסוף באהבה עזה וחמדה
לקבל ההכאה באהבה וברוב חיבה תשוקה וחמדה
לחסות בנועם ה' **על ידי ההכאה זו!**"

קדושת לוי כללות הניסים

If you would have a **clear understanding**, you would **crave** and **yearn** with incredible desire to receive MORE rebuke, punishment, pain, and challenges from Hashem, for that is the most efficient way to ensure that you will become elevated and become closer to Hashem! After all — isn't that the purpose of your life?

Okay, of course you (probably) aren't on this amazingly high level, and it even sounds pretty absurd to a regular person like you and me.

However, when we internalize this concept into our very being, we will at least not shudder and cringe when we receive G-d-sent challenges. We can elevate our attitude to ACCEPT and (as much humanly possible) look forward to our next challenge. Why? Because we believe that these difficult times are truly OUR OPPORTUNITIES to reach heights that would otherwise be unattainable to us.

Authentic Yiddishkeit understands that when Hashem gives you a "נסיון." He is actually extending an invitation to build the next floor of your personal skyscraper. Your job is to accept the situation and build yourself up by facing the challenge and overcoming it to the best of your ability.

With the proper understanding, you can learn to accept and even smile when you encounter painful situations. Really? Yup! You would even smile if you were bitten by a snake! Nooooo waaaaay!!!! Way!

POISONOUS SNAKES AND HAPPINESS

The Torah tells us that in the desert the Yidden sinned against Hashem and were consequently attacked by vicious poisonous snakes. Many people died. The survivors ran to Moshe and pleaded with him to pray for them to be saved. Moshe prayed to Hashem and Hashem commanded him to make a copper snake and display it before the people:

”והיה אם נשך הנחש את איש
והביט אל נחש הנחשת וחי“

במדבר פרק כא:ט

"And whoever will be bitten by a snake shall gaze
at the copper snake and he will live."

There is one truly amazing word in this *pasuk*. Can you guess which one it is?

(Hint: It rhymes with "shmihuyuh"!)

”ויהי־ה לשון שמחה.“

מדרש בראשית רבה מב:ג

The word "ה-והי" is used in the Torah as an expression of **joy** and **happiness**!

Now that we know this important fact, let's reread the *pasuk* in the right spirit: "And whoever shall be **HAPPILY** bitten by a snake ...."! HEY!!! Hang on a second .... **HAPPILY BITTEN?** What can possibly be **HAPPY** about being bitten by a snake!?

SWEET POISON

Can you imagine the scene: Reuven was screaming in pain and knew that he could die because of the venom soaring through his veins from the poisonous snake that just bit him. He was so HAPPY about this that he asked his wife to mark the occasion by baking a special "snake cake"!

"והי-ה לשון **שמחה** על הנשיכה
לצד **התועליות** הנמשכות מהבטת אל נחש הנחושת ...
אשר יכיר בהם בעל הנס!"

אור החיים הקדוש במדבר פרק כא:ט

Let's understand: The snake only bit someone who rebelled against Hashem. Now just imagine for a moment how incredibly "off track" this guy must have been to actually speak out against Hashem!

But after this person was bitten by a poisonous snake and knew that he would surely die, he ran to be miraculously healed by Hashem through gazing upon the copper fake-snake that Moshe Rabbeinu posted. That certainly set him straight!

Once saved, this open miracle brought him to recognize his great sin and repent! Once healed from his crooked ways, his life was changed for the better and he then certainly thanked Hashem for this second chance to live a pious life! He went from "poison" to "pious"!

Now we can understand why the biting itself is referred to with a term reflecting "happiness" — for this was a great event in this person's life!

TURNING POINT

Simcha was spiraling out of control. At fifteen years old he already became an all-out rebel. It was on a snowy Friday night that his life took a major turn. He stole his father's car and picked up some friends. He was driving way too fast without paying attention to the icy roads. Music blaring throughout the smoke-filled car, he tore up the winding dark country road. On a sharp curve, he hit an icy patch and lost control of the car. The car was spinning around ... everyone was screaming ... the car flipped over and rolled ... windows shattering, and it jumped the guard rail ... falling off a cliff ... the car fell almost 200 feet. Silence. Simcha blacked out for almost an hour and woke up to the EMT first responder. They managed to pry him from the vehicle and strap him to a stretcher. They flew him by helicopter to the nearest emergency room. Over time, the pieces came together and the depth of the situation sank in. None of his friends survived. Simcha was the "lucky one" but he would lose both of his legs.

Ten years later, Reb Simcha — as he was now known — became one of the most inspirational leaders of the generation. He travelled to every Yiddishe neighborhood and dedicated his time to reach out to every rebellious teenager. No one was as effective as Reb Simcha in helping troubled teens. He did more good than anyone in his generation and brought back thousands of kids to the path of Torah. He would emotionally say that his personal road to a successful happy life began on that cold icy night. Losing his legs ... is what got him to change his direction and walk — no — run — toward Hashem.

NOW HERE'S THE ICING ON THE SNAKE CAKE!

"לשון 'יהיה' שהיא אותיות שם 'יהו־ה'

שהוא רחמים גמורים תמיד מורה על השמחה."

לחם לפי הטף

The letters of וה־י־ה are the same as the letters of: יהו־ה that always represents the pure MERCY of Hashem! This proves (once and for all!) that the event of the sinner being bitten by the poisonous snake was a GIFT from a MERCIFUL LOVING FATHER!

YOU AND ME

So too with each and every one of us: Every time we experience any kind of difficulty or challenge, we must strive to look at it with the attitude of **happiness**, since we believe that this is a tailor-made **OPPORTUNITY** to improve our lives and straighten ourselves out.

"ואוהבו שחרו מוסר (משלי יג)

זה הקב"ה שאהב את ישראל דכתיב (מלאכי א')

אהבתי אתכם אמר ה' שהוא מרבה אותן ביסורין!"

שמות רבה (וילנא) פרשה א'

When Shlomo HaMelech says that "a loving father is one who chastises his child," he is referring to Hashem Who loves Klal Yisrael so much and therefore He constantly makes them suffer.

At first glance we would wonder HOW constantly making someone suffer is the PROOF that Hashem loves us.

But we already understand that inner growth is the **KEY** to living a worthwhile life that you will ultimately be proud of. Therefore, the chance to attain inner growth — which can only happen by going through various challenges — is a **gift** and an **opportunity** presented to us by Someone Who cares about us and wants us to grow.

"אמר הקב"ה לישראל: בני
לא תהיו סבורים שאני עושה אתכם כעבד
שאדונו מבקש למכור אותו קוריסין בכל מה שמוצא
אלא כך אני מביא עליכם יסורין עד שתכינו את לבבכם אצלי!"

דברים רבה ג:ב

Hashem says to Klal Yisrael: "My **child**, don't think that I am treating you like a slave whom I want to sell and discard; rather the only reason I bring suffering upon you is so that you should properly refine your heart to better serve Me."

After a person realizes how much he benefited from the painful experience, he will surely give thanks to Hashem for sending him this difficult, yet life-altering growth process which *helped* re-route his GPS and led him to a more elevated level of faith and purpose.

Authentic Yiddishkeit believes that a person who is **fortunate** enough to be "bitten" by Hashem is ...

18

ACCEPTANCE

*How to digest your challenge
without getting indigestion*

"לעולם יהא אדם רגיל
לומר כל דעביד רחמנא
לטב עביד!"

תלמוד בבלי מסכת ברכות דף ס:

*"A person should always
be ready to say that
whatever Hashem
does is for the
good!"*

HASHEM

sometimes challenges us in order to see
how we will internally react to the test:

"ודע אחי: כי העשר נסיונות שנסה המקום את אברהם אבינו,
לא היינו משבחים לו עמדו בהם
לולי שהיה מקבל הכל מאלהיו **ברצון ובטוב לבב**!"

ספר חובות הלבבות שער ח' שער חשבון הנפש פרק ג'

We would not praise Avraham Avinu for passing the ten challenges had he not truly **ACCEPTED** them with a willing and open heart. As it says: "And his **heart** was found to be loyal before You."

"וישכם אברהם **בבקר**!"

בראשית פרק כב:ג

When Hashem commanded Avraham to sacrifice (=kill, =murder) his beloved child as some kind of spiritual offering, the Torah testifies: "Avraham woke up early in the morning!" Why? Because he was **excited** to be able to serve and fulfill the will of Hashem!

"והעלהו שם לעלה,
לא אמר לו שחטהו, לפי שלא היה חפץ הקב"ה לשחטו
אלא שיעלהו להר לעשותו עולה, ומשהעלהו אמר לו הורידהו."

רש"י פרשת וירא כב:ב

The truth is that technically speaking, Hashem never even told Avraham to actually KILL Yitzchak; He only said to "**bring him up** to the altar for an offering." Avraham could have tried to wiggle out of the situation by claiming that he was not commanded to actually slaughter his child, only to "set him upon the altar."

Yet Avraham realized that if Hashem told him to "bring him up," then Hashem's will was probably that Yitzchak should actually be slaughtered — and therefore he was ready to do that for Hashem — even though he was not specifically commanded to do so!

"כשם שהיה לי להשיבך ולא אמרתי לך כלום
רבונו של עולם אתמול אמרת כי ביצחק יקרא לך זרע, ועכשיו אתה אומר
והעלהו שם לעולה, וכבשתי יצרי ולא השבתיך, אף אתה כשיהיו בניו של
יצחק חוטאים לפניך ונכנסים לצרה, זכור להם עקדת יצחק אביהם
וסלח להם ופדה אותם מצרותם!"

מדרש תנחומא (בובר) פרשת וירא סימן מו

After the Akeida, Avraham prayed to Hashem: Even though I could have questioned You; first You told me that Yitzchak would carry on my legacy, and then You commanded me to slaughter him thereby ending that promise!? — and yet I didn't, in that merit may my descendants be forgiven and spared even when they sin before You and deserve to be punished.

This shows us that the main merit earned by Avraham was not for being ready to execute his beloved child, but for **not internally questioning** an apparent contradiction in Hashem's words.

In fact, a few of the ten challenges received by Avraham did not actually require ANY action at all. The entire challenge was to see if he would internally ACCEPT the way Hashem ran his life:

"הנסיונות של 'ויהי רעב בארץ'
ומה שנלקחה שרה לבית פרעה ובית אבימלך
שבכלל לא היו ענינים שבבחירה ורק שלא הרהר אחר הקב"ה!"

ספר נתיבות שלום לך לך ס"ט

The challenges of being directed by Hashem to travel to specific places, only to be greeted by a famine or by having his wife abducted, was not a test to see if Avraham would do or not do something; it was only to see if Avraham would **question** Hashem within his own mind and heart.

ELI HAKOHEN

"וַיַּגֶּד לוֹ שְׁמוּאֵל אֶת כָּל הַדְּבָרִים וְלֹא כִחֵד מִמֶּנּוּ.
וַיֹּאמַר: ה' הוּא – הַטּוֹב בְּעֵינָיו יַעֲשֶׂה!
מצודת דוד: הֲלֹא הוּא ה' וְהַכֹּל שֶׁלּוֹ וְיַעֲשֶׂה הַטּוֹב בְּעֵינָיו
כִּי מִי יוּכַל לוֹמַר לוֹ מֶה תַּעֲשֶׂה!"

שמואל א:ג

When the prophet Shmuel told Eli HaKohen that Hashem had decreed that Eli's two sons will both die on the same day and ALL of his descendants for all generations to come will always die before they turn 18, Eli's incredible gut reaction was: **"Hashem is the Master of everything, and He shall do as He sees fit, for who can tell Hashem what is best to do."**

DOVID HAMELECH

"וּכְמוֹ שֶׁהֵשִׁיב דָּוִד לַאֲבִישַׁי בֶּן צְרוּיָה בְּעֵת שֶׁרָצָה לִנְקֹם עֲבוּרוֹ מֵאֵת שִׁמְעִי
בֶּן גֵּרָא עַל שֶׁחֵרֵף וְגִדֵּף לְדָוִד וְקִלְּלוֹ קְלָלָה נִמְרֶצֶת לֹא הִנִּיחוֹ דָוִד וַאֲמַר 'ה
אָמַר לוֹ קַלֵּל וְגוֹ'" וְאָמְרוּ חז"ל **שֶׁעֲבוּר זֶה נִמְנוּ בְּבֵית דִּין שֶׁל מַעְלָה
וּמִנּוּהוּ לְדָוִד שֶׁיְּהֵא הָרְבִיעִי מַרְגְּלֵי הַמֶּרְכָּבָה!"**

ספר שמירת הלשון שער התבונה פרק ו'

When Shimmy ben Gayra cursed Dovid HaMelech and tried to stone him, Dovid's general Avishai ben Tzruyah wanted to kill him. However Dovid HaMelech did not allow Avishai ben Tzruyah to touch him and said: **"Hashem put into his mind to curse and try to hurt me."**

Chazal teach us that because of this incident of incredible tolerance and acceptance of G-d's will, the heavenly angels appointed Dovid to be the fourth leg to carry the chariot of Hashem.

BRINGING IT HOME

The same applies to each one of us. There are some challenges that do not require any **ACTION** on our part; in fact it is specifically through **INACTION** and **acceptance** that the person grows.

Sure you believe that Hashem is good ... it makes sense ... but when you take a step on the street and your foot goes right into a deep puddle of mud and then you fall and bang your head ... you get a ticket or stub your toe ... you may start to think, "Why is Hashem out to get me?" And of course, things can get much worse ... and thus more challenging. We see innocent children die and pious good people suffer ... and all of this challenges our core belief in a GOOD MERCIFUL G-d Who knows exactly how to run the world ... and our lives.

In fact, some of the greatest challenges we get are specifically regarding this belief. The human brain is programmed to respond to pain and difficulty with anger and opposition. Overcoming that with a firm belief in a loving and merciful G-d is in itself the **growth process** leading to becoming a spiritually elevated human being.

Imagine a scale of 1-100: 1 being the least amount of tolerance and acceptance of Hashem's decrees and 100 being the absolute highest. As you go through life, you will be given MANY different opportunities to raise yourself to a higher level.

When you get a level "10" test and you pass — you prove that when something goes "a little wrong" — you can maintain your faith in a loving G-d who is giving you this pain for your benefit. But what about when you are hit with a "30" or "50" — can you still stay strong?

Whenever you feel that you are being tested — think about what LEVEL the test is on and celebrate the fact that by MAINTAINING YOUR COMMITMENT — you have truly GROWN in the biggest way humanly possible.

Your job is to build up, strengthen, and empower your faith and trust in Hashem, to overpower your intuitive human attitude to complain when things don't go your way.

WHAT HELPS YOU COPE WITH STRESS?

   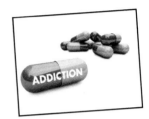

"המדה של שמח בחלקו, שיהודי שמח ומרוצה מהנהגתו יתברך,
שיודע דכל מה דעביד רחמנא לטב עביד ושמח בחלקו שהוא חלק אלוק
ממעל, היא המדה היותר גדולה מכל המדות ונפלאות היא פועלת בלב
האדם, שזה תכלית הכל שיהודי יהיה שמח ומרוצה בהנהגת הבורא!"

נתיבות שלום עניני פורים מאמר א'

The trait of being "Happy with your lot in life" means that you are internally pleased and satisfied with HOWEVER Hashem manages your life. For you believe that WHATEVER Hashem decides will happen to you, is for your GOOD. Living like this does **wonders for your heart** as it takes away your **heartache and pain** when life is not going well.

ACCOUNT MANAGER

Henry Farber transferred all of his assets to a brand-new hedge fund with brokers who claimed that they could earn 20% profit a year.

After several months the vice president of the fund called Henry. "Mr. Farber, I am calling to see if you are satisfied with Ron, your account manager. Is he handling your assets properly or do you feel that someone else can do a better job?"

In the same way, every person must ask himself: "Am I happy with my account manager — Hashem? Am I satisfied with the way that He is running my life, or do I think that maybe I can do a better job myself?

"וזהו פירוש חז"ל:

כל האומר פרק שירה בכל יום מובטח לו שהוא בן עולם הבא;

היינו שהוא מרוצה תמיד מהנהגת הבורא יתברך שמו

ומקבלה בשמחה ומאמין שהנהגת הבורא כולה לטובה -

הרי זה 'בן עולם הבא' פירוש: גם בחייו בעולם הזה

הריהו כבר שרוי בעולם הבא!"

ספר נתיבות שלום חלק ב' רפ"ט

Now we can uncover an enlightened understanding of the words of Chazal: "Whoever sings praise to Hashem **every day** is guaranteed to have a portion in the World to Come."

We all have ups and downs, good days and bad days, happy days and sad days; if you can sing praise to Hashem EVERY SINGLE DAY which means that you can be happy with even the "difficult" days ... **then you are already in paradise!**

"וכל החיים יודוך סלה;

כלומר, שתמיד אנו מודים להקב"ה על 'כל החיים' ['אויף דעם גאנצן לעבען'], היינו על **כל** מה שיש בחיים ועל **כל** מקרה בחיים שלנו!"

ספר נתיבי אמת עניני תפילה

Authentic Yiddishkeit understands that ACCEPTANCE is your ticket to attaining the highest level, both on this world and in the Next World! And that is precisely why the ULTIMATE GOAL of every Yid — even you — is to build up your TRUST in the absolute goodness of Hashem, so that regardless of **WHATEVER** MAY COME YOUR WAY — you can react with FEELING that Hashem, Who is full of mercy, compassion, and unconditional love for you, is now giving you some kind of unique gift and opportunity that is for YOUR GOOD.

"אם יהודי שמח ומרוצה בהנהגת הבורא עמו,

וגם כשכואב לו מאד יודע

שאם הקדוש ברוך הוא מתנהג עמו כך הרי זה טוב,

ושמח בהנהגתו יתברך,

אזי מדה כנגד מדה גם הקדוש ברוך הוא

מקבל אותו איך שהוא מתנהג **ומוחל לו**!"

תורת אבות מובא בנתיבות שלום עניני פורים

If you learn to **happily accept** the way Hashem manages your life, and even when you are in a lot of pain, you believe that since this is what Hashem decided for you, it **MUST BE** what is **BEST** for you (otherwise — why would He do it!?), then in the very same way, Hashem will **HAPPILY ACCEPT YOU** even if you have sinned against Him, and He will FORGIVE YOU for all of your sins!

"וזה התיקון הגדול ביותר לענינים שתשובה אינה מועלת עליהם,

לקבל את הנהגת הבורא בשמחה ורצון."

תורת אבות מובא בנתיבות שלום עניני פורים

This is an incredible "back-door pass" to be **forgiven** for sins that are extremely difficult to repent for!

Every Jew can spot a good deal ...
and this is a really

GREAT DEAL!

19

PERFORMANCE &
PERFECTION

*Understanding how to properly
evaluate and grade yourself*

"כי שבע יפול צדיק
וקם!"

משלי כד:טז

*"The righteous man gets
knocked down seven
times — yet still
he gets up!"*

HASHEM

does not expect the same result
from every person:

"אין הקב"ה
בא עם בריותיו בטרוניא
ולא נתן להם חקים כדי ליגען
וכדי לטרדן מן העולם ... ואין
הקב"ה מביא את האדם בדין
אלא על דבר שנצטוה ובידו כח
לעשות (כדי) שידו מגעת ...."

פסיקתא זוטרתא (לקח טוב) במדבר
פרשת נשא דף פט.

Hashem does not make impossible demands on people and He did not give us rules and regulations to destroy our quality of life. Hashem would never ask someone who has a broken back to lift a 400-pound weight and carry it for a mile!

"שהרי הקרבנות לא אמר לישראל
להביא איל וצבי ויחמור אלא מן הגדלים בעדרו."

פסיקתא זוטרתא (לקח טוב) במדבר פרשת נשא דף פט.

The proof is that when Hashem commanded us to sacrifice animals, He did not ask us to bring animals that were hard to find or hard to catch!

Can you imagine an old Jewish Rabbi with a white beard running after a deer because he wants to bring a sacrifice? Or wrestling with a hippopotamus to shlep him up the ramp of the Mizbei'ach (altar) and try to slaughter him with his fingernail? Or imagine if you had to catch a tiger! Or an alligator ... or a shark! Yoiysh! This would be a DANGEROUS RELIGION!

Throughout your life, you will face various challenges. Sometimes you will stand up to them and other times you won't. Your job is to do the best you can, and when you fall (and you will) your mission is to then GET UP!

The right way to look at it is that you get paid (for example) $100.00 for every time you get hit and don't fall down, but you get $1,000.00 for every time you fall down and then you GET BACK UP AGAIN!

As long as you don't give up and keep trying **YOUR** hardest in any given situation — then you are doing the will of Hashem and you are a **HERO!**

SO WHAT DOES HASHEM WANT FROM US?

HE WANTS US TO TRY AND NEVER STOP TRYING!

"מי יכול להגיע לתשובה כהלכתה? אך הרי מחוייבים לשוב בתשובה –
אלא הדרך כמאמר חז"ל לגבי חמץ: 'בודק בחורין ובסדקין **עד מקום
שידו מגעת',** וביאור הדברים, שאם יהודי בודק **עד מקום שידו מגעת הרי**
עשה חובתו, אבל אם גם זאת לא עשה וכלל לא בדק
לא יצא ידי חובת מצות בדיקה."

ר' נח מלכוביץ זי"ע מובא בספר נתיבות שלום חלק ב' עמוד רל"ב

Before Pesach we are commanded to search for and destroy any bread in our possession. However, if you have a hole in your floor or wall, how are you supposed to retrieve every crumb? Are you supposed to start breaking your house down in order to find every last tiny crumb? Are you meant to act like an undercover agent searching for every terrorist hiding in the mountainous terrain of the Pakistani border?

Certainly not! The only requirement is for you to check "as far as your hand can reach." If you have short stubby hands with thick fingers that can't fit into the small cracks — then you do not need to call a skinny-fingered friend to come help you!!! As long as you try to the best of your ability and truly search for those crumbs as much as you can, then you have **fulfilled your obligation** even if there are crumbs in the walls or floors!

THE SAME APPLIES TO ALL ASPECTS OF SERVING HASHEM:

If you take it seriously and really try **"YOUR"** hardest, according to **YOUR CURRENT ABILITY** — not someone else's ability and not even your ability on a different day — **YOUR CURRENT ABILITY** — then you have **fulfilled your ENTIRE responsibility!**

JUDGING EFFORT

Reb Feivel was a sixth-grade Rebbi for over 30 years. As usual, he sat down in the quiet teacher's office to mark the latest test, when suddenly he fell into a deep sleep. He dreamed that an old man with a long, flowing white beard appeared and offered to assist him with marking the tests.

As they went over each test, the answer each boy wrote was mysteriously blank and in its stead a number magically appeared that rated how much effort the boy put into finding the correct answer. The old man taught Reb Feivel the mystical secret of how to mark each test based only on the effort each boy put into the test! When the Rebbi handed out the graded tests — boy, were the boys shocked!

Just imagine if Hashem would grade our tests in school! The brilliant boy who easily remembers everything and has the ability to spit out all the information with virtually no effort would be shocked at his weak grade. Whereas the child who always tries so hard but is up against so many obstacles would also be amazed at his fantastic mark! In Hashem's eyes, it is this student who is the מצויין (excellent student) and he is the one who **truly deserves** to be the valedictorian of the class!

UNLIMITED TOLERANCE

Ari was looking for a supervisor to oversee his many companies. Tovya, a sharp and capable fellow, had been out of work for over a year and applied for the job. The interview went extremely well and Ari agreed to pay Tovya a salary of $180,000 a year plus benefits. After the first week, Tovya came into Ari's office, huffing and puffing.

He said, "Listen, Ari, I'm so appreciative that you hired me but I have a big problem ... my wife just became ill and needs to be hospitalized for at least six months! I have no one to help me with my ten kids! I need to get them to school every day, do the shopping for them ... cook supper for them ... there is just no way that I can work every day for a full day!"

Ari looked at Tovya compassionately, and said, "Don't worry about it — I completely understand your situation. Just come in for a few minutes each day and I'll keep your salary and bonus exactly the same!"

After a few more weeks, Tovya approached Ari's once again. "I have bad news ... the doctor said that my wife needs to live in a warmer climate, so we must move to California and I won't be able to come in to work anymore!"

Ari looked at Tovya with tremendous compassion and said, "Oh — don't worry about it! Just come in whenever you can, even if it is just ONE day a year! And don't worry — I will keep your salary AND your bonus in place!"

* Note: please do NOT try this with your boss!

Doesn't it sound IMPOSSIBLE for a boss to react that way? Would you like to have a boss who is as understanding as Ari? Well, guess what? YOU HAVE ONE!

THINK ABOUT THE FOLLOWING:

"וְהָגִיתָ בּוֹ יוֹמָם וָלַיְלָה."

יהושע א:ח

We are obligated to learn Torah ALL day and ALL night. When it comes to marking your diligence in Torah study, what do you honestly think your grade will be? How many hours do you really learn a day and how many at night? Do you even come close to learning "ALL" day and "ALL" night? If not, do you think there is any way that you could be rewarded for learning ALL day and ALL night?

"דהיינו **למאן דאפשר** אבל למאן דלא אפשר -
כל הקורא קריאת שמע שחרית וערבית בכוונה
מעלה עליו הכתוב כאלו קיים והגית בו יומם ולילה!"

מנחות צט:

You bet! The commandment to learn ALL day and night is ONLY for someone who CAN! However one who cannot do so can fulfill his obligation by properly reciting *krias Shema* once in the morning and once at night, and Hashem considers it the same **AS IF YOU LEARNED TORAH ALL DAY AND ALL NIGHT!** (WOW! That's a pretty awesome deal!)

"אכן קריאת שמע שחרית וערבית
אין הכוונה כמו שאנו מתפללים אלא בתפלה בכוונה כראוי
נמצא שגם זה אי אפשר לכל אדם לעשות עבור הטרדות והמניעות."

ערבי נחל דברים שבת ר"ח אלול

But hang on a minute — what if it's simply TOO difficult for you to properly concentrate for the few minutes that it takes you to recite *Shema* each morning and night? Is there NO OTHER WAY for you to fulfill your obligation to learn Torah ALL morning and ALL night?

"והקב"ה רחום וחנון חפץ חסד הוא והמציאו חז"ל תרופה
ודרש רבי יוחנן (חגיגה ה:) מאי דכתיב 'ואותי יום יום ידרושון' (ישעיה
נח:ב) וכי ביום דורשין ובלילה אין דורשין? אלא כל העוסק בתורה יום
אחד בשנה מעלה עליו הכתוב כאלו עסק כל השנה כולה!"

ערבי נחל דברים שבת ר"ח אלול

Don't worry! Hashem, the All Merciful, is on your side! He wants you to win the game of life! Therefore, if you study Torah just ONE day in the year — Hashem considers it as if you TOILED IN TORAH THE ENTIRE YEAR!

"כי מזה ניכר ונראה שברצונו לעסוק תמיד בדברי תורה
רק הדאגות אינן מניחות לו - ומצרף הקב"ה מחשבה כמעשה!
... וזהו מחסדי הקב"ה וצדקותיו."

ערבי נחל דברים שבת ר"ח אלול

For by giving up ONE day to sit and learn, you reveal that in truth your inner will is to learn ALL day EVERY day! You show that if you COULD you WOULD! Therefore, Hashem counts your inner desire as if you actually did it!

This is the supernatural, eternal, everlasting, perpetual, infinite, incredible kindness and understanding of Hashem!

Unlike anything that you will encounter in this physical world, Hashem only judges you by your **EFFORT — NOT BY RESULTS!** No two people are the same, and Hashem knows and completely understands each and every one of us, with all our flaws, deficiencies, and problems, and He judges us **only based on exactly what we are currently capable of doing!** WOWOWOWOWOWOW!

 **HEAVENLY GRADES** *Reb Feivel had an interesting way to mark the tests of his sixth-grade class. Each boy was judged only according to how much effort he put into his studies. No one knew why*

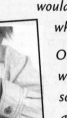

he did this, and when asked about this unique system, he would mutter something about an old man with a long white beard!

One day while marking the tests, Reb Feivel was faced with a difficult situation. Shloimie was going through so much in his life that if he had shown any effort at all, Reb Feivel would have given him 100. But he knew that poor Shloimel'eh had not put even one stitch of effort into this test. He had no choice but to give him a "0."

With a heavy heart Reb Feivel handed out the tests. As he got closer to little Shloimie, tears welled up in his eyes. Reb Feivel knew that Shloimie wished that he could concentrate and do well. He wished that he could have studied for the test and at least put in some effort so that he could have gotten a good grade based on his effort! With tears rolling down his cheeks, Reb Feivel handed Shloimie the test. Shloimie looked at the grade and with rosy cheeks and a big smile he said: "Oh, thank you, Rebbi!"

"Thank you Rebbi?" Reb Feivel was shocked and confused at Shloimie's elated response! The Rebbi looked at the paper and right there in front of the "0" was a "1" and a "0"! Shloimie had miraculously received "100" on his test! But how?

That night, the old man with a white beard appeared to Reb Feivel in his dream. "Ah, Feivel, Feivel ... you should have known that for this specific boy in his specific situation, giving it 'all he got' was just pushing himself to show up to school! I'm the one who added the 1 and the 0 to his mark!"

THIS IS THE WAY OUR LOVING FATHER IN HEAVEN GRADES OUR LIFE!

"אמר רבי יהושע בן לוי:
כל העונה אמן יהא שמיה רבא מברך **בכל כחו**
קורעין לו גזר דינו."

תלמוד בבלי מסכת שבת דף קיט:

If someone says "*Amein, may His great Name be blessed, etc* ... " with all **"HIS"** energy, all evil decrees against him are ripped up.

"דקדקו בזה לומר 'בכל כחו' ולא אמרו ב'כח גדול' וכדומה
להורות שכל הנדרש מן האדם הוא לעבוד בכל הכוחות שברשותו!
ואף אם הוא חלש - די בכך שהתאמץ לפי מידת כוחו
ובזה כבר זכה לקריעת גזר־דינו"

נתיבי אמת על עניני תפילה

The Gemara does not say, whoever praises Hashem "the loudest" or "the best"; rather, it just says "with all of **YOUR** strength." This is to teach us that you are not being compared to anyone else! But even more so, you are not even compared to YOURSELF at other times! If you feel weak and you push yourself to reach your current maximum concentration level, you have fulfilled all that is required of you, and you can successfully shatter any evil decree!

TWISTED REALITY

If we would look around a shul and watch how each person davens, we would most likely award "Best Davener" to the person who "looks" like he is davening the best; shukkeling, saying the words out loud, all into it, etc. .... But when Hashem judges us, He may very well pick someone completely different. There may be a person sitting in the back who is hardly into it but he pushed himself to just "show up," or someone who is having tremendous difficulty concentrating but he manages to keep trying to pull himself together whenever he possibly can.

"כי בעבודתו ובהתאמצותו על אף חולשתו
חביב הוא ביותר בעיני הקב"ה ודי בכוחותיו הדלים
לפעול אותה סגולה שהגיבור זוכה בה רק בהשקעת כוחות מרובים!"

נתיבי אמת על עניני תפילה

Even when your service is lacking in physical or emotional strength, it is lovingly accepted by Hashem and calculated according to the EFFORT that you exerted in performing this service. Therefore, your weak service can accomplish AS MUCH as what another person who is stronger can only accomplish with much more work.

We need to internalize that our Creator does not require **perfection**. Had Hashem wanted perfection, He would have created robots instead of humans! Then we would never mess up! We would ALWAYS show up on time for davening! We'd NEVER talk Loshon Hora! We would ALWAYS control our desires — actually — we wouldn't even HAVE desires!

Authentic Yiddishkeit believes that all that is required of you is to do the BEST that YOU can do at that particular moment! Therefore, when you feel that you have no energy in you — whether you are drained physically, mentally, emotionally, or even spiritually — you should be inspired when you realize that all you have to do right now is push yourself with whatever energy you can muster up, and with that seemingly "small" service you can hit 100% of your requirement from Hashem's perspective!

The reason that this is such a foreign concept to us is because NOTHING in our world works this way! School doesn't work this way, relationships don't work this way, and your job certainly doesn't work this way!!! Therefore, from when we are young children it is ingrained in us that we only get credit for what we ACCOMPLISH!

AN UPHILL BATTLE

The new dynamic camp director always came up with exciting night activity games. One night he picked five of the strongest counselors and brought them onto the camp

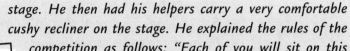

stage. He then had his helpers carry a very comfortable cushy recliner on the stage. He explained the rules of the competition as follows: "Each of you will sit on this cushy recliner for five minutes and you will get a point for every time that you stand up. But of course, there is a catch ...." He then called up Shmerel Schmerling, the weakest, nerdiest kid in camp. Shmerry walked onto the stage, holding his suspenders while chewing on a pen cover and proudly waved to everyone. "Shmerryberry [as he was fondly called] will stand in front of you and keep pushing you down, making it really hard for you to stand up. You job is to stand up in spite of his efforts to push you down." This didn't look so hard. A strong 280 lb, 6'2", 23-year-old counselor, against a scrawny 100 lb, 4'8", 10-year-old boy.

You were one of the five mighty counselors chosen. Your turn came and you sat into the deep cushy recliner. Ready ... set ... go!!! It was so hard to muster up the strength to get out of the deep cushy cushion and try to stand, and since you were so off balance, all this puny weakling had to do is give you a small push and down you went! Your whole bunk was cheering you on — but it was just sooo hard to keep pulling yourself up. But you didn't give up. You kept trying but you kept ending up right where you started from! You realize that this is probably impossible — you will never be able to stand up against these odds — but you still didn't give up! You kept trying over and over to pull yourself up and out of the deep comfortable cushion and then try to stand ....

After your turn, the other contestants also had their turn and they also could not manage to actually stand up. Then the judge wanted to announce the winner. Everyone was confused because NONE of you actually managed to get up

even one time — so how could ANY of you be the winner!
But then he announced that YOU WON! Why? Because
the real game was to see how many times you would TRY
to once again face terrible odds and TRY to stand up!!!
You tried to get up more times than anyone else! So YOU
are the WINNER!

Authentic Yiddishkeit believes that FALLING doesn't show anything other than the Yetzer Hora was TOO strong for you to win! GETTING UP shows that your inner desire and strong will is to still be in the game of life!

All Hashem wants from you is to just keep trying...
and trying...
and trying...
and trying...
and trying...
and trying...
and trying...
and trying...
and trying...
and trying...

PARTING WORDS OF ENCOURAGEMENT:

"בעת שהאדם עומד נבוך ומייאש נגד
תכונות וטבעים שאינו רואה איך יוכל לשנותם:
גם בזה צריך בהירות הדעת
שלא עליך המלאכה לגמור,

ולא נצחונות דורשים ממך
אלא יגיעה ועבודה בכל כוחותיך!"

ספר נתיבות שלום חלק א' עמוד כ"ו

"When you find yourself confused and ready to give up
because you simply don't see how you can ever really change,
you need to have CLARITY to know that:
It is not incumbent upon you to FINISH working on yourself
and no one ever demanded VICTORY from you —
only that you to try hard and work with all your might!"

FACING THE BATTLE OF
YOUR LIFE

Every person is smack in the middle of an intense and fierce battle in which he is surrounded by the enemy from all sides!

‫"ונמצא שהוא‬
‫מושם באמת‬
‫בתוך המלחמה‬
‫החזקה ...‬
‫עד שנמצאת‬
‫המלחמה‬
‫אליו פנים‬
‫ואחור!"‬

מסילת ישרים פרק א'

20

HEART & SOUL

Understanding what
really *counts!*

"קוּדְשָׁא בְּרִיךְ הוּא
לֹא בָּעֵי מִינָן אֶלָּא:
לִבָּא!"

זוהר הקדוש חלק ג׳ קס.

*"Hashem wants just
one thing:
YOUR HEART!"*

HASHEM

**has the ability to set us free;
all we need to do is convince Him to help us!**

"במקום המחשבה
שם הוא האדם!"
בעל שם טוב זי"ע

A person's true place is **where his thoughts are**.

We are used to thinking in terms of the physical world. If you are physically at the Kosel in Yerushalayim — then that is WHERE YOU ARE; whereas if you are at work in Manhattan — then THAT is WHERE YOU ARE. But the truth is that "YOU" are not your "physical body," "YOU" are a soul and your soul is not confined to your physical location.

Therefore, even though YOU might be physically at work in Manhattan, "YOU" can transplant the real "YOU" to a completely different atmosphere and environment. "YOU" are NOT BOUND by the physical world to determine where YOU are.

So even when you are physically at work in your office or doing mundane tasks such as grocery shopping, YOU CAN REALLY BE at the cave of R' Shimon bar Yochai!

On the flip side, even when you are learning or *davening*, if your mind is "somewhere else" — then that is TRULY "WHERE" YOU ARE! Your BODY might be in shul — your lips might be muttering beautiful words — but "YOU" are "somewhere else"!

Therefore, as we talk about the fight that each of us has with our Evil Inclination, it is not ONLY applicable for the sins that you actually commit, it is also about the battle raging within your mindset!

GETTING INTO THE "SPIRIT"

The holy Torah is a **training manual** in which Hashem imparts to us the right way to live our lives. It is not just an instruction manual about what to do and what not to do — rather, a person should strive to digest and internalize the **spirit** of His Divine will.

If Hashem says that something is wrong, disgusting, depraved, sickening, etc. — if your mindset would be pure and holy, then you would internally FEEL the same way. If Hashem says that something is DANGEROUS for you and can cause you spiritual cancer, then you must not lust after it on ANY level.

Therefore, even if you are not actually acting out on a certain sin (which is super!) you might still be **bound** to it in your mind, and there is much work to be done to separate yourself — the real YOU — from the evil, bad corruption that has taken root in YOUR mind.

Authentic Yiddishkeit believes that true freedom is **TOTAL CONTROL** over not just your actions, but also your **MIND** — because your mind is **WHO YOU ARE**.

"אל תאמר שאין תשובה אלא מעבירות
שיש בהן מעשה כגון זנות וגנבה אלא כשם שצריך אדם לשוב מאלו
כך הוא צריך לחפש ב**דעות רעות** שיש לו ....."

רמב"ם פרק ז' מהלכות תשובה

A person should not think that he must repent only for **ACTS** of sin! Rather, a person must also repent for **THOUGHTS** of sin. In fact, THOUGHTS of sin are actually **more difficult** to rectify than ACTS of sin, because when a person is immersed in corrupt thoughts, it is very difficult to separate himself from them.

LET'S GET PRACTICAL

"ולא יסמוך במה שלא עבר עברה מימיו
הרי מסתמא כל כוחותיו קשורים בו יתברך - שאין ראיה לדבר...."

הרב הקדוש ר' מענדל מויטבסק זי"ע בפרי הארץ פרשת כי תשא

Even if there are sins that you have never succumbed to and you may feel that you have no practical connection to them — you may be more tied to them than you want to believe:

"כי אולי לא בא לידי נסיון
או מחמת שאר דברים המונעים אותו כמו הבושה או מה שיהיה,
מעתה מה בכך שלא עבר עברה אם שורש העון עצמו אינו נמחק מלבו
הרי קשור בו ... והרי הוא הוא!"

הרב הקדוש ר' מענדל מויטבסק זי"ע בפרי הארץ פרשת כי תשא

Listen carefully: Even if you never actually come to perform a certain sin, it is possible that the sin exists — alive and well — right there inside of you and it just never actually happened because the opportunity did not present itself! Maybe you were never truly challenged, or maybe you were too embarrassed to sin, or maybe there was some other reason that prevented you from acting out on your desires.

In other words, you might feel that you are 100 percent committed to Hashem. However, if in a certain situation you would sin, then although in the practical physical world you did not sin and you have no "action" to be sorry about, the fact still remains that there is a major breach in your loyalty to Hashem.

At the end of the day, that rebelliousness and unfaithfulness to purity and holiness are very much alive right there inside you — and you cannot claim that you are completely internally faithful to Hashem.

"כי האדם יראה לעינים וה' יראה ללבב!"

שמואל א' פרק טז:ז

A person's vision is limited to what he can see; however, Hashem sees all that is in a person's heart. (UH OH!)

TWO-FACED

Special Sergeant McGrady was the top bodyguard of the president of the United States. As he stood there with his hands on his AKA semiautomatic machine gun, he was dreaming about how much he would love someone to kill the president since he hated him so much!

As far as people can see, he is doing a wonderful job. However, what do you think would happen if the president would get a birthday present from NASA of the latest technologically advanced version of BTS (brain thought scanner) and it would openly reveal what the bodyguard is actually thinking?!

In the very same way, if Hashem tells us not to DO something — of course it's wonderful when we do not perform that sinful act. However, Hashem has one of those amazing "thought" scans — and He can see what we are thinking inside us!

TICKING TIME BOMBS

A sleeper cell refers to a cell, or isolated grouping of sleeper agents who belong to an intelligence network or organization. The cell "sleeps" (lies dormant) inside a target population until it receives orders or decides to act. While most Axis espionage agents sent to the UK during World War II were almost immediately caught and neutralized, a few, who had infiltrated an area long ahead of time, and set up a clock repair shop or something else innocent that was also near a naval base, were activated only when there was a specific operational requirement. Source: Wikipedia

Inside the crevices of your mind may lie "sleeper cells" of the evil enemy that consist of things that you have seen and thoughts you have had. Over time this corruption has taken root, gotten comfortable, and fortified itself within you. They may lie dormant for years living comfortably within your mindset, but if you don't **root them out**, they may surprise you someday.

WHO, ME?

This sheds light on why there are times a person can perform a sin that is really beneath the level he is on and he even shocks himself! He wonders, "Where did THAT come from?"

It is true that until now the sinful **action** may never have materialized, but in your imagination you have done this sin many, many times. In fact ... you can probably write a book on it! So if and when this sin rears its ugly head, don't act all that shocked and surprised — for this sin has been incubating inside you for years!

The whole point of Hashem teaching us in the Torah what "to do" and what "not to do," is in order to RAISE our mindset out of the gutter and to become elevated humans who think in line with what Hashem has taught us is correct and proper.

Hence, when Hashem says that something is WRONG or an ABOMINATION and you still dream about doing it (even though you will surely be rewarded for controlling your desires and not acting out on them), can you honestly say that your "mindset" is in line with G-d? Putting aside your "actions" for a moment, do you completely "think" and "feel" like a Yid should?

"וזה ענין מה שאמרו חכמינו זכרונם לברכה
'הרהורי עבירה קשים מעבירה' (יומא כט.)
כי הרהורי עבירה הם שרש הרע הנמצא בעצמותו!"

נתיבות שלום

Now we understand why "thoughts of sin" are considerably **more dangerous** than actual acts of sin. For these invisible secretive thoughts are where moral and ethical corruption have freely taken root inside you without restriction!

"... המחשבות הן נעלמות ואיש אינו יודע מזה
והריהו יכול ללמוד עם מחשבות [רעות] ולהתפלל עם מחשבות רעות
ולשבת עם אחים יחדיו **באין איש יודע מה שבלבו!**"

נתיבות שלום

Since no one knows what you are thinking, you can sit and learn Torah with impure thoughts flying around your mind, you can be *davening* with impure thoughts, you can be smack in the middle of mussar seder or you can be sitting at a Rebbe's "*tish*" and no one knows what is on your mind! (Except maybe the Rebbe!)

This is the danger of impure thoughts: Since they are not rooted in the physical world, they have no boundaries in time or space, and so they are **unlimited**!

"ואם כשאדם חוטא **במעשה** יש לו לכל הפחות שברון לב
יודע שעליו לחזור בתשובה הרי פי כמה קשים הם **הרהורי עבירה,**
שגם שברון לב אין מחמתם שאינם נחשבים בעיניו לחטא!"

נתיבות שלום

Additionally, when a person actually sins, at least he feels bad about what he did and knows that he must repent. But thoughts of sin are more difficult to eradicate because a person does not consider them to be "real" sins and so he doesn't feel so bad about them. Therefore, these thoughts slowly creep into your mind and become very much a part of you without the resistance you would put up toward actually DOING what you are thinking about!

"בפיך ובלבבך לעשותו (דברים ל:יד)
דלא כתיב 'ובמעשיך' שהעיקר מצד האדם הוא בלבבך ...."

פרי צדיק דברים לראש חודש אלול אות ג'

People say, "You are what you eat."
We now know that "you are what you think!"

"... הכל תלוי בלב כי בו משכן
הנשמה וכל האיברים גרירי בתריה!"

תורת חיים מסכת סנהדרין דף קו:

The reality is that **everything** depends on one's mind, for that is the home of the soul, and the physical limbs merely follow and carry out the will of the mind.

So whereas you might have originally wondered, "Hey — what's the difference what I am 'thinking'?", now we realize that ALL that really matters is WHAT YOU ARE THINKING! What you think is what you are! In fact, the only significance of your "actions" is because they are a physical manifestation and materialization of your thoughts!

And so, whether you have sinned and want to change your ways — or even if you have not brought out the sin but you know that beneath the surface you are CONNECTED to sin and you are not entirely committed to the way of Hashem, in both instances the solution is the same, because both problems stem from the same source: your corrupt mindset that is BOUND AND GAGGED!

SET ME FREE

"הוציאה ממסגר נפשי להודות את שמך!"

תהלים קמב

Dovid HaMelech writes:
"Release my soul from the chains that bind me,
so that I may praise your name."

THERE ARE TWO PARTS TO THIS MESSAGE:

1. Our pure holy soul is bound by thick chains preventing us from acting the way we truly want to act and being who we truly want to be.

If only these chains would be removed —
I would be sooo good!

2. A person who is bound and gagged cannot be satisfied and grateful for all the good that Hashem has given him.

If only these chains would be removed —
I would be able to truly appreciate all the good in my life!

ADDICTIVE MINDSET

When a person quits smoking, even though he doesn't "smoke" any more, he still has the mindset of a "smoker." He is a "smoker" fighting his addiction.

Similarly, there is a very big difference in the mindset of an obese person who lost weight and a naturally skinny person.

The same applies to any mindset that imposes itself on you. Even if you manage to control it — you are still an escaped slave at risk of being caught once again in the web of your addiction.

There are three types of people; IN CONTROL, OUT OF CONTROL, and CONTROLLED!

Our hero, Dovid HaMelech, taught us that we must cry out to Hashem: Have MERCY on me and UNCHAIN me so that I may be mentally and emotionally free to soar to you!

Ahhh ... how incredibly GOOD I would be ... how HAPPY I would be to serve You ... if only You would unbind me ... even just a little ... even for a short time ... I would run to You ... I would sing Your praises!

PROOF OF OWNERSHIP

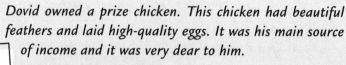

Dovid owned a prize chicken. This chicken had beautiful feathers and laid high-quality eggs. It was his main source of income and it was very dear to him.

One night Chaim stole the chicken and plucked out all the beautiful feathers so that Dovid would not to be able to identify his chicken.

The next day, Dovid realized that his chicken was missing and began searching desperately for it. Lo and behold — he found it in Chaim's chicken coop. He ran over to Chaim, grabbed him by the lapels, and demanded that he give it back to him! Chaim retorted: "Leave me alone — this is not your chicken!" Poor Dovid had no way to prove that this was his prized chicken, since his chicken had beautiful feathers and this one had no feathers at all! Dovid thought for a few moments and then responded; "I will prove to you that it's mine: If you open the door to the coop and let it roam free, you will see that it will come to me!"

Source: Dubna Maggid, Tehillim 117:16

We look very different today than we did 4,000 years ago when Hashem selected us to be His chosen nation and gave us His holy Torah, and we have certainly fallen very far from the lofty spiritual levels of holiness and purity of the golden days of our glorious history.

Yet as far as we may have strayed, we know deep down that if Hashem would release us from the thick bonds of the יצר הרע (Evil Inclination) that pollutes and contaminates us on a daily basis then — BOY-OH-BOY — would we run straight into His awaiting embrace!

LEARNING FROM A SEADOG

"כל שבים טהור חוץ מכלב המים מפני שהוא בורח ליבשה,
לפי שכל שאר בריות שבים אין אחד מהם בורח ליבשה

כשבאים לצוד אותם אלא כלב הים בלבד.״

ר׳ עובדיה מברטנורא משנה מסכת כלים יז:יג

Although the seadog spends MOST of its time in the ocean, since it runs to dry land when it senses danger, it is considered a LAND animal.

״אל מקום שאדם בורח בשעת צרתו

ניכר שׁשם שרשו!״

ר׳ צדוק הכהן מלובלין מובא בספר פתגמים נבחרים דף י״ד

This clearly drives home an incredible point: If you want to know a person's **essence**, don't focus on where he spends MOST of his time and how he USUALLY acts; rather, look at how he acts and where he runs when he senses that he is in danger! For that is the measure that correctly describes what the person is REALLY all about!

Where does a Yid run when he's in danger? He runs to Hashem! Danger breaks the chains that normally hold us back from running to Hashem. Once unbound, our true essence becomes revealed and we act the way we REALLY wanted to act ALL along.

AND SO WE INVITE YOU ON A JOURNEY

Fasten your seatbelt as we delve into your psyche to discover what is holding you down and preventing you from reaching your potential. Then you will be able to program your **GPS** and reach your **final destination!**

״ועל זה התפלל דוד המלך עליו השלום:

הוציאה ממסגר נפשי — **משעבוד לחדות!**״

נתיבות שלום עניני פסח מאמר י״ב אות ד׳ עמוד ע״ר

This is what Dovid HaMelech prayed for when he begged Hashem: "Release my soul from the chains that bind me!" Take me out from being mentally bound, overpowered, suppressed, restricted, and controlled — and set me psychologically free!

21

HINDSIGHT IS 20/20

*Enlightening our lives
by studying the past*

"גלות מצרים הי־ה
שורש לכל הגליות
לכן מזכירין בכל יום
יציאת מצרים."

שפת אמת פרשת שמות תרל"ג

*"The Egyptian exile is the
foundation of all future exiles.
This is why we mention
the redemption
from Egypt
every single
day."*

HASHEM

**rescued us from the intense
slavery of Mitzrayim:**

"ומן הידוע שהיו ישראל במצרים
רעים וחטאים מאד!"

רמב"ן שמות פרק י"ב

Chazal teach us that when we were in Mitzrayim,
we sank to a very low spiritual level.

HOW BAD WERE WE?

"כשמת יוסף:
הפרו **ברית מילה** – אמרו: **נהיה כמצרים!**"

שמות רבה (וילנא) פרשה א'

After Yosef died, we stopped performing a *bris* on our children!

Why? Because we wanted to **be like** the Egyptians!

"כל מצרים מטונפת **מעבודת כוכבים** שלנו!"

שיר השירים רבה פרשה ב'

Furthermore, the land of Egypt was FULL of our idols!

"ותמלא 'הארץ' אותם:
נתמלאו **בתי טרטראות ובתי קרקסאות** מהם!"

מדרש אגדה שמות פרק א:ז

And ... the theaters and clubs were filled with Yidden!

I'm sure you get the picture — and it sure ain't pretty! During the first 100+ years that we lived in Egypt, **before** they began to persecute us, we became deeply entangled with the Egyptian people; socializing with them at their theaters, partying with them at their clubs, worshiping idols, and generally living like our Egyptian neighbors.

"בשביל ג' דברים נגאלו ממצרים:
שלא שינו שמם, ולשונם, ומלבושם!"

מדרש ויקרא רבא לב:ה מובא בספר מנחם ציון פרשת בשלח

Yet, amazingly, we did manage to keep three things: our Jewish names, our Jewish language, and our Jewish dress code! Now, even though keeping these three distinctions is what gave us the merits we needed in order to bring about our redemption, let us imagine how ridiculously confused we were:

"ונתאר לעצמינו היאך הי-ה נראה:
הולך לו היהודי לעת ערב ונכנס לבית הטאטראות
לרקוד כשהוא לבוש בלבוש שחורים ואולי אפילו 'שטריימל' לראשו!
לנגדו עומד המצרי עם לבושו הדק וכך הם רוקדים יד ביד ומשתכרים!"

ספר לב שלום מר' שלום שבדרון זי"ע פרשת שמות

Try to imagine what the scene looked like: A Yid went out at night to party at the new Egyptian disco "Mubarakoo." But since he didn't change his dress code, he wore his black pants, white shirt, and even perhaps his *shtreimel* as he partied the night away, dancing hand in hand with the scantily clad Egyptians, while getting drunk with them! (Some *melaveh malkah* that was!)

IDENTITY CRISIS

As Laibel entered the club, the lights and sounds hit him in the face. He spotted his buddy Chaim Yoisef dancing wildly right in the middle of a whole group of goyim, with a bottle of Old Williamsburg in his hand and his curly payos bouncing up and down.

Chaim Yoisef excitedly called out to him in perfect Yiddish: "Nee Laiybel'e — kimm chap a rikeedah!" (Come dance!)

(Egypt 2238 or America 5838?)

The sad fact is that after living in Egypt for 210 years, our spiritual situation had thoroughly deteriorated as we drifted far off the path of our holy ancestors. We were ALL "at risk"!

Unfortunately, the concept of living a spiritually uplifted Yiddishe life and the dream that one day Hashem would appoint us to be His chosen people had all but faded away. We were shattered and battered physically, emotionally, and spiritually.

Throughout our long, bloodstained history of exile, there were many times that we, Klal Yisrael, found ourselves under the authority of murderous tyrants. They abused their superior physical power to oppress us with harsh decrees in order to prevent us from learning Torah and performing mitzvos (commandments).

For example, in the time of the miracle of Chanukah, the Greeks did not allow us to learn Torah, perform mitzvos, or even perform a *bris* on a newborn child! These "atrocities" were punishable by death! Even in recent times, the Communists outlawed circumcision and didn't let us follow our Torah! These "atrocities" were punishable by life in prison!

Yet the response of the Jewish nation to those difficult circumstances was always to show our steadfast willingness to risk our lives to fulfill G-d's commandments and sanctify Hashem's name!

QUESTION #1

"הרי לא מצינו שהכריחו אותם המצרים
לעבור על התורה, והיתה בידם הרשות להתנהג כרצונם,

אם כן: **איך זה הגיעו להיות משוקעים במ"ט שערי טומאה??"**

נתיבות שלום עניני פסח מאמר י"ב זמן חרותנו אות ב' עמוד רס"ח

In מצרים there were no decrees that forced us to follow the spiritually contaminated ways of our captors.

So we need to figure out what exactly pushed us to abandon our beautiful, fulfilling Yiddishe lifestyle? Why were we found cheering at the stadiums and partying in the bars and clubs together with the local gentile population and not teaching our children to follow the ethical and moral path of our holy forefathers?

QUESTION #2

"ויוציאנו ה' ממצרים:

לא על ידי שליח לא על ידי מלאך ולא על ידי שרף

אלא הקדוש ברוך הוא בכבודו ובעצמו."

הגדה של פסח

When the Torah says that Hashem took us out of Mitzrayim, it means that Hashem did it "Himself" — without sending angels or any other messengers.

"מה איכפת לן אילו היתה יציאת מצרים

על ידי מלאך או שרף או שליח?"

מדברי נתיבות שלום עניני פסח מאמר י"ב אות ג' עמוד רז"ט

The question is: What practical difference does it make whether Hashem took us out "Himself" or if He had sent a messenger? The bottom line is that Hashem would have arranged for us to be saved from the bitter slavery of Mitzrayim.

QUESTION #3

"כי **בחוזק יד** הוציאך ה' ממצרים."

שמות יג:ג

The Torah says: "With a **mighty hand** Hashem took you out of Egypt."

"מה שייך למעלה שצריך כביכול ל'חוזק יד'
וכי יש דבר קשה לפניו יתברך?"

נתיבות שלום חלק ב' עניני פסח ד' רמ"א

Let us understand: What does it mean that Hashem used His "mighty hand" to save us — is there anything "difficult" for the Master of the universe? Couldn't He just use His "regular hand" to get the job done?

Hashem manages the earth, the sun, the moon, the stars, and all the galaxies every single day! But He needed His "mighty hand" to shlep a few Jews out of Mitzrayim??

QUESTION #4

"אחד מחמשה יצאו וארבעה חלקים מתו בשלשת ימי אפלה
שלא היו רוצים לצאת ממצרים!"

מכילתא בשלח פר' י"ח ד"ה ויסב

Incredibly, when the time of redemption arrived, there were "many" Jews who simply did not want to leave Egypt. This was not just a small number; rather, it was — are you ready? Brace yourself: a whopping 80 percent majority of Klal Yisrael did **NOT WANT** to leave Mitzrayim! (We warned you to brace yourself!)

We need to understand; How is it possible that 80 percent of Klal Yisrael — about 2.4 million of our brothers and sisters — made the awful decision to remain enslaved in Egypt! Who in their right mind would choose slavery over freedom?

"והיוצאים לא היו כל כך סרבנים
ועם כל זה יצאו כמוכרחים."

תולדות יצחק שמות פרק ל"ב

And even the 20 percent who **DID** agree to let Hashem rescue them from Mitzrayim were not really excited about leaving and Hashem had to kind of nudge them out!

Be honest — does this make ANY sense to you?

QUESTION #5

"ויאנחו בני ישראל - מן העבודה"

שמות פרק ב:כג

The Torah says, "The Yidden moaned in pain from the work."

So come on — ask us the question like a real *yeshivah bachur*: How can we have just said that 80 percent of Klal Yisrael did not want to leave Mitzrayim when the Torah specifically tells us that Klal Yisrael was screaming out in pain from the servitude?

"שהיתה קשה עליהם
ויזעקו ותעל שועתם לשמי מרום של ה׳
ויאמר במאמרו: להושיעם מן העבודה!"

כתר יונתן שמות פרק ב:כג

The answer is, yes, it is true that we cried out in pain — but only for the **cruel slave labor** to end!

Now hang on a second; once we were crying out in pain because we were being beaten mercilessly by our Egyptian captors, and the "fun" of mingling and partying with the Egyptians was OVER — why did we not scream out to Hashem to have mercy on us and end the miserable exile and bring us to Eretz Yisrael!?

QUESTION #6

"ויהי בשלח פרעה את העם
ולא נחם אלקים דרך ארץ פלשתים - כי קרוב הוא,

כי אמר אלקים: פן ינחם העם בראתם מלחמה ושבו מצרימה!
רש"י: יחשבו מחשבה על שיצאו ויתנו לב לשוב!"

רש"י שמות פרק יג:יז

When we were taken out of Egypt, Hashem did not lead us by the way of the Pilishtim even though it was the shortest route to Eretz Yisrael. Why? Because Hashem was worried (so to speak) that when we would encounter war we'd get cold feet and **want to return to Egypt!**

Now hang on just a second; Hashem was worried that we would — whaaaaat??? Go back to Egypt? Are you kidding me? Weren't we just freed from intense, horrific, inhumane slavery! Go back? The Egyptians were putting our babies into cement walls! Go back? Paroh slaughtered 300 Jewish babies every day just to soak in their blood! Go back? Did we forget how we "moaned and groaned" in agony just a few days before?

NEVER AGAIN

October 1939: The Nazis took over Poland. Young Moshe had witnessed horrific brutality at the hands of the Nazis that would haunt him for the rest of his life. Miraculously Moshe had managed to be smuggled out of the concentration camp and he joined a partisan group hiding in the forest. After a year, he obtained false documents with a new Polish name and address. He was now as free as any Polish citizen. On the way to work each day, he would pass by the concentration camp and was able to see the electric barbed wire fence, barking dogs, and the Nazi guards in the towers. You can be sure that Moshe would NEVER have the slightest urge to voluntarily go back to that place!

We need to understand; Why did Hashem have to worry about us EVER even thinking of returning to the horrific nightmare of Egypt?!

QUESTION #7

"**עבדים** היינו לפרעה במצרים,
ואילו לא הוציא הקדוש ברוך הוא את אבותינו ממצרים
הרי אנו ובנינו ובני בנינו **משועבדים** היינו לפרעה במצרים."

הגדה של פסח

We all know the famous words of the Haggadah: "We were slaves to Paroh in Mitzrayim, and if Hashem would not have rescued us from Mitzrayim, then we, our children, and our grandchildren would still be enslaved to Paroh in Mitzrayim."

"כלום יתכן כדבר הזה? הרי הקדוש ברוך הוא
כבר הבטיח בברית בין הבתרים שיוציאם ממצרים?"

של"ה הקדוש מובא בנתיבות שלום חלק ה' עניני פסח דף רס"ח

The obvious question is; How could we say "... if Hashem would not have rescued us we would still be slaves ..."? Didn't Hashem specifically promise Avraham Avinu that after 400 years of exile the Yidden would be freed from slavery?

LET'S REVIEW THE QUESTIONS

Question #1

"**איך זה הגיעו** להיות משוקעים במ"ט שערי טומאה?"

What exactly pushed us to abandon our beautiful and fulfilling lifestyle and spiral down to such a low spiritual level?

Question #2

"**ויוציאנו ה'** ממצרים: לא על ידי שליח לא על ידי מלאך
ולא על ידי שרף אלא הקדוש ברוך הוא בכבודו ובעצמו."

What practical difference does it make if Hashem would have had taken us out "Himself" or if He would have sent a messenger to free us?

Question #3

"כי בחוזק יד הוציאך ה' ממצרים."

Why did Hashem need to use His special "mighty hand" and not just use His "regular hand" to yank us out of Mitzrayim?

Question #4

"שלא היו רוצים לצאת ממצרים!"

How is it possible that a whopping 80 percent of Klal Yisrael preferred to stay in Mitzrayim and even the 20 percent that chose to leave were not even excited to leave?

Question #5

"ויאמר במאמרו: להושיעם מן העבודה!"

Why did we not scream and beg Hashem to rescue us and bring us to Eretz Yisrael as He promised Avraham Avinu!?

Question #6

"פן ינחם העם: יחשבו מחשבה על שיצאו ויתנו לב לשוב!"

After we got out, why did Hashem have to worry about us EVER thinking about returning to that horrific nightmare?!

Question #7

"הרי הקדוש ברוך הוא כבר הבטיח
בברית בין הבתרים שיוציאם ממצרים?"

How could we say "... and if Hashem would NOT have rescued us ..."? Didn't Hashem specifically promise Avraham Avinu that after 400 years of exile the Yidden would be freed?

Obviously, we really need to figure out what on earth was *really* happening in Mitzrayim!

In order to properly understand this (and many other interesting insights!), we invite you on a journey deep into the subject of

Galus Mitzrayim (Egyptian exile) so that we can truly understand what our servitude in Mitzrayim was really all about. We will (hopefully!) emerge with a greater understanding of what we are all going through in our **current** *galus* and (hopefully!) find tangible ways **to greatly improve our daily lives.**

22

ATMOSPHERIC COMBUSTION

Understanding what is shlepping you down

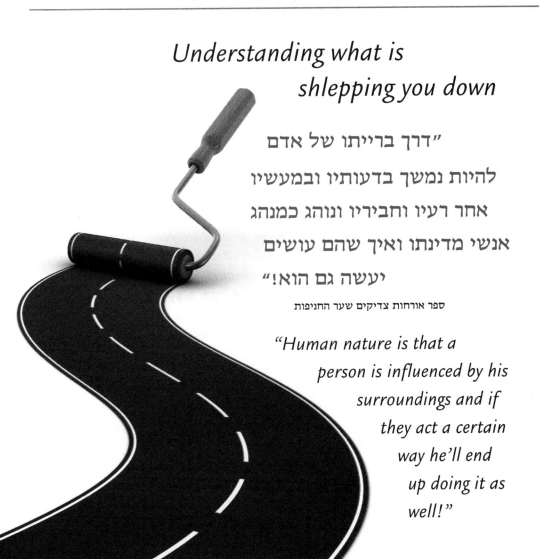

"דרך ברייתו של אדם
להיות נמשך בדעותיו ובמעשיו
אחר רעיו וחביריו ונוהג כמנהג
אנשי מדינתו ואיך שהם עושים
יעשה גם הוא!"

ספר אורחות צדיקים שער החניפות

*"Human nature is that a
person is influenced by his
surroundings and if
they act a certain
way he'll end
up doing it as
well!"*

HASHEM

had to reformat the hard drive
of his precious nation:

"עבדים היינו לפרעה במצרים."

דברים פרק ו:כא

The Torah says, "We were **slaves** to Paroh in Egypt."

When we think of what it means to be "slaves" in Egypt, we assume that our freedom and rights were taken away, and that we were forced to physically work for our Egyptian captors. Long hours, little pay, and NO say.

SLAVERY

The encyclopedia describes slavery as: The systematic exploitation of labor; a social-economic system, slavery is a legal or informal institution under which a person is compelled to work for another. Slaves are held against their will from the time of their capture, purchase, or birth, and are deprived of the right to leave, to refuse to work, or to receive compensation in return for their labor.

HOWEVER, AS YOU ARE ABOUT TO FIND OUT,
OUR ENSLAVEMENT IN EGYPT
WAS SOMETHING MUCH MORE THAN THAT:

"עיקר עניינה של גלות מצרים הי-ה

מה שישראל היו 'משועבדים' שם 'לגמרי'

בכל מהותם ללא שום עצמות – אפילו במחשבה!"

נתיבות שלום עניני פסח מאמר י"ב אות ב' עמוד רס"ח

Although our enslavement started out just as "physical" captivity, over the course of time the Egyptian culture and thought processes infiltrated our pure Yiddishe mindset **to the extent** that we became *psychologically* trapped into **thinking** like our Egyptian captors.

This means that as the years and decades passed, we lost our **personal freedom of choice** to **DO** — and to even **THINK** — in any way that was not in accordance with the Egyptian lifestyle and culture.

"ישראל היו במצרים כעובר במעי אמו שאינו מסוגל בכוחות עצמו לשום דבר ואינו כלל מציאות בפני עצמו אלא כולו נתון בתוך אמו, כיון שהיו משועבדים לפרעה לגמרי ברוחם ובגופם!"

נתיבות שלום עניני פסח מאמר י"ב אות ב' עמוד רס"ח

Just as an unborn child has no control over his own life and his existence is completely dictated by his mother, in the same exact way; the Egyptians turned us from "slaves subjugated to the Egyptian people" into "Egyptian slaves."

We lost our **Jewish identity** and **Jewish mindset**, and we became completely משועבד (sub'JEW'gated) to פרעה and מצרים.

This is an amazing accomplishment for a captor to attain, for the natural response of a slave in captivity is to "despise" his captor!

In fact, throughout our history, Klal Yisrael suffered from many captors, tyrants, and dictators, and we never felt any "closeness" to them at all! We certainly didn't let them CONTROL our minds!

On the contrary, we always looked at them and their culture with disgust and disdain! In fact, the more they **physically** controlled us and hurt us — the **further** we distanced ourselves from them emotionally, psychologically, and especially spiritually!

Yet by the time our redemption came around, we were (almost) completely **bound** to the all-powerful psychological influence of Paroh and Mitzrayim.

The Hebrew word that describes this full existential enslavement is משועבד, which means an **all-encompassing** state of captivity that **completely** controls the slave; physically, emotionally, and psychologically, thus incapacitating the slave's internal capacities of thought and decision making.

LEARNING FROM STOLKHOLM SYNDROME:

Wikipedia: In psychology, "**Stockholm syndrome**" is a term used to describe a paradoxical psychological phenomenon wherein hostages express adulation and have positive feelings toward their captors that appear irrational in light of the danger or risk endured by the victims.

While uncommon, the FBI's Hostage Barricade Database shows that roughly 27 percent of victims show evidence of Stockholm syndrome.

To properly illustrate the concept of "psychological slavery," we present to you the following true stories:

FREELY TRAPPED

1. Patty Hearst was kidnapped by the Symbionese Liberation Army. After two months in captivity, she actively took part in a robbery they were orchestrating. Her unsuccessful legal defense suggested that she suffered from Stockholm syndrome and was coerced into aiding the SLA. She was convicted and imprisoned for her actions in the robbery, though her sentence was commuted in February 1979 by President Jimmy Carter and she received a presidential pardon from President Bill Clinton on January 20, 2001.

2. Jaycee Lee Dugard was kidnapped and held captive for 18 years by Phillip Garrido. When first interviewed by parole officers who were suspicious of her abductor, she did not reveal her identity. Instead, she told investigators she was a battered wife from Minnesota who was hiding from her abusive husband, and described Garrido as a "great person" who was "good with her kids."

3. In 2003, 11-year-old Shawn Hornbeck was abducted by Michael Devlin. After four years in captivity, he was miraculously found in Kirkwood, St. Louis, only 50 short miles away from his home.

What was so shocking about this abduction was that the kidnapper frequently left Shawn free to move around on his own — and yet the boy never tried to escape! In fact, Kirkwood locals testified that they saw Shawn biking around the area on his own and hanging out with friends he made during his abduction. He looked so naturally content that they never even suspected that anything was wrong!

Why didn't Shawn use his apparent freedom to escape or at least contact authorities or his parents? The explanation is: The captor, Michael Devlin, somehow managed to penetrate Shawn's own mind and influenced him into keeping himself in captivity.

Once "Stockholm Syndrome" or "slave mentality" takes over a person's mindset, the person is no longer the same "free thinking" person as before he was captured — with the exception of being physically trapped. Rather, his own mind has become manipulated to the degree that he has lost his own identity and control over who he really is! That is why such people do not even try to escape!

NOW LET'S APPLY THIS TO MITZRAYIM:

"כך היו פרעה ועמו טמאים ומטמאים את ישראל ...."

פרקי דרבי אליעזר פרק ל"ט

Paroh and his nation were spiritually contaminated and they defiled the holy nation of Klal Yisrael!

Now we finally can understand that the main challenge of the Egyptian exile was **NOT** the "physical" oppression (as we once thought!); rather, it was the transformation of **our own mindset** causing us to become completely "משועבד" (***Mitzrafried***™) without any independence — even within **our own** mindset and thought process!

"עצם המציאות שהיו משועבדים לגמרי
לרוח המקום השפל ביותר בעולם היא מצרים ערות הארץ
הפכה אותם ממילא להיות משוקעים במ"ט (49) שערי טומאה!"

נתיבות שלום עניני פסח מאמר י"ב זמן חרותנו אות ב'

This is the sad truth about what happened to us in Mitzrayim: we became completely "משועבד" to the decadent רוח המקום — **ATMOSPHERE** — of Egypt, which at that time in history was ערות הארץ, the immorality capital of the world.

 **BRAINWASHED** *Imagine that a sweet, pure, innocent boy is abducted and locked up in a room, surrounded by huge television screens for five years.*

After you physically release this poor child, he will certainly be mentally affected by what he saw and heard. In fact it is safe to say that his entire outlook on life will be substantially altered!

Although the Egyptians did not create evil decrees to prevent us from learning Torah and performing mitzvos, it was the intense CULTURAL ATMOSPHERIC PRESSURE that **systematically influenced** us and shoved us down the slippery slope toward the lowest levels of impurity.

Over the course of 210 years, the Egyptian lifestyle and culture

affected and infected our own identity, thereby causing us to fall to the lowest levels of spiritual impurity; the 49th level of טומאה (spiritual contamination).

Our values, morals, ethics, priorities, attitude, and outlook on life deteriorated from the pure *derhoiben* (uplifted) Yiddishe perspective we once had, and the despicable, immorally decadent Egyptian culture reprogrammed what we knew to be true and false, right and wrong, good and bad, beautiful and ugly, *aiydel* and *grub*.

Think about this: 49 out of 50 is 98 percent. So if we fell to the 49th level of *tumah* out of 50 levels, this means that 98 percent of our mindset had already been taken over by spiritual filth and contamination, thereby leaving us with only a tiny 2 percent of our original pure Yiddishe mindset!

"כי היו במצרים במ"ט [49] שערי טומאה ואלו חס ושלום
היו נשקעים בשער הנ' [50] לא היו יכולין ליגאל."

אר"י ז"ל מובא בשפת אמת במדבר שבועות

Just as when a person is 100 percent brain dead, the brain cells can no longer re-grow, the same concept applies to the spiritual mindset. Therefore, as long as we had even just 2 percent of our Yiddishe mindset intact, we would be able to once again grow, regenerate and re'JEW'venate. However, if we would have reached the 50th level of טומאה and our minds would had become 100 percent **Mitzrafried**™, then we would have been *fried* forever!

"ולכן גם נקראה מצרים 'בית עבדים':
מקום שהפכו בו אנשים לעבדים!"

נתיבות שלום עניני פסח מאמר י"ב אות ב' עמוד רס"ח

Now we can understand why מצרים is constantly referred to as "בית עבדים — house of servitude," for this is the suitable descriptive title of what Mitzrayim really was!

The land of Egypt was not just a country where they happen to have a nation of slaves **working** for them — rather, it was an efficiently run **manufacturing plant** that specialized in successfully transforming freethinking humans into psychologically trapped zombies with no mind of their own!

"ידוע דברי חז"ל (רש"י שמות יח:ט) שלא הי' אף פעם עבד שברח ממצרים. ואולי הטעם הוא מכיון שהמצרים היו יודעים **איך לשעבד המוח לגמרי**, ממילא מעולם לא בא להעבדים **אפילו המחשבה** לברוח משם!"

מדברי הנתיבי אמת שליט"א

Perhaps this is why Chazal say that NO ONE EVER escaped from Mitzrayim. This was not because of their superior security forces and electric barbed-wire fences that **physically** trapped their slaves; rather, it was due to their amazing success in converting their captives' minds into total sub'JEW'gation to the point that NO ONE EVER EVEN THOUGHT ABOUT TRYING TO ESCAPE! (Exactly the thought process of every addict!)

"וזה שנאמר:
'וגם ראיתי את 'הלחץ' אשר מצרים לוחצים אותם'
היינו לחץ השעבוד שאינו שליט לא על המחשבה ולא על הדבור **אלא כל מהותו ומציאותו משועבדים!**"

נתיבות שלום שלום עניני פסח מאמר י"ב אות ב' עמוד רס"ח

The Torah says, "... and I have seen the *pressure* with which the Egyptians have been *pressuring* them." Let's think for a minute; what *pressure* is Hashem referring to? Is it merely the pressure to physically show up on time to work and work really hard? No vacation days?

But you, dear reader, already understand that the "pressure" mentioned here refers to the intense *psychological* **pressure** of the enslavement that did not merely take away our freedom of action and freedom of speech; rather, it stripped us of our entire **identity** as we became משועבד לגמרי, completely swallowed up and entrapped within the Egyptian culture and way of thinking.

BRAIN SCAN

Imagine if we could invent a "spiritual" brain scan. We would set it up so the Yiddishe brain cells would light up in yellow and the goyishe brain cells would light up in orange.

Let's say our fellow Yid named Shmuel would be kidnapped by a goy. It would certainly be possible for Shmuel to become physically enslaved by a gentile and lose his physical freedom and yet his brain can remain completely "yellow." However, if the gentile would befriend Shmuel, watching television and movies with him, sharing his books and magazines with him, etc., etc., then the goyishe influence would start to seep in and we would slowly begin to see small blotches of orange light up on our "spiritual brain scan."

At first it would just be a little blotch here ... a little there ... on the outskirts of the brain. But after some time, we would find that the infected orange area spread out and even took over some small sections of the brain. Over time, we would witness Shmuel's spiritual deterioration and see that the orange overcomes more and more of the brain, eliminating any trace of yellow.

Now imagine if 98 percent of the brain changed to a deep shade of orange and there is only a tiny 2 percent of the entire brain that still lights up yellow! Now you understand our situation in Mitzrayim!

"כי **בחפזון** יצאת מארץ מצרים."

דברים פרק טז:ג

Now we can finally understand the incredible danger we were in at the point when Hashem swooped down to rescue us from the claws of the Egyptian enslavement, and why Hashem had to get us out of there "quickly," after just 210 years of slavery.

The onslaught of the *psychological* Egyptian enslavement had already pushed us to the **brink of extinction** — for once the pure Yiddishe brain was completely ***Mitzrafried***, the person was just a shell and there was nothing left worth redeeming!

FRIED BRAINS

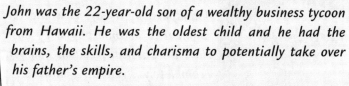

John was the 22-year-old son of a wealthy business tycoon from Hawaii. He was the oldest child and he had the brains, the skills, and charisma to potentially take over his father's empire.

At 18 he moved to New York to start college and he fell in with the wrong crowd. He began using addictive substances and his life spiraled completely out of control. He was once a bright young lad with a bright future ahead of him, but a few months of substance abuse ate away at his brain cells and he was hardly able to think straight!

Eventually John checked into a top-notch rehabilitation center and after a full year of intense rehab and therapy, his brain cells seemed to somewhat repair themselves. His wealthy family was convinced that it was now safe to bring him back home and they hoped he would get back on track. But just before they came for him, he fell again and this time he fell harder and eventually the substance abuse caused irreparable damage to his brain cells.

After that point, even if his family would come to "rescue" him from his horrific lifestyle and bring him to a beautiful new life with every opportunity in the world — it would be too late for him. His brains cells were permanently damaged (fried!) and there was no longer the potential for him to ever recover and lead a normal life.

"Studies show that drug abuse can lead to a buildup of proteins that cause severe nerve cell damage and death in essential parts of the brain."

Source: Neuropathology and Applied Neurobiology, June 2005

RECALCULATING SLAVERY TIME

Based on the above, we understand that Hashem had to rush us out of Egypt after just 210 years, because otherwise there would have been no one left to rescue! We would have been spiritually brain dead!

However, how could Hashem justify this early release in accordance with His original decree that we were to be enslaved for 400 years?

The answer may very well be: Had our servitude been only **physical** day labor, then we would have been there for 400 years as scheduled. However, since the Egyptian slavery spread to an all encompassing **emotional** and **psychological** לחץ (pressure) which was constantly upon us day **and night**, Hashem counted the nights as well!

NUMBER CRUNCHING

However, this presents a mathematical question: If we count the psychological שעבוד as well as the daily physical labor, then why did we end up being freed after 210 years and not after 200 years?

Maybe we can answer: When we left Egypt, we numbered 603,550. The לויים numbered 22,273. This is around 3 percent of כלל ישראל who were not part of the physical שעבוד מצרים. However, they still suffered psychological pressure from watching their brothers and sisters deteriorating before their very eyes!

For the rest of us, even though on the physical level we were completely enslaved, psychologically speaking we were on the 49th שער הטומאה, which, as we explained, means that 98 percent of our brains were "Mitzrafried." This means that we still had control over the 2 percent of our Yiddishe mindset that was not yet mentally enslaved.

So, the Leviim, who formed 3 percent of Klal Yisrael, were

*enslaved psychologically but NOT physically, and 2 percent of the rest of us were not psychologically enslaved. Together you have 5 percent of Klal Yisrael whom the מצריים did NOT yet manage to enslave! Doubling our enslavement from just physical to both physical and psychological would entitle us to be redeemed in exactly 50 percent of the original decreed time. 400 years divided by 2 would be 200 years. However, the שעבוד was not exactly "twice" as hard, since 5 percent of us were not משעבוד to the Mitzreeyim, so 400 divided by 45 percent comes out to exactly 190 years that were **deducted** from the original decree!*

"אילו לא הוציא הקדוש ברוך הוא את אבותינו ממצרים וכו'
הפירוש: שהיינו נשארים לתמיד 'משועבדים' לקליפת פרעה
ואף אם **בפועל** היו בני חורין עדיין היינו **משועבדים** לפרעה במצרים!"

נתיבות שלום חלק ב' עניני פסח דף רס"ח

That is what it really means when it says: "If Hashem had not taken us out at that moment, we would have been enslaved forever!" For if we had lost that tiny remaining 2 percent of our Yiddishe mindset and become completely **Mitzrafried** — then even if Hashem would have set us **physically** free at the end of 400 years in Mitzrayim, we would have remained **psychologically and spiritually משועבד** (bound) to the spiritual decadence of the Egyptian mindset FOREVER!!!

NOW LET'S SEE HOW ALL THE ORIGINAL QUESTIONS ARE ANSWERED:

A MIGHTY HAND

"ולזה הפירוש: 'בכח גדול וביד חזקה' מוסב על 'ישראל'
שלא היו רוצים לצאת ממצרים

וְעַל כָּרְחָם הוֹצֵאת אוֹתָם בְּיָד חֲזָקָה וּבְהֶכְרֵחַ גָדוֹל!"

תולדת יצחק שמות פרק ל"ב

This is why the Torah says that the redemption was with "great strength and a mighty hand." This is not referring to Hashem's "difficulty" (so to speak) with the Egyptian captors — nah — that was a cinch! The real problem was US YIDDEN!

Eighty percent of our brothers and sisters were already completely *Mitzrafried* to the extent that they did not EVEN WANT to leave מצרים, and even from of the remaining 20 percent who agreed to leave — 98 percent of their brains were unfortunately already *Mitzrafried* to the point that they weren't even eager to leave!

"אֶלָּא לִרְמוֹז עַל יְצִיאָה כָּזוֹ לְנַתֵּק אֶת הַנֶּפֶשׁ רוּחַ וּנְשָׁמָה מִכַּבְלֵי הַשִּׁעְבּוּד שֶׁהִיא צְרִיכָה לִבְחִינַת חוֹזֶק יָד!"

נתיבות שלום עניני פסח רס"ט

Since we had sunk to such a low level and we didn't even really want to get out of that sick place, the simple physical rescue mission turned out to be more like a full-blown **extraction** from the *psychological grip* of the Egyptians, and that required "great strength and a mighty hand"!

DIGGING DEEP

After the three-hour surgery the dentist came out and told the worried mother that although the surgery was extremely complicated everything was now all right.

The mother couldn't understand why simply pulling a tooth should be such a long and difficult process. What took the dentist three long hours to do?

The surgeon explained that when he started to pull the tooth he found that its roots were deeply intertwined with the roots of the surrounding teeth and therefore the simple "pull" turned into a full-blown "extraction."

"אז שהיו ערום וערי-ה היתה הגאולה **בחזקת יד** ...

... במצרים משוקעים במ"ט שערי טומאה ועבדו עבודה זרה

ועל כן נקראת גאולת מצרים '**חוזק יד**' וזדרוע נטויה."

שו"ת חתם סופר חלק ז' סימן מ"ב

It certainly would not have been *difficult* for Hashem to rescue a worthy nation *anxiously awaiting* rescue. However *we* had become so deeply rooted in the corrupt mentality of the Egyptians that their immoral mindset had thoroughly taken control of our minds and twisted itself deep into the roots of our psyche.

THE DIFFERENCE BETWEEN MITZRAYIM AND ALL OTHER EXILES:

And now we can understand the distinction between *Galus Mitzrayim* and all our other exiles:

"וזה ההפרש בין כל הגלויות לגלות מצרים:

כל הגלויות שעברו בני ישראל התבטאו רק בכך שהגויים

היו יותר חזקים מישראל ומצירים להם אבל עם זאת

לא היו משועבדים להם!

נתיבות שלום ענייני פסח מאמר י"ב אות ב' עמוד רס"ח

Every other exile can be described by saying that the goyim were physically "stronger" than we were and they abused their might to make our lives miserable — but we were never ever "**משועבד**" (psychologically) bound to them! On the contrary, our mindset and emotions were completely independent, and we despised them and their culture!

"רק במצרים היו 'גוי בקרב גוי' – משועבדים לגמרי'

עד שאפילו חלק המחשבה מה ואיך לחשוב

גם כן הי-ה משועבד למצרים!"

נתיבות שלום ענייני פסח מאמר י"ב אות ב' עמוד רס"ח

However, in Mitzrayim, we were a nation swallowed up "inside" another nation and the **influence** of the cultural atmosphere took control over our pure Yiddishe thought process and sank our Jewish battleship.

"ויוצא את עמו ישראל 'מתוכם' לחרות עולם."

תפילת מעריב

We say in our prayers: *"... and Hashem brought out His nation Yisrael from within their midst to everlasting freedom."*

Seemingly, "מתוכם" (from their midst) is extra, for could it not have just said, "And Hashem brought out His nation Yisrael to everlasting freedom"?

"והכוונה מלת 'מתוכם'
מורה באצבע **שעיקר** הגאולה תולה בזה:
שהוציא עמו ישראל **מתוכיותם** של המצריים!"

אור המאיר דברים פרשת דברים ד"ה ולזה תמצא

The answer is that not only is this word NOT "EXTRA," but, on the contrary — it is the MOST IMPORTANT word in the *pasuk*! For it is this specific word that fully describes our redemption from Egypt — for Hashem truly **extracted** His beloved nation literally from **"within"** the Egyptians! Not only did Hashem extract US out of Mitzrayim, He also had to extract the Egyptian influence out of our mindset!

AND NOW WE UNDERSTAND WHY HASHEM HAD TO RESCUE US HIMSELF!

"ויש לומר דמלאך או שרף יכולים להוציאם ממצרים רק **בפועל**,
אך מכיון שגם הנפש רוח ונשמה משועבדים היו **לגמרי** לקליפת מצרים
לא הי-ה ביד שום מלאך ושרף או שליח להוציאם, רק הקדוש ברוך הוא
בכבודו ובעצמו יכול הי-ה **לנתקם** מכבלי השעבוד."

נתיבות שלום עניני פסח מאמר י"ב אות ג' עמוד רס"ט

Angels could certainly have been dispatched to do a "pick up" and **physically** transport us out of מצרים. However, our situation in מצרים required far more than a mere "physical" rescue since we needed to disconnect and free our **mindset** from the morally corrupt and spiritually bankrupt **perspective** of the Egyptian culture which **took over** our pure Yiddishe way of thinking that distinguishes us from the rest of the world. Only Hashem could do that!

"אילו לא הוציאם 'הקב"ה' בכבודו ובעצמו
אלא הי-ה מוציאם על ידי מלאך או שרף או שליח
הרי אנו ובנינו ובני בנינו **משועבדים היינו** עד היום לפרעה במצרים!"

נתיבות שלום חלק ה' עניני פסח דף רס"ח

Now it's *gevaldig!* Since we required not just a "physical" redemption but especially a "psychological" redemption — which, as stated, can ONLY be done by Hashem Himself — therefore we are saying; had Hashem not been the One to take us out Himself and instead He would have sent an angel or messenger to rescue us from slavery, then, even though we would have been "physically" "FREE," we still would have remained internally *Mitzrafried* and psychologically משועבד to Paroh and Mitzrayim forever!

This point is seen clearly in the episode of Lot; we find that Hashem dispatched angels to physically yank him out of סדום and airlift him to a safe location. However even after taking Lot out of Sodom, the immoral ways of Sodom were not removed from within Lot's corrupt mindset!

AN ANGEL COULD TAKE LOT OUT OF SODOM ...
BUT ONLY HASHEM CAN TAKE SODOM OUT OF LOT!

When a person develops a dependency on anything at all, aside from the actual dependency and desire for that obsession, the person's **mindset** also becomes increasingly **affected** as he goes through many psychological changes, drifting far from his original normal thinking mind. Merely stopping the action does not automatically correct and straighten out the twisted mindset that resulted from years of abuse.

Just as when you need to reformat a computer hard drive in order to completely remove viruses that corrupted and crippled the operating system, the יד ה' (hand of G-d) was necessary to liberate and reformat our **mindset**, thus returning it to its previous state of Yiddishe purity.

NOW WE CAN TRULY UNDERSTAND WHY WE USE A DUAL DESCRIPTION WHEN WE THANK HASHEM FOR TAKING US OUT OF MITZRAYIM:

"נודה לך ...

ועל שהוצאתנו מארץ מצרים — ופדיתנו מבית עבדים."

ברכת המזון

Thank you Hashem for *taking us* "physically" out of Mitzrayim and for *redeeming* us "psychologically" from the effects of being in the house of slavery!

NOW ALL THE QUESTIONS ARE ANSWERED!

Here's a list of all the questions ... let's see if you can answer them!

Question #1

"איך זה הגיעו להיות משוקעים במ"ט שערי טומאה?"

What exactly pushed us to abandon our beautiful and fulfilling lifestyle and spiral down to such a low spiritual level?

Question #2

"ויוציאנו ה' ממצרים: לא על ידי שליח לא על ידי מלאך ולא על ידי שרף אלא הקדוש ברוך הוא בכבודו ובעצמו."

What practical difference does it make if Hashem would have had taken us out "Himself" or if He would have sent a messenger to free us?

Question #3

"כי בחוזק יד הוציאך ה' ממצרים."

Why did Hashem need to use His special "mighty hand" and not just use His "regular hand" to yank us out of Mitzrayim?

Question #4

"שלא היו רוצים לצאת ממצרים!"

How is it possible that a whopping 80 percent of Klal Yisrael preferred to stay in Mitzrayim and even the 20 percent that chose to leave were not even excited to leave?

Question #5

"ויאמר במאמרו: להושיעם מן העבודה!"

Why did we not scream and beg Hashem to rescue us and bring us to Eretz Yisrael as He promised Avraham Avinu!?

Question #6

"פן ינחם העם: יחשבו מחשבה על שיצאו ויתנו לב לשוב!"

After we got out, why did Hashem have to worry (so to speak) about us EVER thinking about returning to that horrific nightmare?!

Question #7

"הרי הקדוש ברוך הוא כבר הבטיח
בברית בין הבתרים שיוציאם ממצרים?"

How could we say "... and if Hashem would NOT have rescued us..."? Didn't Hashem specifically promise Avraham Avinu that after 400 years of exile the Yidden would be freed?

**We're sure you did a great job!
Now let's see how all of this information pertains to
EACH ONE OF US!**

23

TWISTED REALITY

Getting sucked into
your surroundings

"לעתיד לבוא תהיינה שתי
גאולות; אחת: להוציא את
ישראל מן הגלות, ושניה: להוציא
את הגלות מישראל! והאחרונה –
קשה מן הראשונה!"

ר' אברהם מרדכי מגור (אמרי אמת) זי"ע
מובא בספר פתגמים נבחרים

"When Mashiach comes there will
be two forms of redemption: One to
take US out of galus and the
other — to take the galus
out of US! And the
second one is more
difficult than
the first!"

HASHEM

sets up every stage of our exile to consist of various levels of physical & psychological challenges:

"1: ויושע ה׳ ביום ההוא את ישראל מיד מצרים
2: וירא ישראל את מצרים מת על שפת הים
3: וירא ישראל את היד הגדולה אשר עשה ה׳ במצרים ...
4: אז ישיר משה ובני ישראל את השירה הזאת ...."

שמות יד:ל

The Torah says:
(1) And Hashem saved Israel that day from the Egyptians, (2) and Israel saw the Egyptians dead upon the seashore, (3) and Israel saw the great hand that Hashem inflicted upon Egypt ... (4) then Moshe and Bnei Yisrael SANG this song ....

"יש להתבונן בסדר הפסוקים האלה שלכאורה הקדים המאוחר:
הזכיר ראשית ׳וירא ישראל את מצרים מת על שפת הים׳
ואחר כך ׳וירא ישראל את היד הגדולה אשר עשה ה׳ במצרים׳
והלא את היד הגדולה אשר עשה ה׳ במצרים ראו תחילה?"

ספר נתיבות שלום עניני פסח דף רפ״ב

The order of #2 and #3 seems to be backward; first they saw Hashem's mighty hand and only after did they see the Egyptians dead on the seashore, so why does the Torah first say that Klal Yisrael saw their Egyptian oppressors DEAD on the seashore and THEN they recognized what Hashem did to them beforehand?

Furthermore, why did we wait until we saw all the Egyptians dead on the seashore to sing praises to Hashem? Why didn't we sing praises to Hashem as we left Mitzrayim after 210 years of being enslaved and trapped within their borders??

SLAVES ON THE RUN:

"במיתת המתעוללים בהם לשעבדם נשארו הם בני חורין
כי עד עת מותן היו ישראל כעבדים בורחים!"
ספורנו שמות יד:ל

The explanation is: Even after we physically marched out of the land of Egypt and we were technically "free," as long as the forces of Egypt that abused us for so long were alive and well, the Jewish mindset was that of עבדים בורחים, slaves on the run.

Every step toward our new free life was taken while looking over our shoulder, worried that our Egyptian masters will somehow once again grab us and bring us back into captivity.

Therefore, although **PHYSICALLY** free — we were still not **PSYCHOLOGICALLY** free people, since running away from someone or something still means that they are controlling you!

"כי רק לאחר ששברו את קליפת מצרים — הגיעו לתכלית של:
וירא ישראל את היד הגדולה אשר עשה ה' במצרים!!!"
ספר נתיבות שלום ענייני פסח דף רפ"ג

It was only after our oppressors were officially pronounced DEAD that we were truly FREE of their PSYCHOLOGICAL stranglehold!

Only at that time — with the PSYCHOLOGICAL shackles broken and the nightmare truly over — were we able to reflect back with a clear mind and express our appreciation and gratitude for everything that Hashem did for us throughout the entire redemption process.

NOW WE UNDERSTAND THE ORDER PERFECTLY:

(1) And Hashem saved Israel that day from the Egyptians, (2) and *(once)* Israel saw the Egyptians *(physically)* dead upon the seashore *(and the nightmare was truly over)*, (3) and *(then)* Israel *(was psychologically free from the grip of their masters and able to look back and they)* saw the great hand that Hashem inflicted upon Egypt ... (4) *(now they could truly appreciate what Hashem did for them and so ...)* then Moshe and Bnei Yisrael SANG this song ....

TODAY'S GALUS

"גלות מצרים הי-ה שורש לכל הגליות
וגאולת מצרים הי-ה הכנה לכל הגאולות
לכן מזכירין בכל יום יציאת מצרים!"

שפת אמת שמות פרשת שמות [ג"לרת]

Our exile in Egypt was the source of all our exiles, and the redemption from Egypt is the source of all future redemptions. This is why we remind ourselves of Yetzias Mitzrayim every single day of our lives.

When we carefully study what transpired in Mitzrayim we will uncover what brought about our redemption, and we will discover practical steps to bring redemption to OUR OWN lives:

In today's day and age, we are once again exposed to the lowly ideals of our surrounding society and these ideals slowly (not so slowly) creep and seep deep into our minds and eat away at our pure Yiddishe mindset.

On a constant and continuous basis, each and every Yiddishe *Neshamah* is exposed to an increasingly immoral world that brazenly flaunts that which was considered "private" even by their standards — just a short few decades ago.

We are each exposed to more immodesty and immoral behavior than any of our grandparents could have possibly been exposed to — even if they had been looking for it!

DEADLIEST WEAPONS

Several years ago, there was a debate between two radio personalities about what the United States should do about Cuba. One claimed that the only way to deal with Cuba was by increasing "sanctions" against them! The other person said that "sanctions" never work! All it does is make the country more isolated and more resentful, which in turn makes them harbor more animosity toward America, which in turn gives the dictator even MORE power!

The moderator then asked: "If you believe that sanctions won't work, then how do you suggest we deal with Cuba?"

He responded brilliantly: "I suggest that we send in our two most powerful weapons; McDonalds and Blockbuster! In just a few short years the Cubans will become Americanized and we won't need to worry about them anymore! The influence of McDonalds [that represents the concept of "fast food" and the destruction of family dinner time and the transmission of values from the powerful father seated at the head of the table], along with the influence of Blockbuster movies [which would fill their time and minds with fantasy and lustful desires] would AUTOMATICALLY CHANGE their Cuban mindset and transform them into ... Americans who happen to be living in Cuba!"

THIS IS A LIFE LESSON FOR US TO INTERNALIZE:

"דרך ברייתו של אדם להיות נמשך בדעותיו ובמעשיו
אחר ריעיו וחביריו ונוהג כמנהג אנשי מדינתו."

רמב"ם הלכות דעות פרק ו' הלכה א'

A person's thoughts and actions are naturally INFLUENCED by his friends and acquaintances and "**a person fashions himself after the people of his country**."

Do you think you are not affected by the society that surrounds you? Think again!

UNDER THE INFLUENCE

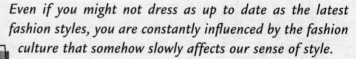

Even if you might not dress as up to date as the latest fashion styles, you are constantly influenced by the fashion culture that somehow slowly affects our sense of style.

Glasses that were once fashionably "in" are now completely "out" and look like a silly joke. Just imagine attending a fancy wedding, immaculately dressed in accordance with the style of 30 years ago! Everyone would stare and laugh at how "silly" you look!

Ties go thin, then wide, then thin; glasses go round, then square, then big, then small; hairstyles go from flat to poufy; the colors and cut of our clothing all have dramatically changed and continue to change decade after decade. Remember bellbottoms?

*Amazingly, our own internal opinion of what WE think looks nice completely changes solely due to the influence dictated by the fashion world that surrounds us, to the extent that a stylish **expensive** name-brand outfit from 30 years ago would be nothing more than an absolutely hilarious Purim outfit!*

OSMOSIS

Regardless of how sheltered a person may try to be — we are all constantly being **attacked** and influenced by the values and lifestyle of McDonalds and Blockbuster!

"ואתם תהיו לי ממלכת כהנים וגוי קדוש."

שמות פרק יט:ו

The description of the Jewish people is that we are a גוי קדוש (a holy nation). "גוי קדוש" is not just a nice catchy title, but it is the very foundation of our nation's existence and it defines our very essence!

Therefore, there is nothing more painful to a holy Yiddishe *Neshamah* than to be immersed in the filthy atmosphere of an impure, hedonistic, and adulterous society.

The constant influence of the world around you is slowly eating away at your pure Yiddishe mindset, dripping in thoughts and ideas that corrupt and dull your spiritually sensitive nerve endings.

BOILING POINT

The "**boiling frog**" theory states that although a frog placed in boiling water will jump right out in order to save itself, when placed in cool water that is heated very slowly, it will continually become accustomed to the gradual rise in temperature and will never make the decision that it is time to jump out — and it will eventually be boiled alive!

The story is generally told in a figurative context, with the upshot being that people should make themselves aware of gradual change lest they suffer a catastrophic loss.

Source: Wikipedia

If we simply "go with the flow," then we are in terrible danger of slowly drifting away from our connection to holiness without even being aware that a battle has been waged and a battle has been lost.

WE CAN FIND THIS CONCEPT CLEARLY IN THE TORAH:

"ולוט ישב בערי הכִכָּר ויאהל 'עַד' סדום"

בראשית יג:יב

When Lot split from his uncle Avraham Avinu and went his own way, it says that he pitched his tent "UNTIL SODOM" — meaning until the border of Sodom. After all, Lot had been living with the holy Avraham for so many years and therefore would never consider being an actual citizen of the lowest spiritual place on earth!

"ויקחו את לוט ... והוא יושב 'ב'סדום"

בראשית יד:יב

However, in the VERY NEXT chapter, the Torah tells us that Lot and his belongings were captured: "and he was living **IN** Sodom"!

In fact Chazal teach us that on that very day he was appointed as a judge! This means that he was enough of an expert in their laws to represent the government and enforce their corrupt values on the citizens! He really understood and internalized their lowly ideals!

So we need to wonder — what happened to him? How did he go from being an "outsider" to becoming an "insider"?

"ונראה לבאר:

אולי בתחילה לא חשב לוט להתיישב **ממש בסדום עצמה**

ולהיות 'סדום'ני**ק**' בכה שפל המצב הנורא

אלא רק לחיות בשכנות לסדום!"

ספר נתיבי אמת בראשית יד:יב

Perhaps the answer is as follows: Although Lot was attracted to the wicked lifestyle of Sodom, after living for so many years near the holy and charitable Avraham Avinu, he could not bring himself to actually move into such a despicable, impure, and selfish atmosphere!

"אמנם השכנות עם הרשעים אנשי סדום שהיו 'רעים וחטאים לה' מאוד'

משכה אותו יותר ויותר עד שעמד ונתיישב ביניהם ממש **ונעשה אחד מהם!**"

ספר נתיבי אמת בראשית יד:יב

However, just living **NEAR** the "exceedingly wicked sinners" was enough to pull him in closer and closer until he became *mamesh* one of them!

The Torah shows us that in a relatively short span of time — from one chapter to the next — Lot transformed into a full-fledged "*Sodom'nik*"!

LET'S BRING THIS CLOSER TO HOME

Sadly, we can see this same concept by looking at our current situation. Imagine a non-religious Jew heading to the beach on Shabbos in his Porsche convertible with his *goyishe* wife and two puppies, while smoking a cigar and munching on a fresh bacon-and-egg sandwich.

If משיח (Mashiach) would approach him with the "great news" that Hashem finally decided to "rescue" him from this "horrible" גלות and bring him to Jerusalem to live a holy pure spiritual life — would he follow?

The horrific heartbreaking truth is that there are currently about five million unaffiliated Jews in America who would **not** be at all interested in being "rescued" from this horrible exile! (About 80 percent of us — eerily, the same percentage as way back in Mitzrayim.)

We see clearly that far worse than the **physical** exile itself is the "**disease**" that slowly infects our spiritual brain cells and eats away at our Yiddishe consciousness to the point that we become oblivious to the fact that we are even in exile!

LOST HOPES

There was once a wealthy billionaire who was forced to expel his beloved son from his home. After many years, one of the close family friends happened to meet the son.

After chatting with him, he asked the son, "Is there anything you would like me to ask your father on your behalf?"

The son replied; "That's a great idea; it really gets cold at night in my basement apartment — can you please ask my dad to send me a small heater?"

Upon hearing these words, the friend could no longer contain himself.

He broke down and cried; "Have you strayed so far that you have already disconnected yourself from remembering who you are and where you belong? Why not ask me to beg your father to allow you to come back home?!"

Adapted from Nesivos Shalom, Purim, p. 79

As time passes, we tend to forget where we came from and who we are. When we have a chance to speak directly to our Father, the King, we should not ask Him for things to make us **comfortable away from our home**; rather, we should beg him to finally **bring us home**!

EMPTY WORDS

A famous story is told of a simple man who led a very inspirational Seder on Pesach night. Finally, at the end of the long evening, they came to the emotional words that we all say, "לשנה הבאה בירושלים — Next year in Jerusalem!" The man burst out in song, clapping and dancing with great emotion. He was enjoying a real spiritual moment.

His transcendent spirit was disturbed by the soft sounds of his wife sobbing. Puzzled, he asked, "What's wrong?"

She sobbed, "I don't want to go to Yerushalayim! I love it here! I love my nice big house and my new luxurious car! I don't want to live in those tiny claustrophobic apartments in Meah Shearim! I don't wanna do sponja!"

He turned to her with a warm reassuring smile and said, "Relax — it's only a song!"

Psychological slavery / victim mentality / Stockholm syndrome occurs when the victim loses his own identity to the point that he doesn't even complain anymore about being a slave! How sad! He becomes limited to dreaming about having an easier life as a slave but loses the capacity to even dream about once again living as a "free" person.

Our job is NOT to relax...

Because this is much more than just a song!

24

CONTROL TOWER

Who is really in control
of your control tower?

"כי זו תכלית יעודו
של אדם מישראל
להיות בן חורין."

נתיבות שלום חלק ב' עניני פסח

"The ultimate goal and purpose
of a Yiddishe person
is to be completely
FREE."

HASHEM

created a world and gave you the choice
to be FREE or to be CHAINED down:

"אמר רב אבדימי בר חמא בר חסא:

מלמד שכפה הקדוש ברוך הוא עליהם את ההר כגיגית ואמר להם:

אם אתם מקבלים התורה מוטב, ואם לאו,

'שם תהא קבורתכם.'"

תלמוד בבלי מסכת שבת דף פ"ח

When Hashem gave us the Torah, He lifted a mountain over us and proclaimed, "If you accept the Torah — that's great; however, if you don't accept the Torah, then 'שם — over **there**' 'קבורתכם תהא — shall be your burial place.'"

"והמפרשים הקשו מה הכונה 'שם' תהא קבורתכם;

הלא ההר הי־ה על גביהם והוי ליה למימר

'פה' - היינו תחת ההר - תהא קבורתכם?"

הלקח והלבוב רי"א

(1) The question is: If the mountain was being held right above the people, then why does it say "שם — over **there**" will be your burial place, it should have said that if you don't accept the Torah, then "פה — right **here**" will be your burial place!?

(2) Furthermore, does it really make sense that Hashem *threatened* us that if we don't accept the Torah He will actually drop a mountain on us and kill us all? What kind of *kiruv* approach is

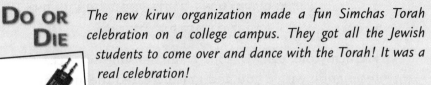

that? Can you imagine if we started using tactics like this to get people to accept Torah life?

DO OR DIE

The new kiruv organization made a fun Simchas Torah celebration on a college campus. They got all the Jewish students to come over and dance with the Torah! It was a real celebration!

After all the dancing was over, the rabbi in charge gathered all the students into a room and spoke to them about the beauty of Yiddishkeit.

When he was done he made them an offer: Sign up now and completely accept the Torah way of life, or ... I'll lock you in this room and blow up the building!

(3) Finally, why the violence? Didn't we already say "נעשה ונשמע" (we will do and we will listen) — we already agreed to happily accept the Torah?

LOOKING FOR ANSWERS

"בעת מתן תורה הקיפם השם יתברך בני ישראל בגיגית
היינו: שלא יהיו תוך אויר העולם ויהיו נבדלים מהעולם
ומהשפעת האויר המזוהם של כל האומות."

הלקח והלבוב רי"א

When Hashem gave us the Torah, He lifted the mountain over us to create a spiritual force field that sheltered us from the rest of the world. The message was: As long as we place ourselves under the influence of the Holy Torah, the Torah will be a protective shield that will shelter us from the negative influences of the outside world.

"כך הקב"ה אמר להם לישראל:

בני, בראתי יצר הרע ובראתי לו תורה תבלין

ואם אתם עוסקים בתורה - אין אתם נמסרים בידו

ואם אין אתם עוסקין בתורה - אתם נמסרים בידו!"

תלמוד בבלי מסכת קידושין דף ל:

Hashem told us: My son, I am the One who created the Evil Inclination within you and I also created the antidote to it — the Holy Torah! If you toil in Torah you will not be controlled by the powers of evil; however, if you do not toil in the Holy Torah — you will find yourself in the grip of the powers of evil!

The lifting of the mountain was not a threat; rather, it was a message from Hashem, Who showed us very clearly that as long as we stay under the protective shield of the Torah by living a true Torah life and conforming to its guidelines, the Torah will protect us from spiritual illness and destruction.

"אמר להם השם יתברך:

'שם' היינו חוץ לגיגית מקום שאין האויר טהור באותו מקום מנותקים

מקדושת התורה שהאויר שהאויר של עולם הזה שולט ואי אפשר לחיות חיים

נצחיים של תורה 'שם תהא קבורתכם' ונקראים מתים!"

הלקח והלבוב רי"א

However, if you leave the protective shield of Torah life, then שם = over **there** — on those *shmutzy* filthy and disgusting streets, where you are vulnerable to the spiritually contaminated world, "over there" will be your spiritual burial place!

The **MORE** we step out of the protective shield of Torah life, the **MORE** susceptible we are to psychological and spiritual diseases from the contaminated atmosphere of the society around us.

"והנה פשוט הוא שאם הבורא לא ברא

למכה זו (יצר הרע) אלא רפואה זו (תורה) אי אפשר בשום פנים

שירפא האדם מזאת המכה בלתי זאת הרפואה ומי שיחשוב להנצל

"זולתה אינו אלא טועה ויראה טעותו לבסוף כשימות בחטאו!"

מסילת ישרים פרק ה'

Even a small child can understand that if the Master of the universe created only one remedy (THE TORAH) that can possibly treat this disease (THE YETZER HORA), then it is impossible to cure this disease ANY other way! Anyone who thinks that he can try some kind of "alternative approach" to treat this disease is simply making a foolish mistake and one day will realize that he deceived himself and wasted his life trapped in the web of sin.

The bottom line is: There is no possible way for you to successfully navigate the many difficult spiritual challenges you will encounter in your lifetime if you leave the protective shield of the Torah.

HANG ON FOR A WILD RIDE

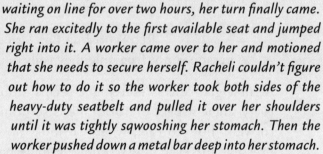

ENJOYING THE RIDE

Little Racheli was so excited to finally be big enough to experience a ride on the grown-up rollercoaster. After waiting on line for over two hours, her turn finally came. She ran excitedly to the first available seat and jumped right into it. A worker came over to her and motioned that she needs to secure herself. Racheli couldn't figure out how to do it so the worker took both sides of the heavy-duty seatbelt and pulled it over her shoulders until it was tightly sqwooshing her stomach. Then the worker pushed down a metal bar deep into her stomach. "Hey — what are you doing? This is so uncomfortable — how am I supposed to enjoy the ride?!"

The worker answered, "Silly girl – I'm doing this to keep you safe – so that you can really enjoy the ride."

It's true that the seatbelt is very uncomfortable and the metal safety bar pushing against your stomach is extremely annoying, but you know that without these restrictions, no matter how hard you try to hang on for dear life, you will eventually be thrown from the ride and ... !

Those who are properly strapped in and restricted do not have to worry about getting hurt and they can enjoy the ride immensely as they fly through the air waving their hands. Whereas the one who cannot accept the restrictions and removes the restraints — for him the ride will be nothing but terror and will surely end in misery.

Authentic Yiddishkeit understands that life is very much like a rollercoaster, with all kinds of sharp turns, crazy ups and downs, and unexpected drops. **Torah life is the seatbelt; sure, it's restrictive but deep down you know that it's the only SAFE WAY to get through life — and even get to enjoy the ride!**

"אמר רבי יהושע בן לוי:

אין לך 'בן חורין' אלא מי שעוסק בתלמוד תורה!"

משנה מסכת אבות פרק ו' משנה ב'

Reb Yehoshua Ben Levi says:
"A person is not **free** unless he toils in the study of Torah."

At first glance this statement seems strange, for we know that every single aspect of Torah life is scrutinized and dictated: how to walk, how to talk, where to look, how to think, how to get dressed, and even how to cut your fingernails! This religion leaves no detail of life unrestricted!

So let's think about this for a moment: Wouldn't the description of a "free" person more accurately describe the person who *threw away* all the rules and regulations of the restrictive Torah lifestyle? That person is "free" to do whatever he wants, whenever he wants, and with anyone he wants to do it with! So why of all things, does the Tana say that only the Torah Jew is: "FREE"??

YOU MUST ADMIT WHAT YOU ALREADY KNOW DEEP IN YOUR HEART:

True freedom is not the common superficial meaning that a person is "FREE" to DO whatever he wants at any given time. Rather, **TRUE FREEDOM** is the ability to **choose** what is best for you and to **follow through** with it!

A person with no **inner strength** and **self-control** is NOT FREE at all! When faced with life's choices, he can "only" choose the easiest way out — even if he believes that it is NOT the best thing for him! He is stuck. He is bound. He is trapped!

LET'S ANALYZE THIS

Diet: If a person decides to restrict what he eats in order to lose weight or for health reasons, and instead of overcoming his urges he goes around eating whatever he wants; he is **NOT FREE**.

He can put on a big smile and show off how much he can stuff himself with the wrong foods and be in complete denial over his situation, but the reality is that **he simply does not have the self-control to actually do what he knows is in his best interest.**

Character: If someone has no control over his temper, he cannot choose how he will react. Even if he knows that he could lose his job, his friendship, his marriage, etc. ... nothing will be able to stop him from reacting with explosive anger.

He is certainly "free" to explode with anger, but he is **NOT FREE** to choose the best reaction for his own best interests.

Culture: If a person can decide what he likes and what he does not like, and then based on his personal taste he makes his purchases, we can say that he has **control** and **freedom** over his life.

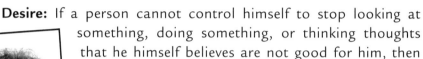

However, if his style is dictated by society (people he never even met!) to the extent that he even purchases things that he himself knows are ugly or overpriced — then he is actually a "slave" to the culture that took away his personal freedom of choice!

Desire: If a person cannot control himself to stop looking at something, doing something, or thinking thoughts that he himself believes are not good for him, then he has lost control over himself and he is a "slave" to the desire.

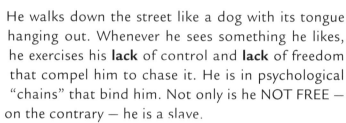

He walks down the street like a dog with its tongue hanging out. Whenever he sees something he likes, he exercises his **lack** of control and **lack** of freedom that compel him to chase it. He is in psychological "chains" that bind him. Not only is he NOT FREE — on the contrary — he is a slave.

CATAGORY	SPECIES
Mammals	5,490
Birds	9,998
Reptiles	9,084
Amphibians	6,433
Fishes	31,300
Insects	1,000,000
Spiders and scorpions	102,248
Molluscs	85,000
Crustaceans	47,000
Corals	2,175
TOTAL	**1,298,728**

Hashem created over a million different species. But ONLY ONE — the HUMAN — was given a unique gift: THE POWER OF SELF-CONTROL. Although the human has the same physical urges as every other animal, he has the G-d-given ability to use the **power of self-control** to control those ANIMAListic urges.

Therefore #1: When you are in control of your ANIMAListic urges, then you are "living" the HUMAN experience. However, if you are at the mercy of your ANIMAListic urges — then you are living the life of an animal.

Therefore #2: To the degree that you have control over your ANIMAListic urges — you are experiencing life as a HUMAN.

Therefore #3: Living life to the MAX actually means: having MAXIMUM control over yourself.

Once you have the knowledge that something is not good for you, when temptation arrives (as it surely will), you have two ways to meet that challenge: you can either succumb to the temptation and fulfill your desire of the moment (like an animal), or you can upgrade out of the ANIMAL kingdom and act like a HUMAN and utilize your self-control.

If you succumb to the desire, you will indeed enjoy the **temporary** pleasure; however, it will be replaced by the gloomy feeling that comes from the realization that you cannot control your own self and you are no better than the average chimpanzee.

Whereas, if you refrain from the temptation, then you will feel **permanent** pleasure, satisfaction, and inner happiness that you will always be able to look back and be proud of. By restraining yourself — you BUILD YOURSELF to attain the MAXIMUM HUMAN EXPERIENCE!

THIS IS CONTRARY TO THE WAY MOST PEOPLE LIVE THEIR LIVES

Let's say a person has high cholesterol and the doctor directs him not to eat his favorite food: Cajun French fries! If he succumbs to his urges, all he has is: the temporary pleasure of eating Cajun French fries.

However, if he would resist the temptation and control himself, he exercised "self control," thereby tapping into the immense pleasure of enjoying the **maximum human experience** that G-d gave him, which is: the freedom to choose and control your own life. On one side is the urge. On the other is LIVING the MAXIMUM human experience!

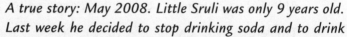

THE REAL THING

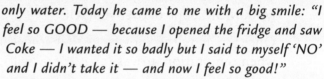

A true story: May 2008. Little Sruli was only 9 years old. Last week he decided to stop drinking soda and to drink only water. Today he came to me with a big smile: "I feel so GOOD — because I opened the fridge and saw Coke — I wanted it so badly but I said to myself 'NO' and I didn't take it — and now I feel so good!"

Little Sruli didn't understand WHY he felt so good. I explained to him that he just learned a valuable lesson that most people don't learn till they're much older (unless they read this book!): A person feels internally good about controlling himself MUCH MORE than he would have enjoyed the temptation! The GREATER the temptation — the BETTER you will feel about yourself after you control yourself!

By learning how to control yourself — even with regard to small, insignificant challenges — you thereby strengthen your ability to control yourself, and this prepares you to succeed with even more difficult challenges. So you feel good about what you have done and you help build up your inner self-control, which will help you win more battles over your future desires, which will bring you even more pleasure as you become a person with self-control. It's an "un-vicious" cycle — perhaps the only one of its kind!

Authentic Yiddishkeit believes that "self–control" is the epitome of achieving the highest level of living the HUMAN experience and will give you the most satisfaction you can have in your lifetime. Want to really enjoy your LIFE? Utilize SELF-CONTROL!

WHAT ARE YOU? A SLAVE OR A KING?

"מלך: ראשי תיבות ידוע:
מוח לב כבד."

חתם סופר מסכת פסחים דף ז.

The word מלך (king), is spelled מ then ל then ך. This hints at the proper chain of command within a healthy person. For a person's מח=מ (mind) must control his לב=ל (heart) that controls his emotions, and his emotions must control his כבד=כ (liver), which the holy *Sefarim* say is the source of a person's תאוה (desires). Such a person is a מלך (king) over his own life.

However, if a person's desire controls his emotion, and his emotion controls his mind, then he is the opposite of a מלך (king) who has control over his personal empire. This useless *shmeh-geh-gee* has become a "slave" who cannot even control his own self.

MAGNETIC PULL

True text conversation between a father and his 15-year-old son:

Hi Dad - i bought a belt! Its very nice but its x me! (it's a fake ferragamo!!) personally i x need it or want it but theres still somethin pullin me - my friends r all wearing this stuff - i don't feel left out but i just wanna fit in! whatcha think?

Hi - I hear your struggle. In the end - you need to figure out what YOU want YOUR life to be without ANYONE else influencing you. I love you either way.   Daddy

Thanx Dad! Think im gonna keep it! I have enough self

"שהיה יודע לכוין אותה שעה שהקדוש ברוך הוא כועס בה ...
כמה זעמו? רגע!"

תלמוד בבלי מסכת ברכות דף ז.

When Balak brought Bilaam to curse Klal Yisrael, Bilaam knew that in order to produce maximum disaster, he had to calculate the timing of his curse to be said at a specific moment that he knew Hashem would be angry.

"ואם תאמר מה היה יכול לומר בשעת רגע?
יש לומר: כַּלֵם!"

תוספות מסכת ברכות דף ז.

Tosafos ask: Even if he could somehow properly pinpoint that specific moment, what could he possibly say in one tiny second to sufficiently damage *Klal Yisrael*? Tosafos answers: The word he intended to use was "כַּלֵם" which literally means, "destroy them."

On a deeper level, he cursed the Yidden with the one word that would unravel our mindset and lead us to total confusion and destruction: incredibly, the order of the letters of the word "כַּלֵם" is: כבד=כ (desire), לב=ל (emotion), מח=מ (mind)!

The biggest possible curse is when the chain of command within us is reversed so that our *desire* controls our *emotion* that controls our *mind*. For with this inverted chain of command we would never be able to survive as a pure and holy nation! We would still have our STRENGTH — but we wouldn't be able to use any of it properly!

"ויהפוך ה' את הקללה לברכה: ונעשה: מלך!"

ערבי נחל דברים כי תצא דרוש ה ד"ה ופירש בדרך

When it says afterward that Hashem "turned around" the curse to a blessing, this means that Hashem flipped around the word from "כלם" to "מלך" ensuring that His holy nation would retain the proper chain of command!

Authentic Yiddishkeit understands that ONLY the person who **has control** over himself is truly "free"! He is the one who is FREE to pick ANY path that he believes is right and he can control himself to stay on track to accomplish whatever goals he sets for himself! Making decisions about your life and actually following through with them is the **ultimate human experience**.

The goal of a Torah Jew is to build up his **inner strength** in order to achieve true "freedom" to exercise control over his mind and body. Every time the Torah Jew exercises his "freedom of choice," he flexes his psychological muscles and proves once again that HE is in control!

A person who follows his impulses and desires may think that the Torah Jew is *nebach* tied up by all the restrictions and lacks the FREEDOM to do whatever he wants. **However — the complete opposite is true!** It is the one following his every impulse who has no inner "freedom" to choose to live a "higher" life for an elevated purpose. Can he control his language? His eyes? His mind? Does it require any psychological "muscle" and self-control to always pick the EASIEST choice and do whatever feels good? Is he really showing off his "freedom" — or is he is trapped and bound because he simply has no self-control?

CHAOS IN THE SKY

The incoming planes were ordered to circle around the command center until further notice. One by one they entered the circle of planes as they followed the instructions given to them by air traffic control.

The teenagers who had hacked into the airport's computer system laughed hysterically as they heard the pilots frantically radioing the tower: "Come in! Come in — what's going on here — who is in charge of the control tower?"

Now it's time for you to ask yourself:

**If you are not defining and controlling your life;
then who is?**

25

LOSING ALTITUDE

Your engines are shutting down
and you're losing control.

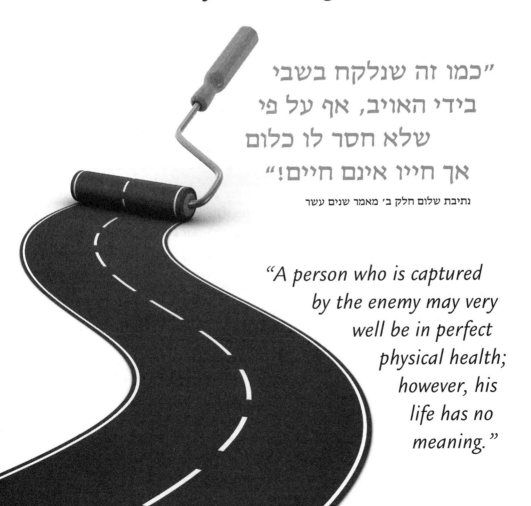

"כמו זה שנלקח בשבי
בידי האויב, אף על פי
שלא חסר לו כלום
אך חייו אינם חיים!"

נתיבת שלום חלק ב' מאמר שנים עשר

"A person who is captured
by the enemy may very
well be in perfect
physical health;
however, his
life has no
meaning."

HASHEM

took a holy Jewish soul straight from heaven and placed him smack in the middle of World War Three!

STEP 1: INBORN PULL TO BAD

‏"יש מסית שבא עם האדם מיום היותו בעולם ...‏
‏והוא מסית להאדם להרע."‏

‏אור החיים הקדוש דברים יג:ז‏

To begin with every single person has an inborn pull to do bad. Every child naturally wants to do things that he is told not to. Everyone has an Evil Inclination pulling him down.

CRUISE CONTROL

A true story: There was once a yeshivah bochur who was not behaving properly. The wise Rosh HaYeshivah called him in and asked: "Nu ... so what will be with you?"

The boy answered: "I'm letting my life roll."

To which the wise tzaddik responded: "Nothing ever rolls uphill!"

STEP 2: NEW PULLS TO SIN

‏"עוד יולד באדם כח מסית ב' באמצעות העבירה.‏
‏אם עבר על מצוה אחת תוליד בו כח החפץ רשע.‏

והוא סוד מאמר: עבירה גוררת עבירה!"
אור החיים הקדוש דברים יג:ז

Each time you sin, you create an inner pull within you to do more bad. Just as someone develops a stronger urge to smoke each time he takes a cigarette, so too each time you sin, you build up an internal urge to sin again.

You think YOU are taking a cigarette ...
but the truth is — the cigarette is taking you!

You think YOU are taking a drink ...
but the truth is — the drink is taking you!

IN THE VERY SAME WAY:
You think YOU are taking a SIN ...
but the truth is — the SIN is taking you!

STEP 3: A NEW INBORN PULL TO SIN

"עוד באמצעות נטות האדם לדרך לא טוב, יסובבנו קנות כח ג' שהוא:
נפש רעה כדרך שיזכה האדם בתוספת נשמה יתירה בהתעצמותו בדרכי ה'
כמו כן באמצעות דרכים הרעים יקנה תוספת נפש רעה להחטיאו!"
אור החיים הקדוש דברים יג:ז

After you keep on sinning over and over, you acquire a new evil soul (addictive voice) that becomes an OFFICIAL member of your thought process and now has a seat at the table and a vote in all that you do. It really feels at home.

This is very similar to what happens to someone who becomes addicted to something.

THE PROCESS OF ADDICTION

No person is born an addictive smoker. Addiction happens only after a certain number of cigarettes are smoked, whereupon at that point the person becomes mentally and physically **dependent** on them.

At first, when a person decides to smoke, he has complete freedom of choice to make a conscious decision whether he wants to smoke or not. Even if there was an **outside** "external pressure" influencing him, like peer pressure, there was no **internal** drive to smoke.

However, as the person continues to make the decision to smoke, each "friendly" cigarette he "chooses" to smoke brings him closer and closer to the point where he will eventually **lose** the ability to "choose" to NOT smoke. It will become "natural" for him to smoke and he will no longer go through the decision process each time he takes a cigarette. It's just what he does. It's the way he is. No longer is he just "a person who smokes" — now he is "**a smoker**"!

No longer is there just an *external* voice calling out to you ... such as; a friend, someone you are trying to impress, the cool kids in the neighborhood rebelling against authority, etc. ... rather it is now your OWN *internal* voice demanding to be pleased. Listen closely to that voice of temptation calling out to you and you will hear that it sounds like: "YOU"!

Once a person is officially "a smoker," every decision in his life is affected by his addiction. A smoker might actually turn down a better job, give up marrying the right person, and ruin many golden opportunities throughout his lifetime, all because he is משעובד — **bound** and **gagged** — to his new boss: a stick of poison.

You see this clearly whenever you see a smoker standing outside shivering in the freezing cold, smoking a cigarette between his chapped and shaking hands!

IT'S BAD ENOUGH THAT IT CAN KILL YOU ...
... IT DOESN'T EVEN LET YOU LIVE!

At this point, even if he were to decide to quit smoking, he would require a tremendous amount of commitment and effort. He may need all kinds of patches, chewing devices, therapy, and even perhaps hypnosis. He becomes exposed to the pain of constant challenge and failure as he tries to wrestle back control to stop doing the very thing which he himself freely "chose" to do so many times before.

This is why we will always hear a smoker say "I NEED a cigarette," for it is his "I" that "NEEDS" and craves and demands the addiction. The slogan "I NEED" becomes so powerful that it controls the rest of the person's mind.

At this point the "I NEED" motto becomes the central factor in every decision he makes. This explains why addicts are completely self-centered — since their entire world view revolves around their own needs:

"אם התאוה שלי בא לפני האני שלי;

כל שכן שהתאוה שלי בא לפני האני שלך!"

יין שרף ונתיבי אמת

Once the concept of "I NEED!" comes before your own personal needs and comforts, then it will certainly take precedence over OTHER PEOPLE's needs!

At this point your entire focus is about your **needs,** and you evolve into a **self-centered** person. You come to internally believe that YOU are the center of the entire universe and the entire universe revolves around YOU!

Now that this is who you are, who you became, what you somehow evolved into, your new life revolves around feeding your newly acquired "needs" that you just can't live without. You think the whole world runs around YOU and you lose your sensitivity to the needs and feelings of others. It's ALL about YOU — ALL the time!

TWISTED PRIORITIES *A wealthy lawyer parked his car at the side of the road and opened the door of his new BMW. Suddenly, a speeding car*

appeared from nowhere, hitting the door and ripping it off the car. The lawyer was outraged. When the police arrived at the scene, the lawyer whined, "Officer, look what that person did to my new Beemer! You have to find him and arrest him!"

"You lawyers are so materialistic, you make me sick," the officer snapped. "You're so upset about your stupid BMW that you didn't even notice that your left arm was ripped off in the accident!"

Finally noticing his missing arm, the lawyer gasped, "Oh no! — My Rolex!!"

So now we understand clearly how addiction starts out as an outside influence with very little control over the person, yet it ends up being the all-powerful deciding factor of the person's life. Even a sophisticated intelligent mature person ... can end up making foolish decisions like an impulsive immature child. The homeless guy standing next to the billionaire in the cold, smoking a cigarette, shows that BOTH are ultimately controlled by the same small-minded addiction.

NOW LET'S UNDERSTAND HOW SIN DOES THE SAME THING:

"יש הרבה ענינים המשעבדין את האדם."

נתיבות שלום עניני פסח דף ע"ר

There are many things that can restrict a person to the point that he is no longer a free man:

Family and Peer Pressure:

"ואם זה שהוא משועבד לסביבה שׁשּׁרוֹי בתוכה, או משועבד לביתו
ושאר תנאים ומצבים שהאדם נעשה משועבד להם ...."

נתיבות שלום חלק ב' עניני פסח דף רס"ט

As we explained before, every person is affected by his surroundings. He is affected by the people in his life and all the various factors that are in his life. Which Yeshivah he is in, which shul he *davens* in, the location in which he is brought up, where he spends his summers, etc.

Just as the inborn tendencies given to you by Hashem make up who you are, so too everything about the way you were brought up and the people you encountered have a real effect on who you are.

For example: Two people with the same exact internal make-up, will lead completely different lives if one is born into a Chasiddishe home and one is born into a modern home. If a child is born in Yerushalayim where he is surrounded by smokers, it does not mean that if he had been born in Monsey he would be smoking by age 12.

Many bad habits actually come from a person's **surroundings and upbringing,** what he has learned from family members, and what has been taught to him by his friends.

When you think about it, **people do not actually choose most** things about their life. They are "placed" into a specific family living in a specific area and they live that specific life with their personal "tool chest" of inborn character traits.

External Thoughts:

"ואם בהילוך מחשבתו
שנעשה משועבד וקולט הלכי מחשבה זרים שאינן שלו
ומאבד את הילוך המחשבה היהודי המקורי חס ושלום!"

נתיבות שלום חלק ב' עניני פסח דף רס"ט

Aside from your inborn character traits, and aside from the behaviors which you picked up from your family and surroundings, as you go through life you encounter all kinds of situations that cause you to think and act in a certain way.

For example: You can have naturally good character traits; however, if you become interested in the lowlife behavior you see on the streets around you and you constantly think about it — it will change your inner self.

The source for this outside influence comes from the **society** around you and a person can become **affected** and **infected** by sights and experiences he encounters throughout his lifetime.

Aside from each of the above-mentioned influences, you are also affected by a **mixture** of each influence, with endless combinations of pain and confusion.

"הצד השוה בכל אלה שהוא
משועבד לפרעה במצרים שורש הקליפה!"

נתיבות שלום חלק ב' עניני פסח דף רס"ט

The bottom line is all the same: Somehow you lost control and ended up משועבד — addicted/subservient to outside influences that pulled you away from being able to exercise control over your own mind, your own actions, and thus over your own life, as represented by the quintessential example of the most powerful king of all addiction: Paroh the king of Mitzrayim — the king of minimizing a person and squeezing him into "Mitzarim = boundaries!"

THIS IS A DEEP INSIGHT INTO THE TRUE AMBITION OF THE EVIL SNAKE!

We are used to fighting an Evil Inclination that (1) entices you to think and perform sins, and (2) tries to prevent you from performing mitzvos. However, the truth is that the cunning Yetzer Hora has a much more dangerous agenda in store for you:

"יותר מכל פיתוי והתגברות בעניני סוד מרע תאוות ומדות רעות או
במניעת עשה טוב, עוד יותר מזה נועץ יצר הרע את צפרניו במוחו ולבו
של יהודי להטרידו ולבלבלו בנתיבי הדעת לצמצם ולהקטין את תפיסתו
הרוחנית עד **שכל עבודתו בקטנות הדעת!**"

נתיבות שלום חלק א' פרקי מבוא דף י"א

Even more than (1) pushing you to sin and (2) preventing you
from doing mitzvos, the evil snake digs its fingernails deep into
your heart and mind to **bamboozle** and **confuse** you. It does this
in order to minimize your spiritual vision so that even when you
finally do something spiritual — it is done on a very shallow and
small-minded level!

"הולך יצר הרע ומסבכם ומכניס בהם ערפול ומבוכה עד שכל עבודתו
לקוי-ה בחוסר בהירות ואינו מבין מה חובתו בעולמו אשר ה' אלוקיו דורש
מעמו ועל ידי כך קוצץ ממנו את כל כנפי רוחו שלא יוכל להתעלות!"

נתיבות שלום חלק א' פרקי מבוא דף י"א

Once you are pushed down to a shallow level in your relationship
with Hashem, even the mitzvos and good deeds that you do are
done with a lack of clarity, feeling, and intensity. Eventually your
connection to Hashem becomes diluted and you forget what your
life's mission is really all about. The snake let the air out of your
tires.

At this point the Yetzer Hora can sit back and relax, because
through this molestation of your spirit it has **clipped your spiritual
wings, thereby grounding your ability to soar.** How sad indeed.

TO BRING THIS OUT CLEARLY:

Let's put aside all your past sins. And let's put aside any of your
character flaws. And while we're at it, let's also put aside all the
positive mitzvos and Torah learning/observance that you did NOT
properly pursue and actively partake in until now.

With all those things on the side, there should not be much of a difference between you and the greatest sage who ever lived — right?

Now, the next time you do any mitzvah, look at yourself from the outside and think about HOW you are performing it. Will you perform that mitzvah with the same connection, inspiration, and elevation as a pure holy Tzaddik?

IF NOT, THEN PLEASE THINK ABOUT THIS ...
WHY NOT? WHAT IS HOLDING YOU BACK?

ABSENT MINDED

Yidel always made it his business to daven with a minyan even during busy business days.

One day he got to shul just in time for Shemonah Esrei. He shuffled back and shuffled forward and started turning pages. Looking around the small shul, he surveyed the people around him. Hey, is that Avi? I haven't seen him in a long time! I wonder how he's doing? "Atuh kudosh ...."

After feeling the familiar vibration in his shirt pocket, he pulled out his Blackberry. As he rounded "slach lanoo," his right hand softly patted the left side of his chest while his left hand softly scrolled to pick up his email: News update: The Yankees just agreed to trade Julio Mariolesia for 12 million dollars. "Oh shoot! Shema Kolaiynu ...."

Bow down ... "Modim ..." check text ... "Yidel we r all here — where r u?" Cruising past "Sim Shalom," he sent a quick reply "running late — be there in 15," shuffle back ... shuffle up. Kedushah. Gone like the wind.

Let's break this down: Yidel took time out of his hectic day to "speak directly to G-d." He obviously believes in Hashem and believes that he can talk to Hashem. If so, why did he perform this "act of connecting to G-d" on such a small-minded and watered-down level???

This is exactly the point that we are trying to bring out. Aside from previous acts of sin, and aside from the prevention of your positive deeds, there is a much more serious "game" going on:

"כל עיקר התגברות הרע אצל האדם
היא בעת חשכות וצמצום הדעת וקטנות המוחין
כשהוא הולך חשכים ואין נוגה לו ומשל לסומא החשוב כמת!"
נתיבות שלום חלק א' פרקי מבוא דף י"א

The main threat of the powers of evil is to create situations where you feel depression and darkness that restrict and compress your ability to think clearly, at which point you are like a blind person who is compared to a dead person!

Authentic Yiddishkeit understands that the REAL GOAL of the evil snake is to deflate you and water down your relationship with Hashem so that even when you manage to do something good, you do it with a very superficial mindset, thus losing your opportunity to connect with G-d as you could and should! This glides you further down the slippery slope toward disconnection.

Of course you aren't *davening* now as best as YOU can — because in your mind you don't really have a close relationship with Hashem! And what made you come to that conclusion? Your previous sins!

YOUR SINS are what prevent you from feeling completely connected to Hashem and calling out to Him wholeheartedly in your time of need.

YOUR SINS cause you to think that perhaps you are not the person Hashem really meant to call "My beloved precious son!"

YOUR SINS block you from feeling elated when you learn the Holy Torah and from feeling enthusiastic while doing mitzvos.

When you disregard the will of G-d and you set your petty fleeting desires as a priority, then you are swimming against the natural tide of alliance with your Creator. Your life becomes a gerbil wheel as you run aimlessly on the treadmill of pleasure, getting nowhere fast. Your potential has been grounded.

This is the real reason the snake wants you to sin — not just for the few points of commission that it gets for causing you to do a sin — but much more so for weakening your entire grasp of spirituality and sinking your spiritual battleship!!

"ובלא זה אין לאדם כל חיות,

וחוץ מיסורים אין לו מאומה בעולם התלאות ותמיד חסר לו;

כי בתאוות העולם הזה הרי מי שיש לו מנה רוצה מאתים."

מרן בעל בית אברהם זי"ע נתיבות שלום עניני סוכות מאמר ראשון קצ"א

Once you feel disconnected from G-d, you will feel that you have no spunk left in you. The world increasingly becomes a dark and depressing world, with one letdown after another. Life becomes full of pain and anguish, and you always feel that you are missing out on the spice of life. You feel empty.

As you become dispirited and deflated, you lose the ability to clearly see the hand of Hashem. Then, your life begins to lose true meaning, and internal happiness escapes you — and THAT IS WHAT THE EVIL SNAKE WANTED ALL ALONG!

"לא תיתכן חיות ליהודי אם מרגיש

שמחיצות מפסיקות בינו לבין אביו שבשמים."

נתיבות שלום עניני פורים

It is not possible for a Jew to feel alive while he feels that there is a brick wall between himself and his Father in Heaven.

This is the secret war going on in our lives and this deep concept is really what our exile is really all about. For as long as someone feels completely connected to Hashem, it would not matter whether he is bringing a sacrifice in the Bais HaMikdash or walking into the gas chambers of Auschwitz.

"משמעותה של גלות היא
מה שיהודי מרגיש עצמו רחוק מהשם יתברך ....
... ומחו ולבו אטומים ומחיצה של ברזל מפסקת בינו לבין השם יתברך."

נתיבות שלום חלק ב׳ שבת עמוד פ׳ז

The main aspect of our being in exile is that our hearts and minds are clogged and numb and we **feel** as though there is an iron wall dividing us from Hashem. This is what being in exile is really all about: being in chains!

26

CONFUSION

What is the worst state to live in?
The state of Confusion!

"רבי שמחה בונים מפשיסחא:
'שצרוך האדם לגמור בדעתו
תמיד כאילו איש אחד עומד
לנגדו וגרזן בידו להתיז ראשו [כנגד
יצר הרע אמר כן]. ובאם שאין זה
בדעתו, הוא סימן שכבר התיז
את ראשו.'"

קיז מבשר חלק א נח י"ג

REB BUNIM M'PSHISCHA:

"You must imagine the Yetzer
Hora standing in front of
you with an ax ready to
chop off your head.
And if you don't
feel that way —
that means it
already did!"

HASHEM

created you on a much higher level than an animal but you can end up living like one anyway:

"יש לפעמים אשר מרגיש בענין מסוים שהפך להיות **משועבד לרע**, דהיינו שפרט זה אינו אצלו בגדר תאוה בעלמא **אלא הוא משועבד לו לחלוטין!**"

ספר נתיבות שלום עניני פסח דף ע"ר

You may find that regarding certain specific sins (thoughts or actions), you are not just dealing with a typical desire that is pulling you to sin; rather, you have reached a point that you have become completely משעובד (bound/addicted) to them.

HOW DID THIS HAPPEN?

"הכל משום שאין זו התגברות יצר הרע בעלמא **אלא הוא הפך להיות משועבד לגמרי בענין זה** עד שאינו שליט על עצמו כלל להתנתק מהרע!"

נתיבות שלום חלק ב' עניני פסח דף ע"ר

There has been a major shift within your mind. No longer are you overtaken by an **external voice of temptation** that is trying to convince you to transgress the will of G-d; rather, the sin **infiltrated your very existence** and now you find yourself **internally** drawn to these sins!

At this point you are actually a slave. You lost the self-control to detach yourself from them! You are now משועבד (bound/addicted) to them and at their mercy! You work for THEM!

Once you are trapped, you can't see clearly anymore. What is important seems silly and what is silly seems important. Everything is blurry. Where is G-d? Where are the good things in your life? How come peace and tranquility elude you? How come you can't appreciate the good in your life?

SWEET 'N SOUR

A person can become physically sick and things that are sweet will taste sour to him, and sour or spoiled things will taste sweet to him.

> "נפש רעבה שאינו מרגיש תענוג בעבודת ה' ואין לו תענוגים דקדושה,
> אדם זה מחפש תענוגים רעים וכל מר מתוק לו."
>
> ספר נתיבות שלום חלק ב' עניני שבת עמוד צ"ט

In the very same way, one who no longer feels spiritual pleasure, will seek out "bitter" pleasure and it will seem "sweet" to him.

Everything is turned around. Sweet wonderful spirituality (like Torah, mitzvos, Shabbos, and Yom Tov) tastes disgusting, whereas vulgar, vile, disgusting temporary physical pleasures suddenly seem quite nice and sweet. You find yourself smack in the middle of a hostile takeover as you try to run from the power that is trying to take over your mind.

"ומהאי טעמה יש עניינים מסוימים אשר כל כמה
שיהודי מקבל על עצמו וחוזר ומקבל אינו מועיל לו – והוא חוזר ונכשל!"
נתיבות שלום חלק ב' ענייני פסח דף ע"ר

This is why when it comes to these specific sins, even if you make a clear decision that you truly want to improve, your inner resolve and willpower are simply **not strong enough** and you will continue to stumble over and over again.

Your בחירה (power to choose) is now irrelevant, because no matter what you choose — you can't follow through with it, since your addiction controls how you act! It is at the wheel … the driving force of your life. Your **GPS** has been hijacked!

"יש מסגר הסוגר על מדות המח ויש מסגר על מדות הלב ...
נתון הוא במסגר לפי שמשועבד לכוחות הסטרא אחרא!"
נתיבות שלום ענייני פסח מאמר י"ב אות ד' עמוד ע"ר

There are many forms of "chains" that bind a person. There are chains that bind a person's ability to **THINK** and there are chains that bind a person's ability to **FEEL**, etc. … there are many different ways that a person becomes bound and gagged and completely משועבד to the forces of evil that surround him.

When you follow your יצר הרע (Evil Inclination) to think or perform עבירות (sins) that you already decided are wrong for your life and are not what you really want — that shows that you do not have the ability to control your own self.

You may be living in a "free country"; however, you are NOT "free." Your mind is chained down, bound and controlled by outside influences that have infiltrated your mindset and have become who YOU are. Inside your conscience you're suffering because you know that you've lost the ability to control your own self. And that hurts!

Deep inside, you are full of incredible emotional pain! You have lost control over your own identity and now **you lack an identity.** Who are you really? What do you truly stand for? Who is really in charge of making decisions for you? You know this is not the way you really want to live your life — you want to be better — why can't you just grab hold of yourself and regain control over your own mind!? You are DOWN and OUT and this is EXACTLY where the Evil Inclination wants you!

MISGUIDED

Shimmy was late, again, for a meeting. He had to be in Manhattan in forty-five minutes. OK, no problem ... he jumped into his car ... and entered the address into his trusty GPS. Shimmy didn't know that his arch enemy Simon, was out to get him. Simon, a technological evil genius, managed to break into Shimmy's GPS frequency and now he was able to direct Shimmy in any way that he wanted! Shimmy got on his Bluetooth and partook in an important conference call, while blindly following whatever his GPS told him: turn left ... turn right ... turn right ... turn left .... Simon was having so much fun making Shimmy go round and round! After two hours, Shimmy missed his meeting and found himself under the tracks in a dangerous neighborhood ... out of gas!

In the beginning you utilized your *"free will"* to follow the external temptation. However, after continuing to choose this thought or action over and over, this EXTERNAL TEMPTATION slowly transformed itself into becoming an **internal and integral** part of your very being. It somehow became a **part** of who you are and it became **your natural** way of thinking or acting. Eventually you lost some — or most — and sometimes even ALL — of your G-d-given right to "free will"!

Looking back, you will remember the days when you began your journey. In hindsight, those original urges were so small! If only you would have utilized your self-control to withstand those relatively small urges — you would have SPARED YOURSELF from much BIGGER urges! From MORE challenges! From MORE pain! How foolish you were to give in and open that door.

Now the urge is entirely different from the first few times you casually utilized your freedom of choice without thinking about the long-term consequences. Your mind now NEEDS these thoughts. Your body now NEEDS these actions.

Now, in spite of your decision to change your ways, you may find that you've lost the power to carry out your new will. You have become powerless. At this point YOU are the bad influence in your OWN life! This urge is now YOUR OWN urge. It is now a part of who YOU are and it becomes extremely difficult to wrestle control back from it.

Just as one introduces a person by his descriptive title: "a doctor," "a lawyer," "a rabbi," "a ben Torah," "a businessman," "an insurance salesman," etc., **YOU** have now become: "a smoker," "an alcoholic," "a drug addict," "a compulsive gambler," "a בעל תאוה" (glutton), "a בעל גאוה" (haughty person), etc., and this addiction is wedged deeply in your mind, affecting every decision you make — whether you realize it or not!

Once you are controlled by something other than your own intellectual sound mind, this outside influence (which is now an **inside** influence) will bring you new interests, opinions, and desires that you have no way to stop.

REAL BAD INFLUENCE

Motti had a very pure Yiddishe mind and unclean thoughts were foreign to him. However, he spent a lot of time with Josh, who always told him unclean jokes and looked at life through a filthy lens. After a while Motti didn't need to hear these jokes from Josh, for his own mind produced them for himself!

Once this crooked mindset becomes the starting point of your thought process, you will base all your decisions on top of this warped and crooked foundation! At this point you will use all of your G-d-given intelligence, wiSODOM, and logic to defend crooked ideals and false concepts. Your internal "calculator" is broken and you are living a completely false life!

A COCKTAIL OF CONFUSION

"אותיות הראשונות של **בלק** ובלעם הם 'בלבל' והאחרונות הם 'עמלק' כי זה גם קליפת עמלק להכניס את האדם **בבלבול** הדעת **שעל ידי זה הוא כולו ביד היצר הרע!**"

זוהר הקדוש ח"ג רפא: מובא בנתיבות שלום חלק ב' עניני שבת דף פ"ט

The first two letters of the names Balak and Bilaam create the word בלבל, which means confusion, and the last two letters create the word עמלק, which represents everything that is "against" what Yiddishkeit is all about!

Authentic Yiddishkeit understands that the biggest threat to a Jew's spiritual well being is **"CONFUSION"**! For once in a state of confusion, you are completely in the Yetzer Hora's clutches.

SIP BY SIP At 30 Ruby did not expect to pick up any addictions. He always enjoyed a l'chayim here and there but he never drank too much and usually never drank during the week. As he went through some difficult times, he began to take a shot after Shacharis to get the day going. He found that after work he was very tense, and so he started to take a shot or three when he got home. He felt that it was simply the "best" way to deal with his children, since he needed to be more patient with them.

After a few months, he found himself finding more "good"

reasons to take a shot here and there throughout the day ... like — if a good thing happened! Or if a stressful situation happened! Or if nothing happened! Slowly but surely, the dependency crept up on him and he became a full-fledged alcoholic.

Looking back, he realized that each one of his friendly "shots" that he happily welcomed into his life were actually all in on this scheme the whole time! Each little individual weak shot was part of this coup d'état and now they all ganged up on him and took over his mind and destroyed his self-control! He is now at completely at their mercy!

What was once a simple, easy decision (not to do certain acts, not to think certain thoughts, not to look at certain things) now requires incredible commitment and T.M.E. (time, money, and effort!) to get the assistance you need because **you lost control over your own mind!**

Each time you do not successfully maintain control over yourself, your future ability to control yourself fades away. At this point, regarding these specific thoughts or actions, you are no different from any addict who lost control of his life.

Once you lost the ability to control yourself, you became a split personality. It used to be that once you made a decision about what is best for you, you were able to follow through with it! Meaning: If you came to the conclusion that something was BAD for you — you were able to STOP doing it. If you came to the conclusion that something was GOOD for YOU — then you were able to START doing it. Life was so simple in those days.

But now things have changed quite a bit. You may decide what is right for you from an intellectual or moral standpoint, but there is another part of **YOU** that is in **CONTROL** of what you actually end up doing. This evil part of you does not allow YOU to follow through with your commitments and resolutions. You become a living, breathing hypocrite, since you now have thoughts or actions that are not in sync with what YOU truly want for yourself.

You will find yourself confused: Hey! Didn't I already decide to DO this good thing!?! Hey! Didn't I already decide that I should have these good thoughts!?! Hey! Didn't I already come to the conclusion that I don't want to do those bad things!?! Hey! Didn't I already decide NOT to have these kinds of bad thoughts!?! What HAPPENED after I made my decision??? Who's really in control here???

ITCHY YITZY

Mosquitoes bit poor Yitzy all over his face and it was itching like crazy. He knew that the best thing for him would be to hold back the urge to scratch, and he tried so hard not to. But then he just couldn't hold back any more and he lost control. He scratched and scratched and, boy, did it feel good. He thought that he really "fixed" his problem, but only one short minute later that same crazy itch returned — with a vengeance!

Yitzy clearly understood that giving in to the urge to scratch only helps for a really short amount of time and then makes his situation even worse than it was before — and yet — all day he kept finding himself scratching away. His good friend told him, "Yitzy — if you just don't give in to the urge to scratch, in a few days this will all be history." But Yitzy simply couldn't control himself. He kept scratching — it kept itching — he scratched more — it itched more — scratch — itch — scratch — itch!

Two days later his face was a mess. His scratching caused the bites to bleed. Then his skin became infected and he had to buy all kinds of anti-infection creams. After about a week scabs began to form. That was good news. But if you think the original irritation was itchy, boy-oh-boy, were these itchy scabs itchy! Yitzy — now known as Itchy — just couldn't control himself and he kept scratching off the scabs, preventing the healing process from completing. Thus he entered a vicious cycle. Scratching. Bleeding. Creams. Scabs. Scratching. Bleeding. Infection. No more scabs. More bleeding. More creams. Infections. Puss. Creams. Bandages. Finally scabs. Scratching. Bleeding. And back to the beginning.

Because of Itchy's lack of self control, the relatively minor problem that should have been gone after a few short days, turned into a huge life-altering situation that ended up scarring Itchy for the rest of his life.

You were meant to be a king over your own personal empire. However, the outside influences that you yourself happily invited into your own castle orchestrated a hostile takeover and demoted you to not having any influence in determining your final destination! This out-of-control behavior (addiction) rips you up inside and causes inner turmoil and emotional pain, and it destroys the quality of your life!

Now you find yourself being bossed around by external corrupt and immoral ideas that are now sitting in YOUR executive chair in the penthouse of YOUR mind.

OVERNIGHT NIGHTMARE

Yankel founded a company. After a few short years of incredible success, Yankel took his company public. When the company hit some challenges, there was a sudden hostile takeover — and overnight the shareholders voted him out of his position of power.

The next day Yankel came to work as usual. He had no

idea of what happened. As he pulled into the executive parking lot, he could not find his parking space with his name on it. When he entered the building, the elevator operator told him that he may not ride the presidential elevator to the executive offices; rather, he must take the freight elevator down to his new cubicle in the shipping department!

As bad as this situation was for Yankel, it was even more painful because the guy who orchestrated the hostile takeover and took over as the new President and CEO — was a homeless kid who Yankel personally liked and had invited to join his company!

Being shoved aside by the thoughts that you yourself happily invited into your life — is extremely painful! Now you are forced to think thoughts that you no longer want — and yet you cannot find any way to stop yourself! You are your own worst enemy.

Ultimately, the worst condition for a human being is to lose the control over his own mind, for if you are not controlling yourself, in what way are you better than an animal?

THIS IS THE PROBLEM WITH SINNING OVER AND OVER:

"דאמר רב הונא:

כיון שעבר אדם עבירה ושנה בה – **הותרה לו.**

הותרה לו סלקא דעתך? אלא נעשית 'לו' כהיתר."

תלמוד בבלי מסכת קידושין דף כ'

If you sin over and over, it seems permissible to you.

The simple explanation is: After you sin over and over, when faced with doing that sin again, you become numb to the severity of the sin and it will no longer strike you as such a terrible thing to do.

HOWEVER, FASTEN YOUR SEATBELT FOR A DEEP LESSON:

"אדם השולט בעצמו ובתאותיו
נקרא 'אסור' כיון שהוא קשור מדיני התורה
לעומתו, אדם שאין לו שליטה עצמית נהי-ה 'מותר' בלי גבולים!"

ספר נתיבי אמת

The Hebrew word for something that is tied and bound is **אסור**, whereas something that is loose and unbound is called **מותר**.

Someone who follows the restrictions, rules, and guidelines of Torah life is called **אסור** (bound) since he has control over himself. Whereas, someone who constantly gives into temptation is called **מותר** (unbound), since he has lost proper control over himself:

"כיון שעבר אדם עבירה ושנה בה פעם אחר פעם
אז מחריב הוא את כל הקשרים שיש לו מן התורה
וממילא נעשה 'לו' רצה לומר: האדם גופא - כהיתר!"

ספר נתיבי אמת

When you keep on sinning over and over again, you damage your inner self by weakening your spiritual "seatbelt" and loosening the straps that secure you to a happy, pure Torah lifestyle.

All of these sins "**נעשה "לו**, cause the person himself to become **"כהיתר"** like an unbound animal who is not capable of utilizing any self-control.

Even though no one else can see it, there is a full-blown war going on in your mind. There are scuffles, skirmishes, kidnapings, undercover agents, double agents, terrorist attacks, suicide bombers, and perfectly orchestrated attacks.

Your self-esteem and self-worth deteriorate as you struggle with the fact that you do not have the ability to control your own being! You are a slave to a faceless master that you cheerfully invited into your mind. Your new master has no morals, no values, no pity, and no boundaries. He is relentless, persistent, unyielding, and ruthless. He is ... the new YOU.

Your life becomes one of great confusion, frustration, and guilt. You try to find ways to blame outside circumstances or other people for your own inability to follow through on your own החלטות (resolutions). You feel like a loser.

THIS FRICTION CAN TEAR YOU UP AS YOU WATCH YOURSELF SLIPPING INTO YOUR OWN PERSONAL EXILE:

"וזה משמעות גלות פנימית:
כשהנשמה אינה שולטת על נפש הבהמי שבאדם
ואז הוא בבחינת שביה – שהוא התחלת הגלות!"

ספר נתיבות שלום חלק ב' פ"ח

You have entered your own personal inner exile, as your holy Yiddishe *neshamah* loses control. You are becoming a CAPTIVE at the mercy of these forces that are fighting you tooth and nail to control your life!

At this point you can only dream of a time that you will actually be able to determine for yourself the way you want to act and have the life you really want to live.

You dream and dream and dream ....
You may have dreams, but they are far from reality.
Right now you can't pull yourself up ....
You are powerless ...

and — boy — does that hurt!

Looks like you need an:

EXTREME SPIRITUAL MAKEOVER!

HOW TO LIVE
LIFE TO THE MAX
M.H.E.
MAXIMUM HUMAN EXPERIENCE

A person
is alive to
conquer his
nature ...
for if not,
then what is
the purpose
of life?

"כי מה שהאדם
חי הוא לשבר
את המידה
אשר לא
שבר עד הנה
- ואם לאו
למה לו
חיים?"

גאון על משלי

INTRODUCTION

MAKE A LEGAL U-TURN

*Maybe it's time to pull over
and reprogram your destination.*

"זכאין אינון מאריהון
דתשובה דהא בשעתא חדא
ביומא חדא ברגע חדא!"

זוהר כרך א' בראשית פרשת חיי שרה קכט.

*"Fortunate are those who
repent, for in one year, one day
and even one moment
you can change your life!"*

INTRODUCTION

WASTED POTENTIAL

Everyone knows there is nothing more sad than seeing someone waste his G-d-given "potential." If you know someone who was given the gift of brilliance and he could have been a famous educator, professor, doctor, musician, etc. ..., and he is living an unimportant average life, it hurts you to see the waste of human potential. When you see the son of a rich man who was given the chance to take over his father's company and live a rich, successful, important life and he threw it away chasing petty desires, we can all sense the loss of potential.

You may be are aware of the potential lying deep inside of you. If you look in the mirror and think about how your life could have turned out if you hadn't thrown away the opportunities Hashem gave you, you will find yourself in tremendous pain. This bitter feeling makes a person feel depressed.

Even if you would try to mask it with smiles and you would try to make everyone think that you are enjoying life and having a great time, you would mourn the loss of your potential every thinking day of your life. The pain can be so great that you would even need to look for ways to dull or numb the pain.

The truth is; if you do not take advantage of your full potential and become all that you can be, you actually "kill" that potential within you: you KILLED that piece of life that G-d gave you.

Thus we can say that fulfilling your personal potential is the epitome of achieving the highest level of living the HUMAN experience and will give you the most satisfaction you can have in your lifetime. Want to really enjoy your LIFE? Fulfill your potential!

But what happens when you find yourself LOST and CONFUSED? Have no fear, GPS will guide you back, step by step, to a life of meaning!

You might be thinking:
This all sounds great, but ... can I really turn around?

TURNING YOUR LIFE AROUND

"כרחק מזרח ממערב
הרחיק ממנו את פשעינו."
תהלים פרק קג:יב

Dovid HaMelech writes:
"As far as the east is from the west,
so has Hashem removed our transgressions from us."

"אדם יכול לחזור בתשובה בתוך זמן מועט מאוד...
'כרחוק מזרח ממערב' שאינו רחוק כלל ורק שצריך להסב פניו ויהי-ה במערב
'כן הרחיק ממנו את פשעינו.'"
חתם סופר החדש ליקוטים קידושין מט:

A person can repent and change his life in a very short amount of time! Just as a person facing east only has to turn himself around to be completely facing west, so to, even if you find that your life is on a path of sin and abuse of your *middos*, all you have to do is **MAKE A LEGAL U-TURN** and change the direction of your life!

Is it easy to turn yourself around? Of course not! But at least you should know that if you do the difficult work involved and you follow the steps required — you CAN actually change and can unlock the potential which Hashem gave you.

"ויאמר ה' אל אברהם:

לך לך מארצך וממולדתך ומבית אביך אל הארץ אשר אראך."

פרשת לך לך יב:א

"Hashem said to Avraham: For your own sake, leave your hometown, your relatives, and your father's house, and go to the land that I will show you."

"יש אצל האדם מידות רעות המושרשות בו מצד הארץ שנמצא בה ...

ויש מידות רעות הבאות מצד המשפחה ...

"ויש פגמים הטבועים בדם שאותם קשים ביותר לעקור ...."

מדברי נתיבות שלום פרשת לך לך דף ס"ד

As we previously explained; (1) the land where a person lives influences his character, (2) a person absorbs bad traits from the way his family behaves and from their outlook on life, and (3) there are also imperfections that are part of one's internal make-up (DNA), and those are the hardest to transform!

"וזאת אמר הקב"ה לאברהם

שיעקר המידות הרעות וישרש אחריהן יותר ויותר עמוק

עד שיגיע 'אל הארץ אשר אראך' היינו שיגיע לתכלית הדביקות בה'!'

מדברי נתיבות שלום פרשת לך לך דף ס"ד

This is what Hashem was telling Avraham: In order for you to reach "the promised land," meaning YOUR full potential, you must disconnect yourself: מארצך = from your land, וממולדתך = and from your family, ומבית אביך = and your DNA — what you got "from your father"!

The same goes for each one of us: The only way you will truly change and reach **your potential** is if you are willing to FIGHT AND CHANGE every single aspect of your life, from your surrounding

אלקי ישראל / יעקב בגדו שברו של ה' יתגלה אליקין

area — to the negative influences of your family — to your very essence. Just as the Torah showed us about Avraham Avinu: only by waging a FULL-SCALE WAR ON ALL FRONTS can you truly change and reach the "promised land."

U-TURN

After traveling FOUR DAYS to get from Brooklyn, New York to Portland, Connecticut (a trip that should have taken four hours), Yeshai finally realized that when he had programmed his GPS, he accidentally entered Portland "Texas" as his destination!

The realization that he wasted so much time for so long and that he was so far off course was very frustrating for him. He lost time and money (on tolls and gas), and wasted days of his life cruising 70 mph down a beautiful highway ... the wrong way! He thought to himself — how could I have been such a fool?

What should he do now? Keep driving toward Texas? Pump up the music, put the pedal to the metal, and pretend nothing is wrong?

There is only one way for him to get back on the right track. He needs to pull over and re-enter his destination — the right one this time! He will need to immediately make a U-turn! It will cost him even more money to get back on track. However, if he reprograms his GPS and follows exactly what it tells him to do — he WILL reach the correct destination!

The same is true in real life. One day you might wake up and realize that you have been cruising on the highway of life ... but in the wrong direction! You will feel like ignoring your instincts and just keep on cruising ... change is SO hard ... you'll pump up the volume to drown out your inner conscience. But deep down you know that it will not lead you to a happy and satisfied life. It's your life — you have to reach your potential and be all that you can be ....

AGAINST THE TIDE

Irwin, a senior citizen, was driving down the freeway when his cell phone rang. Answering, he heard his wife's voice urgently warning him: "I just heard on the news that there's a car going the wrong way on the freeway — please be careful!" He yelled back: "it's not just one car — it's hundreds of them!!!"

"וזוהי גם כן הדרך לכל יחיד **העמל ומתייגע כל ימיו**
להשתחרר מכל השעבודים דסטרא אחרא ואינו עולה בידו."
בעל בית אברהם זי"ע מובא בנתיבות שלום חלק ב' דף ע"ר

Surely there must have been times in your life that you were motivated and inspired to improve and yet ... you were not as successful as you had hoped. Hmmm ... how did that happen? That's frustrating! Why have you never been successful in truly breaking free from the influence of evil that binds you and prevents you from reaching your potential?

COMMON MISTAKE

At 300 solid pounds, Jerry finally got sick and tired of being heavy and he committed (once again) to losing 100 pounds. Each day he weighed himself the first thing in the morning and the last thing at night. Every time he lost a pound, he wrote it down in his journal: "Today, Monday January 3rd, I lost one pound" ... "Today, Thursday January 6th, I lost 3 pounds!" and so on.

After a year of hard work, Jerry wanted to see how many pounds he had lost. So he added up all the pounds that he "lost" and it totaled "100 lost pounds" — and yet when he went on the scale, he weighed 350! How can this be?

Jerry immediately went to Staples and bought a new calculator! Again he added up all the pounds he had lost — but he ended up with the same result! Frustrated, Jerry called his accountant for an emergency meeting to figure out where he went wrong with his numbers!

The accountant studied the entire situation and then presented him with the answer: "My dear Jerry, although you had days that you did very well and you really did lose weight, since you did not fully stick to the diet, there were other days that you GAINED weight! You only added up the pounds you lost without adding back in the pounds you gained! After studying the entries we noticed that you began each week with a renewed commitment to lose weight and you did lose a few pounds each Sunday, Monday, etc. ..., but then between Thursday night chulent, Erev Shabbos 'toi-ah-meh-hoo,' Friday night Shalom Zachor, Shabbos morning Kiddush — including; herring, kishka, kugel (potato, lukshin and of course salty noodle and sweet yerushalmi!), chulent, pastrami, some more chulent, and then 11 yummy deserts all 'l'kuvid Shabbis Koidesh!' you gained them all back — and then some!"

You might conclude that over the year Jerry did not lose a single pound — however, that conclusion is simply not true! Each time he successfully controlled himself, he really did lose weight! He did try hard hundreds of times and he did actually accomplish each time that he tried! There were many days that he successfully controlled himself and he really did lose 100 pounds over the year!

Yet in the end he was not successful in netting an actual loss of pounds because **he did not wage an all-out war**.

At the end of a full year of hard work, including depriving himself hundreds of times and constantly building up his strength to renew his commitment over and over again, Jerry found that he weighed even MORE than before an entire year of hardship! What a waste of energy!

THE SAME APPLIES TO YOU:

"הסיבה לכך היא בגלל שממשיך על עצמו תמיד הארות קטנות,
ומקבל על עצמו קבלות קטנות שיש בהן אחיזת החיצונים
נמצא שעדיין הוא משועבד לרע."

בעל בית אברהם זי"ע מובא בנתיבות שלום חלק ב' דף ע"ר

Although there were many times that you managed to pull yourself together to try and strengthen yourself and attempt to improve, you were only able to wage a weak revolt with minimal firepower.

Therefore, at the very same time that you tried to pull away from the evil within you, since you were still attached to the evil — it constantly pulled you back in! You may have tried to get up and walk one way — but your "life" was on a path going the other way!

AGAINST ALL ODDS

As the store closed and Koby was about to leave the building, he realized that he had left his cell phone on the 10th floor! The elevator had already been shut down for the night, so he would have to climb ten flights of stairs. It would be a lot of work but he would do it. However, when he reached the stairwell he found that it was under construction and blocked off.

The security officer saw him flustered and told him, "Don't worry, son, just go down the hall, make a left, and you'll see the escalators." Koby's heart gladdened at the thought of sailing up the ten floors with little effort;

> *however, when he reached the escalators he found that there was a slight technical problem. When it comes to closing time and the company wants to empty out the building, they program all the escalators to go DOWN! Realizing he had no choice, he started running up the escalator!*

Think about how much effort it takes to walk against the direction of the escalator. Even as Koby makes the effort to raise himself up and he lifts his foot to go up, at that same exact time the escalator has already pulled him down. When he gets tired and takes even a short break — he will lose so much of his hard work in a short amount of time! Koby is up against a constant unrelenting downward pull that never ever gets tired.

Is it doable? Perhaps ... but it would take incredible strength that only a few people have. Wouldn't it be so much easier if the escalators would have been joining his efforts to pull him in the right direction???

Similarly, if your life is constantly being pulled down, then trying to stand up for yourself and make the climb against the tide will not be enough to allow you to successfully change.

So you try. You fail. You try again — but you fail again. Then you get sick and tired of trying and sick and tired of yourself — and then it's even harder to try. You begin to develop negative thoughts, like: "Why bother to try if I'm just going to fail again?" "I obviously have no self control." "I am a big loser ...."

DONUT TRAP *As every dieter knows all too well; the reason that you gained weight was not because you messed up on your diet plan and ate ONE donut ... rather, it's because once you felt like a failure — you finished the whole box!*

You cannot expect to easily take back control over your life once you have already **lost control** to the forces of darkness that have invaded your control tower. In fact, your dark invader LOVES when you keep attempting weak and unplanned minor attacks against him, so that he can crush your spirit and show you once again that you can **never** win back any control! This pushes you deeper into despair and depression, thereby placing yourself further in his control.

There is nothing more satisfying to a ruler than the opportunity to crush a tiny weak rebellion and flex his mighty muscles to show everyone under his rule who is really in charge.

Please don't give him that satisfaction. You cannot afford to once again get excited and motivated to "try" improving your life, for it is senseless to waste your energy and emotional stamina on waging **tiny battles** to improve yourself, only to be knocked down once again.

Therefore, as you read the next section of our book, if you start using the skills we teach you to begin fighting right away, you will once again only be waging a weak revolt using concepts that are still relatively new to you and not really ingrained in your inner psyche. These new ideas will never be strong enough to fight against the deeply entrenched thoughts controlling your corrupt mind and the result will most likely be that once again you will lose.

— THE UNIQUE GPS APPROACH —

We want you to try a different approach and patiently plan a sophisticated full-fledged attack from a point of strength and control, and then once-and-for-all make a life change. It's the only way to really win.

YOU need to pull over, ANALIZE **ALL** ASPECTS OF YOUR LIFE, and truly reprogram your destination — the right one this time!

Much focus and determination are needed in order to put yourself on the truly right path toward the life that **you want** to be proud of — once and for all!

We suggest that before you take any action to improve your life, you should absorb the CONCEPTS in the next section; spend a few quiet minutes each day reading and re-reading, thinking and re-thinking, living and breathing these new concepts into your being by reviewing the step each and every day until you completely internalize it.

The idea of working on individual concepts is to focus and completely **internalize** one idea at a time and then build on that knowledge as you move on to the next step. Just as an army must have the ability to attack by air, sea, and land in order to overthrow an entrenched enemy, only utilizing the **power of ALL the steps** fused together deep within you, and with Hashem's help you will be able to tap into a power far greater than you ever experienced and overthrow the evil regime that took control of your life, and propel yourself to greatness.

UP, UP, AND AWAY

A spaceflight begins with a rocket launch, which provides the initial thrust to overcome the force of gravity and propels the spacecraft from the surface of the Earth. Once in space, the motion of a spacecraft — both when unpropelled and when under propulsion — is covered by the area of study called Astrodynamics. Source: Wikipedia

---

ATTAINING SPIRITUAL ASTRODYNAMICS

Only after you completely **internalize** all the steps can you plan the day that you will unleash all your power and put them into motion with a unified attack on all fronts. You will have ALL the necessary tools to give you the initial thrust to overcome the force of gravity that has been keeping you grounded all these years.

This may be the very first **REAL WAR** in which you truly take on the evil within you and make a real effort to completely change and improve your life once and for all!

Everything must be "on the negotiating table" and open for introspection. Everything which you do "just because" that's the way people these days do it ... or that's the way you were brought up ... or the way you naturally do things ... must be up for honest evaluation.

You must be willing to take the necessary — albeit painfully difficult — steps "אל הארץ אשר אראך," toward the new life that Hashem wants you to have "היינו שיגיע לתכלית הדביקות בה'," which is to reach the ultimate purpose of truly being connected to Hashem!

CONCEPT ONE

This is NOT the real me!

CONCEPT ONE

"וייצר שתי יצירות: יצירה מן התחתונים ויצירה מן העליונים ...
מלמטה: אוכל ושותה כבהמה, פרה ורבה כבהמה, מטיל גללים כבהמה,
ומת כבהמה, מלמעלה: עומד כמלאכי השרת, מדבר, ומבין, ורואה
כמלאכי השרת."

בראשית רבה פרשה יד:ג

Hashem took a lofty, angelic נשמה (soul), which has the superior power of intellect, reason, morality, long-term vision, etc. ... and inserted it into a physical, animalistic body.

SO HERE'S WHAT YOU'RE UP AGAINST:

Since you were created with the same physical needs and basic instincts of every other animal, you have bodily needs and an inborn pull toward living a physically pleasurable life. This is completely foreign to your holy נשמה (soul) which is not bound to any form of גשמיות (physicality) whatsoever, and is craving accomplishment, growth, purpose, clarity, and it yearns to connect to its source: Hashem.

So to start off with — it's like you have a **split personality disorder**! One side pulls you one way — and the other side pulls you the other way. Day by day, year after year, these two sides inside you are having a tug of war. Your ANIMAL craves physical pleasure, and your SOUL craves spiritual pleasure — and neither has any concept of what the other enjoys!

אשרי שלא-ל יעקב בעזרו שברו על הי אלקיו

BUT WAIT — THINGS GET EVEN WORSE:

Originally, Hashem created the יצר הרע (Evil Inclination) as a constant **exterior** force pulling us toward fulfilling our animalistic needs and desires. However:

"עד שאכל מן העץ ונכנס בו יצר הרע."

רש"י ישעיהו פרק ה'

When the exterior Evil Inclination, represented by the נחש (snake), caused Adam and Chavah to sin by eating from the עץ הדעת (Tree of Knowledge), the evil snake actually **entered inside them**. From then on every single one of us has that evil slimy **snake** squatting deep inside of our consciousness!

ALLOW US TO SKETCH THIS OUT FOR YOU:

(just to make sure you reeeeealllly get this concept once and for all!)

→Mitzvos→Chessed→Torah→Purity→Holiness→Hashem

The pits←evil←sin←desires←bad thoughts←

... and you were wondering why you have stress?

This is a lot to deal with and it's okay if you feel a little overwhelmed. You just realized that you are literally a wild **beast** with physical needs and urges similar to that of all wild beasts, and then on top of that, you also have a twisted, cunning, slimy **snake** lodged deep within you! Yuck!

But now that you have the facts straight, we can get to work! Your job is now to **split** your **external** image, represented by your current actions and thoughts under the influence of the combined powers of the **beast & snake,** from your pure **internal angelic** self that is yearning to be so good ... so holy ... and so close to Hashem.

This means that even if on the **exterior** you **seem rebellious**, you must now understand that in essence "YOU" are not a rebel! Although you may be thinking or acting in a way that seems as if you are spiritually contaminated, you must now comprehend that intrinsically "YOU" are pure and holy!

"ישראל נקראו צדיקים:
ועמך **כולם צדיקים** (ישעיה ס')."

ויקרא רבה (וילנא) פרשה ה'

"Yisrael is called righteous," as the Navi says: "Your nation is all righteous"! Righteous? Did the Navi really say that EVERY JEW is righteous?

YES! It is the **cunning snake** that causes you to stumble and sin in the first place, and then it turns the tables on you and tells you how low "you" are, convincing you that surely Hashem is not interested in you after what you just did! However, this is a LIE!

Your response to the evil master must be: **NO!** This is not true! I am great! I am pure! I am holy! I have an eternal pure SOUL which is an actual piece of Hashem!!! I would have never sinned if not for YOU! It is YOU that is the root of all evil — not me! Look at what YOU did to me! If not for YOUR influence over me I would always ACT like such a good, pure, holy Tzaddik! YOU are the underlying cause of each and every one of my sins! Just because YOU tripped me up that does not prove that "I" am low and "I" am bad — it just proves how bad and evil **YOU** are! If I had the ability to slaughter you once and for all and never sin again — I certainly would!

SOUL SURVIVOR

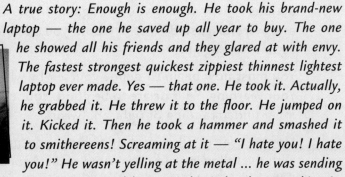

A true story: Enough is enough. He took his brand-new laptop — the one he saved up all year to buy. The one he showed all his friends and they glared at with envy. The fastest strongest quickest zippiest thinnest lightest laptop ever made. Yes — that one. He took it. Actually, he grabbed it. He threw it to the floor. He jumped on it. Kicked it. Then he took a hammer and smashed it to smithereens! Screaming at it — "I hate you! I hate you!" He wasn't yelling at the metal ... he was sending a message to its evil boss. He hit it harder. Punching it. Kicking it. Faster. Tears rolling down his cheeks as he vented his frustration on this technologically advanced version of the evil snake that slithered into his life and wrapped itself around his neck ... nearly choking him to death.

Think of how you feel on Yom Kippur, after just a few hours of disconnecting from being controlled by your BEAST and SNAKE. Remember how good you want to be and how close you want to be to Hashem.

Now realize that whenever you fall short of that lofty spiritual level, it is solely the work of the relentless beast/snake within you. It's time to take off your CLOWN costume and meet the REAL YOU!

Once you separate your exterior from your TRUE PURE HOLY ESSENCE, you can no longer judge who YOU are by your sinful thoughts and actions — which are nothing more than your beast/snake grabbing control of the wheel and forcing you to act against your true inner will!

The truth is that the only reason you ever sinned in any way is only because your mind became numb and overcome with a spirit of foolishness that caused you to go against your better judgment and inner will. After all, who in his right mind would want to sin against the will of his Creator? And for what? And after so many times that you sinned and felt regret and disgust because of your actions — why would you sin again? If you accidentally ate dirt and were disgusted by it — would you go and eat it again? And again? And again?

You must now begin to define yourself by who YOU REALLY ARE. Your yearning. Your desire to be good. Your concept of truth. Your inner understanding of right and wrong.

However, after all is said and done, you may still be struggling with the following question: Am I really a good and pure soul who falls only due to the יצר הרע burning inside me like a raging fire, or have I already been transformed to a bad, twisted and immoral human being? — Who am I?

FORTUNATELY,
WE HAVE 3 QUICK AND EASY WAYS FOR YOU TO TELL:

1. If you really are corrupt, then why would you be interested in changing yourself? Why are you reading this book? Did you think that this book is going to teach you: "How to get rich quick"?

Obviously, the concept of improving your life must have appealed to you. That says something about who you really are. You are not happy with your current status and you are looking for ways to raise yourself up and become closer to Hashem. That's pretty amazing!

2. Here's another way to know how incredible you really are deep down:

Imagine that a blank piece of paper appeared in front of you right now and a pen materialized in your hand. Suddenly you hear a heavenly voice: *"Sign your name on this piece of paper and I will guarantee that you will never sin again!"*

Would you sign up for that?

You wouldn't even think twice about grabbing this amazing

opportunity! This is a **clear indication** and deep insight into your internal רצון (will). You just proved to yourself that YOU WANT TO BE GOOD!

3. Here's another way to see how pure and amazing you really are:

If YOU really were immoral, then when you succumb to lowly sin, it wouldn't bother you and you wouldn't be filled with remorse about it! If you have the feeling of regret after you sin, it must mean that YOU really are a moral person and that is precisely the reason why you feel so very bad about what you did! It only hurts to fall from a HIGH place!

It's time for you to face the facts: You are an amazingly sweet and pure Yiddishe soul who just wants to be good and would love to be connected to Hashem! Yup — that's the real you!

HOWEVER, YOU MAY ASK:

How can you GPS people tell me that ALL the bad that I do comes from an OUTSIDE source — what about the fact that I have בחירה (the power to choose) and I seem to be the one choosing to do bad over and over again?

DANGEROUS ENEMY

Joe was set for the boxing match of his life against Mickey the reigning heavyweight champion. Aside from being a great boxer, Mickey was also very cunning and he would use any and every trick to win. Mickey found out that Joe had a set schedule for the day of his boxing matches. At 2:00 Joe would work out for 2 hours. Then at 4:00 he would take a nap for 2 hours. At 6:00 he would sit in the Jacuzzi for 30 minutes and follow that up with another 30 minutes in the steam room. At 7:00 he would jump rope and be ready to fight at 7:30.

On the day of the match, sneaky Mickey secretly set the

heat in Joe's private dressing room to go up to 90 degrees at 4:30 and then to drop back to normal at 5:45.

At precisely 6:00 Joe's coaches came into the room to wake him up and found him in a deep sleep and drenched in sweat. They couldn't understand why he was so weak. Continuing with his set routine he sat in the Jacuzzi and then the steam room. But instead of rejuvenating him, it just drained all his energy. By the time 7:00 rolled around, he was hardly able to jump rope and at 7:30 he entered the ring with no energy.

Needless to say, Mickey won in the very first round and it seemed to all of the spectators that Joe couldn't even put up a fight against the mighty Mickey. However, we know that the truth is that Joe's inability to properly fight Mickey — was ALSO because of Mickey.

The same applies to you. Your lack of ability to put up a good fight — is ALSO due to the undermining of the Evil Inclination!

"יהודי הוא בעצם משועבד להשם יתברך,
ואם הוא חוטא אינו אלא מקרה מחמת שהכשילו יצר
אבל אינו משועבד לכוחות הסטרא אחרא!"

נתיבות שלום חלק ב' עניני פסח דף ע"ר

Authentic Yiddishkeit believes that your **inner** essence is pure and holy and that is who you **really** are, since your holy נשמה = soul cannot be affected and cannot be corrupted by your **external** behavior.

Recognizing that your life has somehow been hijacked and you are now being forced to think or act contrary to who you really are inside is the very first step toward your personal redemption and recovery.

CONCEPT TWO

*Recognize that YOU cannot
continue like this!*

CONCEPT TWO

STEP ONE revealed that there is a deep rift between your sinful actions/thoughts and your pure holy essence.

The more that you realize how true STEP ONE is and you constantly reveal your pure inner self, the more UNHAPPY you will be because you will feel the friction between your exterior actions and your interior essence! You will begin to feel that you are not really content with the way that you are currently leading your life and you will begin to feel that you must change your actions/thoughts to match who you REALLY are deep down!

HAVE NO FEAR — THIS IS A GOOD THING!

"כל עוד שיהודי אינו משלים עם המציאות,

ומצפונו מייסרו על מצבו הרוחני, ומרגיש כי חיים כאלה אינם חיים,

נפשו תובעתו לעמול ולהתייגע כדי להגיע להתחדשות, ואז אינו אבוד:

כי תביעת הנפש הבוערת בקרבו וזה שאינו משלים עם מצבו

היא כח הקוסטא דחיותא הגדול ביותר ומזה תחילת הצמיחה החדשה!"

מרן הקדוש מקוברין זי"ע מובא בנתיבות שלום עניני פסח דף רנ"ח

When you do not ignore the screams emanating from your inner essence to wake up and realize that you can't continue living life the way you do now, that fire raging inside of you is the SPARK that will IGNITE your passion to fight for your G-d-given right to live a life that you will be truly proud of!

As long as you are not content with your current spiritual status and you feel that to continue living this way is just not an option — then you are not a lost cause!

"שהגרוע ביותר הוא כשיהודי משלים עם מציאותו
הרוחנית כמות שהיא - ושוב אינו חותר לשנותה!"

מרן הקדוש מקוברין זי"ע מובא בנתיבות שלום עניני פסח דף רנ"ח

Whereas if you smother the anguish emanating from within your soul and try to convince yourself that you are at peace with your current spiritual level, this will result in your inability to dig deep down and muster the courage to change yourself! You will just continue to live a smelly life!

This is an important revelation, because as long as you think you are content with your spiritual life, you will never be able to truly change and improve yourself. In fact, as long as you are not completely and utterly **disgusted** with your spiritual status, you will never be able to really change the direction of your life:

ODORLESS OR ODOROUS

I could hardly take the horrible stench as the garbage truck drove by, but the garbage man seemed oblivious as he held onto the back of the truck with his nose right next to the disgusting garbage while eating his lunch!

"משול למה הדבר דומה: לאדם שנפל לבור עמוק,
שכל זמן ששומעים אותו בוכה וצועק הרי זה סימן שעודנו חי ושרוי בהכרה,
מה שאין כן אם אין שומעים אותו, אות היא שנפילתו היתה קשה כל כך
עד שאבד את הכרתו!"

נתיבות שלום עניני פסח דף רנ"ח

This is like a person who fell into an extremely deep pit. As long as the rescue team hears him crying and screaming, they know that he is alive and alert. However, if he's not screaming to get out, this shows that the fall caused him to lose touch with reality.

Furthermore, just imagine if they call down to him: *"Don't worry, help is on the way,"* and he replies: *"Help?? I don't need any help; I'm fine down here — YOU need help!"* — that would mean that the impact of the fall caused such severe damage that he doesn't even know that anything is wrong with him!

"והיא המדה גם ברוחניות: כי האדם מישראל שיש בו הכרת אלקות הריהי גורמת לו יסורי נפש התובעתו להתעלות ולא להשלים עם מצבו-ה וזאת היא **הקוסטא דחיותא** לצמיחתו המחודשת!"

נתיבות שלום עניני פסח דף רנ"ח

The same applies with regard to spirituality: The more that you recognize how far away you are from where you want to be, the more confusion, inner pain, and suffering you will feel. You will feel sick and disgusted from the way that you currently live your life.

However, when this grief is used properly, this deep pain can positively **motivate** you and thrust you onto the correct path of life. As the famous saying goes, "Change only happens when you are sick and tired of being sick and tired."

HOW YOU KNOW RIGHT FROM WRONG

When you take the time to really listen to your inner voice — instead of trying to drown it out and tell it to just be quiet because "everything is fine" — you will hear very important messages emanating from your pure soul.

You do not need outside sources to teach you right from wrong. Deep down, your pure soul knows **exactly** what is right and what is wrong. However, what is necessary is for you to honestly listen to your soul.

TUNING IN

Did you ever listen to your own heartbeat? You know it's constantly there and it is audible — yet you don't usually hear it. So how can you hear it? First you need to shut out all the outside "noise" — go into a quiet place and put your hands over your ears, and after a short time you can actually hear the beating of your heart. (Or you can just use a stethoscope!)

When you finally allow yourself to be affected by your inner turmoil and pain, you will then be able to tap into an **inner strength** that you never knew you had. This will give you the strength to overcome ALL the obstacles and challenges that are blocking you from improving your life.

No external source can give you the motivation to change and the power to do so. The answer lies right inside you and the POWER lies right inside you, as long as you take the time to truly listen to your spiritual heartbeat emanating from your soul. First you must shut out any external "noise" that can sidetrack you. With time and practice, you will learn to constantly be in touch with your soul's messages and you will learn how to live a life that pleases your soul.

TUNING IN TO HEAVENLY SIGNALS

"בכל יום בת קול יוצאת מהר חורב
ואומרת שובו בנים שובבים."

זוהר הקדוש ח"ג קכ"ו מובא בקדושת לוי דברים פרשת כי תבא

Every day a heavenly voice cries out from Har Chorev (Sinai):
Return, My wayward children.

"ממה נפשך: אם היא יוצאת מדוע אין שומעים אותה

ואם אין שומעים אותה לשם מה היא יוצאת?"

מובא בתולדות יעקב יוסף ובדגל מחנה אפרים (פרשת ויקרא) בשם הבעל שם טוב הקדוש זי"ע

וכן הוא בספר חרדים מצות התשובה פ"ז סגולה ששית עי"ש.

The question is: If this heavenly voice cries out every day, then why don't we hear it? And if we aren't able to hear it — then why does the voice cry out every day?

"ותירץ שהבת קול היא המעוררת אותם ההרהורי התשובה

המתעוררים לפעמים מאליהם בלבו של יהודי!"

The answer is that this heavenly voice is like a radio signal that is being transmitted all the time; however, only a radio tuned into the right frequency can hear it! Our pure holy soul is that device and it hears this heavenly voice every single day! In fact when we feel the inner urge to better ourselves — that is because we felt that signal resonate within us.

If you can learn to connect and listen to your inner unsatisfied soul begging you to break the status quo and finally have the courage to step up and change your life, then you will have the strength to follow through with a new plan to pull yourself out of even the most difficult and perverted lifestyles!

TUNING INTO YOUR INNER VOICE IS THE BEGINNING OF YOUR PERSONAL REDEMPTION:

"אתחלתא דגאולה ממצרים היתה ככתוב:

ויאנחו בני ישראל מן העבודה ויזעקו וגו'."

נתיבות שלום ענייני פסח דף רס"ח

The Torah notes that the beginning of our redemption from the Egyptian exile was sparked by the "moans and groans" of Klal Yisrael.

"משהגיע זמן הגאולה עזר להם הקדוש ברוך הוא שיוכלו כבר להיאנח."

נתיבות שלום ענייני פסח דף רס"ח

When the time for our redemption arrived, Hashem **lightened the load** of our enslavement in order to allow us to wake up and realize how far we'd fallen from the kind of life we wanted to live, and this allowed us to moan and groan about our unfortunate situation!

"אך מקודם לא יכלו אפילו להיאנח לפי שהיו משועבדים כליל למצרים ולא היתה להם אפילו מחשבה עצמית לכאוב ולזעוק על צרות רבות כאלו!"

נתיבות שלום עניני פסח דף רס"ח

However, until the time for redemption arrived, the situation was so terrible that we could not even groan and complain about our situation. We were completely משועבד = sub'JEW'gated to Mitzrayim and controlled by our warped exterior beast to the point that we were not even capable of tapping into our own internal thought process and at the very least cry out to Hashem about our horrific situation!

SHOCKING REALITY

*The last time I succumbed to my addiction, it had gotten really bad. **It took me a while to actually want to receive treatment — I didn't want the help.** When my mom finally realized I had a problem, she knew something had to be done. She made me get help. **It was so hard** to realize my addiction and even harder to kick the habit, but I was able to while receiving assistance in a residential treatment center.*   Source: http://www.drugstory.org

If a person stands on your foot, you say, "Excuse me — you are on my foot!" However, if someone drops a very heavy box on your foot, you scream, "Hey! Get this off my foot!!" But if a tractor-trailer backs up on your foot, the pain will be so severe that you will not be able to utter a sound.

TOO PAINFUL TO FEEL

June 8, 2007. A 16-year-old boy named Tonpo Dorjee visiting the U.S. from Tibet was involved in a horrific car accident and both his legs were crushed between a Honda Civic and a light pole.

Medics on the scene pointed out that Tonpo was talking but he wasn't screaming due to the extreme amount of pain he was in!

Source: NYDailyNews.com

LET'S BRING THIS HOME:

As you go through life, most of the time your exterior beast will manage to silence your interior pure voice so that you seem to be complacent and happy with your spiritual level. However, now we know what you can do to REVERSE YOUR SITUATION and bring redemption and salvation to your life:

"כמו בגאולת הכלל כך גם בגאולת הפרט זאת היא הקוסטא דחיותא
ושורש הגאולה: אם יש ליהודי תביעת הנפש ויסורי מצפון ואינו משלים
בשום אופן עם המציאות והוא מבקש ומחפש את כל העצות איך
להתחדש בצמיחה מחודשת הרי זהו כח הגאולה המוציא אותו
אפילו מהמצבים הקשים ביותר ומביאו לצמיחה חדשה!"

נתיבות שלום עניני פסח דף רנ"ט

Just as the redemption of Klal Yisrael came about by beginning to moan, so too, this applies to the redemption of every individual. Once you realize that this is not the real you (Concept One) and you begin to listen to the pain and confusion deep inside you that pushes you to realize that you cannot continue to live this way (Concept Two), then even though you don't yet have the self-control to improve your situation, at least you can express your inner pain by **moaning** about it, which will bring you the power to pull yourself out of even the worst conditions and situations!

"השער לעבור ממצב של גלות למצב של גאולה,
היא **האנחה** העמוקה שיהודי נאנח מפנימיות לבבו
על שנתרחק מאביו שבשמים!"

נתיבות שלום מאמר שני דף מ"ג

Authentic Yiddishkeit believes that tapping into your inner pain and allowing yourself to express your sincere yearning to improve your life and become closer to Hashem is the vehicle that will carry you from exile to redemption.

Exposing your inner pain over the fact that your life has somehow been hijacked will motivate you to STOP floating through life being forced to think or act contrary to who you really are inside. This is the second step to your personal redemption and recovery.

BEWARE!
THERE IS A DANGEROUS SIDE EFFECT TO EXPOSING YOUR INNER PAIN

Even though this is a necessary step to change your life, tapping into your inner pain can be a very dangerous game. The יצר הרע (Evil Inclination) is certainly not going to allow you to simply reflect on your life and then actually change yourself for the better! You can rest assured that it will use your good intentions to work AGAINST YOU, and it will try to do whatever it can to make sure that you do not walk away from this moment of introspection with any real motivation to change.

THE EVIL PLAN

As you feel the inner pain that comes from your yearning to improve and elevate your life, the evil snake will attempt to cause you to feel frustrated and confused so that you don't actually change.

You will then return to the same old actions and thoughts, and you will conclude that spending time and effort thinking about your situation is a complete waste of time! You will be convinced that you CAN NEVER change and improve! You are "stuck" for life! The snake wins again! So let's not let that happen — K?

HERE'S A TOOL THAT WILL REALLY HELP YOU:

"שברון הלב של איש יהודי
מחמת גודל החטא צריך שיהי-ה תמיד **מעולם הבנין**
ולא מעולם החורבן שיגרום לו יאוש ועצבות חס ושלום!"
נתיבות שלום עניני ראש השנה דף קכ"ז

REMEMBER! When you feel heartbroken over your many sins, this must always come from the עולם הבנין = world of **CON**struction and never from the עולם החורבן = world of **DE**struction which could easily lead you to יאוש = giving up and עצבות=depression.

After proper introspection from the **"world of construction"** which looks at your situation through the lens of the עולם הבנין=world of building, you should feel **refreshed**, energized, motivated, and full of hope! You are **stronger** than before, you are **smarter** than before, you are on the lookout to make sure that you don't repeat the same past mistakes again, and you are ready to lift yourself up even if you fall again! GO! GO! GO!

"כיון שמתוך המרירות סופו שמתייאש ומאבד את התקוה,
שהרי כבר כל כך הרבה פעמים התחיל מחדש, והנה רואה הוא שלא
עלתה בידו, וזה מובילו לחורבן חס ושלום - **ולא זו הדרך!**"

However, when you reflect on yourself from the perspective of the עולם החורבן (world of destruction), you will use your past struggles to depress you and cause you to give up. You won't study yourself in order to figure out where you went wrong and strengthen those weaknesses; rather you will just sulk, feel lower and lower, and think about how worthless it is to even try.

You will hear a voice telling you that you really have no potential to ever really change and you end up just feeling drained and thoroughly **unmotivated** to ever become a better person. Why bother trying "again" after you tried so many times before and you FAILED!?!

After this introspection, you belong completely to the snake as never before as it uses the past losses to destroy whatever defenses you still have against it. You are weaker than before and unable to prevent yourself from repeating the same mistakes again.

The snake is happy for you to sit and think about your sad and low spiritual situation; it may even approach you like a good influence, but it isn't a good friend at all. It just wants to use the powerful tool of introspection to depress and completely destroy you.

"היצר הרע אומר ליהודי:

אחר העבירה שעשית הקב"ה אינו רוצה להסתכל על מצוותיך!

אבל צריך יהודי לחשוב: אחר המצוות שעשיתי אולי הקב"ה

שוב אינו רוצה להסתכל בעבירותי!"

נתיבי אמת פנימי

When the evil twisted snake within you tells you, "After the sins that you did — Hashem is no longer interested in your mitzvos," you should reply, "Maybe the opposite is true! After the mitzvos I did — Hashem is not interested in my sins!"

Think about it this way: If your close friend would open up to you and tell you all about his struggles and difficulties and his yearning to grow closer to Hashem, how would you respond to him? Would you ever tell him, "Ooooh boy — you did that? Man — you are a real lowlife, a piece of garbage! A real loser! You'll NEVER be able to change! You should just GIVE UP now and not even try to improve!"

Can you imagine that anyone who cares about someone would ever tell him that? Of course not! Any normal caring person would LIFT the person up and motivate him to carry on and on and on and on ....

"כי כל דבר שיהודי עושה צריך שיהיה **מעולם הבנין**,
ובכלל זה גם החרטה והתשובה, **ויתמלא בתקוה** שהקדוש ברוך הוא
לא יעזבנו ובודאי יעזור לו לשוב ולהתקרב אליו יתברך!"
נתיבות שלום

Whatever a JEW does — including feeling really bad about his past sins — must only be done from **the world of BUILDING!** After properly analyzing your current position, you should come to realize that even after everything you did — THE DOOR IS WIDE OPEN FOR YOU TO RETURN TO Hashem — and you should be filled with HOPE that Hashem will NOT forsake you!

"יש סוג אנחה בדרגה עילאית: לא אנחה של שברון לב
אלא אנחה אשר שורשה **השתוקקות געגועין וכיסופין** לאלקות!"
נתיבות שלום חלק ב' עניני שבת דף מ"ד

The אנחה (anguish) and inner yearning MUST NEVER be a negative and depressed moaning from a broken spirit that is helpless and can only sulk in his own misery, have a pity party, and do nothing positive to start to grow and improve!

Rather, a Yiddishe *"krechtz"* is a deep inner motivation that comes from a positive yearning to take a stand and really CHANGE your life and become closer to Hashem!

"ותראהו והנה נער בוכה ותאמר מילדי העברים זה (שמות ב')
שמבכייתו הכירה שהוא יהודי:
כי ראתה שבוכה בכי של **תקוה** ולא בכי של יאוש
ותאמר מילדי העברים זה – זוהי בכיה יהודית!"
נתיבות שלום בין המצרים בשם מרן הרמ"ח זצ"ל

The Torah says that Basya the daughter of Paroh saw the child crying and she said: "This child is a Jewish child." She was able to know that this was a Yiddishe child specifically from listening to the type of crying emanating from the child! She heard a cry of HOPE and not a cry of surrender and depression, and she said: "This must be a Yiddishe child!"

You must beware of the danger of giving up and depression, and instead remain focused on the great importance of your inner motivational yearning to become better!

Let us allow ourselves to moan and cry motivational and inspirational tears of yearning for our individual salvation and the salvation of all of Klal Yisrael.

CONCEPT THREE

Digging deep and really changing

CONCEPT THREE

Many people have tried to lose weight, stop smoking, quit substance abuse, give up drinking, become more religious, and make various other important life changes. ALL of them really WANT to change, yet MOST of them keep falling back to their previous behavior. WHY?

OH NO- NOT AGAIN!

*The effect of incarceration on former prisoners has been a very common topic of discussion for many years. In most cases, it is believed that many prisoners will find themselves **right back** where they started, in jail.*

In the United States, 68% of males and 58% of females are rearrested, and 53% and 39% respectively are re-incarcerated (2003).   Source: Wikipedia

*83% of smokers
who quit smoking start again!*

Source: NYC.GOV

*81.8% of alcoholics
who quit drinking start again!*

Source: spiritriver.com

*80% of drug addicts
who quit drugs will relapse within one year!*

Source: chacha

So let us analyze this: **WHY** is it that most people are **NOT** able to permanently change their lives — even once they come to the realization that they HATE what they are doing and they REALLY WANT to stop???

If you are successful in figuring this out, you will be UNSTOPPABLE, because you will be in possession of the secret to successfully make ANY LIFE CHANGE that you ever decide to make — and the **ability to stick to it FOREVER!**

SO HERE IT IS; THE SECRET TO SUCCESSFUL LIFE CHANGE:

When you **DO** anything, that action comes from a **THOUGHT** that is generated by a **MINDSET**.

Therefore, the only way to REALLY CHANGE is to identify the ORIGIN OF THE CORRUPTION within your mindset — the first spot where you parted from the healthy outlook on life:

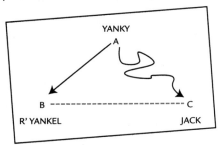

Yanky and Jack represent the same person. He started off as a pure precious Yanky, but somehow drifted off the right path and began to live life as Jack. In order for Jack to truly be like the R' Yankel he was meant to be, he cannot just walk from where he is now (point c) to where he would have been had he stayed on the correct path (point b); rather, he needs to walk all the way BACK to the point at which he started to veer off (point a) and then follow the correct path. There are no shortcuts!

When you feel the urge to sin, the main question you need to figure out is: How did you end up on such a low level that you would really even consider doing such a low thing? After all, when you started to veer off track, you never would have even considered this sin to be a possibility for you!

And so, if you are trying to mend your ways, you must dig deep into your psyche until you reach the earliest point that your mindset went off the proper path.

HERE'S A PRACTICAL EXAMPLE OF WHAT WE ARE TALKING ABOUT:

Just not eating fatty fried foods is not enough to help you lose weight and **KEEP IT OFF!** Of course you need to stop the fat intake — but that's just the "first" step! What will make you successful is clearing your mindset of all the **influence** you ever had that affected your mind to want to eat unhealthy and lead an unhealthy lifestyle!

Only when you see a dieter embrace a healthy lifestyle with a new **healthy mindset** generating healthy thoughts and ideas, including drinking water, going to the gym, not eating after 8 p.m., etc., do you know that he is truly serious about changing his weight!

One dieter drools over fried food or delicious cakes and feels like a "nebech" that he is so "deprived," but the other one has emotionally freed himself and "moved on." Even though the fatty food still looks good to him — just like to anyone else — he knows that for him, it's "poison," and therefore it doesn't entice him. It is just NOT WORTH IT!

The thought of exchanging LONG-TERM HAPPINESS AND TRUE

FULLFILLMENT for short-term pleasure is absolutely **ABSURD** to him because it goes **AGAINST** everything he stands for and what he wants to be.

Two people walk by a delicious hot dog stand. They both are really hungry and have the same craving for a delicious fully loaded fresh hot dog. But there's a problem: Both of them have a heart condition and both of them are NOT ALLOWED to eat saturated fat. One can't control himself and he eats it. The other walks away … he has a HIGHER AGENDA than a hot dog. Which one is a winner?

"שנעשה משועבד
וקולט הלכי מחשבה זרים שאינן שלו
ומאבד את הילוך המחשבה היהודי המקורי חס ושלום!"
נתיבות שלום חלק ב׳ קמ"ו

The REAL reason that your life is not what you want it to be is NOT just because of the low ACTIONS that you currently do; rather, it is because your "calculator" in your pure Yiddishe mindset became corrupted. That is why you end up making wrong decisions over and over again that are not in your own best interest!

Furthermore, even once you feel bad about ACTING OUT in a shameful manner and you really do want to change your life around, you may still find that it is difficult to successfully do so until you dig deep into the innermost point of your subconscious to SEARCH FOR and RECTIFY what is corrupted.

REPEAT PERFORMANCE

One of the main reasons criminals [Jack] find themselves back in jail is because it is difficult for them to fit back in with "normal" life [Yanky] …. Many prisoners report being anxious about their release; they are excited about how their life will be different "this time" [R' Yankel], which does not always end up being the case.

Source: Wikipedia

"דתניא ר' אליעזר אומר:

מנין לעוקר עבודת כוכבים שצריך לשרש אחריה

ת"ל: ואבדתם את שמם."

תלמוד בבלי מסכת עבודה זרה דף מה:

Jewish law dictates that if people worship something growing in the ground, such as a bush or a tree, and you want to destroy the idol, it is not good enough to just cut off what is above the ground; rather, you must dig all the way down to the deepest roots and completely rip it out — so that it can never ever grow back again!

ROOT OF THE ISSUE

Weeds creep up and prevent crops from growing properly. Farmers who just cut off the weeds that grow above ground are in a constant battle to deal with the destructive weeds as they re-grow. On the other hand, farmers who are smart use the latest scientific inventions to kill the weed all the way down to its deepest root, so it will never be able to grow again!

Pulling Weeds: Weeding is often considered a dreaded task, especially when it comes to pulling weeds from the ground. However, when it comes down to it, it's the quickest and usually the most effective way to do it! Most annual weeds should be pulled by hand, unless they have already grown too far out of control. The important thing to remember when pulling weeds from the ground is to make sure you pull not only the weed, but also its roots. Many deep-rooted weeds can grow up to 6 inches into the soil, and if not removed, those roots can grow back again. When digging-out the weed, make sure that you remove as much of the root as possible. Remember, the root should be completely removed, even to its root depth. If the roots are 6 inches deep, make sure you dig the roots up from that depth as well.   Source: www.allaboutlawns.com

"וצריך ראשית להקדים את
הסור מרע ולפרוש ממעשיו הרעים."

ספר נתיבות שלום עמוד קמ"ו

Of course, when you are finally ready to crack down and really change your life, you will have to STOP doing the things that you know bring you down. Because as long as you are involved in these destructive actions, how can you really expect to separate yourself from them? How can you raise yourself up while being pulled down? How can you climb a mountain with ankle weights on?

However, people often make a tragic mistake and think that "stopping" the action is the "FINAL" step to recovery, when in fact, not only is that not the "FINAL" step — it is the very "FIRST" step!

Certainly you need to fight "outside-in" and STOP the actual corrupt activity; however, at the very same time, you need to fight "inside-out," changing your inner **mindset** and purifying your **perspective** so that you would not even **want** to perform the sin!

"וכלשון שאמר אחד מן הצדיקים קודם פטירתו:
'פראסט אפגילעבט דעם לעבן'
שאין הכונה על 'החטאים' אלא על **כל מציאות החיים**
שאינם ברמה הראוי-ה!"

ספר נתיבות שלום חלק ב' קמ"ז

This is the ROOT of your problem: NOT just the actual sins that you do — for they are just the outcome of a much larger, greater and deeper problem: the fact that you are living life ON THE WRONG TRACK!

Now it's time to take charge of YOUR LIFE! You must seek and destroy the enemy and every "sleeper cell" that set up a home base within the crevices of your mindset. But fighting one at a time will never work! The only choice is to make a complete LIFE CHANGE that will destroy ALL your enemies in one full-blown assault!

BURN DOWN THE FOREST

"משל לאחד הרוצה לפנות יער עבות מעציו

והי-ה חוטב עץ אחר עץ וראה שימיו יכלו ולא יספיק לגמור

עד שהדליק אש גדולה שאכלה את כל עצי היער בפעם אחת!"

ספר תורת אבות מובא בנתיבות שלום חלק ב, עניני פסח

> **EXTREME SOLUTIONS**
>
> There was once a man who needed to clear a whole forest of its trees. So he went out every day with his ax and proceeded to chop down one tree after another. Although he was working very hard, he realized that even if he would work his entire life, he could still never get the job done! So he lit a huge fire and burned down the entire forest!

The lesson is: As long as you are living the "same exact" life as before, even if you try to become better, you are boxed into that same old mindset and your options are limited! Therefore, you have to be ready to change not just your "actions," but also the entire PATH of your life! You must LIFT your outlook on life once and for all and surround yourself with people who you look UP TO!

CHANGING DIRECTION

"אין כתוב: יעזוב רשע **מעשיו** או **עוונותיו** אלא 'יעזוב רשע **דרכו**' את **הדרך המביאתו לרע**! וזה גם המשך הכתוב 'ואיש און מחשבותיו' שהכוונה להרהורי עבירה שהם בכלל שרש הרע!"

בעל בית אברהם זכותו יגן עלינו מובא בנתיבות שלום

If a person is living with crooks and hoodlums and he decides to straighten out his life, it is obvious that he cannot continue to live among those lowlifes! If a person is living with drug addicts and he decides that he wants to go "clean," it is obvious that he must move out.

IF YOU WANT TO REALLY CHANGE WHO YOU ARE, YOU MUST COMPLETELY CHANGE THE "PATH" THAT YOU ARE ON:

"ויאמר ה' אל אברם: לך לך מארצך וממולדתך ומבית אביך אל הארץ
אשר אראך, ואעשך לגוי גדול ואברכך ואגדלה שמך והיה ברכה!"

לך לך יב:א

This is what Hashem told Avraham: LEAVE — FOR YOUR BENEFIT AND GROWTH! In this atmosphere you cannot become YOU! Get away from your surrounding influences ... your corrupt family ... your friend and neighbors ... your entire city! Because YOU will never become the real YOU if you stay put! You have great potential lying inside you that is being smothered by the surrounding atmospheric pressure.

Understand what is at stake: Becoming who YOU want to be, fulfilling YOUR potential and living a life that YOU will not regret; is there anything that should stand in your way? Is there any sacrifice you can't make for YOURSELF?

You might have to change the way you dress, where you work, where you live, who your friends are, etc. ... etc. ... all the way, deeper and deeper, releasing yourself from anything that is holding you down and preventing you from reaching **your true potential.**

FRESH START

Mottel had a huge storehouse filled with grain. One day, part of the grain became moldy and the mold began to spread and ruin the grain. When Mottel noticed what was happening to his fortune, he started to put in more and more grain to make up for what was rotting away!

In reality, this didn't accomplish anything — on the contrary, the more that Mottel added to this warehouse, the greater loss he will have as the mold spreads onto more

grain and destroys it! Also, he will have even a bigger mess when he will empty out and clean the storage house!

The only correct thing for Mottel to do is to take everything out of the storehouse and thoroughly disinfect it from any drop of mold. Only then can he begin to refill it with good grain. Only then will his stock be safe!

Source: Nesivos Shalom, Volume 2, p. 147

If part of your life is "moldy" and "rotting away," the only true solution is to cut it out of your life once and for all! Otherwise it will always be there, alive and well, and it will continue to spread its influence onto other parts of your life.

Don't take anything in your life as a "given." Start putting **your life** together piece by piece as YOU would like it to be. If you have a **FRIEND** you know is bad for you, cut him out! Don't be stuck with him for the rest of your life and deprive yourself of having the life you should have had! If your **ENVIRONMENT** is holding you back from reaching your potential, then you must consider releasing yourself from those ties as well.

Instead of once again TRYING to improve within your current limited parameters — **it's time to take charge of your life and reach for your destiny!**

"יעזוב את כל הדרך שהולך בה!
שיש שעושה תשובה על פרט זה או אחר אך 'יעזוב רשע דרכו'
היינו שיזנח לגמרי את כל הדרך שהלך בה עד כה שהוא חי חיים ירודים
מאד וצריך לעזוב ולעבור לדרך חיים אחרת לגמרי!"
בעל בית אברהם מובא בנתיבות שלום על חודש אלול

If you are intellectually honest about what you want to change, you must get to the root of the issue. Just as you can't be serious about losing weight so long as your house and office are full of hidden stashes of chocolate bars, so too, if your struggle is with a computer, then how can you really expect to change until you throw it out of your life?

As long as the computer is still a part of your life, your entire struggle is over what you watch on it. You may even think that you are doing great and putting up a decent fight against the Evil Inclination. However, it is the Yetzer Horah itself who set the parameters of your fight! It is making sure that you only put up a fight about the end result and not about the REAL issue at its source! It's happy that you have the computer and you are fighting over how many times you watch inappropriate content. So even your FIGHT is being controlled by IT! It is setting the rules and the boundaries of your fight against it! For once, it's time for YOU to control the parameters of the fight! Say: NO! I don't want to HAVE A LAPTOP!

If someone living in a trailer park decides to elevate his life, get a full-time job, quit drinking beer, get some teeth, and make a "real" life change, he won't be too successful as long as he still lives in a trailer park!

"תשובה על עבירות היא כאמור דבר קל
ביחס לתשובה זו על כל דרך החיים!"
ספר נתיבות שלום חלק ב' קמ"ז

This is really hard work. Stopping the actual act of stealing (for example) is much easier than changing every influence of your life so that you can end your "**urge**" to steal!

A STAINED PAST

" השיבנו ה' אליך ונשובה, חדש ימינו כקדם."
איכה ה:כא

The Navi Yirmiyahu says:
"Hashem, return us to You and we shall repent,
renew our lives like the days of old."

Every sin you do leaves an imprint on your mind. Even after you repent and the actual sins are forgiven, your mind is still affected and infected by what you did and the thoughts that entered your mind.

Therefore, merely stopping the actual sinful actions will not automatically return your mindset and thought process to be pure like that of another person who never did those sins.

KUGEL DAMAGE

In honor of Rosh Hashanah, Mr. Schoenfeld bought his wife a brand-new beautiful white tablecloth. On Erev Rosh Hashanah, he woke up early in the morning and spread out the new tablecloth, and it looked amazing. When his wife would come downstairs she would be in for a big surprise! Then he left to go daven. While he was out davening, his two-year-old son Berel woke up and came downstairs. He opened the fridge and found a potato kugel that his mother had made for yom tov. Rubbing his eyes, he sat in his seat at the Shabbos table and enjoyed himself, eating right on the new tablecloth! When Mr. Schoenfeld returned from shul and noticed what little Berel had done, he worked very hard to take each piece of kugel off of the tablecloth. Obviously, the oily residue could not be removed and the beautiful new tablecloth was ruined.

"חדש ימינו כקדם; מבקשים אנו שהקב"ה יחדש את ימינו 'כקדם',
כקודם החטא! היינו לא רק למחוק את **פעולת** החטא, אלא למחוק אף
את **הרושם** שנעשה בנו על ידי החטא, שנהיה נקיים וטהורים כאילו לא
עשינו בכלל את המעשים הרעים והפחותים נגד רצונו יתברך!"

ספר נתיבי אמת

This is why we cry out: Hashem! Return me to You and renew my mindset back to the way I used to think BEFORE I sinned and brought foreign and low thinking into my mind! Once upon a time I was a pure, innocent, and naive good *Yiddishe* child, but now after all of the many low thoughts and actions, I need You to please give me back my innocence.

Stopping sinful corrupt "actions" is EASY compared to purifying your mindset, which is what's necessary in order to definitively turn your life around forever! SO you have a big battle ahead of you!

Fortunately, you have a very powerful Father to help you:

"עיקר העצה לעקירת שרשי הרע היא ...
לבקש ולהתחנן מלפני השם יתברך שיהי-ה לו לעזר!"

נתיבות שלום

The main advice for someone who needs help to break away from the root of evil that has built trenches within him is to **beg and plead for Hashem to help you!**

**So let's get ready to work hard ...
and don't forget to**

PRAY!

CONCEPT FOUR

Reclaiming the right perspective

CONCEPT FOUR

An animal walks on all fours with his eyes naturally facing ארציות, the materialistic ground. Therefore, his natural view is of the lowest part of the world: the ground. Only with difficulty can an animal temporarily change his natural posture by turning his head upward for a short period of time to allow him to see anything other than ארציות.

SLAM DUNK! *The crowd at the circus event went wild watching an elephant stand on its hind legs and dunk basketballs!*

What is so exciting about an elephant dunking a basketball — after all, there are MANY people who can do that!?

The explanation is as follows; it is unnatural for an animal to stand upright and not face the ground. It takes a skilled trainer a long time to teach the elephant how to do that!

That is what makes it so fascinating to watch!

"נפשו של אדם לא נבראת מן הארץ כשם שנפש שאר הבהמות נבראת
לכך היא [נפש הבהמה] פניה לעולם למטה,
ונפש האדם פניו למעלה!"

מדרש אגדה בראשית פרק ב:ז

On the other hand, humans were created physically upright, giving us the ability to turn our view either upward toward heaven, for a heavenly angelic view of the world, or downward toward earth.

But there's one catch:
You can't see both at the same time.
You have to choose your view:
Heaven or Earth.

When we compare animals to humans there are many similarities; we both have the need to eat, sleep, and take care of our physical bodies. However, Hashem gave us humans the ability to determine where our **focus** will be.

The choice is yours ... will it be a heavenly spiritual view like pure angels or an earthly materialistic view like the animals? Will you focus your life on attaining lofty spiritual heights, thereby building a close connection with Hashem, or is your life focused on the next hot dog?

WHAT TALENT!

The Nathan's International July Fourth Hot Dog Eating Contest is an annual competitive eating competition held at Nathan's Famous Corporation's original and best-known restaurant at the corner of Surf and Stillwell Avenues in Coney Island, Brooklyn, New York. The event is held on July 4, and is regarded as the world's most famous hot dog eating contest and a colorful tradition of Independence Day in the United States. In 2006, over 30,000 spectators attended the event, and an additional 1.5 million households watched it live on ESPN.

The 93rd annual contest was held on July 4, 2008. Six-time champion Takeru "Tunami" Kobayashi and defending champion Joey Chestnut were tied with 59 hot dogs eaten after the new ten-minute time limit, but Chestnut prevailed by winning a five-dog "eat off" held immediately after the contest. Source: Wikipedia

You have the power to choose a path that will lead to an ethical and moral life with a focus on getting closer to Hashem and committing yourself to helping other people and to positively impacting the world around you. Or, you can chose to live your life like a walking talking animal focused on how to best fulfill your own selfish needs and desires at any given time.

Ask yourself:
What is your perspective?

Angel:	0%	10%	20%	30%	40%	50%	60%	70%	80%	90%	100%
YOU:											
Animal:	100%	90%	80%	70%	60%	50%	40%	30%	20%	10%	0%

"רבש"ע: אני מוחל לך עולם הזה ועולם הבא

ובלבד שתאיר עיני ישראל שלא יסתובבו עלי אדמות **כבהמה בלי דעת**!"

הרה"ק מרוזין זי"ע מובא בנתיבות שלום חלק א, פרקי מבוא דף י"א

With this understanding, the Holy Rizhiner Rebbe *zt"l* proclaimed: Master of the universe! I am willing to forgo both this world and the next, if You would enlighten the eyes of the Yidden so they should not wander around the earth like animals!

 HUMAN CIRCUS   *On* חול המועד *the Berenstein Bear Family joined all the other local animals to see the very first "human circus." In amazement they watched Mr. KleinKeppel, the famous human with the tiny head, get down on all fours and crawl around like an animal, chasing a ball and bringing it back to the bear ringmaster!*

WHAT IS REALLY BLOCKING YOUR SPIRITUAL VISION?

When you look at the world through a purely materialistic view, the world appears to be full of loss and failure, hurt and pain, selfishness and emptiness, a world with no rhyme or reason. You only see a world of confusion, inconsistency, and contradiction. A world where G-d is nowhere to be found.

"בעת שדעתו מצומצמת
אינו רואה אלא את עצמו על תאוותיו."

נתיבות שלום חלק א' פרקי מבוא דף ט"ו

As your mindset becomes smaller and smaller, you turn into a petty small-minded creature. Once your mind is condensed and squashed to the point that your perspective on life is shallow and narrow, you cannot see anything at all except your physical needs and sinful desires. When will you fill your next need? Get your next fix?

LIMITED VISION

Imagine that someone makes a huge pile of one million silver dollars. Standing 100 yards away, you will be able to see the entire mountain of silver glistening in the sunlight. How much money can your eyes see? A million dollars.

However, if you take just two silver dollars from the mound and bring them closer to you, the closer they get to your eyes, the more your vision will be blocked from seeing the entire pile, and when these two coins are placed right over your eyes, you will not be able to see anything other than just these two coins. The incredible million-dollar mountain has been completely blocked by two small dollars. How much can your eyes see now? Just two dollars!

A person who is **TRAPPED** into small-minded thinking is commonly referred to as an "addict," but in our case we are not referring to someone addicted to alcohol, substance abuse, or gambling; rather, we are talking about how each of us can become TRAPPED by our own desires.

The more the walls of sin close in on your mind, the more you become **controlled** by small-minded materialistic thinking. We are at risk of relinquishing ETERNITY for PETTY PLEASURES. We may sacrifice the infinite ... for the finite.

"כמעט הייתי בכל רע בתוך קהל ועדה:

'כמעט' - **בעבור הנאה קטנה כשיעור היותר מועט**

הייתי עתה בכל רע בתוך קהל רב ועדה גדולה בפרסום רב!"

מצודת דוד משלי פרק ה:יד

Shlomo HaMelech, wisest of all men, proclaimed: For an insignificant fleeting moment of pleasure, I fell into a world of evil, while still being a proud distinguished member of Klal Yisrael!

The result is that your view of G-d's "million-dollar world" is now blocked out by tiny petty pleasures that are blown out of proportion and have taken over your entire perspective.

Once your life is focused on physical pleasure and/or materialistic goals, you are much closer to the animal kingdom than to angelic beings.

"FEELING" SEPARATED FROM YOUR CREATOR:

"... העניינים הגשמיים והחומריים

הם המכסים מפניו אור אלקותו יתברך שמו

כי על ידם אישיותו מצטמצמת ושרוי בקטנות המוחין."

ספר נתיבות שלום חלק א' דף ט"ז

It is your materialistic desires that prevent you from perceiving a feeling of connection to Hashem! They minimize your ability to see and absorb spirituality, thereby leaving you with a very weak bond with your Creator.

As your feeling of connection to Hashem becomes weaker and weaker, you become even more vulnerable to being sucked into a self-indulging, pleasure-seeking, self-gratifying lifestyle focused mainly on: the pleasure of the moment. You have little concern for anything other than your next petty physical desire, comfort, materialistic need, financial gain, drink, fantasy, sin, etc.

FADING REALITY

As Murray got more and more into gambling, it began to take over his life. He started to miss work and become unsocial. His friends and family tried to tell him that his love for gambling was getting blown out of proportion, but they couldn't get him to stop. Over time his entire life perspective changed and all he could see was gambling. Nothing else was important and he could not live without it. There was no night or day. He would miss family time and important meetings. He even missed his son Murray Jr.'s tenth birthday party. The whole family gathered together but Daddy just called in because he was stuck in a "meeting." The family members who knew better tried to call, text, and email him to please come home at least for the end of the party. At first Murray felt bad, but he just could not stop playing. Finally, he turned off his phone and shut out the world.

"המבט הארצי הוא בבחינת:
'והארץ היתה תוהו ובוהו'
כי הארציות מביא באדם בלבול הדעת."
נתיבות שלום חלק א, דף כ"ז

Looking at the world with a narrow-minded materialistic outlook brings a person to a state of **emptiness** and **confusion**. Your focus on instant gratification changes your perspective little by little, and the sweetness of the "real" world, as Hashem intended, continuously slips away from you. Pretty sad — no?

DISTORTED PRIORITIES

A elderly man had 50-yardline tickets for the Super Bowl. As he sits down to enjoy the game, a guy comes over and asked him if anyone is sitting in the seat next to him. "No" he said, "the seat is empty."

"This is incredible," said the man. "Who in their right mind would have a seat like this for the Super Bowl, the biggest sport event in the world, and not use it?"

Somberly, the elderly man says, "Well ... the seat actually belongs to me. I was supposed to come here with my wife, but she passed away. This is the first Super Bowl we have not been at together since we got married in 1967."

"Oh ... I'm so sorry to hear that, that's terrible! But couldn't you find someone else — a friend or relative or even a neighbor — to take the seat?"

The elderly man shakes his head. "No ... They're all at the funeral!"

Turning you into a small-minded, shallow, self-indulgent pleasure-seeker was the true objective of the Evil Inclination all along!! In fact, all the sinning it pushed you to do was necessary only to bring you into this dire situation! Get it???

SO LET'S GET TO WORK: WHAT IS THE SOLUTION?

"העולם אומר: 'אז מ' קען נישט אריבער - גייט מען ארונטער' אך צדיקים
אמרו: 'אז מ' קען נישט ארונטער - גייט מען אריבער און אריבער!'"

בעל בית אברהם זי"ע מובא בנתיבות שלום חלק ב' דף ע"ר

The world says: "If you can't go over it — go under it," but tzaddikim say: "If you can't handle the struggle on your low level — then jump way over it!"

"כאשר האדם נמצא בין חיות טרף נחשים ועקרבים,
כל כמה שימית מהם לא יינצל כי רבים המה,
ועצתו האחת היא שירימו ויגביהו אותו למעלה ממקום שידם מגעת!"

ספר נתיבות שלום חלק ב' עמוד קס"ז

If a person is walking in the wilderness amongst wild animals, snakes, and scorpions, no matter how many of them he kills, he'll never be safe since there are so many more of them! His only chance of survival is to climb up to a place where they can't get to him!

When life's struggles get too hard, and you can't take the tug-of-war anymore, the only choice you have is to raise yourself ABOVE the struggle! GET OUT OF THERE! Or as the world says: "if you can't handle the heat — GET OUT OF THE KITCHEN!"

"שאו מרום עיניכם וראו מי ברא אלה."

ישעיהו פרק מ:כו

The Navi proclaims:
"Raise your eyes upward and see Who created everything!"

"לכאורה הלא מיתוש קטן אפשר לראות את כח הבורא
שגם אם יתאספו כל המדענים שבעולם לא יוכלו לברוא אפילו יצור קטן כזה
ולשם מה צריך לשאת עינים למרום?"

נתיבות שלום חלק א' דף כ"ז

We should all ask a really simple question: Even if we could gather all the scientists in the world, they could not create even one tiny ant. So why then is it necessary to look "**up to the sky**" in order to come to the realization that Hashem created everything — isn't it obvious from looking **anywhere**??

"אלא הפירוש הוא:
הביטו במבט שמימי: מבט מלא בהירות!"

נתיבות שלום חלק א' דף כ"ז

The deeper understanding is: The Navi is **not** telling us to **physically** "look upward" to realize that there is a Creator.

Rather, his message is: when you look at the world around you "קוק מיט א העכערע בליק"— raise your vision to look from a **spiritually elevated** perspective.

Once you ELEVATE your vision and view the world through a higher spiritual lens, the hand of G-d will be obvious and evident:

"כי אתה אור עולם

ועיני כל נפש זכה יראוך."

נתיבות שלום חלק א' דף כ"ז

Hashem is the light of the world; however only the eyes of pure souls can see Him. The people fortunate enough to live with this perspective are living lives full of light, purpose, and understanding. However, those who are dragged down by materialistic cravings are confined to a low perspective of the world, and their lives are full of nonsense, darkness, and confusion.

"למה הדבר דומה לאחד הנמצא תוך הבית

שכל תחום ראייתו מצומצם בתוך כתלי ביתו

אך ככל שיוצא יותר לחוץ ומתרומם מעל פני השטח

מתגמד ביתו ומקומו כנגד המרחבים האין סופיים המתגלים לעיניו."

נתיבות שלום חלק א' פרקי מבוא דף ט"ו

Being trapped by shallow animalistic thinking controlled by desire and materialism is like standing inside a small room. Even though there's a whole huge world out there, your entire vision is limited by the ceiling and walls that surround you.

However, as you walk out of the room and head to higher ground, your scope of vision will spread out and you will be able to see the world around you.

THE SKY'S THE LIMIT

The sun is over 90 million miles away and since every person can see the sun, this means that human vision can see a distance of over 90 million miles. Yet if you are in a room that is 10 feet x 10 feet, you won't see past 10

feet. What happened to the power of your vision? The answer is simple — the walls blocked it!

However, imagine that you hop into a hot-air balloon and start to float up in the air. As you float above your house, your vision will expand to see your whole house. As you float higher you will see your whole block ... your whole town ... your whole city ... your whole state ... and if you could reach outer space, you would even see the entire earth! The higher you go — the more perspective you have to see what was there all along but was blocked by the "walls"!

PULL YOUR MIND "UP, UP, AND AWAY!"

"כאשר מזדכך ומביט במבט שמימי
רואה את בורא הכל ואין שום חומר מסתיר בעדו."

נתיבות שלום חלק א׳ פרקי מבוא דף ט״ו

As you raise your perspective and pull away from shallow desires, you will begin to view the world through a heavenly, spiritual, and uplifted outlook. Suddenly wherever you look you will "openly" see the hand of G-d Who manages every single detail of the universe.

Just as a person with silver dollars over his eyes cannot **physically** see the beautiful world around him, in the very same way, animalistic worldly desires block a person's **spiritual** vision and he cannot see the beautiful spiritual world around him!

Whereas look what happens to a person who rises above the small-mindedness:

"... רואה את כבוד ה׳ הממלא כל עלמין תוך כל עלמין וסובב כל עלמין
ואין עוד זולתו יתברך ובכל הבריאה כולה ירגיש
כי הוא יתברך הדור נאה זיו העולם ונפשו תחלה באהבתו יתברך!"

נתיבות שלום חלק א׳ פרקי מבוא דף י״ד

When you look at the world with UNBLOCKED spiritual eyes, ALL that you will see is the glory of Hashem Who fills and surrounds the world and there is nothing except G-d. As you look at the entire creation, you will be filled with the understanding that Hashem is the beauty and glory of the world. Your soul will yearn with a burning desire to build a close and loving relationship with Hashem.

BUT WHAT WILL HAPPEN TO ALL THOSE HUGE TEMPTATIONS THAT ONCE CONTROLLED YOUR LIFE?

"אז יהיו אצלו כל ענייני עולם הזה

על הנאותיו תשוקותיו ותאוותיו אין ואפס והכל הבל!

כי אין אדם יכול להיות שקוע בהם רק בעת יחשכו כוכבי נפשו

כשהוא מבולבל בהעדר הדעת ומבטו מצומצם מתוך חשכת דעתו!"

נתיבות שלום חלק א' פרקי מבוא דף י"ד

The only time you can lower yourself to chase cheap worldly pleasures is when the lights of your soul are dim and flickering! In that weak state you can become confused and mixed up and you are in danger of giving up precious diamonds for worthless imitations!

"נפש ... שמרגיש תענוג ושביעה מעבודת ה' ...

נמאסים בעיניו הדברים הגשמיים המתוקים המושכין את הלב!"

נתיבות שלום

However, when your soul feels pleasure and satisfaction from your sincere devotion and connection to fulfilling Hashem's will, all the cheap thrills of the perverted society around you will look disgusting. You will realize how **empty** and **worthless** those lowly worldly desires really are. Those sparkling silver dollars will stop blocking your ENTIRE vision and will start to blend back in with the ENTIRE pile of silver dollars as you regain the proper perspective. Sure, you will still be able to see them — they are there — but you will have the ability to also see the "entire" picture and to understand that they are just a tiny, tiny part of a much larger picture! You will never again let two measly dollars take over your entire vision and block you from seeing a MILLION-dollar world!

THINK ABOUT IT:

What is pinning you down and trapping you? What is holding you back from raising yourself up to live a HIGHER and BETTER life? Only your state of mind. If somehow you could break out — the world would look so different to you, your perspective would change, and therefore your choices would be different!

BROKEN MINDSET

Remember our friend Murray? As long as he was hooked into the mindset of a "gambler," no one could talk to him and reason with him. He was lost! Each time he gambled he lost touch with the real world and locked his mind into a smaller and smaller box.

The only thing that could help Murray would be if somehow he would raise his mindset ABOVE his addiction so that he would once again realize that there is more to life than gambling. As his mind opens up to what's really important, the "significance" of gambling will automatically be diminished and placed back into the right **proportion**.

THIS CONCEPT CAN BE SUMMED UP IN THE FOLLOWING WAY:

"איזה עולם מלא אור ומתיקות: לאלו שאינם שקועים בו
ואיזה עולם חשוך ומר הוא: לאלה השקועים בו!"

מאמר מרן הקדוש מקוברין זי"ע מובא בנתיבות שלום חלק ב' קצ"ב

What a wonderful world full of light and sweetness for those who are not immersed in it, and what a dark and bitter world for those who immerse themselves in it!

There are two sides of the coin: On one side we have people who are subjugated and immersed in blindly following earthly materialistic pleasures. Not surprisingly, these people can NOT find any trace of G-d. They see a world of pain and confusion, anger and hatred. A world full of questions: "How could G-d allow a holocaust to happen?" ... "Where was G-d?" ... "Couldn't G-d make a better world?" and so many more questions.

While those who manage to push down their physical side, thereby raising their spiritual side, live a tranquil life with a clear vision of a world created by a loving G-d Who clandestinely controls every single thing that happens!

Exactly like a seesaw, you can't have BOTH at the same time! The more you PUSH DOWN a life of physical pleasure — the more you RAISE UP your spiritual outlook on life.

"כל מה שיהודי עושה הרי זה 'מנחה':
או שזו 'מנחה לאדוני,' להקדוש ברוך הוא ... שעל ידי זה מתדבק אליו,
או שהיא 'מנחה לעשו' ולסטרא אחרא, ה' ישמרנו."

נתיבות שלום חלק ב' דף ט"ז בשם מרן בעל בית אברהם זי"ע

When looking at life this way, you will come to an incredible realization that absolutely nothing in this world is truly "pareve" — for either it leads you toward a connection to Hashem and a life of purpose and inner pleasure, or it is connecting you to the forces of evil that will lead you down a path toward pain and regret.

We can all easily see that the above statement is true when it comes to very big life decisions or acts that are obviously going to push you in one direction or another. However, after deep introspection, you will realize that this applies to every single action or thought you can have.

"השיקול היחיד המכוון איש יהודי בכל פעולותיו ועניניו צריך להיות:
האם יתקרב על ידם להשם יתברך או חס ושלום יתרחק."

נתיבות שלום חלק ב' דף ט"ו

The single factor that must guide a Yid in every situation is: will this thought or action strengthen my connection to Hashem, or not?

"אבל נדע בלא ספק שמעשה האדם ביד האדם
ואין הקב"ה מושכו ולא גוזר עליו לעשות כך."

רמב"ם הלכות תשובה פרק ה' הלכה ה'

The choice of which direction to focus your life on — is yours. That is called "בחירה." You have the choice to observe the world and decide what kind of person you admire. You have the choice to decide what kind of lifestyle you would like to lead and to place yourself on the path that will lead you toward your goal.

You may not necessarily have the freedom of choice to actually BE at your goal right away with your performance where you would like it to be, but you do ALWAYS have the choice to place yourself on the path going **toward** the direction of your choice and you have the choice to begin to learn what it takes to end up at your goal and to start heading there ... one step at a time!

SO LET US PRAY:

"מן המצר קראתי י-ה — ענני במרחב י-ה."

תהלים קיח:ה

Dovid HaMelech says in *Tehillim*:
"From my distress I called to Hashem;
answer me with abundance."

"מיצר מלשון מיצרים-גבול: 'מן המצר' - כלומר מקו הגבול,

'קראתי י-ה' - הריני פונה אליך וקורא לך: 'ענני' איך? 'במרחב'!

כלומר: הרחב לי את מקומי כדי שאוכל לעשות עוד

ולזכות לעלות לשליבה הנוספת בסולם העלייה!"

מדברי ספר נתיבי אמת עניני תפילה

"מצר" also means a "boundary." Using this meaning, the verse reads: "מן המצר" — When I find myself at the **BORDER** — I'm as far as I can go ... the end of the line ... I'm trapped by thick walls of addiction and sinful thoughts that closed in on me ... "קראתי י-ה" — I call out to Hashem and plead: "ענני במרחב" — please provide me with an **EXTENSION** and expand my boundaries so I can flourish and grow higher!

"כל הון העולם אינו שווה

לשעה אחת שאיש יהודי עומד בישוב הדעת!"

מרן מקוברין זי"ע מובא בספר נתיבות שלום חלק א' הקדמה דף י"ד

Having all the money in the world doesn't come close to having clarity and tranquility of spirit!! This means that if someone would actually give you a choice; you can have 1 BILLION dollars along with a life without tranquility of spirit, OR: a life of clarity and tranquility — a wiser choice would be to take the TRANQUILITY!

Once you tap into this concept — even for just a few minutes — then you will taste the delicious sense of inner tranquility and peace. Your life will change. Your attitude will change. Your stability will improve. You will learn to keep your focus on what really makes you feel good. You will yearn to grow even higher. You will push DOWN your sinful desires and you will RAISE UP your life to a higher spiritual level ....

Of course you cannot do this on your own. When you make a sincere effort, then Hashem weighs in and helps you out:

"האדם בשר ודם ... אינו מסוגל כלל להגיע לקדושה בכחות עצמו
אלא תחלתו השתדלות להשיג בעבודתו מדרגת 'טהור'
וסופו מתנה שלבסוף נותן לו הקדוש ברוך הוא במתנה שנהיה קדוש!"

ספר נתיבות שלום

A human being, flesh and blood, can never reach high levels of
Holiness purely on our own, we must TRY to reach PURITY and
then Hashem gives us the GIFT OF becoming PURE and HOLY!

"על ידי הדברי תורה ש'בפיך'
על ידי זה יהיה נכנס ללב, וזה 'ובלבבך,'
ולגמר המעשה יעזור ה' יתברך!"

פרי צדיק דברים לראש חודש אלול אות ג'

Through your yearning and learning the holy Torah, it will enter
your hearts and then Hashem will then help that your actions will
be correct!

Let us strive for a life of clarity,
Which will carry us to spiritual healing
and to a life of happiness on Planet Earth!

CONCEPT FIVE

Discovering REAL happiness

SECTION FIVE

TRUE HAPPINESS is an extremely important part of human existence, both physically and spiritually:

"העצבות אינה עבירה והשמחה אינה מצוה:
אולם טמטום הלב שהעצבות גורמת - שום עבירה לא תוכל להביא
ולמקום שהשמחה יכולה להביא - שום מצוה לא תביאנו!"

ר' אהרן הגדול מ'קארלין זי"ע מובא בספר פתגמים נבחרים

שמחה (happiness) is not a mitzvah and עצבות (sadness) is not a sin, yet, HAPPINESS can lead you to a place that no מצוה can take you, and SADNESS can lead you to a place that no עבירה can bring you.

But where does happiness really come from? A new car? More money? Physical pleasure? Alcohol? Partying? No rules? Coca Cola? Vacations? Playing cards? Cruises? Designer clothing? Watching TV? Being a sports fan? Chocolate? Drugs?

Let's discover the secret of HAPPINESS so that it can bring us to the highest levels of true pleasure, satisfaction, and enjoyment — in this world and the next!

As you know, a human being is essentially a combination of two parts: a physical beast and a spiritual angelic soul. If you want to please your physical beast, simply take part in any pleasure activity — and guess what? You will feel pleasure! You don't need any book to teach you how to do that — it's simple!

However, "inner happiness" does not come from your physical animalistic side; rather, it comes **ONLY** from your angelic side.

"כל מה שיעמול ויתן להנפש מהנאות ותאוות עולם הזה ...

אין לנפש שום סיפוק מזה ואין לה שמחה מכל זה

כי איזה ערך יש לעניני עולם הזה אצלה אחרי שממקור קודש מחצבתה?"

ספר נתיבות שלום חלק ב' עניני סוכות מאמר א'

As much as you may try to pleasure yourself with worldly physical desires, your angelic soul does not get ANY satisfaction from that — because worldly pleasure does not please your soul!

"משל למה הדבר דומה: לעירוני שנשא בת מלכים,

אם יביא לה כל מה שבעולם אינן חשובין לה כלום, למה? שהיא בת מלך."

מדרש קה"ר ו:ז מובא בנתיבות שלום עניני סוכות מאמר ראשון קצ"א

There was once a poor uneducated man from a hick town who married a princess. He had a big problem! Nothing he could afford to buy her could possibly impress her! Why? Because she was a wealthy princess!

"נפשו של יהודי היא בת מלך, היא חלק אלו-ה ממעל,

ולכן ... כל מה שיעמול ויתן לה מהנאות ותאוות עולם הזה -

הנפש לא תמלא, אין לנפש שום סיפוק מזה, ואין לה שמחה מכל זה!"

נתיבות שלום עניני סוכות מאמר ראשון קצ"א

In the same way, every Yiddishe soul is a piece of G-dliness. Therefore, as much as a person tries to fill up his spiritual soul with worldly pleasures, his soul feels absolutely NO satisfaction from it.

MISSING THE POINT

Yanky was so busy working that he didn't eat all day, and his stomach began to growl. It was calling out to him and asking him to please send down some food. Yanky ignored the call and his stomach began to really ache. He continued to ignore it, and after a while he began to feel weak and dizzy.

That evening he realized that since he was so weak and

dizzy, he must do something to take care of himself! So he decided that immediately after work he would go straight to the sauna because that always made him feel so good! But after twenty minutes in the sauna he felt faint! Now he was frustrated and upset that not only did the sauna not make him feel any better — it actually made him feel even worse! He concluded that he needed a new plan to make himself feel better! So he got a bunch of guys together and went off to play paintball — because that is always so much fun! Yanky felt even more angry and disappointed when this plan made him feel even worse! Since he could not function properly and seemed to be on the verge of fainting, his wife decided to take him to see a top psychiatrist. They did some research and picked out a top doctor; they found out where the doctor lived, drove over to his house, and at 2:30 a.m., they banged on his door! They apologized for waking him up but they explained that it was an EMERGENCY! The doctor listened patiently to the whole story and then said with a straight face: "Yanky, my advice to you is that you should eat a bowl of cereal!"

Yanky exploded! A bowl of cereal? "Doc — are you making fun of me? Do you think I'm going to pay you $800 to be told to eat a bowl of cereal!? Besides, what does 'cereal' have to do with my severe problems!? You don't understand me! I did much MORE than eat a bowl of cereal — I went to the sauna and even arranged a group of friends to play paintball! — and even that didn't work for me!" Yanky stormed out of the doctor's office.

Obviously, when you are physically hungry, no pleasure activity will alleviate your hunger and give your body the sustenance it needs in order to function — not even skydiving!

In the very same way, the next time that you feel a little "down," take a few moments to break it down: What exactly in you is feeling "down"? Is it your arm? Your leg? Obviously it isn't your **physical body** that is causing you to feel down, and so pleasuring your physical body will not make you feel better. Duh! So what is going to boost your spirit and give you the relief you crave?

Here's a hint: It does not need to be fun and often is specifically not an enjoyable, easy, or pleasurable activity.

SELFLESS PLEASURE

Yitzchok recently signed up to volunteer for the Chevrah Kadisha. Late one night he received his first call. Getting dressed and driving over to the chapel, he found himself really nervous to do his very first taharah. Indeed, it was a frightening and extremely difficult experience. Upon leaving the funeral chapel, a feeling of inner satisfaction and pride came over him. He was feeling real inner happiness.

The truth is: **Happiness does NOT come from RECEIVING — IT ONLY COMES FROM ACHIEVING!**

Why? Because when pleasure is happening **TO** you it doesn't do anything to **improve** who YOU are and so it cannot give your soul the internal happiness it craves.

RUNNING ON EMPTY

Shaya was on the highway when he suddenly noticed that he was almost out of gas.

So he pulled over to the very next gas station and got himself ... a nice shiny carwash. Before getting back into the car, he inspected it with great pride. His car sparkled and looked brand-new. He kicked the tires, hopped in, and headed back to the highway.

... Ten minutes later — he ran out of gas!

When you FEEL EMPTY "inside," the first rule is: Stop looking for ways to buff up your "exterior" and begin to focus on FILLING UP with something that will give you the "internal" fulfillment and satisfaction you so crave!

Feeling a little down? Hungry for a little satisfaction? Go visit some old folks in the local nursing home for an hour and see how it makes you feel! Go try it! When you get back, continue reading.

Oh, hi — back so fast? Okay, let's continue: You need to internalize what you already know to be true: you cannot afford to make the terrible mistake of confusing PLEASURE with HAPPINESS — like our friends at Coke would like you to believe! The 2011 Coca Cola advertising campaign slogan is: "OPEN HAPPINESS." Their researchers know that people feel empty and everyone is craving the emotional feeling of INNER HAPPINESS! So they are capitalizing on that and actually trying to convince you that drinking a soda can somehow bring you "Happiness" when in reality there is no way that a drink, food, or ANY physical pleasure can give you any drop of HAPPINESS!

"מדת השמחה אי אפשר ליהודי להשיגה
אלא כאשר מתנער כליל מכל הנאות ועניני העולם הזה
כאשר האדם שקוע בהם לעולם אינו בא על סיפוקו."

נתיבות שלום עניני סוכות קצ"ב

The reason most people can't find internal peace of mind and happiness is because they are simply barking up the wrong tree. They think: "If this makes me feel good, then certainly doing a lot more of it will bring me even more pleasure and that must be the secret to finding happiness!"

However, that is simply not true! As long as you are immersed in the pursuit of worldly pleasures and earthly desires, **you will never ever feel truly happy.**

Need proof? Here it is: In today's world where people have the most *unlimited, uninhibited, unrestrained* pleasure ever known to man since the creation of the world, what do you think is the most prescribed medication? Are you ready for this? **ANTIDEPRESSANTS!**

DEPRESSING STATISTICS

Is America the most medicated nation on Earth? ... Adult use of antidepressants almost tripled between 1988-1994 and 1999-2000.
source: usgovinfo.about.com/od/healthcare/a/usmedicated.htm

"DECEMBER 09, 2007: Nearly 50 to 70 percent of complaints by patients today are depression and anxiety. Antidepressants are disseminated like water."
source: PamelaEgan.com

36 Million Americans are on antidepressants!
source: http://www.paxilprogress.org

How can this be? If you would offer any person who ever lived in any country at any time since the creation of the world to live in today's day and age and in the great United States of America, who wouldn't grab that opportunity? Just think of all the luxuries, comforts, amenities, fun, and freedom that we have! Who would think that living in this amazing time would lead people to feeling down and out? There shouldn't be even a small percentage who need "antidepressants"! Feeling down? Simply go out and have fun! Party all night! Go on a cruise! Indulge yourself in all the pleasures this world has to offer! After all — don't fun and pleasure make you feel happy?

This teaches us a great and very deep lesson: **PLEASURE IS NOT HAPPINESS!** Internal happiness is NOT defined by experiencing "fun," nor can it be obtained through "pleasure." Certainly inner happiness cannot come from sinful pleasure, for anything that brings regret and shame upon reflection cannot bring you "real" inner happiness.

Open your eyes and you will notice many people floating through life wrapped up in all sorts of nonsense. They are not connected to anything that is "real." When we tell someone, "get real," we mean that he should "wake up" and stop wasting time with unrealistic thoughts and become a part of the true reality. Living for the moment does not give you any life after the moment is up, and it is therefore not what we consider to be: **real**.

"נפש רעבה שאינו מרגיש תענוג בעבודת ה' ואין לו תענוגים דקדושה,
אדם זה מחפש תענוגים רעים וכל מר מתוק לו!"

נתיבות שלום

If your soul is starving and does not receive the satisfaction and sweetness of spirituality, then you will search out lowly pleasures and even the most disgusting things will look sweet to you.

Once the foundation and stability of your spirit are knocked out by sinful desires, your spirit is forced to aimlessly drift through turbulence and confusion that cause you to actually "feel" deflated, dispirited, discouraged, depressed, and disheartened, as your inner peace and tranquility are mercilessly ripped away from you.

In the end, instead of feeling satisfied by all the pleasure and unrestricted fun you gobbled up in your lifetime — you end up feeling empty and sad. You may still be able to outwardly appear to be having fun, living the life, putting on a nice show and a big smile, but **internally** you can find little inner peace, satisfaction, or happiness ... and for what?

AFTER ALL IS SAID AND DONE:

 LIFE IN REVIEW *After an entire life of seeking pleasure, Sammy comes up to heaven and they present him with a list of his life's accomplishments:*

9,750 hamburgers, 14,300 hot dogs, 70,000 beers, etc., etc.

Nothing of value for anyone other than himself ... and even that temporary pleasure is now completely worthless!

Authentic Yiddishkeit understands that real happiness can only come when your angelic soul is **content** and **satisfied**.

SO WHY DO PEOPLE HAVE SO MUCH TROUBLE WITH THIS CONCEPT?

The challenge is that when your body experiences pleasure, it mimics the feeling of inner happiness in your brain for that duration and for a short period of time thereafter. Therefore, you do actually feel good; you may really be smiling, and you even can really think that you are "happy."

NUMBING THE PAIN

Danny was depressed. He felt that on a scale of 1-100, his happiness level was down to 30. That night he attended a party and danced his head off. For three hours he partied and felt like he was on top of the world!

The next day, as he sat in his tiny cubicle at his dead-end job, he was back down to a feeling of 30, and feeling the drop from the previous night's high to his current low amplified his gloomy feeling. Wallowing in his depressed state of mind, he made the only logical decision to bring happiness into his life: "Tonight, I'm going back to party!"

Many people try to become internally emotionally HAPPY and CONTENT through pleasure activities, but that does not work **because it does not enhance who they are.**

Furthermore, the pleasure they feel from the high is only temporary, and once it wears off they feel even worse than before. At this point they have to do more pleasure to bring back that feeling of pleasure. When that wears off, they need to look for more, and more. Always numbing their emptiness ... but never filling it.

Also, when you are filling your soul, if you achieve only half of your goal, you will still feel half of the pleasure for what you did accomplish. However, when it comes to the fake pleasure, the reality can never be as good as your fantasy, and therefore you will always feel that you came up short and you need to seek more.

Another distinction between pleasure and happiness is that once you get used to an act of pleasure, it can no longer satiate you and bring you the same feeling. Therefore, you always have to up the ante to try to fill your empty void, since the previous activity doesn't do it for you anymore.

Whereas if something makes you feel **internally happy**, you will continue to search for more, since you HAVE so much and you want even more of the good feeling. You are BUILDING on what you have!

If you want to experience internal happiness, all you have to do is go down the correct road. Make a list of things that make you proud and do them! Simply put: Do the things you would be proud to tell your teachers and parents about — and the things you will be happy your children and grandchildren will one day find out about!

Those are the things that will bring you the feeling you are desperately looking for! If something is "real," then you will feel "real" good about it one day later, one week later, and ten years later. That's REALLY "THE REAL THING!"

But notice that there is one common denominator in all things that give you a feeling of pride and accomplishment: It takes **effort**. It takes **commitment**. It takes **determination**. Almost always the trademark will be that it is something that was **difficult** for you to do and usually it **does not** feel physically good.

PLEASURE OF PRIDE *Going on a rollercoaster is the perfect example of good clean pure FUN. However, we all know that finishing a project — any project — brings a certain feeling of pride and accomplishment that triggers a feeling of internal happiness. You smile from the inside out!*

The fact is that you will feel more **inner-satisfaction, pride, and happiness** after completing a 20-minute challenging project than from receiving two hours of physical pleasure.

If you are faced with the following choice, which one would you pick: Help a stranded family of ten change a flat tire on the side of the road in the freezing cold OR enjoy a two-hour massage?

This sums up your entire life. If your answer is the flat tire — then your entire life is facing the right direction. However, if you answered "massage," then you now know why you are not internally happy.

The bottom line is: You cannot have both instant gratification and internal happiness. You have to choose which one you want — and live a life that leads you to your goal. In order to acquire long-term feelings of inner happiness and pride, you must give up the quest for immediate pleasure and instant gratification.

NOW WE CAN UNDERSTAND WHAT IS REALLY MAKING YOU FEEL SO DOWN:

"וזה מקור העצבות המקננת בתוככי הנפש,

שהאדם מחפש כל מיני סיבות מדוע הוא תמיד נעצב אל לבו,

והאמת היא שהנפש היא התובעת ממנו את סיפוקה והיא אינה מתמלאת,

אין לה כל שמחה מהנאות ותאוות עולם הזה!"

נתיבות שלום עניני סוכות מאמר ראשון קצ"א

The emptiness deep inside you is your **SOUL** that is calling out to be fed a yummy spiritual meal! It is **craving** a little spiritual sustenance.

When your soul feels hungry and empty, it sends you a signal, a "groan," and you feel a little "empty." Something is missing. At this point, you can chose to ignore it or try to fill it up with something that cannot satisfy it — but that won't work and it will just get more and more empty.

"וכל כמה שמוסיף למלא

הנאותיו ותאוותיו הנפש **מתעצבת יותר** ...."

נתיבות שלום עניני סוכות מאמר ראשון קצ"א

And the more that you try to "fill yourself up" with worldly pleasures and sinful desires, hoping to drown out the emptiness of your soul, the **more** your soul continues to get weaker and weaker ... sicker and sicker ... more empty and more depressed ... since you are not treating the problem with the right solution.

Let us analyze this and explain why this is so: Imagine that you want to make your left pinky feel good. While you are making it feel good, where exactly are you experiencing the feeling of pleasure? The answer is that only that specific left pinky feels good. Your other fingers don't have any benefit from it and neither does any other part of your body. So your mind experiences the feeling of the pleasure that your left pinky is feeling.

However, think for a moment: Who are "you"? You are not your pinky, or your toe. You have a heart, a mind, and a holy pure soul ... how can you pleasure **THEM?** Why settle for only a small amount of temporary pleasure focusing on just one spot — when you can get so much more?

Now think of the feeling you had when you did a good deed, enjoyed a great session of learning Torah, prayed really well, or overcame a challenge; how can you describe that feeling? Where exactly did you feel that pleasure? Was it located in just one part of you or did YOUR **ESSENCE** feel uplifted and happy?

Understand that if your heart and soul are not truly happy, nothing you do for yourself will make you feel content and you will waste your life, only to one day look back with regret, sorrow, and the immense pain of a wasted life. A wasted opportunity.

However, when you do the right thing, your **ESSENCE** is being pleasured and this gives YOU a feeling of inner satisfaction. **SATISFACTION (not pleasure) = REAL HAPPINESS.**

JUMPING THE GUN

After being on a waiting list for almost 6 months, we finally got reservations at the best restaurant in town. We didn't eat anything all day in anticipation of this amazing long-awaited experience. As soon as we sat down, I began filling up on the bread, drinks, dips, and salads. The same as in any restaurant. By the time the main dish was served — I was stuffed! However, my wife waited patiently until the incredible main dishes were served and she truly enjoyed the amazing delicacies. I lost out on the reason I traveled to this expensive restaurant, for the simple cheap pleasure that I could have gotten anywhere ... just because it got to the table first! Why would any "smart" person fill up on bread when you can enjoy the most delicious ribs in the world!?!

What fools we are to withhold a lifetime of true pleasure and satisfaction from ourselves! How could we constantly get suckered into grabbing the quick, short-lived, temporary physical pleasure specific to just the limbs involved, and lose out on experiencing the true blissful inner happiness of building a satisfying life that we can be truly proud of.

Billions of people are searching for "inner happiness" and yet they miss this very simple point: If you want to attain "outer happiness," then you should do things that make your "OUTER" feel good; however if what you really need is "inner happiness" — then how on earth could focusing on pleasing your "outer" ever help you attain that goal?

You need to allow yourself to find "inner happiness." This means putting your "inner" first and opening a line of clear communication between you and your "inner" so that you can clearly know what it wants, craves, and needs. When you focus on giving your "inner" pure voice what it truly needs and you don't do the things that it tells you NOT to do because it makes it feel bad and sad and depressed, then indeed you shall find the treasure that the entire world is searching for ... real "inner happiness"!

The key is: The only way to have "inner happiness" is to make your "inner" happy! And how can you make you "inner" happy? By achieving! And what is the greatest possible human achievement? Connecting to the Almighty!

PLUG INTO THE SOURCE OF ALL SPIRITUALITY AND GET RECHARGED!

THE FINAL COUNTDOWN

Asher was in the middle of an important business call when he noticed his cell phone battery was almost drained! He didn't have any other phone and couldn't afford to lose the call. It started counting down: shutting down in 30, 29, 28, 27 ... he panicked as he desperately tried to find his car charger ... 17, 16, 15 ... "Are you listening, Asher?" —

> *"Umm ... yes — I'm here."* Fumbling around, he found it
> *... 9,8,7,6, he plugged it into the car charger, now it needs*
> *to get connected to the phone ... 3, 2 — CONNECTED!*

"כי כל מה שיהודי מרגיש שחסר לו

הרי זה משום **שרחוק** מהקדוש ברוך הוא!"

נתיבות שלום עניני סוכות מאמר ראשון קצ"א

A healthy person feels empty and depressed only when he feels distant from Hashem, for if you would feel connected and close to Hashem, you would not feel that you are missing anything at all!

"כי עמך מקור חיים: **על ידי שיהודי 'עמך'**

שדבוק בהשם יתברך ואז מקור חיים מלא חיות!

ומרגיש אז את עצמו קרוב להשם יתברך ...

והרגשה זו ממלאת אותו בשמחה!"

מרן בעל בית אברהם זי"ע נתיבות שלום עניני סוכות מאמר ראשון קצ"א

Authentic Yiddishkeit believes that your ability to feel internally happy and truly enjoy your life depends on the degree that you are connected to Hashem. Hashem is the Source of all life, therefore, when you connect to Hashem, you connect to the SOURCE of all life and therefore you feel full of life.

I know what you're thinking:
Okay, great ... so how can "I" get close to Hashem!?

Lucky for you ... there's a clear answer!
Just read on ....

CONCEPT SIX

How YOU can bond with the Almighty?

CONCEPT SIX

If you cannot connect with someone,
then how can you have a relationship with him?

WISHFUL THINKING

Motty decided to do something special for his future in-laws. He went to the florist and carefully selected the nicest red roses for them. He knocked on their door with his heart overflowing with joy. His future father-in-law opened the door and he presented him with the gorgeous bouquet. HAAAAAAACHOOOOOOO!

"What's wrong?"

"I'm allergic to flowers!"

"Oh. Sorry — I didn't know." Motty left and 25 minutes later he was at their door again. He smiled broadly and presented him with a gorgeous box of assorted Swiss Chocolates.

He frowned apologetically. "Sorry, but I'm allergic."

"Oh — okay, no problem."

Ten minutes later, at the door: "Assorted nuts?"

"Sorry ... allergic."

"Cotton candy?"

"Nope — diabetic."

IF YOU DON'T KNOW WHAT SOMEONE LIKES ...
HOW ON EARTH CAN YOU PLEASE HIM?

"ועתה אם נא מצאתי חן בעיניך

הודעני נא את דרכך ואדעך למען אמצא חן בעיניך..."

שמות פרק לג:יג

Moshe said to Hashem, "If I find favor in your eyes, please teach me Your ways so that I can understand You, so that I can please You and find favor in Your eyes ...." Moshe understood that you cannot have a "relationship" and "connection" with Hashem if there is nothing you can do to please Him.

Doing something for someone else accomplishes two things:

1. It shows the person that you want to please him, which makes him appreciate you.

2. It shows you how much you are willing to go out of your way to please that person, which then brings out your love and connection to that person.

But how can we connect with Hashem, Master of the universe, who does not "need" anything from anyone!? This is why Hashem created an entire system of do's and don'ts, so that by following His commandments and living the "kind" of lifestyle presented to us, we are then fulfilling His wishes and thereby connecting with Him.

"תכלית כל התורה והמצוות ועבודת ה׳

היא השגת בחינת דביקות בה׳, והרגשת קרבתו יתברך ...

כלשון הזוהר הקדוש: 'תרי"ג עיטין' פירוש: עצות איך לקיים מצות ובו תדבק."

נתיבות שלום הקדמה חלק ב׳

The sole purpose of ALL of the Torah, ALL the 613 commandments, and ALL of our service to Hashem is to help us be able to **connect to Hashem** so that we can feel His closeness to us.

"והקטרת את כל האיל המזבחה
עלה הוא לה' **ריח ניחוח** אשה לה' הוא."

שמות פרק כט:יח

The Torah instructs us to burn an entire ram on the altar as a sacrificial offering to Hashem, and tells us that: "**It is a satisfying aroma**, a fire offering to Hashem."

Now hang on just a minute: What exactly is the "satisfying aroma" to Hashem? Does Hashem Master of the universe enjoy the smell of freshly smoked BBQ ram?

"ריח ניחוח: נחת רוח לפני שאמרתי **ונעשה רצוני**!"

רש"י שמות פרק כט:יח

The answer is: The "pleasure" Hashem has is because He told us to do something — and we did His will! That is what is pleasing to Hashem! When Hashem "sees" or "smells" our loyal service to Him being done in accordance to His Divine will: that is PLEASING to Him!

When you connect yourself to G-d through fulfilling His wishes, you attach yourself to the **SOURCE** of all life, and that is what gives you the feeling of satisfaction and contentment you so crave. You are not just living: YOU ARE ALIVE!

"כאשר יהודי מקיים מצוה כגון שמתעטף בציצית או מניח תפילין
אף אם אין לו בשעה זו הארת הדעת ורגשי הלב - הרי עצם קיום המצוה
שזוכה לקיים את רצון ה' צריך להיות אצלו
התענוג הגדול ביותר מכל התענוגים!"

נתיבות שלום חלק ב' דף שמ"ח

Therefore, when you perform any mitzvah, even if your mind is not clear and you aren't in the mood of doing it, the mere fact that you are now going to **fulfill the will of G-d** and thereby connecting yourself to Him, should give you the greatest sensation of LIFE!

HELPING YOUR HERO

Over 50,000 showed up to the outdoor concert. Young Baruch was so excited to be able to see his favorite singer perform live on stage. Baruch'l begged his father for the best tickets and his dad came through with tickets right next to the bandstand! Suddenly, in the middle of the best song the singer shouted out to him. "Hey kid — get me a ¼-inch to ½-inch cable splitter from the engineer!"

Baruch ran like crazy to find the engineer and get the cable — even though he had no clue what it was — and he ran back as quickly as he could, busting passed the usher and jumping over people in his way, in order to get his favorite singer what he needed as fast as humanly possible. The singer crouched down to take the cable, and with a wink said, "Thanks, kid!" Little Baruch was in heaven!

If doing the will of someone we look up to makes us feel happy, shouldn't doing the will of our Creator make us jump for joy?!

"כן כאשר יהודי מקיים מצוה ואומר אשר קדשנו במצוותיו
אף שאיננו יודעים כלום ולא מבינים מאומה ...
על ידי הכוונה הזאת מגיע לשורש המצוה!"

נתיבות שלום חלק ב׳ דף שמ"ח

So too, when you have the opportunity to fulfill any commandment of Hashem — even if you really don't understand anything about what you are doing or why you are doing it — the simple pure understanding that you are going to do this thing because it is Hashem's will — is the point of the mitzvah!

"בזמנים שיהודי סגור ומסוגר ואינו יכול לעורר הארת המוח ורגשי הלב
והוא חושב בלבו איזה פנים יש כבר לעבודתו ולקיום מצוותיו לתפלותיו

ושבתותיו? **מחשבה זו היא טעות מעיקרא!** ... דבחינת 'נעשה' אף בלא
הארת הדעת ורגשי הלב הוא תכלית רצון ה' והתענוג הגדול ביותר!"
נתיבות שלום חלק ב', דף שמ"ח

Even when you are not in the mood and you think to yourself, "How
is this prayer, mitzvah, Shabbos, or learning Torah going to look
in Hashem's eyes?" — this thinking is completely and utterly false
from start to finish! Because the LESS you are in the mood, the
MORE that shows that you are doing it EXCLUSIVELY because you
want to follow His Divine will — therefore it is even more impressive
to Hashem that you have no self-interest and enjoyment and the
result is that you have an even better opportunity to connect!

JUDGING THE EFFORT

*If you ask your son to please shovel the snow around the
house, with whom will you be more impressed? A son who
is 6 foot 4 inches, 200 pounds, with bulging muscles, who
can lift a car and is strong as an ox, or, your weak, sickly
son, who weighs less than the snow on the shovel, who
gets out from under the covers to struggle with fulfilling
your wishes? Who will get a better "tip"?*

So too, Hashem is far MORE impressed with our service when it is
DIFFICULT for us, specifically when we are NOT in the mood, when
we CANNOT properly concentrate, when we DON'T understand
what we are doing or why He required us to do it ... and we do it
just because we know that it is HIS WILL and we want to connect
to Him!

THIS CONCEPT GOES EVEN FURTHER;

"אפילו כשעומד במלחמת היצר הרע הקשה
וממלחמה קשה הרי יוצאים מוכים ופצועים בכל זה

אשרי איש־לא יקרב בדרו שהרו לא הי אלקיו

הוא מאושר כולו בזה שזכה להלחם על קיום רצונו יתברך!"

נתיבות שלום חלק ב' דף שמ"ח

Even when you find yourself in an intense internal battle with the Evil Inclination, and as with any raging war it is impossible not to be wounded and hurt, still you should feel completely lucky and internally happy that out of all the millions of people in the universe, YOU are fortunate enough to be one of the FEW ELITE people that at least TRY to fight for the will of Hashem!

WILLING TO HELP

I was walking down the street when I found myself surrounded by four thugs, I yelled, "Someone help me," yet people kept their distance and went about their business.

Suddenly one thin weak guy ran over to try and help me defend myself. He got beaten up really bad, but that only made me more impressed that he was willing to come to try and help me — knowing full well that there was no way he could truly win the fight! Can you imagine how I felt about him? He KNEW he would LOSE — and yet he still TRIED TO FIGHT!

In the same way, even if you sin against the will of Hashem, think about this — WHY are you even involved in this struggle to begin with? After all, there are billions of people who completely ignore the will of Hashem! At least YOU showed up! YOU are trying and YOU care and YOU feel bad that you didn't do better!

Certainly YOU are a HERO in Hashem's eyes! When you understand this properly, you should be filled with a deep sense of inner pride and satisfaction that you merited to be from the tiny population who even TRIES to fight off the Yetzer Hora and fulfill the will of Hashem!

Just by TRYING — you SUCCEEDED!

Since you SUCCEEDED — you are CONNECTED!

By realizing you are CONNECTED — you become HAPPY!

You now see how upside-down things are from the way you were thinking! Even in your WORST situations when you feel so down and out, if you do what you can, then your beloved Father will smile down on you, beaming with pride!

But it gets even better! When you look back at your life, you think that the most impressive parts are the ones when you were on your highest spiritual level and felt connected to Hashem. Read on and you will be amazed to learn how false that really is!

"כי אצל האדם יש זמנים של עליה וזמנים של ירידה ...
אחר כל עליה באה ירידה ואחר כך שוב עליה."

ספר נתיבות שלום חלק ב' עמוד שמ"ט

Every single person goes through ups and downs. After every "up" comes a "down" and after every "down" comes an "up." There is no way around this. We are "programmed" to think that we can only try and connect to Hashem when we are on an "up," and so we fall apart and disconnect when we are on a "down." We feel "low" and dirty. We feel embarrassed and ashamed. But most of all ... we feel alone.

"יש דבקות מתוך גדלות, כאשר יהודי מרגיש את גדלות הבורא ומתענג
על ה',ויש דבקות בה' דוקא כאשר יהודי נמצא בשפל המצב!
וזהו תכלית קבלת התורה, שישראל יהיו
תמיד דבקים בה' כחשיכה כאורה."

ספר נתיבות שלום חלק ב' עמוד שמ"ט

However, you must internalize that just as there is a way to connect to Hashem from a spirit of greatness, so too there is a way to connect to Hashem specifically when you are in a low and dark situation!

ANYONE can agree to serve Hashem when he feels amaaazing and energized! But the GREATNESS of a Yid is when you agree to serve Hashem even when you don't feel any personal satisfaction from it! This is the ultimate purpose of leading a Torah life: finding your purpose and connecting to Hashem even when you are going through a DOWN. Even when life is rough and you feel disconnected.

"וזוהי גדלותם של ישראל אשר הקדוש ברוך הוא התפאר בהם על כך
שהקדימו נעשה לנשמע: היינו ש'נעשה' עוד קודם ש'נשמע',
שגם בזמנים חשוכים וירודים נהיו דבקים בה'!"

ספר נתיבות שלום חלק ב' עמוד שמ"ט

This is the greatness of the Jewish people that Hashem praised them for: we said "WE WILL DO!" even before we said "WE WILL HEAR"! That means that even in the difficult and dark times that we all go through, when we can't HEAR! We can't FEEL! We will still do what we CAN do and connect to Hashem DAVKA (specifically) from that low level!

"ואתם הדבקים בה' אלקיכם
חיים כולכם היום!"

דברים ד:ד

The holy Torah says:
"You are connected to Hashem your G-d —
you are completely alive today!"

We already learned that you can ONLY feel ALIVE and TRULY HAPPY when you feel CONNECTED to Hashem. But we have a problem — if every person goes through UPS and DOWNS, and when you are on a "down" you succumb to the persuasion of the lowly slimy snake that ensnares you to sin against Hashem, then does that mean that every time you hit a down you must feel disconnected, unsatisfied, and UNHAPPY? NO!!

"שם ה' הוא בחינת גילוי ורחמים ושם אלקים הוא בחינת דין וצמצום
וזהו ואתם הדבקים: שלעולם אתם דבקים בהשם יתברך,
הן בחינת בה' והן בחינת אלקיכם!"

ספר נתיבות שלום חלק ב' עמוד שמ"ט

You CAN always connect to G-d! Whether you are on an UP and
you feel close and connected to G-d ("Hashem") — and even when
you feel pushed away and disconnected from Him ("Elokim")!
You are CONNECTED to G-d in EVERY WAY; therefore you are
completely ALIVE! You can ALWAYS feel spiritual electricity pulsing
through your veins as you are constantly connected to the power
supply of all spiritual power EVERY DAY in EVERY SITUATION!
Therefore, you can ALWAYS FEEL HAPPY AND SATISFIED!

"יסוד השמחה הוא:
להאמין כי בתוך כל ההסתרים
הקדוש ברוך הוא אתו ואני ה' השוכן אתם גם בתוך טומאתם!!!"

נתיבות שלום ענייני פורים מגילת אסתר - מגילה לנמצא בהסתר פנים אות ד'

Thus, the KEY and source of human happiness is to truly believe
that in **ALL** situations of difficulty and darkness and even if you
are immersed in spiritual lowness and corruption, Hashem stands
right there by your side!

Once you believe that regardless of your status — Hashem is
always right there with you — then you will realize that under ANY
circumstances you can always plug right into that great source of
LIFE — and then you will be connected to the SOURCE of calm,
serenity, peace, harmony, tranquility, and clarity, and you will have
entered a place of true satisfaction and **real internal Happiness!**

**All you need to do
Is follow your:**

GPS!

Dear reader: You are about to engage in the war of your life! Literally! This is the all-out war to finally win *yourself* back from captivity and regain control over your life!

However, it takes change. And change ain't easy.

In fact, change hurts. A lot.

But NOT changing ...
hurts even more!

OK, Now What?

Get up and FIGHT!

OK, Now What?

When you finally make the decision to "fight" and improve your life, an internal feeling of joy and pride will blossom within your essence and you will be full of enthusiasm as you look forward to this new stage of your life. You understand and expect that it may be a little difficult to get used to the new standards you set for yourself and to start to utilize self-control, but since you are doing the right thing, you probably expect the process to be a sweet and exhilarating experience ... **boy, are you in for a big surprise!**

Here's some tips on what to expect and what to look out for:

A "BITTERSWEET" EXPERIENCE

"חולי הגוף טועמים המר מתוק ומתוק מר, ויש מן החולים מי שמתאוה
ותאב למאכלות שאינן ראויין לאכילה כגון העפר והפחם
ושונא המאכלות הטובים כגון הפת והבשר הכל לפי רוב החולי."

רמב"ם הלכות דעות ב:א

A person can become physically sick and encounter a strange phenomenon: sweet things will taste bitter and bitter things will taste sweet. At this point, even if you would bring him the sweetest food in the world, it will taste bitter to him and he will have no pleasure from it — and on the contrary, he will enjoy and appreciate bitter disgusting food much more!

"כך בני אדם שנפשותיהם חולות
מתאוים ואוהבים הדעות הרעות ושונאים הדרך הטובה ומתעצלים ללכת בה

והיא כבידה עליהם למאד לפי חליים!"

רמב"ם הלכות דעות ב:א

In the very same way, after being separated from holiness and purity for so long, you may have become spiritually ill. The side effect may be that the wonderful beautiful delicious sweetness of the correct way of life — may actually taste bitter!

"ויבאו מרתה,
ולא יכלו לשתות מים ממרה
כי מרים הם."

בשלח טו:כג

The Torah says: "And they came to Marah, but they could not drink the waters of Marah, because **they** were bitter." Meaning, the WATER was bitter.

"אמר ר' לוי למה 'כי מרים הם'?
הדור היה מר במעשיו!"

מדרש תנחומא פרשת ויקהל סימן ט'

However, a deeper lesson is brought down in the holy *Sefarim*. It wasn't the WATER that was the problem —, it was the PEOPLE!

"לא שה'מים' היו מרים כפשוטו אלא ה'אנשים' היו מרים -
שעל ידי פגמים נהפך 'להם' המתוק למר!"

נתיבות שלום חלק ב' דף פ"ד

At this point in their journey, the Yidden had not studied Torah for three consecutive days. After not being in touch with spirituality for three days, when they encountered WATER (water refers to Torah) it tasted BITTER to them — but not because something was wrong with the water, rather, כי מרים הם — THEY — THE PEOPLE — were bitter! Once THEY were bitter, they could not taste the SWEETNESS of the water, which is referring to Torah.

Since you have been disconnected for so long to whatever spiritual level is ABOVE where you are currently at, even when you try to reconnect, Torah and Mitzvos will not taste so delicious to "you." But keep in mind: there is NOTHING WRONG with the Torah ... Torah is sweeter than honey to those who are immersed in it ... it is YOU who has strayed from the proper path and it is YOU who has a spiritual sickness that causes YOUR TASTE BUDS to become twisted.

Don't let this discourage you! As you become spiritually healthy, your old habits and materialistic animalistic pleasures will taste bitter to you and the beautiful Torah life will taste sweet to you!

UP AND RUNNING

"דהנה כאשר יהודי מתחיל לעסוק בעבודת ה'

נעמדים בפניו בכל יום מכשולות חדשים ונסיונות קשים ומרים

כדאיתא (קדושין ל:) שיצרו של אדם מתרבה ומתחדש עליו בכל יום מחדש

עד כי נדמה לו שזה למעלה מכוחותיו ואינו מסוגל להתגבר!"

ספר נתיבות שלום חלק ב' עניני פסח דף רע"ט

As you begin to fight to get closer to Hashem, brand new challenges and problems will arise before you, to the point that you feel that it is not realistic for you to achieve your goal! You will start wondering, why did I sign up for this life change? Why did I buy GPS? Why is Hashem making this so hard for me?

> **GROWING PAINS** *Jonathan started to learn karate. In the beginning, he was the weakest kid in the class and everyone was able to beat him up, but after a whole year of working hard, Jonathan became the top kid in the class. There was NO one in the entire white belt class who could win a fight against the*

great mighty Jonathan. Then, the teacher graduated him into the yellow belt class. Jonathan entered the class with confidence and with a smirk on his face. But when he entered the ring to fight — he lost to every single kid in the class! How could this be? Just one day before he was on top of the world and everyone in his class feared him — and now he was suddenly thrown to the bottom of the class and he couldn't win anyone!?

Jonathan begged his teacher to please let him go back to the white belt class so that he can remain undefeated... but the teacher wouldn't hear of it! Jonathan thought: Why did I sign up for this? Why did I decide to push myself? But he didn't quit. After a whole year of hard work, Jonathan climbed his way to the top of the class. Every time he entered the ring against another kid in the class, he overpowered them! He was stronger, faster and smarter than anyone in the yellow belt class! He felt on top of the world. Until — his teacher graduated him into the green belt class and once again he was hopeless and defenseless.

Imagine that someone decides to change his life around and lose weight or build muscle. He feels so great putting on his sneakers and signing up at the gym. He looks around at all the people leaving the gym with smiles on their faces! No one is *kvetching* and complaining! What a great life!

He thinks that since he made the right "life choice" to improve his situation, that now things should be easy for him — how much fun it will be! I'll go every day, I'll "work out," I'll lose weight, I'll feel good, I'll look good!

But we know that that is not the case! On the contrary! Now that he signed up to improve his life, he is BEGINNING his difficult and sometimes even painful journey! He is greeted at the gym by a big burly personal trainer pushing him PAST his current limits, because the only way to GROW is through challenge. Until now he RAN AWAY from physical hardship and difficulty and so his body will not be able to tolerate any little strain! He has NO endurance! And so he feels that this is IMPOSSIBLE for him! His experience will be full of: "OY! I can't do this"!

However, everyone else at the gym will be smiling as they watch the "new kid" look so lost as he struggles through his new challenges. Although the new guy is going nuts and feels like storming out of there never to come back again, everyone else smirks, remembering, "That's exactly what I looked like!" and they know that as long as he doesn't give up — he'll become like they are now.

BLOWING HIS BRAINS OUT

For his afikoman, little Shaya asked his parents to buy him a trumpet and get him private lessons. He was so excited with his new shinny trumpet and he could hardly wait for his first lesson. However, when his parents picked him up from the lesson they were shocked. Little Shaya wanted to put the trumpet under the car and have them run it over! He looked terrible! His lips were puffy, purple, and deformed, and he was pale from trying to blow this metal thing and not getting anywhere after a whole hour!

In the very same way, as you enter the army of Hashem and you take this big step to reform your life and "sign up" for greatness, you will be greeted by NEW challenges that you have never experienced and you will feel like you cannot possibly win.

You may experience feelings of frustration: What was I thinking? Did I really think I could change my life? Things were so much easier for me before I tried to improve myself! Where is Hashem? Why is He making things HARDER for me? Didn't I finally make the RIGHT decision?!

"... אין דבר שיהודי
אינו מסוגל להתגבר עליו!"

ספר נתיבות שלום חלק ב' עניני פסח דף רע"ט

You need to know and trust in your internal strength. There is nothing that you cannot conquer with patience and commitment!

Over time, you will get stronger, quicker, and smarter, and you will be able to conquer your new challenges on your new level. And eventually you will even feel the urge to grow even higher. Once again your courageous decision to grow closer to Hashem will be greeted with new smashing blows by a Yetzer Hora that has been in that class forever. It is stronger, quicker and smarter than you and it will try to make you regret your decision to move up the ladder! But with time, you will learn to overpower those challenges as well, and move higher and higher. YES — YOU CAN and YOU WILL, with Hashem's help!

Now your focus must be to just STAY ON TRACK! You know what is right — don't let anything or anyone talk you off your goal.

Aside from that, there is another reason that things will be difficult for you:

THE DEEPEST DARKNESS

"בכל יום סמוך לעלות השחר החושך מחשיך ביותר חשכת הלילה ...
כי כל דבר טבעי המרגיש שבא כנגדו איזו דבר הפכי לו הרוצה לבטל
מציאותו אז הוא מתחזק ביותר כנגד מתנגדו ופועל בטבעו
כל אשר ימצא בכחו לפעול ...."

כלי יקר שמות ו:א

The darkest part of the night is just before daybreak. This reveals a phenomenon that Hashem instilled in **everything** He created: Whenever something senses a threat to its existence, it gathers all of its strength to fight against that force!

So too, the Yetzer Hora senses that it is about to lose a valued customer! Therefore, as you try to improve your life and raise yourself HIGHER ... EXPECT IT to throw anything it can at you to distract you and knock you off your goal.

When that happens, you should smile a calm and knowing smile. Now you know that it knows that you are for real ... change is around the corner ... if you just hang on and don't give up ... the sun WILL soon rise and push away all the darkness in your life.

FILLING YOUR VOID

When you STOP doing the things that bring you down, your life will feel empty. In order to grow, you need to FILL the void in your life with GOOD thoughts and GOOD acts.

FILLING THE VOID

Tommy went to the dentist with a cavity. First the dentist cleaned out the dirt, then he drilled out the rotten part of the tooth and made a nice clean hole. Can he just leave it like that? Of course not! He must now "fill" up that space with a new strong material that will prevent future tooth decay!

"ונשל ה׳ אלהיך את הגוים האל מפניך מעט מעט
לא תוכל כלתם מהר פן תרבה עליך חית השדה."

פרשת עקב ז:כב

Hashem told the Jews that conquering the land of Israel would be a slow process that would take several years. The question is, why didn't Hashem make ALL the nations in the land run out of Israel all at once?

The explanation is: If all the nations would have emptied out the entire land in one shot, then the small Jewish nation would not have been able to inhabit such a large area. In the interim, wild animals would inhabit the vacant land and then it would have been difficult for us to take back the land from the animals.

Therefore, Hashem gave the Jewish people the land step by step, so that they could conquer an area, occupy it, and then move on to the next portion of the land.

As you break away from your corrupt way of life, you will need to fill the void with positive and productive things. For if you don't replace all negative activities and thoughts with positive ones, you will surely relapse into your old ways.

If you went to the movies every Saturday night, you can't just STOP and sit on your couch every Saturday night staring at the four walls and twiddling your thumbs. Instead, you must turn your Saturday night into a "Motza'ei Shabbos" and go to Rabbi Reisman's enjoyable NAVI shiur!

You NEED entertainment, stimulation, activities, outlets ... so you can't DEPRIVE yourself of them! Just like someone who stops eating non-kosher, must eat kosher food — he can't just starve himself! So too, you must REPLACE all your *treif* activities with kosher activities! You can't just starve yourself!

"וזה ענין: 'סור מרע על ידי עשה טוב' כי הדרך
לעקור את נקודת הרע וזדונו אשר בחובו טמון הוא רק על ידי עשה טוב
שיכנס בכל מהותו לעבדות השם יתברך ואז יהיו ממילא
כל ענייני הרע נמאסים בעיניו!"

ספר נתיבות שלום חלק ב' קמ"ו

The way to truly uproot the נקודת הרע = the "ground zero" of evil buried deep inside your subconscious, is by actively pursuing a righteous lifestyle and immersing yourself in the service of Hashem.

As you immerse yourself in "the GOOD life" you will begin to connect to Hashem and then your inner pull toward sin will become weaker and weaker. As the balance of good over evil shifts in your mind, your priorities and focus will also shift so that sin and corruption will have less of an appeal to you. Over the sands of time, even the idea of sin will disgust you and you will wonder, "Who would be silly enough to give up the feeling of being connected to Hashem for such insignificant things?"

"וכאשר יהודי דבוק בה' מיטהר מוחו על ידי זה ונהפך להיות **מח יהודי**
לבו נהפך להיות **לב יהודי**, וכן אבריו נעשים **אברים יהודיים**,
שהרי כל הדבוק לטהור טהור! על ידי שיהודי מתדבק בה' נוצר אצלו
מציאות חדשה עד שנהפך להיות יהודי **בכל מהותו!**"

ספר נתיבות שלום חלק ב' קמ"ו

As you live a life connected to Hashem, your corrupt mind will transform into a **Yiddishe mind**, your perverted feelings will transform into **Yiddishe feelings** and your entire being will eventually become transformed entirely to be a complete YID from head to toe!

OUR PARTING WORDS

As we already wrote, the Holy Zohar taught us that everything in the visible physical world is created to show us what is going on in the invisible spiritual world. This is why Hashem created the concept of GRAVITY that is a constant pull toward the earth. This represents the constant pull that we each have toward earthly physical pleasures.

However, the world finally discovered that once you break out of the earth's atmosphere, there is NO gravity and everything just naturally floats UPWARD!

This is certainly meant to teach us an amazing insight: Once we somehow break out of the grip of our earthly surroundings, we will naturally float upward and grow closer to Hashem!

"הדבר היחיד שתמיד עולה למעלה
כנגד הכח של ארציות שמושך כל דבר גשמי למטה
הוא הנר - והנר רמז לנשמה כדכתיב: נר ה' נשמת אדם."

כלילת יופי

But what is the one thing on earth that defies gravity? A flame! A flame always flickers upward — even if you turn it UPSIDE DOWN!

Our holy soul is compared to a candle which is always flickering upward, fighting the constant pull of gravity — even while immersed in this UPSIDE-DOWN WORLD!

Regardless of whatever level of spirituality you are on right now, you have a battle to wage: To conquer and push out the evil that has inhabited parts of your life and RISE TO THE NEXT LEVEL!

Now that you've programmed your GPS
you are ready to START your journey ....
Buckle up and stay strong until you reach your

FINAL DESTINATION!

AUTHENTIC YIDDISHKEIT

Navigation for your soul

SECTION 1
Hashem Loves YOU!

Authentic Yiddishkeit believes that Hashem loves a Jew who is on the LOWEST POSSIBLE LEVEL — even more than He loves a perfect holy angel on the HIGHEST level!

Authentic Yiddishkeit believes that whatever situation you will ever find yourself in, you will always retain your title of being Hashem's beloved SON, and Hashem is always ready, willing, and available to communicate with you!

Authentic Yiddishkeit believes that Hashem in His infinite mercy calculates: (1) all the good deeds that you have already done, (2) plus He calculates the ripple effect caused by you and (3) **He even calculates all the good deeds that you will ever do!** CAN YOU STILL THINK THAT HE ISN'T ON YOUR SIDE??

Authentic Yiddishkeit believes that the MORE we distance ourselves from being connected to Hashem — the MORE mercy and patience Hashem showers onto our relationship, so that no matter what the situation is, the door is wide open for us to reconnect to Hashem, our wonderful, amazing, incredible Father in Heaven!

Authentic Yiddishkeit understands that even though kids sometimes think that their parents' ANGER and frustration toward them is a sign that they do NOT love them and care about them, the reality is that the complete opposite is true! For if the parents no longer cared about the child, they would be far LESS angry about the situation!

Authentic Yiddishkeit believes that not only should we not lose any affection for those we must punish, Hashem showed us by example that it is UP TO THE "PUNISHER" to make sure that the "PUNISHEE" never feels that you don't care about him anymore.

Authentic Yiddishkeit believes that Judaism is not just for saints; in fact, much of the Torah speaks directly to sinners and constantly teaches us the same message, over and over! Hashem's response to even the worst sinner is: YOU are my child! I LOVE YOU! I am rooting for you and I am patient beyond your comprehension! Don't ever think that I am sick of you! Come back to Me ... yes — even after what you did I still want you right here next to Me, where you belong!

Authentic Yiddishkeit believes that even when there is no way to win according to normal courtroom proceedings, by truly feeling that Hashem is your loving FATHER, you unleash the enormous reservoir of compassion and mercy that is ABOVE the justice department!

Authentic Yiddishkeit understands that when you actually internally believe that Hashem really is your loving Father — you don't just say it — you really FEEL that way in the depths of your heart — then you tap into a **supernatural power that allows you to receive ANYTHING that you request from Hashem!**

Authentic Yiddishkeit clearly believes that even after sinning over and over, day after day, year after year, all the receptors that connect us to Hashem are still completely intact and ready to be used! They don't become musty, dusty, or rusty!

SECTION 2
Solid Gold

Authentic Yiddishkeit understands that you should not despair and you should not give up on trying to repent, rebuild, and reconnect to Hashem, because every sin you did is only due to **external stumbling blocks** and it does NOT properly represent who you really are, for your **ESSENCE** is a pure soul, and your pure soul is a piece of G-d — so how can you be bad!?!

Authentic Yiddishkeit believes that someone may seem to be "enjoying" himself and "partying" out of control, but that does not mean that he is **satisfied** with his life! In fact, the partying might very well be a manifestation of **tremendous inner pain** that is eating him up to the point that he cannot deal with it any other way. He is not "dancing" he is gasping for life!

Authentic Yiddishkeit understands that no one in his "right mind" would ever willingly "choose" to go against the will of his Creator by engaging in any form of sin. Therefore, your sinning against Hashem was obviously only caused by outside influences that temporarily seized control of your mind and caused you to act against your true inner will.

Authentic Yiddishkeit understands the concept of a mature, normal, functioning adult losing control to the point that he can make incredibly wrong decisions that are inconsistent with his true ideals and life's mission.

Authentic Yiddishkeit believes: If while we clung to worthless idols Hashem still loved us even more than He loves perfect heavenly angels (who never sin or mess up), then He certainly loves each and every one of us — regardless of what sins we are currently doing!!! For our ACTIONS never affect our true RELATIONSHIP with Hashem!

Authentic Yiddishkeit understands the unbreakable, unconditional love Hashem has for each and every Yid to be precisely as we described in scenario #3: **Hashem has been following behind you step by step, even as you descended into the depths of sin, and He is standing behind you RIGHT NOW, anxiously waiting for you to just turn around and feel close to Him again!**

Authentic Yiddishkeit clearly believes that no matter how low you sink, Hashem will **always be on your side!** Believe it or not, there is actually **nothing** you can possibly do to make Hashem **stop** rooting for you — and therefore you can **always** put your full trust in Him. He's on your side! Why should He help you? Because He *wants* to!

Authentic Yiddishkeit believes that no matter what you did in the past, and no matter what situation you are currently in, Hashem is always waiting for you with open arms and there is always a path leading you right back to Hashem. ALWAYS!

Authentic Yiddishkeit believes that since essentially we come directly from the source of goodness, even if we find ourselves completely transformed into a state of impurity and spiritual corruption, we can always return, re'JEW'venate, and reconnect to our pure source of holiness!

Authentic Yiddishkeit believes that no matter how "bad" someone is "acting," you can always tap into his pure essence that has **not been affected** and return him to his place in the "world of building."

Authentic Yiddishkeit believes that only your outer "circuit breaker" can stop functioning properly. However, your internal spiritual wiring is always functional and ready to carry spiritual currents throughout your holy essence.

Authentic Yiddishkeit understands that when dealing with a Yid who has fallen from grace, the focus is not to **improve** the actual נשמה, because nothing is **essentially** wrong with the נשמה — it is still radiating purity and sweetness! Rather, our focus is to remove the **exterior** layers of *shmutz* that are merely **blocking** its glorious shine!

Authentic Yiddishkeit understands that Hashem remains WITH US even if we fall to the lowest possible spiritual level! We must know and remember that we can **NEVER** become separated from Hashem!

Authentic Yiddishkeit believes that EVERY single Yid has a pure נשמה whose internal infinite power can never be tainted, defiled, or removed, even after he may have sinned repeatedly and fallen to the lowest levels of spiritual impurity. EVERYONE .... Yes — **Even you!**

Authentic Yiddishkeit believes that the FURTHER away you are from Hashem, the **MORE MERCY** you need to bring you back home and therefore Hashem is ready to bestow **MORE MERCY** upon you!

SECTION 3
Building Muscle

Authentic Yiddishkeit believes that by remaining steadfast to your belief that the difficult challenge is being presented to you by a loving G-d — **THAT IS THE VEHICLE** that brings you to a closer relationship with Hashem.

Authentic Yiddishkeit believes that a נסיון/test is actually a "challenge" whose **sole purpose** is to give you the "opportunity" to bring out the potential buried deep within you — and which could otherwise never be revealed.

Authentic Yiddishkeit understands that life's difficulties are NOT a distraction that **gets in the way** of your REAL life. On the contrary — those difficulties and challenges are what your life is REALLY all about! It is your specific hardships and challenges that SHAPE who you are and CARRY you to fulfill your personal mission in this world.

Authentic Yiddishkeit believes that EVERY detail of your life — who you were born to, what school you went to, how much money you have, where you live, how many siblings you have, and every single thing that ever happened to you — have all been designed to SET UP YOUR LIFE so that you can reach **your** specific destiny and purpose.

Authentic Yiddishkeit believes that it is not only when someone EARNS 10 million dollars that he has an opportunity to grow and fulfill his life's potential, but even when someone LOSES 10 million dollars, this painful loss is given to him because he NEEDS this in order to reach his potential and complete his life's mission!

Authentic Yiddishkeit believes that even your **character flaws and personality deficiencies** are specifically placed in you by Hashem as part of the "**set up**" that you need in order to fulfill your individual purpose in life.

Authentic Yiddishkeit believes that the foundation of Yiddishkeit is coming to grips with the fact that the Master of the universe is not something that we can understand or figure out. Much like trying to fit the sun into a soda can, it is impossible for a physical, tiny human mind to grasp Hashem.

Authentic Yiddishkeit understands that when Hashem gives you a "נסיון," He is actually extending an *invitation* to build the next floor of your personal skyscraper. Your job is to accept the situation and build yourself up by facing the challenge and overcoming it to the best of your ability

Authentic Yiddishkeit believes that a person who is **fortunate** enough to be "bitten" by Hashem is … ☺ **L** ☺ **U** ☺ **C** ☺ **K** ☺ **Y** ☺ **!** ☺

Authentic Yiddishkeit understands that ACCEPTANCE is your ticket to attaining the highest level, both on this world and in the Next World! And that is precisely why the ULTIMATE GOAL of every Yid — even you — is to build up your TRUST in the absolute goodness of Hashem, so that regardless of **WHATEVER** MAY COME YOUR WAY — you can react with FEELING that Hashem, Who is full of mercy, compassion, and unconditional love for you, is now giving you some kind of unique gift and opportunity that is for YOUR GOOD.

Authentic Yiddishkeit believes that all that is required of you is to do the BEST that YOU can do at that particular moment! Therefore, when you feel that you have no energy in you — whether you are drained physically, mentally, emotionally, or even spiritually — you should be inspired when you realize that all you have to do right now is push yourself with whatever energy you can muster up, and with that seemingly "small" service you can hit 100% of your requirement from Hashem's perspective!

Authentic Yiddishkeit believes that FALLING doesn't show anything other than the Yetzer Hora was TOO strong for you to win! GETTING UP shows that your inner desire and strong will is to still be in the game of life!

Authentic Yiddishkeit believes that true freedom is **TOTAL CONTROL** over not just your actions, but your **MIND** — because your mind is **WHO YOU ARE**.

SECTION 4
The Battle for Your Life

Authentic Yiddishkeit understands that life is very much like a rollercoaster, with all kinds of sharp turns, crazy ups and downs, and unexpected drops. **Torah life is the seatbelt; sure, it's restrictive but deep down you know that it's the only SAFE WAY to get through life — and even get to enjoy the ride!**

Authentic Yiddishkeit believes that "self–control" is the epitome of achieving the highest level of living the HUMAN experience and will give you the most satisfaction you can have in your lifetime. Want to really enjoy your LIFE? Utilize SELF-CONTROL!

Authentic Yiddishkeit understands that ONLY the person who **has control** over himself is truly "free"! He is the one who is FREE to pick ANY path that he believes is right and he can control himself to stay on track to accomplish whatever goals he sets for himself! Making decisions about your life and actually following through with them is the **ultimate human experience**.

Authentic Yiddishkeit understands that the REAL GOAL of the evil snake is to deflate you and water down your relationship with Hashem so that even when you manage to do something good, you do it with a very superficial mindset, thus losing your opportunity to connect with G-d as you could and should! This glides you further down the slippery slope toward disconnection.

Authentic Yiddishkeit understands that the biggest threat to a Jew's spiritual well being is **"CONFUSION"**! For once in a state of confusion, you are completely in the Yetzer Hora's clutch.

Authentic Yiddishkeit believes that tapping into your inner pain and allowing yourself to express your sincere yearning to improve your life and become closer to Hashem is the vehicle that will carry you from exile to redemption.

Authentic Yiddishkeit understands that real happiness can only come when your angelic soul is **content** and **satisfied**.

Authentic Yiddishkeit believes that your ability to feel internally happy and truly enjoy your life depends on the degree that you are connected to Hashem. Hashem is the Source of all life; therefore, when you connect to Hashem, you connect to the SOURCE of all life and therefore you feel full of life.

MEET THE AUTHORS

Yaakov Yosef Shain

is a graduate of the Mesivta of Long Beach who continued his Beis Midrash studies at Yeshiva Zichron Meilech and at the Lakewood East Kollel in Eretz Yisrael.

He attends a Daf Yomi Shiur each morning and is immersed in Torah studies much of each day, managing his import business during the afternoons.

During the summer months Yaakov Yosef is active as the assistant Head Counselor at Camp Hamachane, where his outgoing personality allows him to be a positive influence on younger students.

He advises scores of people from all backgrounds in many of life's myriad issues.

Avi Fishoff

is the founder and director of **Home Sweeeet Home {HSH}**, a well-respected residence for Jewish boys 16-21 whose lives are way off track and out of control.

HSH related contact: **HomeSweeeetHome1@aol.com**
Avi is an Internationally Certified Life Coach and CASAP (Certified Alcohol & Substance Abuse Professional) and is available for private mentoring sessions.

Parenting related contact: **TwistedParenting@gmail.com**

**For questions and positive comments
please contact: GPSforyourSOUL@gmail.com**